PI

4 0

# PEACE BY ORDEAL

Frank Pakenham, Earl of Longford, was born in 1905 and educated at Eton and New College, Oxford. He was a member for six years of Clement Attlee's government and, for more than three years, of Harold Wilson's cabinet as Leader of the House of Lords. He is the author of numerous books, including the biography of Eamon de Valera which he wrote with Thomas P. O'Neill.

Tim Pat Coogan was born in County Dublin and educated at Blackrock College before becoming a journalist. He was editor of the *Irish Press* for twenty years. His publications include *Ireland Since the Rising, On the Blanket, The IRA, The Irish: A Personal Vision, Disillusioned Decades 1966-86* and *Michael Collins: A Biography.*

# PEACE BY ORDEAL

## The Negotiation of the Anglo-Irish Treaty, 1921

FRANK PAKENHAM
(Lord Longford)

With an introduction by Tim Pat Coogan
and a preface by the author

For Olive: what more appropriate title!
Sincerely [illegible]
[illegible]
17/3/92

PIMLICO

To E.P.

PIMLICO

20 Vauxhall Bridge Road, London SW1V 2SA

London Melbourne Sydney Auckland Johannesburg
and agencies throughout the world

First published by Jonathan Cape Ltd 1935
New edition by Sidgwick & Jackson Ltd 1972
Pimlico edition 1992



Printed and bound in Great Britain by
Mackays of Chatham, PLC, Chatham, Kent

ISBN 0-7126-9835-3

# CONTENTS

## PART FOUR



## PART FIVE



## PART SIX



## APPENDICES

# INTRODUCTION TO THE PIMLICO EDITION

*by Tim Pat Coogan*

*Peace by Ordeal* has long been one of my favourite books. It was born in 1935, the same year as myself. I will make no judgement as to which has better stood the test of time. However it is a demonstrable fact that the book has been re-born on five separate occasions (this is the fifth edition) whereas I, alas, have yet to encounter any popular groundswell for the proposition that I should be reincarnated, or re-issued even one more time.

The value of this work of Lord Longford (or Frank Pakenham as he was when he wrote it) may be assessed under various headings. Firstly there is the extraordinary fact that it is the only major book about the single most important agreement ever concluded between Ireland and England: the Treaty which set up the two States of modern Ireland.

That Treaty bowed to the compulsions of the time, one of them being the shared determination of British Conservatives and Irish Unionists that Ireland should be partitioned into two States, a Protestant dominated northern area which contained six counties, and a Catholic controlled south which comprised twenty six.

The consequences of that determination may be seen on our TV screens today. Yet one of the principal motivations for having a Treaty at all was the British requirement to put an end to Ireland's being a source of embarrassing and often disgraceful news.

A study of Longford's book can only assist in the growth of understanding required in today's decision-taking circles if there is to be any hope of our seeing an end to the pornography of violence in the Anglo-Irish relationship.

Through his personal contact with English political leaders of the Treaty period Longford also provides an insight into how Imperial England thought and reacted, not alone towards Ireland but towards the rest of the Empire. It is important to remind ourselves how Westminster once regarded what are now commonplace terms like 'Republic'. And how that regard, or lack of it, helped to bring civil war to Ireland and, *inter alia*, gave rise to today's leading Irish political parties, Fianna Fail and Fine Gael. Each grew out of the opposing sides which fought for and against the Treaty.

The men whom Longford brings to life for us around the negotiating table at 10 Downing Street were titans of their age. Winston Churchill, for example, only ranked fourth on the English team, after Lloyd George, Birkenhead and Austen Chamberlain. Seated on the Irish side were the founder of Sinn Fein, Arthur Griffith, and the Irish Siegfried, Michael Collins.

In his introductory chapters Longford, in graceful style and with sympathy for both English and Irish, explains the often horrific route those men took to get to that table. He explains how they struggled across it, held side-conferences, agonised, recriminated; and how, finally, they walked away admiring each other, whereas when the negotiations began the two sides could not even bring themselves to shake hands.

Longford had access to most of the leading participants on the British side. He was able to see men and minutes. Later he too would sit in a British Cabinet. All this gives him an authority and an empathy which uniquely enable him to analyse the quality of the bargain that was finally sealed in the small hours of the morning of 6 December 1921.

It was a fateful bargain. Birkenhead said after signing it: 'I may have signed my political death warrant.' Michael Collins replied: 'I may have signed my actual death warrant.'

Both men were right. What gives Longford's book the status it has amongst the classics of the Anglo-Irish relationship is the understanding he provides as to why Birkenhead and the British took the risks they did. In fact it is remarkable, given that he was writing in the 1930s, when the great Irish protagonists whom he had not met, Griffith and Collins, were dead, that he is as good as he is on the Irish side also.

However, I must advise the reader that here my viewpoint and that of Lord Longford diverge. The results of my own researches prevent me from endorsing the laudatory view Longford takes in this work and elsewhere of de Valera, who of course survived the civil war and, at the time Longford was writing, had become the revered President of the Irish Executive Council.

This title he was later to alter to that of Taoiseach, Prime Minister, under his own Constitution of 1937. De Valera replaced the Constitution which Collins had drawn up in 1922 because the British had inserted the Crown and an Oath of Allegiance in Collins's more Republican document.

With this imposition, accommodation between de Valera's faction and that of Collins became impossible and civil war the inevitable result. The British acted as they did because they felt that Collins was trying to negate the Treaty by subterfuge.[1] Legally Collins was in fact acting correctly according to the advice he was receiving at the time from his chief law officer, Hugh Kennedy. Politically he was trying not only to escape Lloyd George's grip, but also the trap de Valera had set for him.

'Trap' was the word used by Collins himself after he went to London to commence the Treaty negotiations in October 1921.[2] He had found himself growing increasingly disenchanted with de Valera from the time the latter returned to Ireland from America at Christmas 1920 for the concluding stages of that phase of Anglo-Irish hostilities which ended with the Truce of July 1921.

De Valera had sought to superimpose his will on the Irish situation, having been out of touch with it for the previous eighteen months, when the worst of the fighting had taken place, and he tended to think in abstract terms of how various factions might react to the war. Collins, on the other hand, was preoccupied with the problems of smuggling in the few rounds of ammunition needed to keep it going while at the same time maintaining the undercover intelligence network which was enabling him to cripple the British secret service.

De Valera brooked no rival near the throne. On his return he allied himself with Collins's enemies within the underground Sinn Fein Dail, chiefly Cathal Brugha and Austin Stack, men of great sincerity but without tithe of Collins's ability – an ability incidentally to which Longford pays due homage. One of de Valera's first ploys on returning to Ireland was an attempt to get Collins to leave the country for America, a step which would have crippled the Irish war effort. Failing to do so, he then presided over an inquiry instigated by Brugha into an unsubstantiated allegation that Collins had mishandled Sinn Fein funds.

Later, after various other skirmishings, de Valera had himself declared President of the Republic by the Dail. This in effect confirmed his supremacy over Collins, the President of the secret Irish Republican Brotherhood which, prior to de Valera's return and his subsequent manoeuvrings, had regarded itself as the custodian of the Republic and its President as the real President.

It was the I.R.B. which created the rebellion of Easter 1916 and which, under Collins, masterminded and directed the sub-

1 Downing St., 27/5/22, CAB 21/249 PRO, London.
2 Readers will find Collins's letters on this subject in *Michael Collins* by T. P. Coogan, Hutchinson, 1990; Arrow paperback, 1991.

sequent Anglo-Irish war. However, all of this power struggle remained hidden from the public and from most researchers until 1990 when I published my biography of Collins to mark the centenary of his birth.

Prior to the book's publication there had been very little close analysis of de Valera's attitude to Collins. For instance, the reason why he left him out of the delegation he took with him to London when he went to meet Lloyd George for the first time in July 1921 had gone largely unexamined. Collins was outraged at this slight and argued fiercely that he should have been included in the delegation. De Valera's stated reason for the exclusion was that he did not want British intelligence agents to have an opportunity of taking photos of Collins. (Of course they could have photographed him to their hearts content had he followed de Valera's suggestion that he should go to America.)

More importantly, however, de Valera succeeded in manoeuvring Collins into going to London in October 1921 to face Lloyd George across the negotiating table when the business of concluding a Treaty had to be addressed. De Valera gave different reasons for not going on this occasion. One was that having become President of the Republic he became its living symbol and thus could not allow himself to engage in proceedings where compromise might be suggested. Another was that he likened himself to Woodrow Wilson who, in de Valera's view, had made a mistake in taking part in the Versailles Treaty negotiations personally.

He thus distanced himself from the harsh realities of a debate which, he knew, was bound to involve compromise. Lloyd George had already made clear to him over four successive meetings, during which the two men were alone with each other, the parameters within which the England of that day was prepared to negotiate a Treaty with the Irish. These allowed for an Ireland which would accept the legitimacy of the Belfast parliament, be within the Commonwealth, owe allegiance to the Crown and bear the same constitutional status as Canada and Australia.

This literally meant that Collins 'signed his own death warrant', while de Valera stayed at home, far from the scene of the inevitable compromise. He survived the ensuing civil war over the Treaty terms and lived to validate Collins's 'stepping stone' argument by making the constitutional changes outlined above.

Collins was by no means oblivious to de Valera's attitude. He wrote to a friend two days after the Truce was signed that, far from peace being declared, there would be more agreement in 'the devil's assembly'.[1] But Collins accepted the situation for the same reason that de Valera subsequently accepted the ending of the civil war. He knew that the people wanted peace. Moreover Collins knew that given a period of truce there was no way in which he could re-establish his hitherto secret 'invisible army'.

No war resumed against the British after an internationally hailed truce and a subsequent seemingly fair offer of independence by means of an independent Irish Free State could succeed in military terms. The effort by de Valera's forces to defeat the rag tag and bobtail army of the Free State which continued after Collins's death ended in ignominy. The people had accepted the Truce as the end of the fighting and wanted peace.

The question of getting better terms, an All Ireland Republic by propaganda means alone, after a truce and with Collins's secret army now out in the open meant that in *realpolitik* terms the Irish would have been fighting for the right to kick a gift horse in the teeth where international opinion was concerned.

Accordingly, even at the risk of his own life, Collins went to London determined to make the best bargain he could for the moment: get the British to withdraw their army from the South; make a settlement, as much against the opposition of his rivals in Dublin led by de Valera, as against the British, and then, when the odds were better, use the Treaty as a 'stepping stone' to full independence and a united Ireland.

After his death de Valera did use the conditions made possible by the Treaty to create an illusion of Republicanism in the South. But he fought shy of doing what Collins had done during his brief spell in Government, which was to make a subterranean effort to destabilise the partitioned six county statelet by force.

However, this aspect of Collins's policy, along with much else, only became clear later, when, as I have indicated, the passage of time made possible the research which I was able to carry out when de Valera was dead. A few survivors were willing to talk, and various important documents had become available.

Longford wrote in the thirties. He both consciously admired de Valera and was unconscious of the fact that de Valera misled him.

Longford, who contributed material on de Valera's piety and religious fervour to the authorised biography of de Valera, which was prepared in the first instance by T. P. O'Neill,[2]

1 13/7/21, quoted by Coogan op. cit.
2 *Eamon de Valera* by Lord Longford and T. P. O'Neill, Hutchinson, London, 1970.

actually asked de Valera in writing for his reasons for not going to London to negotiate with Lloyd George.

In his reply de Valera lied point blank, saying that his staying at home was 'generally accepted' and only became an issue after the Treaty was accepted.[1] In reality, it *was* an issue before the Treaty delegation ever went to Dublin, but a hidden one. Collins argued with him in private, both at the house where de Valera was then staying in Glenvar, Blackrock, Co. Dublin and at a private session of Dail Eireann.

This session, on 14 September 1921, discussed a motion by William T. Cosgrave that de Valera, because of his 'extraordinary experience of negotiation' and because he had recently been in touch with Lloyd George should lead the delegation as Chairman. But de Valera still managed to wriggle out of entering the lion's den even though, as he later admitted – in writing, but privately – this was 'against the will of the majority of the Cabinet'.

However, he made that admission[2] close to the time he managed the evasion of responsibility (27 December 1921) when he believed it could not be concealed. But by the time he answered Longford's query, in 1963, the man to whom he had made the admission, Joseph McGarrity, was long since dead.

It is clear, then, that Lord Longford and I disagree, in some profoundly important respects, in our assessments of de Valera. But is it equally clear that *Peace by Ordeal*, written more than half a century ago, is in some ways even more valuable and more relevant now than it was on the day it was first published. The Ordeal of Ireland and of England continues. Much of the reason why the Peace remains elusive is contained in these pages.

1 De Valera to Lord Longford, 14/9/63, Childers pps., 7848/302, Trinity College, Dublin.
2 De Valera to McGarrity, de Valera pps. Ms. 17,440, National Library of Ireland.

# AUTHOR'S PREFACE TO THE PIMLICO EDITION

I first met President de Valera, as he was to become, in early 1932, soon after he came to power, or as one might say, returned after ten years to power. Until I met him, I had never heard anything that was good about him and much that was bad. I was then aged 26, about half his age, working in the Conservative Research Department in London. In British eyes, de Valera was simply regarded as the man who had wrecked the Treaty and caused the Irish Civil War. I heard him referred to pejoratively as a Portuguese Jew and many worse things. My older brother had a few years before returned from Oxford to live at what my eldest son, the present occupant, calls Tallynally Castle. His work for the Gates Theatre lead to a minute's silence in the Dublin theatres in 1961. Later he was to be made a Senator by de Valera, but in the Twenties and Thirties he was friends with leading members of the Cosgrave Pro-Treaty Party, especially Desmond Fitzgerald, father of Gareth Fitzgerald, a very gifted man who, when I first knew him, was a savage critic of de Valera.

I hope that my admired friend, Tim Pat Coogan, will forgive what I am going to say now and what I have already said to him. I would have chosen his Life of Michael Collins as my Book of the Year (1990) in spite of what I regard as its painful unfairness to de Valera. But if anyone wishes to know what I thought about Mr. de Valera before I met him he could do worse than read Tim Pat Coogan's otherwise brilliant book.

Well, I was received by Mr. de Valera and my attitude to him was changed, changed utterly, to lift a phrase from the poet. In case my admiration for him is put down to a boyish infatuation, I can assure you that in my forty years that followed I was more and more deeply impressed by his high-mindedness, sagacity, courage and political acumen. I have said before now, and I will say it again, that to me he will always be the greatest statesman I have ever met.

My own book, *Peace by Ordeal*, was first published in 1935. Speaking with, I hope, proper humility, I can find little if anything that I would want to alter today, though much has been written about it since. I was exceptionally fortunate in my access to those best qualified to pronounce on these matters both in Ireland and England. It is, however, much more obvious to me now than it was then that Lloyd George was indeed bluffing when he issued the threat of an immediate and terrible war. That does not mean of course that if the delegates had refused to sign, the British Army would have evacuated Ireland. Again, Tim Pat Coogan has thrown much new light on the tortured mind of Michael Collins, a genius in his own way but then only thirty years old. Speaking generally I see no reason to alter the thrust of my narrative.

How do I rate de Valera's performance in relation to the Treaty? Certainly no better than beta plus. At that time he was nothing like the statesman that he became. But then how could he be? He was in his late thirties with virtually no experience of government. I should describe his performance as high-minded, but understandably ineffective.

In after years he was ready and, indeed, it seemed anxious to discuss with visitors, including students, the question of whether he should have gone to London himself in October 1921. It will be recalled that he had visited London without result in July. I have always believed that all his life he regretted his failure, for what seemed good tactical reasons, to lead the delegation. He also felt that the tactics employed in London under his authority could have been much improved. After the successful negotiations of 1938, he was kind enough to tell me in the Piccadilly Hotel in London that he and his colleagues had benefitted from reading my book on the Treaty.

But it does seem even clearer than it was to me in 1935 that he was ultimately let down by Arthur Griffith. Churchill, in *The Aftermath*, has immortalised the scene when Griffith, shaking with emotion, announced that he would sign the Treaty if no-one else would. Churchill said in that book, 'A braver man than Arthur Griffith I have never met.' I do not wish to detract from that tribute, nor from Griffith's lifelong services to Ireland, but I said in 1935 that the unilateral abandonment by Griffith of the official Irish was without historical precedent. I would say the same with still more conviction today.

Be that as it may, it was inconceivable that de Valera could in honour sign the Treaty. It would be ludicrous to claim that he was responsible for the civil war but quite as wrong to suggest that he did anything effective to stop it. There was, indeed, nothing he could do once the Treaty was signed; with the IRA, the fighting men, divided bitterly, civil war was inevitable. De Valera *could* do nothing to stop it. He joined the Republican forces in some humble capacity, ready as usual for any sacrifice demanded of him.

It seems to me to speak volumes for his integrity and for the phenomenal belief in him of so many Irishmen and Irish women, that he rose from his ashes, from a humiliation greater even than that of President Nixon, to come back to a position of supreme power in Ireland at the time I met him.

Winston Churchill has said in his book *Great Contemporaries* that if we salute a man as 'great' we are applauding, on the one hand, the impression he makes on all who meet him and, on the other, his achievements. In de Valera's case, as I suppose in most others, it is difficult or impossible to separate the two. The negotiations of 1938 were a triumph for de Valera and, in the long run, I believe, beneficial to Anglo-Irish relations. But de Valera's success owes a lot to the personal relations he established with Chamberlain and, still more intimately, with Malcolm Macdonald, the Dominions Secretary. Macdonald was loud in his praise of de Valera when I interviewed him for the book that Tom O'Neill and I were writing on de Valera. He told me that what he admired most of all in de Valera was his magnanimity, a remarkable tribute to one who had suffered so much from the British and might still be supposed to be in the weaker position.

It was the same with Sir John Maffy, later Lord Rugby, British Representative in Ireland during the crucial years of the war. In his conversations with me, then and later, and confirmed in his public despatches, Maffy was convinced that neutrality was the only possible course for Ireland during the war and that de Valera interpreted it in the direction where his sympathies lay; in other words, on behalf of Britain.

At the end of the war, Churchill poured scorn on de Valera in a broadcast and de Valera was at his impressive best in reply. Randolph Churchill told him later that his father, Winston, had felt that de Valera had got the better of the argument.

Churchill's attitude to de Valera developed, if that is the right word, considerably over the years. He is the villain in Churchill's memorable description in *The Aftermath* of the Treaty negotiations. Soon after the war started and a British warship, the *Courageous*, had been sunk, he encountered me in London. He addressed me in this way: 'Pakenham, friend of Randolph's, welcomed you at Chartwell . . . you can tell your friend, de Valera, that we have treated him with prodigal liberality, with unprecedented generosity. And what does he do in return? He sinks the *Courageous* . . .' But fifteen years later, he was talking a different language and thinking different thoughts. He welcomed de Valera at No.10 Downing Street and his Private Secretary, Sir John Colville, has told us that he was positively thrilled at the thought of meeting Dev.

I pass on rapidly to the years of his Presidency, and the period towards the end when I was helping Tom O'Neill to write his biography. I always felt that de Valera had confidence in me. But he was very guarded in his comments about living politicians and, for that matter, dead ones. I don't think that he ever really forgave Churchill for precipitating the Irish civil war, though he said, without hesitation, that if he had been an Englishman, he would have voted for Churchill in the 1945 General Election. He prided himself on being able to see the other fellow's point of view, a virtue with which he was seldom credited by his opponents.

Frank Aitken, his great friend, told me that the most attractive of all de Valera's qualities was his sense of humour. With me, it took a deadpan form. Towards the end of his life he raised with me, more than once, the question of whether he had been excommunicated during the civil war. I pointed out that Tom O'Neill and I had made it plain that this was not so. Still he persisted. 'I raised the issue with His Holiness, the Pope, and he agreed that I had not been excommunicated.' I could not help asking, 'But supposing the Pope had said that you *had* been excommunicated.' There was not a flicker of a smile as he replied, 'I should have considered that His Holiness was misinformed.'

Twice only he spoke about my family. He felt regretful, guilty one might almost say, that he had not re-appointed my brother as a Senator. I had not been altogether surprised at the time, knowing my brother's extremely independent outlook. President de Valera told me, 'I wished to re-appoint him but the pressures [no doubt from the Party Whips] were too great.' When one of my daughters was killed in a motor accident and I visited him soon afterwards, he told me that his wife, whom I rarely saw, wished to speak to me. Mrs. de Valera clasped both my hands in hers and asked me to give my wife an urgent message. 'Tell her that when I lost Bryan [he was killed in a riding accident in the Phoenix Park], I cried for many days, but now I wouldn't have him back.' My wife drew much comfort from the message.

I come finally to de Valera's religion, about which he never spoke to me directly. When I wrote *Peace by Ordeal* I was still a Protestant, but I knew him for thirty years as a Catholic. I don't think that a more religious man has been a leader of any nation in our time, though de Gaspery might be a rival. By the time Dev was President, he had long been a daily communicant and, once installed in the President's residence, he used to visit the Oratory five times a day. But the last thing that he was, was a bigot. Someone particularly well qualified to speak about his religion told me, 'He would have made such a good Protestant.'

The British Prime Minister, Lord Salisbury, said about Gladstone at his death, 'He kept alive the soul in England.' De Valera would have been the last man to assert that it was necessary for him or any other individual to keep alive the soul in Ireland. But no-one who knew him at all, or had studied his life at all closely, can deny that he was a great Christian man.

# PEACE BY ORDEAL

# INTRODUCTION

*Peace by Ordeal* was begun in 1933 and published in 1935 when the author was still (just) under 30. The opportunity to write it was such as seldom comes to any historical author, hardly ever to one so young and untried. In the last 40 years it can fairly be said to have established itself as the standard book on the Treaty. Two impressive works which have appeared recently—Tom Jones' *Whitehall Diary*, Vol. III, and Robert Kee's *The Green Flag*, a tremendous history of Irish nationalism, appear to treat it as such. One can make this point perhaps without undue self-aggrandisement. I was putting it mildly enough in the Introduction to the First Edition when I wrote "I have been exceptionally fortunate in my material".

Two-thirds of the book are directly concerned with the detailed story of the Anglo-Irish negotiations which began on October 11th, 1921, and culminated in the small hours of December 6th with the signature of the Treaty at No. 10 Downing Street. A friendly chance brought me the priceless boon of a complete set of the Irish official records for the period. That fact alone would have enabled me to make a significant contribution to the history of those events, however skilful or inept my own handling. But my good fortune did not stop there.

In the 1935 Introduction I went on to say that I had had interviews with nearly all the principal actors in the events of 1921 who were still alive when I wrote. "Some told me much, some little, some nothing at all." I said that it seemed to be their unanimous wish that I should not make acknowledgment of them by name. Forty years later there seems no good purpose in drawing aside the veil with one or two exceptions mentioned below. I did, however, indicate the very great assistance rendered by Sir Austen Chamberlain. "Sir Austen Chamberlain though feeling unable to give me the use of his papers had read to me his contemporary notes of the crucial meetings." He would indeed have been ready to let me use his notes unreservedly. I felt it right, however, to warn him that my starting point, and therefore my conclusions might be highly unpalatable to him. He decided then on the compromise indicated; it always seemed to me one of the most generous actions imaginable, though highly characteristic of him. At that time I was gently drifting across from the Conservative to the Labour Party in British politics, not unaffected by Irish sympathies.

I had another still more intimate link with the Conservatives who signed the Treaty. The original invitation to me to undertake the book came from Mr. Peter Davies on the suggestion of the late Lady Eleanor Smith. I was and am great friends with the whole Birkenhead family from whom I have received unvarying kindness over the years. Her brother, the present Lord Birkenhead, was my best man when I married a year or two before I embarked on *Peace by Ordeal*. Their father was dead by that time but I had often heard him speak of his affection for, and appreciation of, Michael Collins. It was, I think, because the subject had so obviously begun to fascinate me that Eleanor Smith suggested to the Publisher that I might be the right person to undertake it even in the absence of other credentials.

In Ireland there seems no reason at this time of day to withhold my gratitude from Robert Barton who gave me more help than any other individual in either country. Through him I met Mrs. Childers and acquired an undying admiration for his cousin Erskine Childers, executed as all are aware in 1922, of whom Mr. de Valera wrote at the time: "He died the Prince that he was. Of all the men I ever met I would say he was the noblest." I had long conversations with Mr. de Valera himself, though he was always at particular pains to avoid imposing his point of view on the youthful author. Then he was truth-loving, kindly, prescient, supremely dedicated. His true greatness revealed itself in later years.

In my own eyes it was, and I am bound to say remains, an attempt at an impartial study. One must admit, however, that in so far as it has had a long-term effect, that effect has been to correct a widespread bias, in England and among many people in Ireland, against Mr. de Valera on account of his part in the story. Others must decide whether it has been found possible to form a more favourable opinion of his rôle without thinking the worse of great Irishmen such as Griffith and Collins. Certainly I took great trouble to present these and others who supported the Treaty in the most favourable light. I was never certain in my own mind at that time whether I would or would not have signed the Treaty if confronted with the ultimate dilemma.

Since then there have been various books about Michael Collins. I may be forgiven for thinking that far the best was published in 1971 by my own firm, Sidgwick & Jackson; written by Marjorie Forester, a young authoress from New Zealand coming fresh to the scene, it has achieved a richly deserved reputation. There is much less available about Arthur Griffith. A good book remains to be written there. If I were writing *Peace by Ordeal* today I would, no doubt, take advantage of Miss Forester's work. Also of that of Rex Taylor and other writers. But in my own eyes at least they supplement rather than substantially correct my account of Collins' rôle in the negotiations proper. A lady who knew him very well at that time and helped him with many speeches, the late Mrs. Llewellyn Davies, gave me an understanding of his point of view which I still feel came close to the truth. I learned from her, for example, his fine sayings that there were to be "no more unattended funerals, no more lonely scaffolds for his men". But she did not like the book when she saw it in proof and I can only hope that she has forgiven me by now. Michael Collins, in so far as he controlled a secret organisation, the I.R.B., has left behind him certain mysteries not yet cleared up. It is in that direction that historical research has still a good deal of ground to cover. Whether the whole story will ever be told remains uncertain.

A British historian who has recently worked over all these topics told me not long ago that Arthur Griffith stood out in his mind as the truly great Irishman. This fits in with Sir Winston Churchill's original tribute in the *Aftermath*—"a braver man than Arthur Griffith I have never met". I would hesitate to claim any deep understanding of Griffith, though in *Peace by Ordeal* there are passages of admiration, however, whose sincerity has not been weakened in a longer perspective. I felt and still feel that the pro-Treaty point of view and in particular the attitude of Arthur Griffith were fully, indeed brilliantly, explained to me by Desmond Fitzgerald, a member of various Irish Cabinets before and after the Treaty. He was a great friend of my late brother Lord Longford and it was certainly no fault of Desmond Fitzgerald if I did not tell the story from the pro-Treaty angle or do full justice to Griffith. No more than Mrs. Llewellyn Davies did he like the book when it appeared, but that did not prevent our friendship prospering. Nothing would convince him that de Valera had not renounced the Republic before Arthur Griffith left for London but there, I am sure, he was wrong. (See *Peace by Ordeal*, page 99.)

The one major point of view that I did not have access to—I am not sure that I have had access to it yet—was that of Lloyd George. The late Lady Lavery who knew the British leaders well and was on friendly terms with Michael Collins took me down to see Lloyd George at Churt. He was delighted to see Lady Lavery, less obviously so to be questioned by me. I asked him with youthful naïvety—"Was Arthur Griffith a great man?" and was told "Pretty big". "And Michael Collins?", "Quite considerable". And so on, all very cagey. Suddenly he saw a way out. He seized a huge bell, conveniently at hand and began shaking it with all his might. At once a number of dogs came rushing in, human beings collected, gales of laughter enveloped us all, and the Irish Treaty was not proceeded with.

But I knew Tom Jones quite well and stayed a night with him in Kent. Curiously enough he did not seem to remember the Treaty events particularly well although his mind and spirit were still full of vitality. At that time his memorable *Diaries* could not be published and may have been out of his reach. I never quite knew what he thought of the picture of himself presented in the book that follows. Once in a house-party at the Astor's house, Cliveden, he said to Lionel Curtis, pointing to me, "He makes us all out terrible villains". But convinced, as he had every right to be, of his own deep-seated love of Ireland he appeared to be able to enjoy the somewhat ambiguous light in which he makes his appearance.

So much for the background of authorship. It seems fair to remark that I could still number on a truncated hand the points of fact which need correction. Perhaps the oddest and most glaring relates to the great emphasis placed in the text on the events of November 12th, 1921. On page 172 a section begins—"If there had been no 12th of November there might have been no Treaty". I am referring to the day on which Arthur Griffith was shown by Tom Jones a vital scrap of paper which was produced by Lloyd George on the last afternoon with crushing effect. No one reading Dr. Middlemass's masterly editions of *The Whitehall Diaries* will dispute the importance of this occurrence. But it turns out to have taken place not on November 12th but on November 13th. It does not make the slightest difference to the significance of what happened but it is better to give the right date than the wrong one. By the time that Dr. O'Neill and I produced our *Life of Mr. de Valera*, 1970, Dr. Middlemass's First Volume had appeared and we were able to make the correction.

Another error has long been on my conscience. In *Peace by Ordeal* I made some not very agreeable references to Mr. Beasley who had already written a comprehensive life of Michael Collins. "Mr. Beasley," I said, "in an exhaustive tome laments the triumph of Griffith and Collins squandered by the perversity of de Valera." I then went on to say that Mr. Beasley and all previous historians of the Treaty agreed . . . "that the Treaty embodied concessions to Ireland that surpassed that country's wildest hopes, and the Treaty, for all the ravages of jealousy, faction, and fanaticism, must be regarded with its potentialities as a final settlement." Mr. Beasley replied with not unnatural sharpness in the Introduction to a new version of his book. I now express regret if I misunderstood him in regard to the matters quoted. I had in mind, of course, Michael Collins's famous contention that the Treaty gave freedom to achieve freedom, but I must concede that he would never have called it a final settlement.

The only other inaccuracy in the text brought to my attention was concerned with John Chartres, Second Secretary to the delegation, which was put right by the *Irish Independent* at the time.

The British documents, the Jones diaries, the C. P. Scott memoirs, Lord Birkenhead's revised version of his father's life and other relevant publications, have taken us behind the British scenes in recent years. Sir Austen Chamberlain had helped me there considerably by the time I wrote.

Taking all this new information, Irish and British together, do I want to alter the main narrative in *Peace by Ordeal* or the summary and assessment of the negotiating performance in Chapter XII? Basically, at the risk of arrogance or complacency, I return the answer "No!". In so far as my mental emphasis has been changed over the years, by later writing, I am much surer in my own mind than I was in 1921, that Lloyd George's famous ultimatum on the last day of the Conference was a total bluff. It is quite obvious now that there would have been no intention whatever of levying "the immediate and terrible war" with the threat of which the Irish delegates were coerced into signature on the spot. But that, of course, is far from saying that the British Cabinet would have agreed to a Republic, even an externally associated Republic, if they had not got their way immediately. It was not until 1949 that India demonstrated that she could declare a republic and be warmly accepted as a leading member of the Commonwealth. One can only assume that if the Irish delegates had stuck together, and insisted, as they were fully entitled to, on reference back to Dublin, the negotiations would have dragged on, with the British army still more or less in control in Ireland. Who can say what would have been the outcome of that situation? At this point the historian departs and the speculator takes over.

Nevertheless, when all is said the imposed signature there and then in London brought its own special tragedy, more or less inevitable. The civil war that followed was a not too distant consequence. One is bound therefore to look closely at the failure of the Irish delegation to refer the matter back to Dublin, as was clearly envisaged when they left Ireland two days earlier. The simple fact is that it still seemed possible at the last Cabinet meeting in Dublin to "stage the break on Ulster", to refuse to sign any treaty, in other words, unless and until the Northern leaders agreed to a United Ireland. Over the years my opinion has varied a good deal as to whether this was ever a feasible tactic and I may change my opinion again. My latest reading of the British authorities suggests that there was a good deal more realism in this approach than I have sometimes thought. But in fact on the last afternoon it was defeated by Lloyd George's melodramatic production of the document assented to by Griffiths on November 13th. It is impossible for me, at least, to believe that if it had not been for that *coup de théâtre* Griffith would never have agreed to personal signature ahead of the others. In fact, the whole ultimatum would have fizzled out. The case for saying that Griffiths was outsmarted by Lloyd George is even stronger than it used to be. But I repeat, the question of whether Ireland could have got better terms at the end of 1921 than those obtained, is still as open as ever.

The story of the Boundary Commission looks more amazing with each new piece of light that is thrown on it. The Jones' *Diaries* confirm the long-held opinion, stressed repeatedly in

*Peace by Ordeal*, that the Irish delegates expected to obtain large concessions in territory, which would have made the Northern area non-viable. What I had not realised until now was that the idea originated with Carson and that he at least expected that it would be the North not the South who would gain. It seems possible that the Unionist leaders persuaded themselves and others that this might prove to be so. Basically, however, the analysis in the text, and particularly in Chapter XII, still seems to hold good.

This is no place to try to write, however briefly, the history of Anglo-Irish relations during the last fifty years. The last chapter of *Peace by Ordeal* begins: "The present position is pitiful." It was written during the period of the economic war. Since then, much has been achieved in Irish affairs. In *The Life of de Valera* (Longford and O'Neill), we quote Professor Mansergh's summary:

"Taken together, the External Relations Act and the new Constitution destroyed the dominion settlement of 1921... After the Agreement of 1938, and six years of neutrality in the war, it was manifest to all that total independence of the Twenty-Six Counties had been secured."

The day was to come when Churchill would call Southern Ireland "a society independent, Christian, cultured and law abiding". But all the time, while the partition issue awaited settlement, Ireland could never be at peace. Ultimately, it was inconceivable that while Northern Ireland remained a part of the U.K., the Catholic minority should continue to be denied the full equality of citizenship which is taken for granted in England, Scotland and Wales.

*Peace by Ordeal* ends with a heart-felt aspiration. "Whatever Ireland's policy, it remains for England to make atonement, for that she has not yet made." But while those words are being written, a British Government has taken an initiative in that direction, which raises profound hopes in all who love Ireland or England, or care for justice in those countries or elsewhere.

June 1972

Frank Pakenham
(Longford)

# Part One

## CHAPTER I

## THE TREATY OF PEACE

"*Spirit of Rumour*: The Treaty moves all tongues tonight."
THOMAS HARDY: *The Dynasts.*

*The changes brought about by the Treaty—The view that it satisfied Ireland—The need for a new approach—The historical origins of Ireland's dilemma in 1921.*

ON December 6th 1921, in the small hours of the morning, was signed at 10 Downing Street a document styled "Articles of Agreement for a Treaty between Great Britain and Ireland," usually referred to as the "Anglo-Irish Treaty." The signature of this document—the first Treaty ever signed (in a phrase of Lloyd George's) "between the two Democracies"—put a final close to the guerilla war which had been devastating Ireland from January 1919, when an Irish Republic had been declared, down to the Truce of July 1921. Its deeper consequence was to transform the whole system under which Ireland had previously been governed and the whole basis of Ireland's relationship to England. The British supremacy over Ireland first claimed in 1172 was virtually ended. The legislative union that had linked the countries since 1800 was dissolved.

Hitherto Ireland (for the moment we pass over the Partition Act of 1920, rejected out of hand by the South) had been one area among many within the United Kingdom; less independent than Scotland; administered from Dublin Castle by a British Lord-Lieutenant and a British Chief Secretary; lacking since 1800 any legislature of her own. Just before the War an attempt had been made to give her a Dublin legislature strictly subordinate to Westminster, where a reduced Irish representation would have continued. And the attempt had brought England within sight of civil war. Now Ireland attained at a bound the status of a British Dominion, and except as regards naval and air defence, the same degree of practical independence.

She achieved a Parliament competent to make laws "for the peace, order and good government" of the country, a Parliament whose wide powers including complete fiscal and financial autonomy, would make unnecessary the retention of Irish membership at Westminster; an Executive Council chosen by and responsible to no English influence or institution, but chosen by and responsible to the Irish Parliament alone;[1] an army of her own to take the place of the British army which would be at once evacuated. She acquired her own police, her own currency, her own flag, the right to define her own citizens. Six counties in the North-East, where a Parliament subordinate to Westminster had under an Act of 1920 begun to function, were given the chance to opt themselves out of incorporation with the South.[2] But whether they availed themselves of the chance or not the new Dominion was to be styled and known as Saorstat Eireann, the Irish Free State.

A year later the new Constitution, passed by England as in conformity with the Treaty, asserted the co-equality of Ireland with the other members of the Commonwealth including Great Britain, and declared that "all powers of Government and all authority, legislative, executive, and judicial in Ireland" were derived from the Irish people alone. In 1923 the Irish Free State was unanimously elected to membership of the League of Nations and in 1930 to a place on its Council. From 1921 onwards she played a leading part in those constitutional advances which, culminating in the Statute of Westminster, have left few if any practical particulars in which a Dominion enjoys less than full autonomy.[3]

The significance of the Treaty which gave rise to these revolutionary changes and, to mention only one other consequence, removed the Irish question from English politics, has not been and is not likely to be minimised in either England or Ireland. Hitherto, however, there has been lacking all detailed narrative of the negotiations and discussions, conducted mainly in London, which led up to signature. With the material for such a narrative at last available, we can for the first time describe the developments and

[1] The British Crown was to be represented by a Governor-General, but it was established from the first that his practical powers would be almost negligible, and that no appointment would be made to which the Irish Government did not assent. Since that time the last vestiges of his practical powers have been removed, and in appointing him the King is now constitutionally bound to act exclusively on the advice of Irish Ministers.

[2] The Six-County Government availed itself of this right (as soon as it had the chance) a year later, and thenceforth Ireland has been divided into two parts: (1) a Dominion of twenty-six counties and three million inhabitants, and (2) an area of six counties and a million and a quarter inhabitants, remaining under the authority of the Imperial Parliament at Westminster, though possessing a subordinate Legislature of its own.

[3] Ireland, however, under the Treaty suffers from Certain Defence restrictions to which the other Dominions are not subject.

analyse the forces and motives of which the settlement was the outcome; connect in the light of them the story of Anglo-Irish relations since December 6th 1921 with what was done that night, and so setting it against its origin and its aftermath give the Treaty its place in history.

The story in so far as it is a simple record of negotiations, a study in diplomatic manœuvre, is beyond our inclination or power to change. Yet in selecting its incidents, allotting its emphasis, pointing its moral, we cannot write to-day exactly as we should have been tempted to write before the events of the last two or three years. Previous historians of the Treaty have brought to their task divergences of outlook only less wide than the variety of their gifts. Mr. Winston Churchill calls on every resource of narrative beguilement to impress us with the courage and realism of both parties to settlement; Professor Alison Phillips, with reckless brilliance, indicts British spinelessness in the face of Irish brutality; Mr. Beasley, in an exhaustive tome, laments the triumph of Griffith and Collins squandered by the perversity of De Valera. But all agree on these two points: the Treaty embodied concessions to Ireland that surpassed that country's wildest hopes, and the Treaty, for all the ravages of jealousy, faction, and fanaticism, must be regarded with its potentialities as a final settlement. This way of looking at things has hitherto, in the absence of any other, been forced on every neutral seeker after truth. Writing to-day we cannot let it go uncorrected.

Previous writers have mostly contended that the Irish people not only ought to have been satisfied, but were in fact satisfied by the Treaty; that as time went by this would become still more plain. Up till a few years ago, perhaps to the Election of 1933 in Ireland, an outsider might have been led into agreeing with them. He might have discovered in the continued and growing opposition to the Treaty Party, little more than a hang-over of revolutionary exuberance, reinforced by personal devotion to a romantic ex-President, general economic radicalism, and natural inevitable reaction against a Government ten years in power. But the result of the last Election, though many varied factors contributed to De Valera's triumph, provided striking and indeed final proof of the continued life and virility of the anti-Treaty tradition—in face, too, of the threat of severe economic sacrifice. In short, it has become impossible to argue that the Treaty satisfied Ireland as a permanent settlement.

The interest of our story will lie accordingly not only in tracing the progress of the rival Delegations towards this great landmark on the road to Irish freedom, but in seeing why this landmark fell so far short of the nation's goal; and this being so, how and why the decision came to be made to call a halt at this point to the nation's march. Why did the Treaty fail to satisfy Ireland? How and why did it come to be signed?

To these questions we shall attempt an answer. On others we provide only the materials for independent judgment. Was Ireland's wisest course in 1921 to agree to Dominion Status? Were the Irish Delegates right to sign in the special circumstances of December 6th? Were De Valera and others right to repudiate the Treaty once it was signed? These and a host of other problems defy agreed conclusion. They will perplex and harass to the end of time, as too will that other eternal speculation: What would have happened to Ireland if the Treaty Delegates had refused to sign?

We do not, indeed, presume to condemn or praise the signatories, on either side, of the Treaty. Their action bears a twofold aspect. It marks on the one hand the greatest step forward yet in Irish emancipation, on the other a decisive stage in the tragedy that a few months later was to engulf Ireland in civil war. A tragedy of which twelve years of intestine strife and an economic war with England are present-day reminders; a tragedy that can never close until England and Ireland find a relationship accepted voluntarily by each and so permitting friendship to grow between them.

How far did each of the principal actors share in the work of emancipation? How far by accident, error, or injustice, in the development and enhancement of the tragedy? These problems should be simpler when this book is read. But by the year 1921 circumstances had imposed a narrow context within which men could move. To appreciate the achievements of those who brought about the Treaty, still more to forgive the failings in their handiwork, we must look back across many centuries. We must learn why Ireland, small, isolated, inoffensive, should have found herself in 1921, in an age of self-determination, confronted with this peculiar dilemma: either she must expect a war of extermination from a neighbouring Empire of friendly congenial citizens, or she must disestablish her declared Republic, surrender her national honour in the eyes of half her Government, and face the possibility, the certainty it soon proved, of civil war.

## CHAPTER II

# THE UNFINISHED CONQUEST

"The too just discontents of Ireland."
MACAULAY.

I: *Ireland's liberation a triumph of national exertion—The centuries of suppression—Irish Nationalism in the modern sense—Its methods—Its demands.* II: *The great opportunity of 1886—Twenty years of "firm government"—The pre-War deadlock.* III: *England's last chance missed—Sinn Fein and the 1916 Rising—Executions, conscription, repression—Sinn Fein sweeps the country—Establishes a Republic—England committed to the principle of self-determination.*

### I

ENGLAND invaded Ireland in 1172; in 1921 she renounced effective authority over all but a corner of the island. There had been Irish Parliaments before—from 1782–1800 one had enjoyed theoretical equality with Westminster—but there had been no Irish Parliament since 1800, and in its strongest days its membership had been drawn from a small Anglo-Irish caste, its executive appointed from England. In 1921 for the first time since 1172 "the old inhabitants of the island" were to be allowed to govern themselves. This sweeping transformation represented when it came the surrender to a people of three million by one of fifteen times their number. It goes without saying that somewhere in the centuries of subordination Ireland put forth prodigious efforts, that England underwent prodigious changes of heart.

The Irish efforts in their recent intense and successful form flowed from a corporate sense of political nationality. In what era this sense originated is a question on which opinions differ. Some would have us believe that Ireland retained her nationhood intact through the seven hundred years of subjection; others that we need go no further back than Grattan and Wolfe Tone and the end of the eighteenth century for the origins of Irish Nationalism in the modern political sense. But the issue between them is for us immaterial. Let us accept the latter version, an account more agreeable to the critics of Ireland. Let us agree that it required the Nationalism of the French revolutionary era to give Irish Nationalistic tendencies political expression in a conscious unified form. What all authorities have established is the existence from 1172 onwards of a fertile soil in which with full and just cause political Nationalism might grow. All along there were the two distinct races in the island, all along there was the savage discrimination against that one to which the vast majority of the population belonged.

It is no part of our purpose to harrow feelings with a recital of Ireland's sufferings and wrongs. We pass over the successive settlements by wholesale violent dispossession under the Normans, under Mary, Elizabeth, and James I, and under Cromwell—the last bringing down the proportion of land held by Catholics from much more than fifty to little more than five per cent. We pass over, too, the outlawing of the natives, whether under the Anglo-Norman code which left the Irish "outside the law," or the penal code of the seventeenth and eighteenth centuries under which the Catholics were forbidden to buy land (or lease it except on intolerable conditions), and under which, in the words of an Irish Lord Chancellor of the time, "the law did not suppose any such person as an Irish Roman Catholic to exist."

We pass over the stifling commercial restrictions imposed by England on Irish Parliaments till 1779, representative though such Parliaments were of none but Protestant interests. If the student of Anglo-Irish history has not been revolted by the tale of these things in the pages of the great Unionist Lecky, assuredly the time for melting or rousing him is past.

Professor Alison Phillips, disgusted one takes it with the plaints of his adopted country, strives gallantly to say what can be said for England. He urges that "the penal laws . . . were less cruel than the contemporary laws against the Protestants in France—to say nothing of Spain." That, too, is the gist of Lord Midleton's defence. But Lecky has once for all exploded the analogy. "That code," he wrote, "has a character entirely distinctive. It was directed not against the few but against the many. It was not the persecution of a sect but the degradation of a nation." And there is this other point for Englishmen. The morality of the ages in question may have condoned oppression and persecution, but not treachery or breach of faith. England seldom kept faith with Ireland. To give only two instances, she observed the Treaty of Limerick of 1689 as little as she observed Pitt's Compact that the Act of Union would be immediately followed by Catholic Emancipation.

To write thus is not to condemn the English character, a national character as upright and compassionate, in recent centuries at least, as any on which historical records throw light. But it is to demonstrate what is indeed self-evident, that in dealing with Ireland, England's policies have fallen far short, not only of her own highest professions, but of her own criteria of normal public conduct. And the reason is simple. From the beginning she was attempting a hopeless task. England refused to mingle herself with Ireland as the Normans had mingled with the Saxons; she set out instead to colonise her as later she colonised North America. But in spite of everything the Irish retained a permanent and distinct identity, and one that in the early stages the English found very infectious. They provided a proposition different in kind and tougher than any elsewhere encountered, a white race so equal in everything but open military power that there was no possibility of their succumbing to a Red Indian fate. They retained their language, their culture, their customs, their national dress, their racial pride. The poet Spenser would have exterminated the lot of them, but they could not be exterminated, and the task of ruling them came to involve conflict with every conception of British humanity and justice.

How far was a course possible for England before the nineteenth century that would have given her the advantages of military domination and the main rewards of plantation, and yet appeased incipient revolt and made Ireland her loyal friend? The point is academic. In actual fact, this hope, if hope it was, was stifled from Elizabeth onwards. Compared to the land-grabbing of the New Adventurers who now invaded Ireland, occasionally in a thin guise of religion, all previous confiscation had been a joke. Fresh tyrannies led to revolt, revolt to further suppression; and "Catholic disloyalty," "Protestant insecurity," and "British firmness" pursued one another down the centuries. By the end, then, of the eighteenth century there existed ample reasons for the uprise of political Nationalism among Irish Catholics. There were the common attributes and there were the common wrongs.

But by this time the Catholics had been brought too low to inspire their own resurrection. For the risings of 1798 and 1803 two Protestants were primarily responsible, Wolfe Tone and Robert Emmet. The United Irishmen, instituted by Tone to bring all religions together behind the demand for Parliamentary reform, found their chief strength in the Presbyterian North; and Hill, Orr, and MacCracken won their Province the lasting soubriquet of "Rebel Ulster." From now on the part played by the Protestant or Presbyterian Irish, the middle nation, complicates the story. At times they find most in common with the English; at times, feeling themselves Irishmen before all else, with their Catholic fellow-countrymen. And they act accordingly. After 1886 Ulster becomes a special problem; she holds up Home Rule in 1914, admits Partition in 1920, preserves her exclusion in 1921–2, and still, a decade and a half afterwards, bars every approach to unity. In the South, from the Union onwards, the Protestant class ranks as Loyalist to England. But most of them stay Irish in everything but political aspiration. And many of them add fresh glories to the Tone-Emmet tradition.

The main tide of Irish Nationalism rolled on, excited by the Nationalism of Europe, encouraged by the enlightenment of England, enraged by fresh economic hardships—among them the famine of 1846–8, and the subsequent halving of the population. Its methods were several. Some were peaceful. Catholic Emancipation in 1829 was won by extra-Parliamentary if constitutional agitation. It opened the way to pressure inside Parliament. For a time dissensions intervened. From 1870, however, Butt was evolving a new Parliamentary formation, and when the agricultural labourer was allowed for the first time to vote in 1885 Parnell became master of a solid eighty-six votes at Westminster.

But the tradition was never lost of physical resistance. 1848, the year of revolutions, saw Smith O'Brien's much-ridiculed escapade. In 1858 was founded the Irish Republican Brotherhood or Fenians, a secret society pledged to establish an Irish Republic by force, and in 1867 they did battle for their principles with no more success than Smith O'Brien. Economic action opened up a more respectable avenue. Davitt, an old Fenian, founded the Land League in 1879; no-Rent Campaigns followed, and the stratagem of the boycott. From 1880 all three streams of the National Movement united behind Parnell. He was at once political dictator, friend of the Fenians and their American supporters, and the first President of Davitt's Land League.

Parnell's fall and death suspended unity. By 1914 the movement had progressed along many paths. The Parliamentary wing was more or less controlled by Redmond. Among the I.R.B. the veteran Tom Clarke was handing on the doctrine of revolt to a band of rising youth, Padraic Pearse their prophet-to-be. Land agitation had been damped down by remedial legislation. Its political place was filled by revolutionary Republican Socialism, inspired by James Connolly, centring in the towns. And then there was Sinn Fein founded by Griffith in 1905 to achieve the practical emancipation of Ireland by abstention from Westminster, passive resistance and concentration on national ends; its purpose much helped by the great cultural revival after the foundation of the Gaelic League in 1893. These and other streams contributed to an immense yet diffused flood of Nationalist purpose. Their vitality was not in question. When Carson armed the North to defeat Home Rule, Redmondites and I.R.B. drilled shoulder to shoulder in an opposition army. And amid the great industrial struggles of these same years just before the War, James Connolly founded his Citizen Army of urban workers.

So much for the different methods of the National Movement. (They dictated usually its immediate sectional divisions.) The ultimate objectives have been no less varied and are harder to assess to-day. Tone had called for an Irish Republic. O'Connell preached only repeal of the Union, that is, restoration of an Irish Parliament with its 1782–1800 powers. Thomas Davis and the Young Ireland group of the forties preached complete practical independence (Griffith called Davis his mentor), but Davis's words can be quoted to prove that he at least did not seek the overthrow of the Imperial Parliament, "with its Imperial power." The official programme of the seventies, Butt's Home Rule, fell short even of repeal, for it did not ask more than an Irish Parliament subordinate to Westminster. Nor on the face of things did Parnell, nor in his English speeches, Redmond. The I.R.B. stood for a separate Republic and nothing short of it, but numerically they were always a handful. Sinn Fein under Griffith aspired only to the Austro-Hungarian relationship. Thus Lloyd George had a strong debating case in 1921, when he claimed against De Valera that "in demanding that Ireland should be treated as a separate sovereign power you are advancing claims which the most famous National leaders in Irish history have explicitly disowned."

Yet a deeper reading of the leaders in question bids one be careful. The most profound conviction of every Irish leader since Tone has been a belief in the inalienable right of Ireland to choose, like every other nation, her own form of government; and to decide her own paramount problem of how far she wishes to be associated with or under the tutelage of England. Different leaders may have stressed differently how far Ireland was willing to go at any particular moment in association or tutelage. Different leaders may have formed different views of how high at any particular moment it was expedient to pitch their claims. But none, if their writings are any witness, or if students of their lives are to be believed, imposed any limit whatever on Ireland's right of self-determination, both at the moment and at any time to come. Every Nationalist thinker has apprehended what the genius of Parnell enunciated: "No man has a right to fix the boundary to the march of a nation."

Still the very fact that Lloyd George was able to score with this particular thrust must influence the course of our discussion. Why was it possible even to argue in 1921 that an official claim by Ireland for independence, *i.e.* exclusion from the British Empire, was something unprecedented in Irish history? Republicans may retort that the argument was absurd, that the claim to independence had been pressed continually, frequently by resort to arms. Alternatively that the claim had always expressed the real or underlying will of the people, though not till now had it been feasible for the whole country to prefer it. But they must forbear a little. No Englishman will hear history read that way. He will insist that Ireland's national demand in 1921 was far greater than at any previous time.

The rest of this chapter will be concerned accordingly with England's efforts in the last seventy years to liquidate the obligations incurred by past errors, to dispose as honourably as possible of the phenomenon presented in a democratic age by the "grim uprise of a submerged race." Irishmen must be content to hear the story told on the assumption that it might have been possible to satisfy Ireland at any time before 1918 by much less than the independence demanded in that year and even than the Dominion Status granted in 1921. The story told this way reflects, it must be confessed, no greater credit on England's political genius. For it raises this inevitable question. If Ireland could have been satisfied by lesser concessions than were afterwards demanded, why was not prompt and generous action taken earlier? Why did not England make the lesser concessions while there was still time?

## II

Two dates are usually mentioned when limited concessions might have proved finally effective, 1886 and 1914. In both years these questions were at stake—did a means exist of satisfying the Irish national demand short of giving her independence? If a means existed, could England bring herself to adopt it?

In 1886 the first question seemed to admit an affirmative answer. The Irish agricultural population had voted for the first time at a recent election. The result everywhere except in the North-East corner had been a unanimous poll for Home Rule. And it was at least possible that Home Rule would provide a permanent settlement. Sweeping land measures of 1870 and 1881 had relieved some of the more pressing economic hardships. All Nationalist sections obeyed or respected Parnell, the Irish were ready to be grateful, disillusionment was still some way off. A moment, if ever there was, to evoke and stimulate statesmanship.

And England was readier than she had ever been to hand back a big share in their government to the "ancient inhabitants." Drawing partly on her own experience, partly on European sources, she had learnt much in the eighty-six years since the Union about the rights of depressed classes and of subject nationalities. Fear had sometimes accelerated wisdom, yet we cannot discount the colossal progress. Catholics had been emancipated in 1829; the Franchise altered out of recognition in 1832, 1867 and 1884; Canada had attained responsible government in 1847, so in the following decade had the Australian Colonies and New Zealand.

By 1886 there would have been nothing to take the breath away in a declaration for Home Rule by either British party. For several years the air had been thick with talk of "some kind of local Board." Parnell had been led to give the Conservatives his support at the recent election. He proved to have been mistaken in understanding certain "conversations" as guarantees of Home Rule. But the Conservatives must have meant something; the gulf cannot have been enormous. On the other side was Gladstone. Whatever his failings, however we detract from his motives, we are not likely to question his sense of the turning-points of history. He was a man fit for such things. "Ireland," he said, in closing the speech with which he moved the first Home Rule Bill, "Ireland stands at your Bar, expectant, hopeful, almost suppliant. Her words are the words of truth and soberness. She asks a blessed oblivion of the past and in that oblivion our interest is deeper even than hers. She asks also a boon for the future, and that boon for the future, unless we are much mistaken, will be a boon to us in respect of honour no less than a boon to her in respect of happiness, prosperity and peace. Such, sir, is her prayer. Think, I beseech you, think well, think wisely, think not for the moment but for the years that are to come before you reject this Bill."

No appeal could have shown truer prevision, though it would be years before this became plain. But the Bill stirred bitter passions. Ulster's special problem had not been separated off, therefore the case against betraying a Loyalist minority could be made out that much more strongly than in 1921. It was only four years since the Phœnix Park murders; agrarian outrage was a contemporary horror; the violence was hailed as Jacobinical, and every Conservative revolted at the appearance of surrendering to it.

Again, the right of small nationalities had not yet won their place in the Unionist creed of morality. It needed the Great War and the violation of Belgium to add imagination to logic and make that place assured. At this time Joseph Chamberlain, a name to conjure with among the very poor, could see no reason why a few million Irish should have more claims to self-government than the same number of Londoners; Lord Salisbury, rising far above all traditional inhibitions, could yet feel "rightly or wrongly no desire to satisfy the natural aspirations of Ireland." Finally the grant of a subordinate legislature was held to constitute in a hundred different senses a threat to the integrity (so much might be conceded), and, what was less demonstrable, to the honour and safety of the Empire.

Joseph Chamberlain led the Liberal Unionists into opposition, the House of Commons threw out the Bill and the opportunity passed. Henceforward for twenty years, with a brief heroic Gladstonian interlude, the Conservatives administered firm government with one hand, while with the other they poured out economic assistance in the effort "to kill Home Rule with kindness." The policy was logically conceived and courageously and consistently carried out. It had a long run and every chance, for during its earlier years the Irish Parliamentary Party were absurdly at variance. It was a political experiment of exceptional interest carried out under exceptionally favourable conditions. And politically it was a complete failure.[1] "Ireland in 1906," quotes Lord Midleton with enthusiasm, "had never been so quiet for six hundred years." Yes, but despite all the splits and factions that had disfigured the Irish Party England had made no inch of inroad on the unanimity of the demand for Home Rule. By 1906, Unionists should have realised that their policy for the South had failed and should have concentrated on saving Ulster.

As is well known they made no such selection. From now till the War, both parties played the party game with increasing rigour

[1] On the economic side a handsome start was made with the work of compensating Ireland for the past. The period conferred great and lasting economic benefits, land purchase the greatest of all. The only political concession of importance was the grant of elective local authorities—a most valuable improvement, but one which naturally did nothing to satisfy the National demand.

and ruthlessness. To thwart the popular will the Conservatives relied on devices such as the Lords' Veto, then perfectly legitimate, but which we should now consider as obsolete as the dodo. Yet they at least clung to the rock of principle. The Liberal record was less dignified. From 1906 to 1910 they were independent of Irish support and emitted accordingly only a most unsatisfying Councils Bill. From 1910 to 1914 they were in sore need of Ireland and strove at each fresh stage to gain her services at the lowest price. Tossed this way and that, half colleague, half counter, on the seas of British social reconstruction and British constitutional revolution, Ireland found little in British government to venerate or be grateful for. Englishmen will vary in how they distribute the shame that belongs to the period, but they will surely all agree on this; from 1906 till 1914 England, under the stress of party conflict, showed herself unfitted to govern Ireland.

The end of that chapter is familiar. A Home Rule Bill, making no provision for the exclusion of Ulster, but conferring on a Dublin Parliament only very limited powers,[1] was introduced in 1912 and passed through the House of Commons by the beginning of 1913. Even without the Irish vote, it commanded a majority in the Commons, but the Lords rejected it by ten to one and it could not pass over their veto till the summer of 1914. When that time came, however, the situation had been transformed by Ulster's preparations under Sir Edward Carson for armed resistance to the death. Already in 1912, a solemn covenant had been signed throughout Protestant Ulster, and open drilling had begun. 1913 saw armed parades and the establishment of a provisional Government with a Military Committee attached. Spring 1914 disclosed the refusal of leading British officers to march against Ulster if called upon, and the great gun-running into Larne. Meanwhile the South had retaliated with their own volunteers—unarmed till July 1914 when Erskine Childers ran a consignment of arms into Howth.

Carson dared the British Government to prosecute him, but the

[1] The Irish Parliament was to have no influence on foreign affairs, no part in the fixing or collection of Customs and Excise, very little control over finance, no control over police for six years. Ireland was to have no army or navy of her own. In all these matters except the first (foreign affairs), the Dominions had by this time achieved complete practical autonomy. Compared with the Bills of 1886 and 1893, this Bill of 1912 gave Ireland less immediate financial autonomy, but control of her police at an earlier date. As regards representation at Westminster, she had one hundred and three representatives under the Union, she would have had none at all under the Bill of 1886, eighty under the Bill of 1893, and under the Bill of 1912, forty-two, *i.e.* rather more than half of what would have been appropriate on a reckoning according to population.

Liberals, looking round at an armed and desperate Ulster, and an England conceivably on the road to civil war, gradually yielded. An amending Bill was added in June 1914 to the Home Rule proposals. In principle the attempt to force Home Rule immediately on the preponderatingly Orange counties was abandoned.

Still the surrender, for which there were intelligible reasons, but which came at least two years too late, did not end the deadlock. The question of what areas were to be excluded from the South seemed insoluble. The King called an all-party conference at Buckingham Palace in July. Nothing came of it. Various incidents raised feeling in both countries to the pitch of fury. For the first time in modern British history the leaders of the Government and the Opposition were not on speaking terms and had to communicate through third parties. It took the outbreak of the Great War to displace the issue from English minds.

Redmond at once offered the Irish Volunteers for the defence of Ireland against the common enemy. "For this purpose the armed Catholics of the South will be only too glad to join arms with the armed Protestant Ulstermen." Home Rule was placed on the Statute Book, but it was not to come into force till a year after the War and a pledge was given that Ulster was not to be coerced. So Carson had won.

Even if the South could have been got to agree to an exclusion of the North-East, Home Rule had never the same chance in 1914 as it had had in 1886 of satisfying Irish Nationalism. Even before the incidents of 1912–14, a youthful manhood was stirring that had lost faith in English politicians and English political institutions. The disgust at what was reckoned Liberal treachery completed the disillusionment. Ulster's claim for separate treatment provoked resentment and yet won a curious respect in the South. Nothing but contempt was felt for the Liberal Government that had allowed the measure to which it was most deeply committed to be overturned by display of arms, by threats of force and by admitted treason and sedition. By 1914 only a miracle could keep Irish Nationalism within the bounds of the Redmondite horizon.

## III

England nearly got her miracle. The Great War gave her an unforeseeable opportunity. Irishmen flocked to the colours, among them Erskine Childers, already an advanced Nationalist.

The cause of Belgium, the rights of small nationalities, appealed to Irishmen; German autocracy and alleged aggressiveness revolted her; there was still enough community of feeling with England to lend glamour to the task of fighting beside her for common ideals. Who knows how it might not have increased if the British War Office could have seen its way to consider, ever so little, Irish national sentiment? Instead Ulster was in all respects encouraged and pampered; she was allowed to form her own division, choose her own officers. The ardour of the South was in every way damped down. They were told in so many words that one had to be careful about arming rebels. The Irish Volunteers were denied recognition, equipment and training. Even when the principle of an Irish division was at last accepted, distinctive badges were for long withheld. Redmond's son was refused a commission. Enthusiasm for recruiting languished as one rebuff followed another; and the country turned its ear to new voices and other counsels. This was how matters stood when England settled down to war.

For close on fifty years she had recognised in the state of Ireland the sorriest blot on her Imperial administration; had admitted its consequence in the enfeeblement of her Empire near its very heart by the persistence of such "a plague-spot of disaffection and sedition." She had tried coercion and she had tried largesse. But gradually her elected House had attached itself to the view that here was a political need that craved political satisfaction. It had passed a measure of self-government, limited, but what was asked for at the moment. That was two years ago; yet Home Rule still seemed as far off as ever and Ireland under fresh resentments was moving further from England every day. Perhaps it was just bad luck that Home Rule should have been introduced in a form that Ulster could force to be amended, bad luck that the War should compel suspension of the amended Bill, bad luck that the exigencies of serious recruiting should brush aside political punctilios. It may or may not have been so. What is certain is that the period of Liberal administration, especially that from 1910 to 1915, sounded the death-knell of British supremacy in Ireland. Such supremacy, so nerve-racking, so nervy, could never be tolerated again.

From now on the period belongs increasingly to that movement on which England, official and unofficial, has conferred the generic name of Sinn Fein. In 1921 Lloyd George hailed the Delegates of the Republic of Ireland as the "Sinn Fein Delegates." "Surely you are not a Sinn Feiner?", they still ask Irishmen, meaning "Surely you want the English back." The instinct is a sound one in so far as it distinguishes *toto cælo* from the Parliamentary movement all those forces that from 1914 onwards renounced hopes of progress by way of Westminster, set out to use the cover of the War for a special effort at final liberation, and determined not to rest until they had eradicated all effective British interference with the domestic government of their country.

Yet the distinctions within the movement were sharp and significant. Sinn Fein proper, the child of Griffith, would usually be called the Right Wing; the I.R.B., still secret and oath-bound, the Left. Neither, when they saw their opportunity to strike, would be deterred for a moment by British authority or law. But Sinn Fein drew its method from the passive resistance used by Deak to obtain legislative equality for Hungary; and its goal, a dual monarchy with England, from the same source. The I.R.B. were Republican or nothing; physical force too, and an armed rising, were of the essence of their creed. Very likely the rising would be stamped out, but under Pearse's teaching they saw in their own deaths the blood-sacrifice that would rouse their countrymen.

The Irish Volunteers[1] were not officially connected with either Sinn Fein or I.R.B. Their titular chief was Eoin MacNeill, Professor of Ancient Irish History in the National University. Intellectually, however, the members owed much to the educational work of Griffith and Sinn Fein, while the I.R.B. moved within its ranks, an active nucleus organising and inciting to revolt, prepared, if need be, to set aside the official leaders. In considering the whole movement, Sinn Fein, I.R.B. and Volunteers, it should be remembered that at the beginning of the War it contained no single Member of Parliament.

Then came 1916 and the Easter Rising, countermanded by Eoin MacNeill when German assistance failed, pushed forward come what might by the I.R.B. This is no place to tell the story of the few hundred young men coming out "in the name of God and of the dead generations" to hold Dublin against an Empire. Nor of what they did and how they died in those seven mad, suicidal, strange, incomparable days, a springtime of rebirth for Ireland. The people of Dublin were irritated by the commotion as quiet citizens well might be. Redmond condemned the rising in the House of Commons (though Dillon shocked Members by suggesting that "it would be a damned good thing if your soldiers were able to put up as good a fight as did these men in Dublin—three

[1] We are talking of that section of the Volunteers that split from Redmond at the outbreak of war.

thousand men[1] against twenty thousand with machine-guns and artillery"). But the executions—all are now agreed—turned the scale of public sympathy. Few, Mr. Churchill reckons them, but there were sixteen of them and they were long drawn out. Only at the last moment were both De Valera and Cosgrave spared. Corroding, Mr. Churchill calls them, and corroding they were. On many a heart till then undecided, they seared Irish nationalism, hatred of England, and the new tireless purpose that would give effect to those emotions. Arthur Griffith, universally respected as a life-long Pacifist, had been dissuaded by the leaders from joining them in the Post Office. Now in his prison cell he heard that men "whom he knew and loved" had been "murdered in cold blood by the English Law." "Something of the primeval man" awoke in him. He clenched his fists and ground his teeth with rage and "longed for vengeance on the murderers." Far away in Chicago, on days when there were several executions, the evening papers were bringing out special editions giving one name only in each to keep the interest lively.

As far as the fighting went the British troops on the whole showed wonderful restraint, but there were some ugly incidents during the week. A British officer was responsible for several stupefying murders. Not till later was it discovered that he was insane. After the rising the deportations, a hundred and twenty-two to convict prisons, and three thousand at random and without trial to internment camps, gave each small circle in Ireland its local martyr and each its vivid notion of tyranny. The internment camp at Frongoch became a great training centre for revenge. Now it was farewell in earnest to constitutional agitation, farewell to everything but arms.

But for two years more the approach retained an aspect of legality. The country soon showed that the day of the Parliamentary Party was done. While the prisoners were still in gaol, Count Plunkett, one of whose sons had been executed and two interned, and McGuiness, himself a prisoner, won by-elections for Sinn Fein. Released in 1917, De Valera gained a resounding triumph in East Clare, and Cosgrave followed him home for Kilkenny. Sinn Fein widened its base to admit all shades of the extra-Parliamentary movement. Its declared aim became the recognition of a Republic, though that once recognised the people were to be allowed to choose what form of government they pre-

[1] Six hundred and eighty-seven men are officially reckoned to have taken part in the Rising on the Irish side.

ferred. De Valera, the one Commandant to survive a rising where he had been the last Commandant to surrender, was elected the new President. He united under him Arthur Griffith, who stood down nobly, and Cathal Brugha, the chief militarist. The Volunteers remained distinct, but they too elected De Valera President. De Valera, then, inspired the country; Griffith was at his elbow, to aid him with a lifetime's plans, while Michael Collins aged only twenty-seven, but future greatness already writ large on him, revived the I.R.B. which De Valera and Brugha had left, and from inside it organised intensively the coming military resurgence.

Meanwhile the British strove desperately amid the press of war to discover ways of pacification. Asquith had visited Ireland after the rising, found "everything including the scenery slightly out of repair in this damnable country," but none the less checked the executions. Lloyd George was now deputed to negotiate with Redmond and Carson. He seemed to reach an understanding, but something intervened—Lord Lansdowne, he tells us—but in Ireland it will always be thought that he had given contradictory promises to North and South. Later the experiment of the "hand-picked" Convention was embarked on. All Irish parties were asked into conference. Elaborate negotiations gave way to elaborate helpless reports. Some say that at one moment agreement was very near, but the public caught no glimpse of it. In any case, the whole affair lacked something of reality; Sinn Fein had abstained from the beginning.

In the country the Parliamentary Party hung on precariously, their organisation holding bravely against the strain. They won by-elections in South Armagh, Waterford, East Tyrone. But the alienation from England soon received a new and urgent impetus. In spring 1918 the British Government decided to extend conscription to Ireland. Sinn Fein and Parliamentary leaders addressed vast indignation meetings from joint platforms, but it was Sinn Fein whose ranks swelled under the menace. A German plot was "discovered" in May and, to their own and everyone's astonishment, De Valera, Griffith, and most of the leaders, were carried off to English gaols. But Collins remained, to scheme and drill and organise more cheerfully and desperately than ever.

Conscription was abandoned, but alienation had by now grown into antipathy. For the rest of the year a British Government, nervous and suspicious with some reason, handled roughly a stirring resentful people.[1] The General Election of 1918 laid bare

[1] In 1920 Sinn Fein issued the following figures of British repression for the period May 1916–December 1918: "Murders, 28 (including 16 executions

the result. Two years before Sinn Fein had been without a single representative with a right to sit at Westminster. Now, fighting on an abstentionist and Republican ticket and the policy of laying their claim before the Peace Conference, they gained every seat but one throughout three-parts of Ireland. Happily Redmond, stricken by blows from many quarters, did not live to see this final massacre of his party.

The victors proceeded to carry out their programme. They abstained from Westminster and refused to recognise British authority. On January 21st 1919 they issued to the nations of the world in Irish, English and French, a Declaration of Irish Independence. They established an "Irish Republic," constituted themselves its legislature (Dail Eireann), appointed an executive from their number, chose De Valera their Príomh-Aire,[1] and began to carry out plans first conceived by Griffith for peacefully supplanting the British Government in Ireland by a *de facto* Government of their own. Their representative quality was, on democratic principles, undeniable; their claim to have behind them the active support of the overwhelming majority of the Irish people was very strong.

In British eyes the position had rotted with a vengeance since 1914, and not in Ireland only are the events of the Great War period reckoned the supreme indictment of British handling of the Irish problem. The muddle over recruiting, the severity over the 1916 Rising, the appearance of trickery in the same year, the limited reference of the Convention, above all the Conscription Bill, a weak-kneed gesture of barbarity that never added a man to the British forces—these things have been ridiculed and censured a hundred times and no doubt they were coarse, tactless bits of work.

Yet it is our personal conviction, probably already made plain, that Britain, barring a miracle, had "lost" Ireland by the beginning of the War. Never again would Ireland tolerate a practical British supremacy over her domestic affairs. 1906–1914 had rendered that out of the question. A sentiment that would otherwise have only

after the Rising, but excluding 21 murders in the 'King Street' Massacre and some other cases in the last days of April); deaths due to prison treatment, 6; armed assaults on civilians, 99; arrests, 4682; deportations, 2064; Courts Martial, 297; sentences, 1402; raids, 271; proclamations and suppressions, 66; total, 8915." (*Daily News*, May 11th 1920.) The figures were, of course, issued with a political motive, but they were never refuted.

[1] Literally First Minister. It was always translated President. The position was that of a Head of the State, who was elected by the Dail and who selected his Cabinet.

gradually emerged was hurried forward by the War. For it created a situation in which those who were not wholeheartedly on England's side were inevitably reckoned against her, in which England could no longer carry out the normal functions of a Government without wounding the susceptibilities of the bulk of the Irish population and estranging many neutral lovers of justice.

"If," it will be protested, "in fighting the greatest war in your history you are menaced close to the heart of your Empire by a plague-spot of sedition and disaffection, how avoid treating it as such?" Yes, no doubt, but how did the "sedition" and "disaffection" come to be?

So much is controversial. The certain fact is that the events of the War period tremendously exacerbated feeling against England and touched deeper chords than any yet of active Irish patriotism. By the end of that period the people were ready to follow through much sacrifice a band of men not long known but of recent inspiring record. Under their leadership the people felt more clearly and immediately than they had ever felt before that Ireland's nationality was something as distinct and inviolable as that of any country in the world. They did not bother themselves much about the footing on which relations between England and Ireland would be placed when Irish independence had been achieved. On the banner of independence their leaders bore aloft they saw written the single word "Republic." When the Republic was recognised the relations between the two countries would no doubt look after themselves.

At last then, after seven and a half centuries, the conquered people had reached the point of full national self-consciousness where the continuance of British interference must appear no less an outrage than the German invasion of 1914 appeared to the Belgians, the point where independence alone could satisfy the national demand. There may have been times (we have suggested that there were), when something less would have been adequate; but readiness to work with England, readiness to accept her ultimate suzerainty, implied towards her some sympathy, some friendliness, some respect. And these towards British Governments, Irishmen could no longer feel.

England on her side had come to lead the world in appreciation of small nationalities. Belgium's wrongs had decided England for war. And they had filled her armies. Now at the Peace Conference it was understood to be the cause of the small nations to which England, through Lloyd George, was specially dedicated; the rights of self-determination which Wilson, amid frantic British approval, had come over to Europe to sustain. Ireland's national claims might have advanced considerably in four years, immeasurably in thirty; but so, it seemed, had England's international philosophy.

# Part Two

## CHAPTER I
## THE WAY OF ENTREATY

> "If arguing makes us sweat,
> The proof of it will turn to redder drops."
> SHAKESPEARE: *Julius Cæsar.*

*The Irish claim rejected by the Peace Conference—The strange war that followed—Impossible to say who began it—Guerilla campaign in full swing by end of 1919—Irish civil achievements by summer 1920.*

BUT it was to be a long time yet before England could dream of applying to Ireland her international categories. Already at the General Election in November 1918 the joint manifesto of Lloyd George and Bonar Law, while paying lip service to the idea of a settlement "on the basis of self-government," had barred any path that led "to a complete severance of Ireland from the British Empire"—the one solution agreed on by the great majority of the Irish population. The Declaration of Irish Independence on January 21st 1919 and the establishment thenceforth of a native system of government in rivalry with the British, were received with unassumed indifference, looked on as gestures of theatrical mummery and not intriguing ones at that. Two years later Lloyd George could only remember of all this period that "when peace came there were gigantic problems which absorbed the mind of each government in the world."

*The Times* found in the incidents of January 21st no immediate occasion for a leading article, but a quotation from the *Irish Times* probably satisfied its readers' requirements. "The Press Gallery," ran the extract, "witnessed a solemn act of defiance of the British Empire by a body of young men who have not the slightest notion of that Empire's power and resources. The more quickly Ireland becomes convinced of the folly which elected them, the sooner sanity will return." Only *The Freeman's Journal* showed much appreciation of what was coming. "If the proceedings were seriously meant and if there was any intention to attempt to carry the decisions into effect, we greatly fear that we are on the eve of one of the most tragic chapters in the history of Ireland."

There was never much chance that Ireland would secure representation at the Peace Conference. It is true that President Wilson had used language which strongly suggested that he would admit the Irish claim to self-determination. The American Senate and the House of Representatives passed resolutions supporting it. Three American delegates from the Irish Race Convention obtained through Wilson's offices British safe conducts for a visit to Ireland, and returned thence horrified by the coercionist régime. But when these latter gentlemen reminded Wilson of his promise to strive for a settlement under which "every people in the world should choose its own master," the President could do little more than join his lamentations to theirs.

"You have touched," he said, "on the great meta-physical tragedy of to-day. My words have raised hopes in the hearts of millions of people.... When I gave utterance to those words I said them without the knowledge that nationalities existed which are coming to us to-day." Still, Wilson had always known that Ireland existed, and there was understandable disillusion in that country when on May 31st the American Peace Delegation finally refused to recommend to a hearing at the Conference "the representatives of the so-called Irish Republic."

During a debate on the Peace Treaties in the House of Commons Joseph Devlin asked Lloyd George why he did not propose to apply the principle of self-determination to Ireland, but the Prime Minister evaded the issue in approved fashion by harping on the Ulster difficulty. Reminded further of the lines on which he had sponsored the national rights of Czechoslovakia, he retorted that after all the Austrian Empire from which Czechoslovakia was freed had been in a broken and moribund condition. *The Nation's* comment hits off the logic of the period. "The present condition is pitiful. In face of it our proclamations of self-determination in Paris die away in a dreary cant and snuffle."

By July, then, of 1919 the claims of a small nation to be governed according to the will of its people had been proved inadmissible so long as a proud and virile Empire felt otherwise disposed—and so long as the small nation confined the expression of its national will to voting at the polls and other pacific means of ventilating grievance.

Ireland changed her methods, and in two years her results were changed. In July 1919 Lloyd George was agreeing with Sir Henry Wilson that Dominion Home Rule for Ireland was "all pure nonsense." In December 1919, by which time sixteen policemen had been killed, he was introducing a mild measure of Home Rule which, besides partitioning the country, conferred on a Dublin Parliament powers no greater than those under the Act of 1914. By October 1920, when a fierce guerilla war was raging, he was promising to break up "the small body of assassins, a real murder gang, dominating the country and terrorising it"; and at the same time dismissing Dominion Home Rule with the question, "Was ever such lunacy proposed by anybody?" In November 1920 "he had murder by the throat."

But in December 1920, within a fortnight of Bloody Sunday, when fourteen British "intelligence officers" were shot in their houses, he was for the first time making serious efforts to get in touch with Michael Collins. In this month, too, he was privately exhibiting leanings in the direction of Dominion Home Rule. In June and July 1921 he was discarding all previous conditions of negotiation, inviting the Irish leaders into conference, agreeing to a truce without surrender of arms, and making Ireland an offer of Dominion Status. This after six months in which the Army had lost three times as heavily as in the whole year preceding, and when Sinn Fein had just burnt down the Dublin Customs House, and begun to extend its "outrages" to England. Those are the overwhelming facts.

Pondering them and the years they illustrate, we shall still find much that is creditable in the English surrender of 1921; plenty of courage and wisdom among the individual statesmen responsible for the Dominion offer, plenty of humanity among the mass of the people that called for a cessation of coercion, when it began to learn the full extent of the crimes that were being committed in its name. But in the offer itself, the offer of Dominion Status, far though it went beyond any previous offer to Ireland, we shall be hard put to it to find much generosity. For it came too late, and it was wrested not presented. The smile that had gathered on English faces when Ireland voted, was not wiped off till Ireland turned to violence. What England had so often and so long denied to Ireland "hopeful, expectant, almost suppliant," she conceded only when she found her savage, ruthless, armed.

The Anglo-Irish struggle from 1919 to 1921 has been looked at from various angles and given a variety of names. It has been likened to the Dutch, American and Italian Wars of Independence, the American Civil War, the Boer War, to the French and Russian Revolutions, to the conflict between the Belgian civil population and the German Army of Occupation, and to innumerable revolts of oppressed nationalities under the old Russian, Turkish, and

Austro-Hungarian régime. One day, no doubt, some scholar in comparative strife will amuse himself by basing a monumental work on analogies such as these. Our purpose is simpler. It includes no close record or analysis of the technical military developments, nor does it aim at recapturing the exaltations or the hatreds of the time. We do no more than set out the main sequence of events, the main devices on which each country relied, and the main political reactions.

Now the first thing that must be recognised is that the Anglo-Irish struggle from mid-1919 to mid-1921, above all from mid-1920 to mid-1921, was in the most vital sense in which ordinary men used the word *a war*. The British Government might continue to the end to deny Ireland belligerent rights, to treat (and execute) her soldiers as rebels, every operation they performed as an "outrage," every loss they inflicted as "murder." They might stop short even at extending Martial Law beyond a comparatively small area, lest the true extent of the "rebellion" should reach the outer world. But Lloyd George once blurted out in the House of Commons that he was fighting a war; while on June 21st 1921 Lord Birkenhead admitted in a considered statement for the Government that there was "a small war in Ireland, in which the British military methods had failed to keep pace with and to overcome the military methods of their opponents." After all, you had two countries passionately attached to contradictory ends. The leaders of each believed that the only means of attaining its own particular end was the organised slaughter of those who assisted the opposing Government. Each country acted on this belief. And what was that but war?

Still it was an odd sort of war. The British showed scant respect for the rules of the Hague Convention. They carried hostages on lorries, they terrorised the civil population, they destroyed the property of civilians when no military necessity dictated. But on the other hand the Irish forces seldom wore uniform or distinctive badges, and (though this omission had been condoned in the Boer War and was frequently imitated in 1919 to 1921 by the British police) they could hardly expect much encouragement from an appeal to any generally recognised code. Each side in fact made its own precedents and used all methods judged essential for victory, in so far as seemed expedient in view of world opinion and in so far as its own humanity permitted.

Consider, for instance, Sunday, November 21st 1920. Not that it disclosed the most characteristic methods of either side, but it does give us an insight into the particular lengths to which each side was ready to carry its general scheme. That Sunday morning, about nine o'clock, fourteen British officers and ex-officers living in Dublin and believed by their opponents to be engaged in intelligence work, and to be aiming specially at the lives of the Sinn Fein leaders, were shot in their beds, or as they were dressing, some of them in the presence of their wives.[1] That afternoon a large crowd gathered at Croke Park, Dublin, for the football match between Dublin and Tipperary. The game was in progress when a body of Crown forces drove up from Phoenix Park in lorries, and began straightway shooting up crowd and players. Twelve were killed, including a Tipperary player, eleven dangerously wounded and fifty-four injured, before a frenzied stampede smashed the barriers and carried the crowd to safety. That evening McKee and Clancy, prominent I.R.A. officers, were hacked about with bayonets in Dublin Castle before being shot against a wall in company with Clune, a man suspected of being a Sinn Feiner. The supporters of each country must realise that the line that their side took on this day was not incidental or exceptional (there was much that was far more cruel) but was integral to policy, as calculated to inspire fear in appropriate quarters.[2]

Who began the war? Most Englishmen would say it was Ireland, and many Irishmen, seeing in the war a desperate move against a long brutal repression, will admit the impeachment with pride. Other Irishmen, however, will argue vehemently to the contrary. Up to quite late in 1919, they will say, Ireland hoped to achieve her freedom by passive resistance only, but the suppression of Dail Eireann in September of that year, the issue of warrants for the arrest of its members, and the subsequent drive against every national activity, left no course open but to take the lives of those whose business it was to destroy the native Government. For otherwise, they argue, the native Government, the expression by this time of the whole National Movement, could not have survived a month.

The discussion on these lines is barren. Our sole conclusion will be this. If England had been prepared to enter into peaceful rivalry

[1] See Appendix 2.

[2] It is true that the Irish deeds were directly inspired from Headquarters, while those of the British police were probably an embarrassment to Lloyd George and Greenwood, if they ever cared to know the truth of them. But the shooting-up of Croke Park and the bayoneting and shooting of McKee and Clancy were a part of the general British policy of "unauthorised reprisals," that is, of allowing the police a free hand. And "unauthorised reprisals" played just the same part on the British side as the execution of what were called spies played on the Irish.

with Dail Eireann for the allegiance of Irishmen, no doubt Dail Eireann would have been happy to compete; but this was always out of the question. We can see now that the attempt to supplant a British by an Irish Government involved always a readiness to fight and a readiness to kill on behalf of the latter. We can detect now in Ireland's manhood from 1916 onwards a growing sense that while the Volunteers would be helpless without the mass of the nation behind them, it would always be the Volunteers from whom at the point of crisis the decisive pressure must come. It was with this kind of prescience that Michael Collins was writing privately in April 1919: "At the present moment things are remarkably high-pitched. It is a most interesting thing to watch from day to day the downfall of the stern Government régime. Not indeed that it is ended, nor even that it won't flash forth occasionally again, but the impotence of the military governors is gradually taking them into a position which is almost chaotic. Certain it is that we are fast reaching the breaking-point, and then..."

As a matter of fact it is impossible to mark off logical stages in the developments that culminated in the guerilla war. 1917 and 1918 had seen more than a thousand Irishmen "arrested without warrant and deported or held in custody without trial; about a dozen Irishmen killed by the bullets or bayonets of the Imperial British police or soldiers."[1] In these years only one policeman had been killed.

But the Declaration of Independence on January 21st 1919 had indicated a state of war with England, and at the first subsequent meeting of the Volunteer Headquarters Staff, Cathal Brugha, their acting chief, was emphatic that a new situation had arisen. "He pointed out to the Volunteers they had now become the army of a lawfully constituted Government, elected by the people, and were entitled morally and legally when in the execution of their duty to slay the officials and agents of the foreign invader who was waging war upon our native Government."[2]

Two days before this private pronouncement Dan Breen and other Volunteers had shot dead two policemen at Soloheadbeg who resisted a raid for gelignite. Now the new principles were authoritatively circulated and the Soloheadbeg affair endorsed by implication in a bellicose editorial in *Ant-Ōglách*, the official organ of the Volunteers. It is true that at this time a large part of Sinn

[1] Report of American Commission of Enquiry, not an unbiased source but here apparently to be relied on.

[2] Beasley, *Michael Collins and the Making of a New Ireland*, Vol. I, pp. 270 and 271.

Fein was still "strongly averse to any kind of bloodshed,"[1] and that by the spring the Dail was going no further against the R.I.C. than publicly to declare them traitors and pass on them a decree of social ostracism. But the incidents of bloodshed multiplied under the stress of Volunteer raiding for arms and of police attempts to arrest Volunteers and leading Sinn Feiners. On July 30th Detective-Sergeant Smith of the "G" (Detective) Division, Dublin Metropolitan Police, was shot dead by official order of Volunteer Headquarters. With the suppression of the Dail in September, and the more or less consistent drive from that time onwards against its personnel and organisation, the issue between Volunteers and British police—the British military were as yet only incidentally involved—had clearly to be fought to a finish.[1]

The accumulated knowledge of the "G" men, or detectives, was reckoned a peculiar menace to the revolutionary administration. "Without their criminal agents in the capital," said Collins, "how could they carry out that 'removal' of the leaders that they considered essential for their victory? The new spy could not step into the old one's knowledge."[2] By the end of 1919 the whole of the "G" Division had been killed off, intimidated into impotence, or induced to lend Sinn Fein secret help.

The year had seen the slaughter of sixteen policemen in all. On December 19th the Lord-Lieutenant, Lord French, was ambushed, but he escaped unhurt. Early in January of the new year Carrigtwohill Barracks in Co. Cork surrendered after a few hours' siege—the first barracks to be captured after serious fighting. By this time there was no concealing the fact that the greater part of Ireland was in a state of guerilla war.

Attacks on police barracks became still commoner and much more successful. By summer 1920 the police had given up all pretence of carrying out their civil duties and had been withdrawn into the larger towns. (One single night the I.R.A., to consolidate and celebrate their triumph, sent three hundred and fifteen evacuated barracks up in flames.) Partly for these reasons, partly under the competition of the Civil and Criminal Courts of the Republic, the British Law Courts became deserted. The Trinity Sessions at Swinford, Co. Mayo, usually lasted five days and before a crowded court a list of twenty to thirty cases would be disposed of. In June

[1] The "British police" at this time were still the old R.I.C.—a centrally organised, well-armed body of Irishmen of magnificent physique and high personal popularity, but associated so largely with political repression that they had come to be regarded as the spearhead of the alien forces of occupation.

[2] Collins, *The Path to Freedom* (1922), p. 83.

1920 the body of the court was empty save for one old woman. No business was done.

It is not often realised in England how far now and later Dail Eireann succeeded in making itself the *de facto* Government of Ireland. Departments of Finance, Defence, Trade and Commerce, Agriculture, Home Affairs, Local Government, Labour and Propaganda were established. Sweeping Sinn Fein triumphs at the local elections of January and June 1920 confirmed national support for these organs. De Valera raised $6,000,000 in America, and Collins £380,000 in Ireland on interest-bearing bonds to provide them with finance. All kinds of supplementary institutions were placed on an effective footing: among them a Land Bank, a Land Commission, Courts of Arbitration to settle land disputes, an expert Commission to plan the fuller utilisation of Ireland's natural resources; most elaborate and realistic of all, a whole new framework of Civil and Criminal Courts and a whole new force of Republican police.

By July 1920 there were few places outside Dublin and North-East Ulster where the King's Writ continued to run. And testimony in favour of the new Courts was astonishingly general. Lord Monteagle praised them, the *Chicago Tribune* praised them, the *Manchester Guardian* and the *Daily News* praised them, the *Daily Mail* praised them; even the *Irish Times* had no complaint to make of them, and plenty of fun to poke at their supplanted rivals. The Commission appointed by the Society of Friends reported: "Moderate people and many Unionists admit the only protection they enjoy is provided by the Sinn Fein police." By this time the Republican administration possessed, as Mr. Bonar Law admitted, "all the symbols and all the realities of a Government."

## CHAPTER II

# THE WAY OF VIOLENCE

"If I were an American, as I am an Englishman, while a foreign troop was landed in my country, I never would lay down my arms, never—never—never."

CHATHAM: *Speech in* 1777.

*The British reply—A year of horrors—The Irish military programme—Examples*

THE year July 1920 to June 1921 saw the British reply to these achievements. The Army became for the first time seriously engaged, and lost altogether in Ireland fifty-three officers and one hundred and twenty-seven men. But these figures were tiny compared to those of the reinforcements steadily poured in, and at the time of the Truce the total strength of the military forces was appraching eighty thousand. Of more immediate concern to Sinn Fein, thousands of ex-Service men at "ten shillings a day and all found," were collected by advertisement in England to fill the gaps caused by death or resignation in the ranks of the R.I.C.; and an auxiliary division of fifteen hundred supposed ex-officers was recruited in the same manner, though at a pound a day instead of ten shillings, to cope with the flying columns of the Volunteers.[1]

When the first of these forces arrived in Ireland a sufficient number of R.I.C. uniforms was not available. The new police, accordingly, were dressed in khaki with black belts and caps, and the first company being sent to Limerick were nicknamed "Black-and-Tans" after a famous local pack of hounds. The name stuck and was often applied generically to Black-and-Tans proper and Auxiliaries alike. The latter, when fully equipped, wore dark-blue uniforms and black Glengarry caps. Both bodies were in practice employed for purposes that General Macready describes as "purely military."

The same year (July 1920–June 1921) saw the passing into law in September of the Restoration of Order in Ireland Act. Under this Act, or provisions made under it, Military Courts of Inquiry were established in place of Coroners' Inquests,[2] Martial Law was

[1] "The whole police force now includes upwards of 15,000 men, of whom nearly 1500 are these Auxiliaries" (*Round Table*, June 1921). The proportion of Irishmen in the police was by this time small.

[2] The latter had shown a propensity to refuse to return verdicts of murder on dead police and soldiers, but to return verdicts of murder against British police and soldiers and in addition against high British authorities when a Sinn Feiner had been killed.

applied in December and January to eight Southern counties, and at the same time in the Martial Law area was introduced a policy of "authorised" or official reprisals. Irish "outrages," *i.e.* attacks on British forces, were to be punished by the destruction, on the authority of a Brigade Commander, of the house or property of anyone who might be considered "implicated in or cognisant of" such outrage. After six months' trial it was appreciated that Sinn Fein could retaliate still more destructively against the property of Loyalists. Shortly before the Truce it was decided to abandon the policy of authorised reprisals.

The year, too, saw the breaking-up or driving underground of many Sinn Fein courts and much other Sinn Fein machinery of government. The authority of the Sinn Fein police was shaken, and one of them who arrested a couple of cattle-stealers got five years' penal servitude for his pains. In the course of this year, too, the British forces reasserted their ability to proceed whithersoever they chose throughout the country—though for the more adventurous journeys they had always to be sure of a good superiority over any forces likely to be encountered. But at the same time it witnessed the perfection of the I.R.A. system of flying columns in the country districts, and in the capital the astounding series of ambushes carried out by the Dublin Brigade. The destruction of the Customs House on May 25th completed and symbolised the utter breakdown of the ordinary processes of British civil administration. Outside the military arena British government now exercised as little restraint as it had long commanded loyalty.

Further, this year and the few months preceding it will always be remembered for certain outstanding deeds of ruthlessness, where all natural feeling was subordinated to the heartless logic of patriotism. On the part of Sinn Fein three performances provoked more horror than the rest. On March 27th 1920 Alan Bell, an elderly magistrate engaged in the proscription of the National Loan, and believed to be connected with the work of arresting its promoters, was dragged from a tramcar and shot, nobody who was present, except one nurse, raising the feeblest protest. On November 21st 1920, "Bloody Sunday," fourteen British officers and ex-officers were shot as already described. Shortly before the Truce, Mrs. Lindsay, an old lady of a well-known Unionist family, gave information that averted an ambush, saved the lives of several British soldiers, and led to the capture of several Irish Volunteers. The British authorities were informed that if the Volunteers were shot Mrs. Lindsay would be treated in the same way. The Volunteers were executed, and Mrs. Lindsay, too, was killed. Volunteer Headquarters did not know until too late, and Cathal Brugha or Michael Collins would have saved her. But perhaps she would not have thanked them. She came of an order that had produced Wellington and Roberts and she died a credit to it.

If we are looking for another tragedy to cast against Sinn Fein, if we require anything intrinsically more pathetic than the wreck made of the old R.I.C., we need go no further than the shooting of Major Compton Smith after a warning to General Strickland of what his fate would be if the execution of certain "Clonmult prisoners of war" were persisted in. In his last letter to his wife he wrote:

> "I am to be shot in an hour's time. Dearest, your husband will die with your name on his lips, your face before his eyes, and he will die like an Englishman and a soldier.
>
> "I leave my cigarette case to the regiment, my medals to my father, and my watch to the officer who is to execute me, because I believe him to be a gentleman, and to mark the fact that I bear him no malice for carrying out what he sincerely believes to be his duty."

Defending the Treaty in the Dail, General Mulcahy, Chief of Staff, argued passionately against any policy that would lead to a renewal of war, and put on Ireland "the responsibility of killing in self-defence the Compton Smiths of England."

The policy behind these executions, or murders, as they were called in England, must be understood.

The official Irish doctrine in its most rigorous form laid down that any traitor or spy was liable to execution, liable, that is to say, to be shot at sight. A traitor was an Irishman, whether policeman or civilian, who actively assisted the Crown forces; a spy was any agent who, wearing no uniform, collected information of military value to the Crown. The latter might be Irish, as the "G" men had been, or they might be English, like the Secret Service man "Jameson," or the notorious *agent provocateur* specially released from prison for the job, or for the most part the officers and ex-officers killed on Bloody Sunday.

It would be absurd to claim that the overthrow of British rule in Ireland was accomplished in perfect harmony with instructions from Headquarters, that mean animus and squalid vendetta never played their part in the local decision who was or was not a spy or traitor; it would be absurd to claim that the Irish executions were never once the murders, planned or casual, that they were invariably painted in England. Many Loyalists will always carry in their hearts the knowledge from individual cases that the rough justice was sometimes no justice at all. Between the beginning of January and the middle of April 1921, Sinn Fein, so Dublin Castle claimed, killed seventy-three civilians, including four women. It is impossible to believe that a military purpose was in every instance served.

But no one should carry away the idea that the Protestants as such were ever submitted to a pogrom of the kind with which Belfast Catholics, whether or not they gave provocation, were all through this period familiar. The figures of civilian slaughter look small even proportionately beside those of the Russian or French Revolutions. Nor is it possible to point to any violent revolution, guerilla war or war of independence, where the insurrectionists combined such passionate ardour with such disinterestedness and self-control. The I.R.A. staked much, as General Macready admits, on absolute sobriety (comparing favourably with the Auxiliaries, whose average wage bill was £5 a week in canteens alone). The I.R.A. police stamped out land-grabbing abruptly and refused to allow a political to become a social upheaval.

Even where the rule condemning traitors and spies was carried out to the letter, humanity kept breaking through. A servant at an inn had given up important secrets entrusted to him and he was shot as a traitor. His wife, thinking him shot by the British, applied to the Irish Relief Organisation for assistance. The application was being turned down when Collins, hearing she had children, intervened in her favour. "The poor little devils need the money." And the mother and the children were kept from knowing how the father had failed.

But while the policy of individual executions was vital to the defence of the infant Government, the main task of the Volunteers was different. That task was to act in units of from ten to forty men in assaults, first on police barracks, and later on bodies of military and Black-and-Tans as they moved about the countryside in lorries. And here the strength of the rival forces is all-important and easy to overlook. British ministers and generals caused their disciples some bewilderment by referring to the I.R.A. at one moment as "a small body of assassins, a real murder gang"; at the next as never attacking except with a numerical superiority of twenty to one (Macready), and as numbering, in a total population of three million, some two hundred thousand men (Macpherson).

Yet there was a sense in which they spoke truer than they knew. Nearly the whole of Southern Ireland was behind the I.R.A. (and as later years have proved, from sympathy not fear), while a large part of the country's youth was formally enrolled for service. But the difficulties were so great of financing wholesale release from civil occupation, the quantity of arms and ammunition was so small that, to quote Michael Collins: "In the whole of Ireland there were not more than three thousand fighting men."

These three thousand inexperienced Volunteers, with very few machine-guns, no artillery, and always inadequate ammunition, were opposed in the later stages by sixty thousand or more British troops and fifteen thousand British police. In these circumstances and against these odds, their mobility, their knowledge of the country, and the support of the inhabitants would not alone have preserved the I.R.A. through two years' guerilla war as an effective striking force. There was needed also a grim yet jubilant idealism, toughening their fibre, lifting their spirit, flowing from a rare conviction that their cause was just, issuing in rare ferocity at bay.

It remains to give a few examples of the warfare they engaged in. At Fermoy twelve Volunteers, armed with revolvers and sticks, overcame eighteen armed soldiers and took their rifles, killing one of them in the scuffle. But on this occasion the troops were taken by surprise and put up little fight; the typical engagement lasted for hours. At Macroom twenty-seven Volunteers ambushed seventeen Auxiliaries and killed all except one left for dead. At Roscarbery thirty-seven Volunteers were surrounded in Burgatia House by about eighty soldiers and Black-and-Tans, and fought their way out without loss. At Roscarbery again a few weeks later the same column captured the strongly-fortified Roscarbery Barracks, "the toughest job of its kind yet achieved by the Volunteers."[1]

At Ballinalee twenty Volunteers under McKeon, a veritable Bayard among blacksmiths, ambushed and routed with heavy loss a party of close on a hundred Auxiliaries out on a reprisal jaunt and apparently in a drunken state. At the same place some time later McKeon with twelve Volunteers fought eighteen Auxiliaries to a standstill and forced them to surrender after three of them had been killed and two mortally wounded. The biggest operation carried out by the I.R.A. was the burning of the Customs House on May 25th 1921. The purpose of destruction was successfully accomplished, but of a hundred and twenty

[1] Beasley, *Michael Collins and the Making of a New Ireland*, Vol. II, p. 181.

Volunteers engaged, seventy were trapped in the burning building and taken prisoner, an irreparable loss.

In none of these fights did the Irish wear uniform, but in other respects no soldier could complain of their conduct. If they were captured after a fight or even found with arms in a Martial Law area, they knew that their lives were forfeit and that they would probably be hung or shot—possibly after torture such as that sworn to on affidavit by Kevin Barry, or a bayoneting such as that accorded Clancy and McKee. Yet they themselves spared their prisoners, and, having no prisons, usually released them. In a few cases, however, they used them as hostages, and in the fight at Macroom they admittedly gave no quarter. But there, it seems, a wounded Auxiliary lying on the ground had fired on the Volunteers after the white flag had been hoisted.

Taking all the Irish methods together, Michael Collins summed them up to General Crozier thus: "England embarked on an underground war of assassination and I replied with the same weapon. England's shock troops were assassinators. Mine were ambushers, but at times we too assassinated. We had no gaols and we had therefore to kill all spies, informers and double-crossers." And at another time he claimed: "We conducted the conflict, difficult as it was, with the unequal terms imposed by the enemy, as far as possible, according to the rules of war."

General Macready could never forgive the Irish soldiers. "It was by no means pleasant," he remembers of his talks with them after the Truce, "to be obliged in the course of duty to associate with men whose methods, apart from their devotion to their cause, can only be characterised as murder and assassination by those who hold that even the art of slaying one's fellow-creatures should be marked by some adherence to the chivalry of bygone days."[1] The *Round Table*, well disposed to Ireland at this time, only defended their methods by recalling the resort of desperate savages to such instruments as poison-tipped arrows. But looking at the matter dispassionately to-day, does anyone seriously suggest that the Irish methods evinced a national cruelty greater than that required for waging an orthodox war, or that any country, however civilised and refined, would eschew those methods if, like Ireland in 1919 to 1921, she found herself fighting for national existence against fantastic odds?

What is true, however, is that the peculiar methods of war adopted by Ireland loosed understandable hatreds on the British side which themselves bred hatreds in return; further, that the

[1] Macready, *Annals of an Active Life*, Vol. II, p. 602.

adoption of the peculiar methods overturned at vital points all conventional notions of what was and what was not murder without putting anything definite in their place. From the spirit of hatred so disseminated, from the shock to ordinary morals so administered, many Irishmen sorrowfully admit that their country is still suffering to-day.

## CHAPTER III

## THE BLACK-AND-TANS

"*Second Murderer*: I am one, my liege,
Whom the vile blows and buffets of the world
Have so incensed, that I am reckless what
I do to spite the world."

SHAKESPEARE: *Macbeth.*

*The British task—Possible expedients—The Policy adopted—The new police—Responsibility of the masters.*

THE British problem was two-fold. First to disperse or annihilate the Irish flying columns, more or less defined bodies of troops scattered about the countryside. This task, in spite of their huge superiority in numbers, they never seemed likely to accomplish. From the spring of 1921, General Macready organised a series of drives similar to those undertaken during the South African War. But though "the effect on the inhabitants" is described as having been "excellent," "the result so far as the actual capture of prominent rebels was concerned was not great." And Winston Churchill admits that by June 1921 to have "restored order in Ireland would have required measures on altogether a grander scale." A hundred thousand new special troops, thousands of armoured cars, cordons of block-houses, and barbed wire would have been necessary; so, too, would have been "a systematic rummaging and questioning of every individual." It would not be true to say that the I.R.A. "outrages" aroused any less resentment or provoked any less retaliation when conducted by a flying column than when they were the product of individuals. Still, a definite means of dealing with the flying columns existed if England was prepared to undergo the financial sacrifices and political reproaches that it involved.

The second task was to defeat that section of the Volunteers that continued to live and operate from among the ordinary civilian population, from whom indeed it was quite impossible to distinguish them. With the paralysing menace these men constituted to the British civil and military administration, there were in principle three obvious ways of dealing.

(1) Punishment (including, of course, execution) could have been inflicted whenever there was sufficient formal evidence to satisfy a Civil or Military Court that the accused was responsible for any share in an "outrage."

(2) Punishment could have been inflicted on all persons suspected on broad grounds of rendering assistance to the enemy.

(3) Hostages could have been held and executed or property earmarked and destroyed if, after warning, the enemy persisted in "outrages."[1]

Now all these methods would have inevitably thrown tasks on the military and police at once brutalising and impossible to carry out with any certainty of justice to every individual. And all of them, especially when they included such powers as those of executing rebels on no charge save that of possessing arms, must have provoked frenzied outcry in an Ireland passionately denying all British right of intrusion. Yet once given the right of a large country to hold in subjection a small nation in revolt against it, such methods as those we have just described would strike one as not incompatible with national decency and honour.

It was not, however, by sticking to such principles as these that the British Government in 1920 and 1921 managed to excite contempt and disgust among every section of civilised humanity to whose ears the atrocities of the British agents floated. Nor can the fact that the British name was dragged lower than ever before or since be attributed to the excesses of a few undesirables acting in gross defiance of authority. A party of Black-and-Tans, capturing six unarmed Volunteers at Kerry Pike near Cork, cut out the tongue of one, the nose of another, the heart of another, and battered in the skull of a fourth. But this kind of lunatic bestiality will be dismissed as exceptional. "One finds," it will be contended, "a few such things in every guerilla war." There is no evidence that the British authorities were anything but shocked by such extreme occurrences in Ireland. After all, there were limits

[1] The British adopted the first two of these three methods, but the third only so far as it could be applied to property. They never indulged in "shooting by 'roster,'" which from his diaries it appears that Sir Henry Wilson recommended.

to what was permitted, even to the Black-and-Tans. Was not the Auxiliary cadet who shot dead Canon Magner and a passing schoolboy put on his trial for murder before being pronounced insane?

Let the freak atrocities on each side be cancelled out. Nevertheless, this peculiar barbarity of British policy remains over: over a long period it explicitly condoned and implicitly pointed the way to arbitrary pillage, arson, assault, and massacre, by organised bodies of its agents.

Sometimes these crimes were a direct reply to a local Sinn Fein "outrage," sometimes not. Behind the whole programme of so-called unauthorised reprisals there was one military purpose and one only, that of rendering Ireland, in the words of the *Police Journal*, "an appropriate hell for rebels"; in other words, the terrorisation of the civil population and the reduction of their support for Sinn Fein. As General Macready puts it: "These unauthorised reprisals had a marked effect in curbing the activities of the I.R.A. in the immediate localities, and on these grounds were justified or at all events winked at by those in control of the police."[1]

Or in the words of the American Commission of Enquiry: "There exists neither under the laws of war nor under the codes of Martial Law in civilised States any justification for assassination, pillaging, or terrorism, as a means of suppressing insurrection. And yet this Commission is reluctantly forced to the conclusion that such forces are relied upon by the Imperial British forces in Ireland to being the Irish people once more under the control of the Imperial Crown."

How pack into the summary catalogue of a paragraph the crimes committed by the Crown forces? In a single week they shot up and sacked Balbriggan, Miltown Malbay, Lahinch, Ennistymon, Trim, and Mallow, murdering as often as not; in a single month they gave twenty-four towns a dose of the same medicine, and they seldom let the pace die down. They burnt property in Cork to the value of three million pounds, including the Carnegie Library and the City Hall, forcing back the fire brigade and cutting the hose; they burnt down sixty-one Co-operative creameries,[2] and sometimes, as at Abbeydorney, the actual incendiaries reappeared to hold an inquiry into the burning. They robbed shops, post-offices, and banks, one of them opening up a depôt

[1] Macready, *Annals of an Active Life*, Vol. II, p. 498.
[2] By April 1921.

in the north of England for goods stolen in the execution of his duty.

They flogged, beat up and murdered, as the mood or the occasion prompted. They tied a seventeen-year-old boy on a triangle and tried to make him talk by daily flogging; they tortured for information to an extent dependent, so General Crozier tells us, "on the ideas of commanders and the rope given to intelligence officers." They tried to "do in" Hugh Martin who gave the facts about them in the *Daily News*; they planned to murder Bishop Fogarty at Killaloe by throwing him into the river in a sack. They murdered among an interminable list of non-belligerents Father Griffin, Lord Mayor McCurtain of Cork, Mayor O'Callaghan of Limerick, ex-Mayor Clancy of Limerick (the last three in the presence of their wives), and Captain Prendergast, an ex-British officer and Christian Brother. Logically, perhaps, it is wrong to mention Annie O'Neill, aged eight, shot in mistake for some young men seen "running away," or Mrs. Quinn shot with her child in her arms. Both of these performances were no doubt what the Prime Minister called the latter, "unfortunate incidents" that always happen in war, though perhaps everybody will not join Sir Hamar Greenwood in acquitting the British forces of all responsibility for the death of Annie O'Neill. Before a single County Court in Clare Judge Bodkin reported that there were one hundred and thirty-nine cases in which it was proved that criminal injuries had been committed by the armed forces of the Government. "In no case was there any evidence to suggest that the victims had been guilty of any offence."

Beside these performances the bombing of Commander Kenworthy's salmon river, which aroused so much indignation among Members of Parliament, pales into an amiable salutation or rough pleasantry at worst. A Divisional Commissioner, afterwards shot dead in the County Club at Cork, explained the new policy to his men. "You may make mistakes occasionally, and innocent persons may be shot, but that cannot be helped and you are bound to get the right persons sometimes."[1] He proved a sanguine prophet.

Most of these outrages were the work of the new police. The military were not guiltless—General Macready admits four occasions when they indulged in unauthorised reprisals. When, for instance, Brigadier-General Lucas was kidnapped and held captive, his men ran amok in Fermoy. But after two years of exceptional temptations to free themselves from its restraints, the

[1] For report of speech see Crozier, *Ireland for Ever*, p. 286, Appendix D.

honour of the Army still meant much to the troops, and few will quarrel with the verdict that General Crozier attributes to the peasants who went through the Terror. "Most British military officers tried their best to hand them out a fair deal, but the police played a dirty game throughout."

What manner of men were these Black-and-Tans and Auxiliaries? The force was raised, Commander Kenworthy has recorded, with the help of an M.P. interested in publicity. "He advertised for recruits in certain Sunday newspapers, and he attracted a peculiar type of individual."[1] "They were selected," Mr. Churchill tells us, "from a great press of applicants on account of their intelligence, their characters and their records in the War." But when he wrote those words he can hardly have had all the facts at his disposal. "A tough lot," is one of the milder judgments passed on them by General Macready. There is reason to believe that some of them were released from penal servitude for service in Ireland, and no doubt at all that a good number of them had at some time or other seen the inside of gaols. Of how many this last is true one cannot say, but a good authority has applied it at a guess to three hundred out of the fifteen hundred soi-disant, though not always in fact, ex-officers, of the Auxiliary Division. Even a superbly indulgent Government could not tolerate all their doings. Several were convicted of robbery under arms, and two were hanged for murder with intent to rob.

On April 19th 1921 Lloyd George admitted that there had been "deplorable excesses," that a certain number of undesirables had originally got into the corps, and that two hundred and sixty-seven of the police had been dismissed as unsuitable, forty-three removed as the result of prosecutions, and in addition twenty-four found guilty and sentenced by Court Martial. Not unnaturally he tried to use these figures to prove that the police were now, in April 1921, not only "gallant" (they had been that all along), but possessed of a "patience and forbearance that would command not the condemnation but the admiration of posterity." That, in fact, they were purged and pure.

But this line of defence will hardly stand inquiry. General Crozier's testimony contradicts it flatly. By November 1st 1920 he had dispensed with the services of over fifty Auxiliary policemen ("ex-officers") for various acts of indiscipline, but "shortly after that time a heavy and hidden hand came down." In February 1921 thirty-one armed police were present at the robbery of Protestant

[1] "It is common knowledge," said *The Times*, "that the Black-and-Tans were recruited from ex-soldiers for a rough and dangerous task."

women shopkeepers in Trim. General Crozier dismissed twenty-six and put five back for trial. His orders were countermanded from above, and General Crozier resigned. Of the twenty-six cadets originally dismissed by him, nineteen were restored to duty, while two of the five awaiting trial availed themselves of the interval to rob a bank at the point of a revolver. When Greenwood was asked why they had not been shut up while awaiting trial, he explained without embarrassment that the prison accommodation for Auxiliaries was already exhausted "owing to the number of cadets under close arrest." So much for the alleged improvement in the police by the spring of 1921.

Sir Henry Wilson, who loathed the I.R.A. if ever man did, made Lloyd George "dance about"[1] by telling him what he thought of reprisals by the Black-and-Tans, and how they must lead to chaos and ruin. "You do not cast out Beelzebub by Beelzebub," said the Archbishop of Canterbury. "Obviously," said Mr. Churchill, "there can be no defence for such conduct except the kind of attack to which it was a reply." But Irishmen, while grateful for the Archbishop's condemnation, will never let the case against the Black-and-Tans stand or fall by the tone of his, and still less by that of Mr. Churchill's, commentary. However much they may have sorrowed over the methods to which their country was driven to resort, they will see no comparison between the ruthless, passionless shooting down of what was regarded as an alien army of occupation, and the wild sadistic cruelty of a gang of hired condottieri practised indiscriminately against men, women, and children—even admitting that on the law of averages a large proportion of those slain and tortured were ready to play a part in the downfall of the British régime.

It may have been the quality of the men chosen, it may have been the nature of the task set them—whatever the cause, the Black-and-Tans and Auxiliaries had done enough long before they left Ireland to dishonour British government, to defile by association the name of the British fighting services and, in the words used by *The Times*, "to make Englishmen hang their heads with shame." Whatever their origin, whatever the provocation, history will record that after a few months in Ireland a large proportion of these, the most active British forces, had ceased for the time to behave or count as responsible human beings—or that so it seemed to those who saw them strutting down the streets of Cork, crazy with drink and nerves, lashing passers-by across the face with riding-whips stolen from the shops.

[1] Wilson's *Diary*, Vol. II, p. 263.

"Scoundrels in uniform," they were called, and the name suited them; but they did not always operate in uniform, and sometimes, as when they visited Kilkenny post-office, they blacked their faces and put on masks and afterwards called Heaven to witness the sneaking vileness of Sinn Fein.

It is difficult, going beyond the individual murderers, castigators, looters, and incendiaries, to allot official responsibility for their crimes. Sir Hamar Greenwood, the Liberal lawyer from Canada, since April 4th 1920 Chief Secretary for Ireland, and Lloyd George, the Prime Minister who appointed, retained, and presumably directed him, pass naturally into the dock. We have no right or desire to pry into their motives; we are concerned only with what went on under their auspices, and their attitude as known by their words.

On September 29th 1920 Lloyd George was dancing with anger at Sir Henry Wilson's suggestion that the Government should accept the responsibility for the murders and arson. "No Government," said the Prime Minister, one eye apparently on the American elections, "could possibly take the responsibility." Two years later Greenwood was boldly telling Lord Riddell that "he had not been responsible for the reprisals in Ireland. On many occasions instructions had been given behind his back, but of course he had had to bear the blame. As a matter of fact, he did not agree with reprisals."[1] And he appears "very bitter at the way in which he has been treated. . . . He finds himself without a position."[1] But neither man can disclaim his responsibility quite so easily.

If we study their speeches throughout the period we shall find them adopting more than one style of reply to attacks on unauthorised reprisals. They begin with simple audacious denials that the reprisals have taken place at all, at any rate in the form that critics of the Government allege. Then as it becomes harder to conceal the truth, as details of the reprisals begin to fill foreign newspapers, an attempt is made to palm them off as well-meaning but misguided attempts to restore law and order; or more commonly, as spontaneous outbreaks in hot blood under immediate unforgivable provocation. After a time Lloyd George makes, or thinks he makes, the discovery that reprisals go down well in England, and the theory that they are unpremeditated is dropped. Crown forces begin to be publicly justified for "going to great extremes." The classic speeches at Carnarvon and at the Guildhall in October and November 1920 are pitched in this key.

[1] See Riddell's *Diary*, pp. 368 and 378.

Public taste proves, however, to have been misinterpreted; protests from the Army in Ireland lead to the substitution of "authorised" for "unauthorised" reprisals as the official policy, and from now on to the end the defence of unauthorised reprisals is usually, though not always, conducted as it had been originally; either the alleged facts are disputed, or else the emphasis is laid on some particular provocation. A new line, too, is struck out. While it begins to be admitted that deplorable excesses (presumably overlooked at the time) occurred in the earlier stages, a reassuring guarantee is given that the number of such excesses is rapidly diminishing under an amazing improvement in discipline.

Over the year, then, unauthorised reprisals are sometimes represented as regrettable accidents, mercifully rare; sometimes as an integral feature of a more aggressive policy. But always the favourite defence of the moment is reinforced with this more crushing retort: whatever the official policy may or may not be, the actual policy being carried out by the present men is winning the war for you. It is impossible to think of any other policy or any other men who would do your work for you half so cheaply, half so quickly, or half so well. For Heaven's sake, don't interfere. As Lord Hugh Cecil summarised the various apologias presented: "There is no such thing as reprisals, but they have done a great deal of good."

Greenwood was happiest in blunt cheery denial. Take for instance what he told the House of Commons on November 1st 1920: "There is no charge with one exception of which I know urged against a policeman or soldier for murder." Yet already twenty-two Coroners' Inquests had returned verdicts of wilful murder or unjustifiable homicide against the Crown forces, and, since Coroners' Inquests had been suppressed, thirty-seven deaths by violence had been circumstantially charged against them. And even Greenwood had admitted under Asquith's interrogation that the police had murdered a couple of men in the "much regretted" Balbriggan reprisal.

He put his foot in it when, on December 11th 1920, a large part of Cork was burnt down with almost insolent publicity in spite of the presence of a military garrison in the town. Greenwood automatically denied that there was any evidence "that the fires were started by the Crown forces"; and he tried indeed to infer from the use made of incendiary bombs that they were the handiwork of Sinn Fein. But when he accounted for the burning of the City Hall by explaining that the fires had spread to it from Patrick Street, he was greeted with a derision which penetrated even his front of brass. For he was expecting the fire to travel a quarter of a mile without touching a house in any of the intervening streets, and jump the River Lee where it was about a hundred yards wide—all this without the north-west wind that alone could have made such a feat conceivable.

No surprise was felt when the report of the military inquiry into the burnings was withheld from the public; still less when it leaked out that the report had fixed the guilt on Auxiliaries. But thenceforth a large element in the House of Commons attached little importance to the unsupported pronouncements of a Chief Secretary, "whose superabundant energy," General Macready tells us, "so often carried him beyond the boundaries of fact that he became as one crying in the winderness."

Greenwood, however, persevered, and if we consult a typical debate we shall find him still harking back to Sinn Fein ambushes six months earlier to excuse men seeing red "who he had never thought would see red," and more generally defending unauthorised reprisals with all his old vigour along each of the official lines in turn. Even supposing his statements correct and his arguments valid (and there was no great disposition among members of the House of Commons to grant anything but the provocation alleged) there was still one thing missing; an assurance that police criminals would be punished. But the case of Balbriggan in September 1920 had made such an assurance for ever impossible. In April 1921 Greenwood was admitting that the town had been sacked by one hundred and fifty police, but "regretted now as he did then that he could never identify those responsible for the crime."

Meanwhile most of the Trim heroes were being reinstated, and the Auxiliaries who burnt half Cork allowed to parade the streets of Dublin with half-burnt corks in their caps. And not long before Greenwood was telling Lord Riddell that the time had not arrived for a settlement. "If we effect a premature settlement, we may lose the benefit of all we have done . . . there are already signs that the Irish people are breathing more freely."[1]

Lloyd George's responsibility was less direct, but if we credit him with all the knowledge that, as Prime Minister, he should have seen was his[2]—ultimately greater. When he spoke at Carnarvon on October 9th 1920, and at the Guildhall Banquet on November 9th, the atrocities at Balbriggan, Trim, and Mallow, for instance, were still fresh in English minds, and it was an open question

[1] Riddell's *Diary*, p. 261.
[2] There are reasons for thinking that in fact it was not till the spring of 1921 that Lloyd George gave the Irish question first-rate attention.

whether the British Government was going to stop or encourage such things. Lloyd George left it doubtful no longer. Here for the first time we meet the immortal "murder gang" in all its glory; here for the first time the weight of a British Government comes down on the side of terrorism by its police.

"There is no doubt that at last their patience has given way and there has been some severe hitting back . . . let us be fair to these gallant men who are doing their duty in Ireland . . . it is no use talking about this being war and these being reprisals when these things are being done [by Sinn Fein] with impunity in Ireland.

"We have murder by the throat . . . we had to reorganise the police and when the Government was ready we struck the terrorists and now the terrorists are complaining of terror. (Loud laughter and cheers.)" And then this jest, surely unequalled on the lips of a British Prime Minister: (one Co-operative creamery after another, life-work of Sir Horace Plunkett, was being burnt down by Black-and-Tans. Sir Horace himself was meanwhile recommending an offer of Dominion Home Rule to Ireland.): I have asked, said Lloyd George, for the name of "a single Irishman who has got the authority to speak for his countrymen who would say he would accept Dominion Home Rule. Sir Horace Plunkett cannot even speak of his creameries." (Loud laughter.)

"At that time," General Macready tells us, "certain figures in high places in London were convinced that terrorism of any description was the best method with which to oppose the gun-men." Six months later the incitements were less blatant, but the connivance was just as unself-conscious and the encouragement no less benign. To a protest by seven Anglican bishops against un-authorised reprisals, Lloyd George retorted on April 19th (in a passage quoted from above) that now that the undesirables had been weeded out the police deserved admiration not blame. If awful things were still happening occasionally—well, "so long as Sinn Fein demands a Republic, the present evils must go on." Nine days later he was once again asking the House of Commons to "make allowance" for "these people trying to do their duty." He was going to defend them. He was certainly not going to make them change their tactics; there were no others which would win the war.

Under these auspices, it is no surprise to find the *Weekly Summary* (official organ of the police, edited from Dublin Castle) quoting with approval such programmes as these: "If in the future any member of His Majesty's Forces is murdered, two members of the Sinn Fein party will be killed. And in the event of a member of the Sinn Fein party not being available, three sympathisers will be killed." Small wonder if even the best elements in the new police, harrassed past endurance, lonely, frightened, bewildered, furious, should have come to see virtue and wisdom in such advice.

To accuse any member of the Government of having deliberately conceived in advance the plan of unauthorised reprisals when they sent the Black-and-Tans to Ireland would ordinarily not have occurred to us. Yet *The Times* of the period does not hesitate to prefer what must surely be this very charge. "The policy of reprisals is now generally admitted in ministerial circles to have been conceived and sanctioned in advance by an influential section of the Cabinet." Whether or not the premeditation was as great as suggested, there is one conclusion we cannot avoid: that, having sent them over, Lloyd George and Greenwood formed the opinion that given time and a free hand the new police, and they alone, would get Sinn Fein under, and that they must be given every chance to do their work in their own way—whatever its ethical drawbacks. For can one not justify everything (including propaganda of any convenient sort) that helps to win a war—particularly when the enemy has begun by infringing the standard rules?

## CHAPTER IV

## PEACE WITH HONOUR

> "Either there was such a rebellion, or there was not. If there was, why is not the nation's quiet secured, and its independence asserted? If not, why have we endeavoured to raise and justify rebellion, by driving an innocent people to madness and despair?"
>
> EDMUND BURKE.

*The British conscience—Discovery that they were fighting a nation—The military situation discouraging to each side—England shocked by the war—Call for negotiations.*

IF bias is detected in what has been written above, let the last few pages be erased from the memory. In any case, let us turn to incontrovertible facts. Whatever the merits of the Lloyd George-

Greenwood policy, the British public could not stand it when they began to know the truth. It would be a long task, though a fruitful one, to trace the stages by which British public opinion swung round to the point when it became less anxious to put down Sinn Fein crime than to stop the crimes that were being committed in the name of the Crown. The *Manchester Guardian* was in the van throughout, and *The Times*, alive since 1919 with varied plans for Irish settlement, was stirred to fury as in the autumn of 1920 reprisal was piled on reprisal. "What echo," it asked of the Prime Minister's speech at the Guildhall, "will reach the world? None that will not be a mockery of the British name." Later it was satisfied that "persistence in the present methods of Irish government would prove utterly irreconcilable with the ideals of this Christian country," and as the spring of 1921 wore on, it launched appeal after appeal for peace on behalf of "that great section of British opinion which refuses to connive at gross illegality and injustice."

In Parliament few outside the central cohorts of the Coalition restrained their disgust at the policy of unauthorised reprisals. The Labour Party based exhaustive indictments of a "criminal," "cruel" and "inhuman policy" on the report of their own Commission. Lord Oxford recovered much of his former majesty to denounce the Government's "condonation of the hellish policy of reprisals." Sir John Simon cast aside habitual reserves and blazed with generous indignation. "The soldiers and constabulary are not responsible for the policy of the country. It is the meanest of subterfuges to exploit the losses and trials of these men when what is really designed is to throw a cloak over a method deliberately approved by their superiors." Among Conservatives, Lord Robert Cecil, Lord Henry Cavendish-Bentinck,[1] and Sir Oswald Mosley crossed the floor; many others, Mr. Walter Elliot, for instance, made no secret of their opposition, and even High Tories like Lord Hugh Cecil,[1] to whom victory over the Irish Government was vital and Martial Law for all Ireland the obvious way to it, would have no truck with the terrorism then in force.

With this stream of dawning awareness, another was united. With a growing consciousness of the nature of the repression went a gradual realisation of who it was that constituted the enemy. Dublin Castle, Greenwood, and Lloyd George, still strove desperately to propagate the legend that there was a sharp dis-

[1] Lord Henry Cavendish-Bentinck also founded the "Committee of Peace with Ireland," which from the first achieved a striking position. Lord Hugh Cecil crossed the floor at the same time as his brother, though for rather different reasons.

tinction between the moderate and extremist elements in Sinn Fein, and that the war was solely against the latter, "the small body of assassins."[1] But by the spring of 1921 confidence in the Castle propaganda was waning. As long ago as October 25th, when Terence MacSwiney died in Brixton Gaol after a seventy-four days' hunger strike, a dim realisation had begun to agitate men's minds that if there was here a military problem at all, it was one of how best to wage war against a spirit. As long ago as November, *The Times* had bravely, if tentatively, pointed towards the truth. "At the Guildhall," it had commented, "the Prime Minister virtually committed himself to a war upon large sections of the Irish people." When, in April, De Valera, on behalf of Dail Eireann, took explicit responsibility for the war policy of the I.R.A., few in England could be kept from knowing that the task of their country was not to suppress crime in Ireland, but to suppress Ireland herself.

Sir Henry Wilson's *Diary* provides telling illustration of how repulsive the war had become to England by the summer of 1921. Times without number Macready and Wilson had represented Martial Law for the whole of Ireland as the one panacea, and cursed the Cabinet wholeheartedly for refusing to permit its imposition. Yet when at the end of May it was decided to carry out this very proposal if a settlement was not reached by July 12th, Wilson (and Macready's attitude was similar) saw little good in it. "Unless we had England entirely on our side, I would strongly advise that we should not attempt Martial Law in all its severity. . . . Unless England was on our side, we would fail, and if we failed, we would break the army. . . . Therefore, unless England was wholly on our side, I was wholly opposed to trying to increase coercion."[2]

Page after page in Wilson's diary, and Macready's autobiography, attempts to explain the strange failure "to get England on our side" in pursuit of a righteous war. They put it all down to a pitiful weakness in propaganda. No doubt the Irish propaganda was brilliantly conducted in the *Irish Bulletin* and elsewhere, by Desmond FitzGerald till his arrest in February 1921, and later by Erskine Childers. But Greenwood, Lloyd George, Sir Basil Clarke, and a large professional staff, had tried hard enough, with far greater resources behind them. Only, the British public had

[1] Lord Riddell's *Diary* suggests that Lloyd George and presumably Greenwood were deceived on this point by their own side's propaganda, long after their eyes should have been opened.

[2] Wilson's *Diary*, Vol. II, pp. 295–296.

come to disbelieve what was told them when it was good propaganda, and to disapprove of it when it was true.

Meanwhile, the military situation was complicated and obscure. Writing five years later, General Macready is confident that the 80,000 troops which, but for the Truce and its preliminary, would have been available by July, would have proved fully adequate for the work in hand, and that the Irish resistance would have virtually disappeared by the winter. But Mr. Churchill treats as of primary importance in its influence on British Government policy a Memorandum not mentioned by the General himself, in which the latter seems to have conveyed a most gloomy impression to the Cabinet. "Unless," he wrote in May, "I am entirely mistaken, the present state of affairs in Ireland must be brought to a conclusion by October, or steps must be taken to relieve practically the whole of the troops, together with a great majority of the Commanders and their staff."[1] And Sir Henry Wilson is mentioned as endorsing this report. What seems clear from these and other sources is that, rightly or wrongly, the British Government had reached the conclusion by June that, even if strict Martial Law were imposed on the whole of Ireland, heavy reinforcements would be required (in addition to anything that was at the moment being sent over). The problem was whether the British people would be prepared for the expenditure of money and the loss of life involved.

On the Irish side, the question was quite different. The 3000 more or less trained fighting men were sadly diminished. For all the active recruits available, it was impossible to fill such gaps as that left by the loss of seventy prisoners in the burning Customs House. But far more paralysing was the shortage of arms and ammunition, a shortage that seemed reaching a head. In May, Liam Lynch, commanding the I.R.A. forces in the South, came up to Dublin to state that, owing to shortage of arms and ammunition, they would be unable to continue the fight much longer. It will always be a moot point how long Ireland could in fact have gone on fighting if the Truce had not come when it did. But in the Treaty debates the opinion of General Mulcahy, Chief of Staff, was emphatic: "We have suffered a defeat."[2]

But even if this be so, Ireland, as Mulcahy demonstrated, had kept fighting long enough to win immense concessions. So long

[1] Winston Churchill, *The Aftermath*, pp. 293–294.

[2] Six months later Ireland's military position had been much strengthened. (Her psychological position is another matter.) General Macready reckons that if war had been renewed in December, not 80,000, but 150,000 British troops would have been necessary for victory.

as she could go on fighting (and she never ceased to fight till England suggested negotiations and agreed to a truce while they lasted), she could not only present the British forces in Ireland with a menace so deadly to their morale that, in the opinion of their Commander, they did not long stay fit for service in the country; she could not only wreck all attempts at British civil administration; she could strike the English people in their most tender spot, their conscience.

English rule in Ireland had long presented a strange denial of those traditions of liberty and democratic government which England had everywhere been foremost to preach and in every white country but Ireland foremost to sustain. But it needed prolonged armed resistance by Ireland, and the inevitable reply to it by England, to make the contradiction conveyed by English rule in Ireland patent and glaring; and to bring it home through mists of prejudice, pride, and supposed self-interest, to the higher nature and reflective mind of the ordinary Englishman.

"If," wrote Professor Dicey in 1886, when putting *England's Case against Home Rule*, "if the time should come, when the only means by which [the unity of the State] is found maintainable, are measures strongly repugnant to the humanity or justice or democratic principles of the English people—then it will be clear that the union must, for the sake of England no less than for Ireland, come to an end. The alternative policy will then be not Home Rule but separation."[1] By summer 1921 that time would seem to have come.

For Irish separation, it is true, England was not yet prepared. An Irish Republic was still conceived to threaten British security at vital points, and, fighting for her life, England might yet call on fresh military resources, find some device to keep her conscience quiet. But except when concession offended the sacred instincts of self-preservation, England was no longer prepared to continue the coercion of Ireland; still less, in the cause of that coercion, to embark on vast new enterprises, prodigal of treasure and men.

The principle of self-determination had been thrust out with a pitchfork at Versailles, but it was coming back into its own now that a small, proud, and determined nation, and a large, proud, and humane Empire, had between them worked out the alternative.

In this chapter we have been digging about among the underlying forces. In the next we return to the surface and examine in some detail the situation as it was in June 1921 and as it developed chronologically from that time. "There are," said Labouchere,

[1] Dicey, *England's Case against Home Rule*, pp. 287–288.

many years earlier, "only two policies for Ireland—Home Rule and Coercion. The rest is intrigue." The British Public had had enough of coercion. But by now Home Rule meant letting Ireland have her Republic. That was out of the question. It was time for a little intrigue.

# Part Three

## CHAPTER I

## JUNE 1921

"Take away the sword;
States can be saved without it; bring the pen!"
BULWER LYTTON.

*The Government's volte-face of June 1921—A Dominion offer maturing since April, but on three conditions—Influences dictating a Peace offer—The part played by the King—The unconditional invitation to De Valera—The negotiation of the Truce.*

IT was now two and a half years since Dail Eireann had issued her Declaration of Independence. For two years Ireland had been pressing that claim with organised force. On the face of things, the future seemed to hold out only an intensification of the combat. Nineteen fresh battalions of infantry and other reinforcements were due to bring the British army in Ireland up to eighty thousand by the beginning of July, and by the 12th of that month, failing a settlement, Martial Law would be proclaimed throughout the whole country. On June 21st a motion by Lord Donoughmore in the House of Lords, calling on the Government to amend the Act of 1920 in the direction of fiscal autonomy, and "to propose and authorise negotiations with Ireland," was resisted by Lord Birkenhead on behalf of the Government in a speech of uncompromising sternness. Yet three days later, on June 24th, Lloyd George was publicly inviting De Valera and "any colleagues" whom he should select, to a conference in London "to end the ruinous conflict" of centuries. History will agree with Mr. Churchill's admission: "No British Government in modern times has ever appeared to make so sudden and complete a reversal of policy."[1]

We must go back several months. Up till April 1921 Lloyd George, like most people who had not visited Ireland, seriously underestimated the Irish resistance. Preoccupied with other matters, he had fallen a ready victim to the Castle propaganda and the reassuring messages of victory from Sir Hamar Greenwood,

[1] Winston Churchill, *The Aftermath*, p. 290.

whose reputation depended on his ability to "finish the rebels off quickly." But the rebels survived many annihilations, and Lloyd George, who had been able to tell Carnarvon as far back as October 1920 that "he had the murder gang by the throat," found, when he turned seriously to Irish affairs in April, no sign that the warfare was nearing its end.[1]

Meanwhile moves towards conciliation had served no purpose in the South. Since the end of 1920 a Government of Ireland Act had been on the Statute Book, under which subordinate Parliaments were to be set up in Dublin and Belfast, Irish representation on a reduced scale continuing at Westminster. Ulster showed herself, if not enthusiastic, at least ready, lest worse befall her, to work the Act. But Sinn Fein, while making use of this Act's machinery to elect a new Dail, left no doubt that few if any members would take their seats in the Southern Parliament. The British Government, if they persisted in the Act, would thus be compelled to fall back on its reserve provision, and throughout the South establish Crown Colony Government.[2]

These considerations combining with the first-hand evidence of agents and visitors to Ireland, among them Mr. Lionel Curtis of the *Round Table* and an unofficial but distinguished group from Oxford, went far to rid Lloyd George of the "murder gang" mentality, and to make him realise that the representatives of the vast majority of the South of Ireland stood solidly behind the Irish methods of warfare. Yet it is plain from Mr. Churchill's account that in April Lloyd George had not yet come to consider seriously the policy of generous concession. "He was still prepared to fight the matter out at all costs, relying on the 'age-long loyalties of the Conservative Party.' " It required an "impressive debate" in the Cabinet to bring him round. Mr. Churchill himself and, more unexpectedly, Sir Austen Chamberlain and Lord Birkenhead, the Unionist leaders, advocated "the fairest offer combined with the most drastic threats." From this time onwards the possibility of a Dominion offer was entertained. It was brought

[1] Even, however, in May his information was still erring on the side of optimism. On the 14th he tells Lord Riddell of "information he had received that Sinn Fein was being got under. There had been a proposal for a truce but he was against it" (Riddell, *Diary*, p. 298).

[2] When nominations were handed in on May 13th for the Southern Parliament it was found that there was not to be a single contest. One hundred and twenty-four Sinn Feiners and four Independents from Trinity College, presumably of Unionist sympathies, were returned unopposed. Lacking a quorum the new Parliament was not able to function. On the other hand, out of the fifty-two members elected for the Ulster Parliament, forty were Unionists. The Ulster Government and Parliament have continued to this day to derive their powers under this "Partition Act."

closer by each friendly move of British opinion, each "Peace with Ireland" or other similar Society, each deputation of Liberal or other M.P.'s who waited on the British Prime Minister.

But thoughts of prestige, his own and his country's, still hampered in three respects Lloyd George's resolve. He had promised to hunt down the murder gang, to "pluck the last revolver out of the last assassin's hand,"[1] and he still clung to the hope of formally at least making the promise good. The only serious "conversations" up to this point (those of the previous December when Archbishop Clune of Western Australia had acted as go-between) had broken down because Lloyd George had insisted at the last moment on a surrender of arms before negotiations proper began. At the same time Lloyd George had made it plain that Collins, Mulcahy, and Brugha were too intimately associated with "murder" to be given safe-conducts as envoys.

In one form or another these demands, especially the second, had persisted. Lord Riddell's diary for April 5th gives an example of the way Lloyd George clung to the "Black List." "The question is whether I can see Michael Collins. The question is whether the British people would be willing for me to negotiate with the head of a band of murderers. It would be rather like a Prime Minister of the day seeing Kelly who was engaged in the Phœnix Park murders." A condition still more important to Lloyd George, and one that it is easier to appreciate, was some preliminary assurance that a Dominion offer would stand a fair chance of acceptance. For without it he would have drawn down upon his head opprobrium and ridicule from the War Party in England without serving any purpose whatever in Ireland, except to cheer Sinn Fein and stiffen her demands.[2]

With these terms of reference a trickle of emissaries began descending on Dublin. Towards the end of April Lord Derby appeared at the Shelbourne, trusting to horn-rimmed spectacles to sustain an alias of "Mr. Edwards." De Valera saw in his mission only that of a "political scout," and talked to him no more freely than he would have to a "press-man." In May, Sir James Craig, about to become Prime Minister in the new Ulster Government, arrived in Dublin, and allowed himself, with a courage worthy

[1] This latter phrase was Greenwood's, used in the House of Commons as late as May 22nd 1921.

[2] As matters developed Lloyd George found this very position confronting him. But he ingeniously manœuvred round it. By raising in June the hopes of peace, before presenting in July his Dominion terms, he thrust on the Irish the onus of refusal and so, in a sense, of declaring for a renewal of war.

of his reputation, to be conveyed through circuitous and confusing by-ways, to a secret meeting with De Valera.

Each leader seemed to have been given to understand that the other wished to see him; the conversation drifted on to a discussion of the Act of Union, and De Valera improved the occasion with certain historical analogies—a unique instance in his dealings with British and Ulster representatives, but one sufficient to fasten on him the "Strongbow" legend.

Nothing came of the talk, nor of a visit to De Valera paid by General Smuts in June. Nor was De Valera responsive to the peace talks passed on by Duggan, formerly Army Director of Intelligence, now with Griffith and Professor Eoin MacNeill imprisoned in Mountjoy Gaol. Soon after Lord Derby's visit an invitation to meet Lloyd George at Lord Derby's house had been refused, and on June 14th we have De Valera writing definitively to Collins: "This particular peace-move business has been on for some time. The reply I have sent through other channels is that if they send a written communication addressed to me directly and not through intermediaries they will get a reply."[1]

Other paths to reconciliation were explored. A Catholic Lord-Lieutenant, Lord Fitzalan, gallantly took over from Lord French at the beginning of May, and on the 12th of that month Collins obtained possession of a secret instruction to the Crown forces to improve relations with the inhabitants on "political grounds." But all such activities pale beside those of Mr. "Andy," now Sir Alfred, Cope, once a detective in the Customs service, and at this time, with none of his old talents forgotten, Assistant Under-Secretary for Ireland.

"He had begun his career at the Castle," recalls Professor Alison Phillips, "by summarily dismissing certain old and trusted civil servants whose intimate knowledge of criminal activities was apparently inconvenient, and is now known to have been carrying on negotiations *sub rosa* with the Sinn Fein leaders."[2] General Macready sympathised with Cope as little but appreciated his qualities more. "When Lloyd George made up his mind to open direct negotiations with Sinn Fein, Cope was his agent, and probably no other man could have carried the matter through. Though I could not share his ideals, I always admired the way he hung on to the most disagreeable and dangerous task he had undertaken."[3]

[1] Beasley, *Michael Collins and the Making of a New Ireland*, Vol. II, p. 236.
[2] Alison Phillips, *The Revolution in Ireland*, p. 204.
[3] But "his somewhat irritable shortness of manner and insufficiency of official oil made him decidedly unpopular with many. I can recall my staff

Whom Cope met personally in those days and how much he actually accomplished, must remain for the present a mystery. In the absence of evidence we discount the notion that any great satisfaction was obtained from Irish leaders before the invitation of June 24th. We incline therefore to the view that two months of secret negotiations had possibly brought Lloyd George some encouraging reports about probable attitudes, but no explicit assurances, and that he was nearly as far away as ever from realising the conditions under which he had calculated it would be safe to set on foot negotiations with a Dominion settlement as the goal.

But it was impossible to stand still; to the other sources of depression were added the "despairing counsels" (Winston Churchill) of Sir Nevil Macready, Commander-in-Chief in Ireland, and Sir Henry Wilson, Chief of the Imperial General Staff. For a Government contemplating, if negotiations failed, military measures on an altogether new scale, requiring anything up to a hundred thousand men, it was hardly encouraging to be informed by General Macready that, unless the war was over by October, steps must be taken to relieve "practically the whole of the troops" serving in Ireland "together with the great majority of their Commanders and their staff."[1] The Martial Law too, for which both soldiers had yearned so long, seemed to have mysteriously died on them in the waiting. Now, in the opinion of Sir Henry Wilson, it would be no use, would indeed be disastrous, "unless we had England strongly on our side,"[1] and of that there seemed ever less chance. The two most powerful newspapers in the country, *The Times* and the *Daily Mail*, called louder and louder for peace. And the public for the most part echoed their cry. By now only a small part of England was interested in a victory over the "Gunmen" and few believed it to be beyond the wit of politicians to devise an offer acceptable to Sinn Fein yet surrendering no vital British interests.

The King's visit to Belfast on June 22nd to open the first Session of the Ulster Parliament was itself a factor that counted on the same side. For it symbolised once and for all the safeguarding of Ulster. Now at last it would be possible for a British Government to refuse to recognise any claim of Sinn Fein to speak for Ulster. Now at last Ulster was secure. All these elements in the situation told with Lloyd George and the British Cabinet against a rigid

officers fairly dancing with suppressed rage when talking to 'Andy' Cope on the telephone" (Macready, *Annals of an Active Life*, Vol. II, pp. 492–493).

[1] For fuller extracts see above, pp. 60 and 61.

striving after consistency, and in favour of cutting losses and unashamedly changing front.

In the events of the 22nd to the 24th, however, not circumstances but men played the decisive part. On June 22nd the King was to visit Belfast to inaugurate in person the first Parliament of Northern Ireland. "It is well known," says Mr. Churchill, "that the King earnestly expressed the wish that language should be used which should appeal to the whole of his Irish subjects." What apparently happened was this. A draft speech arrived from Dublin. But to His Majesty its appeal appeared inadequate; its tone fell short of effective humanity. So General Smuts was summoned privately and a new draft was prepared containing phrases soon to become famous. With this speech passed by his ministers the King proceeded to Belfast.

"I speak from a full heart," he said with emotion that no one who heard him forgot, "when I pray that my coming to Ireland to-day may prove to be the first step towards an end of strife amongst her peoples, whatever their race or creed. In that hope I appeal to all Irishmen to pause, to stretch out the hand of forbearance and conciliation, to forgive and forget and to join in making for the land which they love a new era of peace, contentment and goodwill."

The pressure was now as august as it was universal. Reading next morning's papers the British leaders divined independently that a turning-point had arrived, and with it an unrivalled opportunity for a new departure. Chamberlain went out on to the terrace from No. 11 Downing Street. Lloyd George did likewise from No. 10. Chamberlain argued strongly that the spirit of the King's message was incompatible with the whole idea of renewed coercion without one culminating effort for peace. The Prime Minister seemed impressed, but nothing final was settled on the spot. In the crisis Chamberlain, as Leader of the Conservative Party, felt it imperative to know precisely where Birkenhead stood. He was in the very act of telephoning when Birkenhead, who had reached exactly the same conclusion about the necessity for full understanding, walked into the room. Expressing his attitude with his habitual clarity and incisiveness, Birkenhead left Chamberlain in no doubt that the two saw eye to eye on future policy.

The next day Lord Stamfordham, the King's Private Secretary, went to see Lloyd George about Ireland. He explained in advance to Lord Riddell the spirit of his intended representations. "Now is the time to endeavour to bring about a reconciliation. Unless something is done the effect of the King's speech will die away. There is not a moment to be lost."[1] At last Lloyd George had pointers enough. Responding to advice, to atmosphere, and conceivably to encouragement from Cope in Dublin, before evening he had thrown the "Black List" into the waste-paper basket and issued his invitation to De Valera:

> (1) To attend a conference in London in company with Sir James Craig and to explore to the utmost the possibility of a settlement.
>
> (2) To bring with him for the purpose any colleagues whom he might select.

Before replying to Lloyd George's invitation, De Valera invited Lord Midleton, widely respected in both England and Ireland, Sir James Craig and other Loyalist leaders to a conference in Dublin. Sir James Craig alone refused, having already accepted an invitation from Lloyd George similar to that sent to De Valera. The Dublin Conference met on July 4th and adjourned on the 5th, Lord Midleton hurrying to London. It was fortunate that he did so, for otherwise the discussions could hardly have continued. To his report that De Valera was insisting on a truce (with both sides retaining their arms) before negotiations proper began, Lloyd George at first was most unsympathetic, and a renewal of war seemed certain. Lord Midleton in fact had practically written out a telegram to Dublin announcing the uselessness of his return when Lloyd George capitulated. The Dublin Conference was resumed. De Valera accepted Lloyd George's invitation in guarded terms. General Macready was summoned to the Mansion House, passing unarmed through vast crowds. A truce was announced on July 9th and came into force two days later.

From the first considerable confusion existed about its terms, General Macready publishing one version and Sinn Fein another. In particular the question how far the Irish were to be allowed to continue and develop arrangements for obtaining arms was never satisfactorily dealt with. But there was no ambiguity about the agreement that they should retain the existing supplies of arms and preserve intact their military, no less than their civil, organisation. And for the moment their triumph was outstanding. Of no condition preliminary to a truce had Lloyd George made more in public than of the surrender of arms. He had re-emphasised it as late as April in the House of Commons, and even after the peace offer had, as we have seen, striven to impose it in his interview with

[1] Riddell, *Diary*, p. 302.

Lord Midleton. Now he was not ashamed to recognise that, like so many others of his recent promises, it represented an unadvisable project.

## CHAPTER II

## TEMPTATION ON PRINCIPLE

"BANQUO: Speak then to me, who neither beg nor fear
Your favours nor your hate."
SHAKESPEARE: *Macbeth.*

*De Valera's visit to London—Stack's talk with Griffith—Lloyd George and De Valera—The terms considered in Dublin—Smuts's intervention—The terms rejected—The great correspondence—Ireland's academic victory—Psychologically she has the worst of it.*

ON July 12th De Valera left Dublin for London. Among his companions were Arthur Griffith, the Vice-President of Dail Eireann; Robert Barton, Minister for Economic Affairs; Austin Stack, Minister for Home Affairs; and Erskine Childers, acting since Desmond Fitzgerald's arrest in March as Minister for Publicity and Editor of the *Irish Bulletin.* Of these, Griffith had been released from Mountjoy and Barton from Portsmouth Convict Prison. Stack had been on the run for two years and even now had no intention of allowing himself to be photographed. Childers had not actually been on the run, but his house had many times been raided. He had recently been arrested but released after a futile interrogation by Cope. "All the Irish in London seemed to be awaiting the train at Euston and it was with difficulty," remembered Austin Stack, "that we reached our hotel."[1]

De Valera met Lloyd George four times—14th, 15th, 18th, and 21st July. After each meeting he used to call his colleagues together and tell them what had occurred. "The two statesmen seemed to be sizing one another up most of the time," but it was arranged

[1] On many of the succeeding incidents Austin Stack throws light in some hitherto unpublished recollections begun, though they show no signs of it, on the twelfth day of a hunger strike in 1923. In weighing the significance of his account, one must bear in mind on the one hand his pellucid honesty and on the other the difficulties under which he was writing, his hatred for the policy of the Treaty and his antagonism to Collins.

early on that the British were going to submit proposals in writing. From the second interview onwards the Irish had reason to fear that Lloyd George was not going beyond Dominion Home Rule. When the British proposals arrived on July 20th they contained sure enough Dominion Home Rule, and in an extremely qualified form. Stack "at once demurred," and Barton "said very deliberately, 'Mr. President, would it not be treason to the Republic to bear these terms back to Ireland?' " The President took the same line strongly and handed back the original document at his final meeting with Lloyd George next day. The Irish party then returned home.

Stack relates a striking talk with Arthur Griffith during the London visit. "I remember walking out several evenings with Arthur Griffith. I recall one evening in particular. We knew at the time that the British proposals would not satisfy us—at least I did. When we were passing through Whitehall, Griffith turned to me and then looking up at a building said, 'Would you like to take that to Dublin with you, Austin?' I said, 'It is a fine place. What is it?' 'Oh, that's the Home Office,' he replied. I saw the drift only then and I asked Griffith, 'Surely you do not regard it as possible that we should accept the British terms?' 'I think they are pretty good,' he answered. 'But,' I said, 'how could we conscientiously accept the British King—look at the dead who have given their lives for the Republic.' 'Oh, it is your conscience I see that's the matter,' was the answer. We left it at that for the moment."

Griffith apparently repeated the joke on the same spot the next evening. He may, of course, have had no serious purpose, but it would be very natural to wish to obtain representative reactions to the kind of proposal that seemed likely to be in store.

About the actual Lloyd George-De Valera conversations various stories are current. Winston Churchill[1] provides an entertaining anecdote of how "the British Prime Minister, never a greater artist than in the first moments of a fateful interview," was at some pains to make his guest feel uncomfortable in more ways than one. On the top of a lengthy document presented by De Valera (who was introduced by Art O'Brien, representative of the Republic in London), he noticed the heading Saorstat Eireann, and was told "after a pause" that literally it meant Free State. What then, he asked, was the Irish word for Republic? "While the two Irishmen were discussing together in English what answer

[1] See *The Aftermath*, pp. 297–298.

they should give to this innocent question," the Prime Minister turned and conversed with Tom Jones in Welsh, "to the evident discomfiture of their English-speaking Sinn Fein visitors." Eventually, as Mr. De Valera could get no further than that "Saorstat" meant "Free State," the Prime Minister observed: "Must we not admit that the Celts never were Republicans and had no native words for such an idea?" A long embarrassed silence followed.

This version is marred by one palpable mis-statement of fact. It is liable, moreover, to give two false impressions. The "lengthy document" presented by De Valera was in fact a short letter in which De Valera had accepted Lloyd George's invitation, and which happened to be lying on the table. But "a lengthy document" is more in keeping with the most slighting form of the De Valera legend, so down it goes. Nor had De Valera a difficulty over the Irish word "Republic" of the kind Mr. Churchill indicates. True, the Irish before the British invasion were never what we should now call Republicans, but the admission would be of no contemporary detriment. The only doubt in De Valera's mind, as he explained to Lloyd George, arose from the current dispute among Gaelic purists whether the idea Republic was better conveyed by the broader "Saorstat" or by the more abstract "Poblacht." Finally, nothing could be more unfair than to suggest that De Valera and Art O'Brien were English-speaking as opposed to Welsh-speaking Lloyd George and Tom Jones. All four were bilingual. Lloyd George and Jones had acquired the habit of speaking Welsh to one another to avoid eavesdroppers on the telephone. De Valera had long been prominent in Gaelic circles and Art O'Brien was president of the Gaelic League in London. They could easily have talked Irish to one another if there had been any object in doing so.[1]

The Prime Minister's artistry was, however, chiefly expended on other diversions. Lloyd George was seated at the Cabinet table with De Valera more or less at his elbow so that both men could see a vast map of the world hung on the opposite wall. Lloyd

[1] We have tried to make sense of the Churchillian narrative. But it seems that in fact the whole emphasis of the interview was different, and that Lloyd George was not in fact guilty of the indescribable folly attributed to him by Churchill of trying to embarrass or discomfort the guest with whom he was hoping to arrange a settlement. Lloyd George seems on the contrary to have tried his hardest to establish a Celtic affinity between himself and De Valera, and with this in mind to have tried to ridicule the pre-War Irish Party for ignorance of their own language, and the slow Anglo-Saxons who had, however, the wit to appoint a Celt their Prime Minister.

George at once began meditating on the contribution made by some of those who had sat in his present Prime-Ministerial seat to the building up of that far-flung area marked in red. Pitt, Palmerston, Gladstone . . . he trolled out the names. He reflected on the amazing change that in these last fifty years had transformed the relationship of the Colonies to the Mother Country. An Imperial Conference was in daily session. He pointed to the chairs at the Cabinet table which the Dominion Premiers were accustomed to occupy. What, he could not help asking himself and his visitor, would Lord Palmerston have thought if he had been told that within seventy years of his death the representatives of the Colonies would be meeting here, *on equal terms*, the Prime Minister of the United Kingdom. He began enumerating the occupants of the chairs. Here had been Smuts, here Hughes and so on through the list. Twice as he came to a particular chair he paused, then passed it by. He seemed to be expecting the question who had sat there. But no question came, so at last perforce he returned to it. "One chair remains vacant—waiting for Ireland. . . . If she is ready to take her place. . . . The Council Chamber of the Commonwealth. . . ." His peroration satisfied all expectations.

De Valera, so much is evident, was not in the least impressed by Lloyd George, or by any compelling effects that the British Prime Minister attempted to stage. Lloyd George for his part found De Valera impossible to negotiate with. "It is like sitting on a merry-go-round and trying to catch up the swing in front,"[1] he once complained and possibly for that reason he seems curiously to have misunderstood both De Valera's objective and the sacrifices he was prepared to make for it. He seems to have derived no notion from the talks that the fundamentals, to De Valera, were a certain status and a certain definition of status —things which Lloyd George thought it hair-splitting of the Irish to bother about, though suicidal for Englishmen to concede.

Yet De Valera could hardly have been more explicit in refusal. At the third meeting Lloyd George promised to let him have the British terms in writing when they met for the fourth and last time. But De Valera would have none of it. He must see them in advance. And so after much protest and grumbling they arrived late on the night of the 20th. Barton and Childers were half undressed when suddenly their door was thrown open and "Mr. Lloyd George and Sir James Craig" were announced. . . . However, it proved to be only Tom Jones and Sir Edward Grigg, Lloyd George's

[1] Or again "it is like trying to pick up mercury with a fork." Hearing of which comment De Valera retorted, "Why doesn't he use a spoon?"

secretaries, bringing the British document with its qualified Dominion scheme.

Next day De Valera told Lloyd George that he personally could never agree to such terms. He could not even accept the position of carrying them back officially to Ireland, and he accordingly returned them now. Lloyd George tested him with an ultimatum at once, "But you realise that this means war? Do you realise that the responsibility for it will rest on your shoulders and yours alone?" De Valera ridiculed the threat; "No, Mr. Lloyd George," he explained, "if you insist on attacking us it is you, not I, who will be responsible."

Lloyd George tried a different stratagem. "I will publish these terms immediately for the Irish people to see. I will leave the Irish people the chance of knowing what is being offered them." This plan, in flat defiance of previous arrangements, would have placed De Valera in a quandary; for the world would expect an immediate official reply to the British terms; and how could he produce anything adequate on the spur of the moment, with most of his colleagues absent in Dublin? "Go ahead," said De Valera, "but I thought that nothing would be published unless we both agreed." Lloyd George would have brushed the pedantry aside, "That was a little matter. We are dealing with big things now." De Valera answered him, "So I must assume that is how you keep your promises. But have your way. You publish your terms and I will publish my refusal of them."

By this time De Valera was at the door, the document had been left lying on the table. Lloyd George softened his tone. "But won't you give me a considered answer?" he asked. "Yes, certainly," replied De Valera, "if you give me time for consultation with my colleagues, and refrain from publishing in the meanwhile." "Very well," said Lloyd George.

De Valera returned to his Headquarters. A copy of the British terms was obtained from Tom Jones, and the Irish party went back to Dublin.

The British terms must be examined in detail later. Briefly they offered Dominion Status subject to four classified safeguards for British defence, to an Irish proportionate liability for a share in the British National Debt, and to the preservation of Free Trade between Ireland and other parts of the British Isles. The Parliament and Government of Northern Ireland were to retain "all their existing powers and privileges which cannot be abrogated without its own consent." Partition, that is, was apparently to continue as long as Ulster willed it so.

The terms were discussed first by a gathering of Ministers and others invited to the President's house at Blackrock on July 24th, and then more formally by a full meeting of the Ministers. At the first meeting Cathal Brugha was bluntly opposed to anything less than recognition of the Republic.[1] Stack supported him as well as he could but "the impression was forced upon him" that "Griffith, Collins, and Mulcahy, the Chief of Staff, were inclined to view the proposals favourably." No vote was taken. At the second meeting most of those present were again very cautious. Cosgrave, for example, Minister for Local Government, did not give himself away at all. Brugha, however, would have "none of it," and Stack understood Barton "to be with us." On the other hand Griffith was "favourable to the proposals save as to Ulster," and Collins described the offer as "a great step forward." It is hard to see in these last expressions more than *obiter dicta* into which significance was later read. At any rate the Ministers had not the least hesitation in turning the proposals down.

Smuts had been hovering over the parleys with well-intentioned patronage. He now wrote to De Valera in terms ill-suited to appeal to Irish pride. Pointing to the Dominions he indulged in the unfortunate expression "what is good enough for these nations is surely good enough for Ireland," and went on to depict the glorious outcome of South Africa's surrender.

The letter was published, without warning to De Valera, and called down a sharp rebuke from the aged Tim Healy, no political confederate of Sinn Fein. "To enlist the great Boer statesman to string the government proposals into nursery rhymes set to African lullabies for Irish ears was crudely inartistic, to publish the letters in advance of the text of the Cabinet's offer, and thereby give the world a false and unwarranted idea of its generosity, was sheer mischief. It injured the prospect of acceptance as anything wearing the air of trickiness must. . . . It was not helpful that General Smuts should tell Downing Street after his visit to Dublin that he had been dealing with 'small' men. No man is small who braves death for his country, or who is ready to go back to the death in life endured by these men for years."[2]

De Valera despatched an official refusal of the British terms on August 10th, and in spite of a further appeal from Lloyd George

[1] In describing both meetings we make use of quotations from Stack. But on his own admission Stack could later on find no support for his recollection of the compliance shown at these earlier meetings by Griffith, Collins, and Mulcahy. Cathal Brugha was Minister of Defence.

[2] Later Smuts was to earn the thanks of Irish Free State Delegates by generous support at their first Imperial Conference.

and a plain hint from the hitherto sympathetic *Times* that a Republic could not be tolerated, the new Dail, meeting in public and private sessions, August 16th, 17th, 18th, 22nd, 23rd, 25th, 26th, unanimously confirmed rejection. Indeed neither in Cabinet nor Dail itself does a single voice seem to have been raised in favour of acceptance.

A long correspondence followed. De Valera's letter of 24th expressed a readiness on the part of Ireland to appoint Plenipotentiaries if "consent of the governed" were accepted as the basis of the peace. Lloyd George paid lip service to the principle of government by consent, but called it "playing with phrases" to interpret this principle in such a way as to give Ireland right of secession, and refused to discuss any settlement which took Ireland outside the British Commonwealth. But he expressed readiness to meet De Valera and his colleagues if they were prepared to examine how far "the considerations governing the attitude of His Majesty's Government could be reconciled with the aspirations you represent." De Valera's reply was argumentative, and further obstacles were created by a later letter in which De Valera insisted that "our nation has formally declared its independence and recognised itself as a sovereign state," and that "it is only as the representatives of that state that we have any authority."

In such a capacity Lloyd George refused to meet the Irish representatives on the grounds that to do so would involve disloyalty to throne and Empire. De Valera hastily protested that "we have had no thought at any time of asking you to accept any condition precedent to a conference" and expressed a hope that the conference suggested by the British would be free and "without prejudice"—the blessed phrase which all along the situation had called for. Lloyd George jumped at it, and while reiterating the fundamental and unalterable character of the British demand, issued a free invitation to a conference on October 11th with a view to ascertaining "How the association of Ireland with the Community of Nations known as the British Empire may best be reconciled with Irish national aspirations." On September 30th De Valera accepted the invitation couched in these terms, on the understanding that by coming into conference neither side was in any way committed to accepting the position of the other.

Fifteen letters and telegrams in all were exchanged between Lloyd George and De Valera after July 22nd when De Valera returned to Dublin. Two separate debates were entangled throughout, (1) whether England had any right to restrict Ireland's independence or dictate her form of government; (2) on what basis, in view of the apparent cleavage over (1), could a conference usefully be called. The course of the first discussion favoured Ireland, the second England. Not that in either case the disparity was marked. For Lloyd George's letter of August 26th was a model of public advocacy, with its glittering parade of quotations to prove that the present offer far exceeded the demands of Irish leaders of the past, whether it were Grattan, or O'Connell, Davis, Parnell, or Redmond. Nevertheless, once the British had accepted (which they did in this same letter of 26th) the principle of government by consent, they were, if dialectics mattered to them, doomed. Other lines of argument had been open to them, but it was hard to take seriously any interpretation of this particular principle which did not leave Ireland free. It is hardly surprising therefore that the British statement of their case strikes us to-day as shot through with underlying humbug. The *Irish Bulletin* made unaffectedly merry at the expense of a policy which threatened war if Ireland declined as a "free Dominion to join voluntarily a free association of free nations."

In the second controversy, that over the basis on which the Conference should meet, the positions were reversed. Technically, no doubt, De Valera was entitled to argue that the arrangement finally reached subtracted no iota from the Irish claim. While not insisting that they should be recognised as such by the British, the Irish Delegation held fast to the claim that they were the representatives of a sovereign independent state. But psychologically, it is possible to see now, the Irish had lost important ground by the end. The process was cumulative, and the point is worth some labour.

De Valera was concerned with two objectives. (*a*) The status under which Ireland should negotiate. (*b*) The final settlement to which the negotiations should lead. Under (*a*) he at least maintained his position intact, but at the cost of sad prejudice to (*b*); for anyone reading the rival manifestoes will notice one striking difference. Lloyd George pledges his Government to discuss no settlement which involves a refusal on the part of Ireland to accept free equality and loyal partnership in the British Commonwealth. De Valera on the other hand never pledges his Government to preserve the Irish Republic, and indeed in all his messages only mentions the Republic twice.

It is true that in his various letters De Valera rejects the Dominion Status offered in July, records a strong opinion in favour of complete separation, hints at his being ready to accept at most some form of "external association," and insists that whatever settlement is reached must be accepted by the people of Ireland. But to Lloyd George's declaration that there can be no settlement except on Dominion lines he never makes the obvious, the only answer, that in that case there is no use in holding a conference at all, because Ireland never will renounce a Republic and accept the position of a Dominion.

Now De Valera (the responsibility of course belongs to the whole Cabinet) had understandable reasons for refusing to "break" at the moment on the simple question—without or within the Empire. He had in particular half worked out a form of external association by which Ireland would obtain the position roughly analogous in practice to that of a Dominion, but shorn of symbolism felt to humiliate. It would have been quite impossible to do justice to such a scheme in correspondence, and in any case it was far from complete. At this stage therefore the position was reached that the British Government had pledged themselves in no circumstances to allow Ireland to retire from the Empire, while the Irish Government had not pledged themselves in no circumstances to come inside.

In Irish eyes, it is true, the position had been preserved, but in the minds of British progressives and of the outside world (whose opinion would be of tremendous importance to Ireland if there were any threat of the struggle being renewed), a presumption had been established that the final settlement would leave Ireland a member of the Empire. In their minds the demand for a Republic passed into a bluff which ever so slightly England had already called. A Dominion settlement now became the reasonable, a Republic the unreasonable course.

Perhaps then it would be truer to say that three, not two, controversies had underlain the fifteen letters and telegrams. On abstract rights De Valera had secured an agreeable academic triumph. On the question of status at the Conference he had, formally at least, held his own. But in the race to secure opinion favourable to the settlements that they respectively contemplated, De Valera was still waiting for the pistol while Lloyd George was half-way home.

## CHAPTER III

# EVENTS AND PERSONALITIES IN DUBLIN

"There go the young, the gallant, the gifted, the daring: and there too go the wise."

JOHN FINTAN LALOR.

*The new Cabinet in Dublin—Brugha and Stack—Their attitude towards Collins—The choosing of the Irish Delegation—De Valera to remain in Ireland—Erskine Childers to go as Secretary—Griffith's disapproval—The Delegation's "Credentials" and "Instructions."*

THE Conference had been arranged, and its first meeting was to to be held on Tuesday, October 11th, at 10 Downing Street. In this chapter we must glance rapidly at the events of July to October in Dublin and examine the plans and attitudes that were forming. When the second Dail met for the first time on August 16th—the British released all members who had been imprisoned —everyone took the Oath of Allegiance to the Republic. De Valera, re-elected President, made a short speech, afterwards to prove a fruitful source of controversy, and explained the spirit in which he interpreted the Oath. "He was not a doctrinaire Republican"; he had never "cared for forms of government as such"; he had understood the Republic as the symbol of Irish independence and he interpreted the Oath as requiring only that "he should do his best for Ireland." He then announced that a small Cabinet of seven would take the place of the old Ministry. Its personnel, accepted with acclamation, was as follows—Griffith, Foreign Affairs; Cathal Brugha, Defence; Austin Stack, Home Affairs; Michael Collins, Finance; William Cosgrave, Local Government; Robert Barton, Economic Affairs. This Cabinet remained in being until the split after the signing of the Treaty.

Of De Valera, Griffith, and Collins we already know something. Barton, released only in July, will stand out later. So too will Cosgrave, at this time known only for his record on the Dublin Corporation, his pluck in 1916, and since 1919 his activities both wrecking and constructive as Minister for Local Government. But of Brugha and Stack we should say a little in this place.

We have already seen how in 1917 the two wings of the National Movement combined under the leadership of De Valera, and how in that year Griffith, constitutional in method and dual monarchist in aim, had joined with Cathal Brugha, militarist and Republican; their official programme one of first securing the recognition of Ireland as an independent Irish Republic, and then allowing the Irish people to choose freely by referendum their own form of government. Since that time remarkable unity had been preserved, but no one doubted that Griffith, if only because he hated bloodshed and its consequences for the nation, was the moderate; that Cathal Brugha the man of war was the die-hard; or that Stack stood close to Brugha in principles and personal sympathy.

Now Stack made as little pretension as Brugha to be a politician, and lacked, like Brugha, the arts and refinements of statesmanship. Neither perhaps would have risen to political eminence in any but a revolutionary era. Both would have been more suited to a part confined to the revolutionary sphere. Both knew what it was to feel human passions and resentments, and by the middle of 1921 both had become antagonistic towards Collins.

In each case a plausible reason lies ready enough to our hand. Brugha and Stack possessed exceptional physical courage, and Brugha a will like iron. So did Collins, if a man of more volatile type. But Collins further possessed what neither of them had claim to—the organising executive mind. In his determination to see that the war was won he never hesitated to overstep the theoretical jurisdiction of his office, or usurp the legitimate functions of others. There is this anecdote, credible and reasonably substantiated. Stack is at work in his office. Enter Collins. "Got plenty of staff, Austin?" "Yes." "Well I have just received the following," and Collins threw down a large bundle of letters of complaint about Stack's Department. "Your Department Austin is nothing but a —— joke." Stack, a very silent man, said nothing, but next day some friend spoke to him of the "Big Fella"—the name by which they all knew Collins. "Big Fella! He is no Big Fella to me," said Stack, and he added a stronger comment.

With Collins and Brugha it was similar. Brugha as Minister for Defence was nominally responsible for all the armed forces of the Dail. Collins, besides being Minister for Finance, was Director of Intelligence, and in that capacity was referred to by Brugha during the Treaty debates as a "Subordinate in a subordinate Department of my office." Yet Griffith had declared that it was Collins who "won the war," an encomium that drew the loudest cheers of all those vociferous days. In actual fact "Intelligence" came to cover so much and Collins's personality impressed itself on so many that his name, not Brugha's, became the legend in the countryside. It was him, not Brugha, that the military leaders were anxious to see when they visited Dublin for instructions.

And Collins had two other advantages. He gave up all his time to the struggle, working up to eighteen hours a day, while Brugha, refusing a ministerial salary, continued till near the end to ply his trade as a manufacturer of church candles. Again, Collins as the guiding genius of the I.R.B., the secret society from which Brugha had resigned after 1916, was in a position to pull strings here, there, and everywhere, and insert his nominees in positions that fell vacant through death or imprisonment. In these circumstances, while both men had earned the gloomy distinction of "being reasonably suspected of murder," the British assessed the value of Collins dead or alive at £10,000 but set no reward on Brugha.

It would be gross distortion to try to dispose of Stack and Brugha by hints at narrow-minded prejudice. In truth they were of the representative stuff out of which the fight for liberty has always been fashioned. Martyrs, but not self-immolators, they would be happy to die, but not until their lives had been dearly sold. On his father's side Brugha's family came from Yorkshire, and for many years now Brugha had burned with the undying flame of the convert. To toughness and ferocity he added an earnest culture and a natural distinction. Stack had been nurtured in Fenianism, and to many embodied in his person the pure Fenian tradition. "My father," he cried in the Treaty debates, "wore England's uniform as a comrade of Charles Kickham and O'Donovan Rossa, when as a '67 man he was sentenced to ten years for being a rebel. But he wore it minus the Oath of Allegiance." Faced with a present perplexity, he was accustomed to turn for his inspiration to the lives of the glorious dead.

Both had been noted athletes. Stack, captain of Kerry at Gaelic football, when they were all-Ireland champions; Brugha, the smaller man, a renowned light-weight boxer. Both had an inspiring record in the National movement, for reviving the Gaelic games and the Gaelic language. Both had proved their hardihood beyond question in recent years. Stack had no superior as a leader of hunger strikes; Brugha of all the men who took part in 1916 had alone refused to surrender and, continuing to fight until overcome by wounds, was left by the British for dead. Their bullets were supposed to "rattle in him still as he walked," and after the split Cosgrave admitted: "My own conviction is that except for war he is not worth a damn for anything else, but that he is a great man for war I bear witness to, because even when the spark of life had gone out of him, he was as full of fight as when he was going into it."

Both men were modest, simple, kindly and dearly loved. Stack might lower darkly and Brugha's whole person stiffen in silent menace, but it seemed to make no difference. Many would have used about both of them the words that Collins used about Brugha. "Do you know," he said, after Brugha's outburst against him in the Dail, "in spite of it all, I can't help feeling a regard for Cathal." And when Brugha had met his death at the beginning of the Civil War, advancing, gun in hand, and once again refusing to surrender, Collins did not lightly get over it.

How far the suspicions harboured by Brugha and Stack towards Collins had origins as primitive as those suggested—how far they sprung, rather, from the bewilderment felt by men of taut and rigid principles when confronted with an infinitely more fluent-minded and adaptable colleague, we cannot tell. Perhaps the disapproval showed itself for more than at bottom it was. Certainly, in Stack's own *Memoirs*, while there is plenty of political criticism of Collins there is no personal bitterness. But the consequences of the suspicion were unmistakable and serious. From now on Collins had always the sense of two opponents from whom he could expect no fair hearing, and as December drew nearer he saw in the Cabinet a less and less appropriate forum for a full discussion of his ideas.

The choice of Delegates rested in the first instance with the Cabinet of seven. (Later, on September 14th, was added the sanction of the Dail.) It was expected as a matter of course that De Valera would head the deputation. But, says Stack, "he had his objections. He pointed out that he was in a position of head of the State as well as head of the Government, and that his absence would always be a good reason for our Delegates making no hasty agreements in London. And I think he mentioned, and if he did not someone else did, the failure of President Wilson at Versailles. De Valera prevailed."

Stack might have added that he only did so by use of his casting vote, and in face of the votes of Griffith, Collins and Cosgrave—the first small symptom of the coming rift. That tragic consequences flowed from De Valera's absence from the negotiations both friends and enemies of the Treaty would agree to-day. But the strategy was understandable enough. As long as De Valera was in reserve the Irish Delegates could avoid being rushed into any hasty decisions. There would always be someone in Dublin to whom they must refer back, whose attitude could be represented as uncertain and difficult. The strategy failed because of imperfect understanding among the Irish leaders, exploited by Lloyd George with a peculiar ultimatum.

De Valera now proposed Griffith and Collins. Griffith made no demur but Collins for a long time refused. He did not feel himself enough of a politician, and the actual settlement reached was a politician's not a soldier's affair. He suggested, too, that in his absence a good deal of use might be made of his name as of an extremist hard to conciliate. At last he consented, but Brugha and Stack, disclaiming all skill in conference, were adamant that they would not go. Three more men were wanted "to work in well" with Griffith and Collins. Brugha proposed Gavan Duffy as a legal man; Duggan, proposed by Collins, was preferred as more suitable. Collins then proposed that Barton or Childers or preferably both should also go. De Valera said that he had Childers in mind for Secretary. They had no one to match him for knowledge of constitutional procedure and for general secretarial expertness. His suggestion was agreed to and Barton adopted as a member, a position which he only accepted with diffidence and in view of so many refusals. One place was left, and Gavan Duffy, proposed by De Valera, was chosen as a second legal member of the team, which then stood as follows:

Griffith, Chairman; Collins second in command; Barton, economic expert; Duggan and Gavan Duffy, lawyers.

One or two points strike us from this story of the selection. The three members of the Cabinet who eventually opposed the Treaty, De Valera, Brugha and Stack, all had the chance of going, but all refused, De Valera for reasons that did not commend themselves to Griffith, Collins and Cosgrave. De Valera, Brugha and Stack must therefore bear some share of the responsibility for the actions of those they chose to represent them, above all, of Griffith and Collins, whom they chose as leaders. On the other hand, Griffith and Collins had virtually carte blanche in choosing their companions, and had only themselves to blame if they found them unsatisfactory.

This last statement is subject to one important qualification. It is said that Griffith opposed the selection of Erskine Childers as Secretary, and only gave way in deference to De Valera. It is certain that in his heart he disapproved the choice.[1] From now on we shall find it impossible to ignore an antagonism between Griffith and Childers, that furnishes, as it persists and deepens, a wretched parallel to that between Brugha and Collins. In each case deep cleavage of political principle first suspected, then patent, adds poison to personal coolness, and kills all confidence and trust.

Failure to understand the life of Erskine Childers would leave us blind to many of the deeper implications of the Irish cause. His father, a first cousin of Hugh Childers, Gladstone's last Chancellor of the Exchequer, and his mother, a Barton of Glendalough, County Wicklow, both died while he was still small, and he was brought up at Glendalough with the Bartons, a family like his own of five children, of whom Robert Barton was the eldest son. Passing through Cambridge with distinction, he entered like so many Anglo-Irishmen the British Civil Service and worked as a Committee clerk at the House of Commons from 1895 to 1911. He then resigned his professional prospects to work for Ireland, and in *The Framework of Home Rule* contributed a finely reasoned if rather overweighted plea for a species of Dominion Home Rule—a solution far in advance of that favoured by orthodox Liberal opinion. In July 1914, in reply to Carson's heavily capitalised gun-running into Larne, he and his wife smuggled over guns from Liége to Howth in his little yacht the *Asgard*. A few days later came the European War, and Childers, though by now forty-four, at once joined up with the Royal Naval Volunteer Reserve.

Few amateurs could equal the value of what he had to offer. He had been through the South African War with the C.I.V. and written not only a charming memoir of the corps, but the last volume of *The Times* history of the War, dealing with the guerilla phase. These and later books, *War and the Arme Blanche* and *German Influence on British Cavalry*, had constituted him on military questions the acknowledged expert that, with his exhaustive scholarship and faculty of analysis, he became on every subject that he took up. But the book that made his name a household word was *The Riddle of the Sands*, a story of two young Englishmen who discover and frustrate a plan for a German invasion of England from behind the cover of the Frisian Islands. Childers had acquired from yachting a specialised knowledge of the German

[1] Compare Griffith in the Dail, December 15th 1921: "I was Chairman of the Delegation of which Mr. Childers, not with my approval, was appointed Secretary."

coast, and some part of that knowledge appeared in the story.

The War brought him the D.S.O. and the rank of Lieutenant-Commander, and his whole record was conspicuously gallant, a fact that afterwards even his most venomous detractors admitted. Winston Churchill wrote of him as "a man of distinction, ability and courage who had shown daring and ardour against the Germans in the Cuxhaven Raid of New Year's Day, 1915," and there was plenty more, equally ungrudging. But the period of the War for him was one of as much agony as service. The last phase of the Boer War had turned him from Conservatism to Liberalism, but he had clung to the hope that the aims of the Allies were this time what they professed themselves to be, the rights and independence of the small nationalities. He joined up in 1914, a friend has said of him, in the intention of giving British Imperialism one last chance. As the struggle grew more desperate his soul revolted not only, nor so much, from the material horrors of the War as from the Spirit and objects of its pursuit.

In 1917 Childers was seconded for work as Secretary to the Irish Convention, that ill-fated attempt of Lloyd George to settle the Irish question by agreement among all sections of the Irish people. Sinn Fein, the star in the ascendant, abstained. Ulster proved intransigent, and the Conference broke up, Childers working closely with Bishop O'Donnell, signatory of the most advanced "Report." Not until the War was over did he consider his obligations to the British Government liquidated, but early in 1919 he settled in his own fashion the problem that confronts all Anglo-Irishmen, and towards the end of the year he came back to live permanently in the country which he had always regarded as his home. Literary and political circles were well aware that here was a formidable accession to the Irish ranks, and a wider public followed with morbid fascination the author of *The Riddle of the Sands*.

Childers, however, so it is said, was checked abruptly when he approached Griffith and asked to be allowed to serve Sinn Fein in Ireland. Now it was Griffith himself who had originally initiated Childers into active work for Sinn Fein. For it was by Griffith's authorisation that Childers had visited Paris in 1919 on behalf of Dail Eireann to assist the envoys to the Peace Conference. But this was different. Griffith had no use for Englishmen in Ireland. He regarded Childers as an Englishman, a friend of freedom of a type with which Ireland was familiar, and from whose activities abroad Ireland had frequently benefited. He is believed to have outlined to him schemes of discreet propaganda and spheres of useful service in England.

This was not at all what Childers wanted. He was accustomed to taking responsibility and to facing risk. His heart was set on something more hazardous than journalism and gossip in London. Looking back, his life seemed a story of two developments, one of Irish sympathy crystallising into conviction that Ireland, having declared her independence, must defend it in arms to the end; the other of unconscious self-preparation for assisting in the task of defence. And Ireland seemed to want him and to have use for him. He had already acted on the nomination of Michael Collins as one of the five original Directors of the Republican Land Bank. Now, in what was to many the most telling composition of his life, a series of articles in the *Daily News*, he exposed the atrocities of the Crown agents with evidence beyond dispute. He was appointed Chairman of the Rathmines Republican Justices; when Desmond Fitzgerald was interned in February 1921 he was created editor of the *Irish Bulletin*, and Minister of Publicity; at the elections of May he was returned for a Wicklow constituency. But from the moment that he decided to remain in Ireland, Griffith harboured against him feelings of distrust that in London, when he found Childers resolutely opposed to his own ideas of settlement, hardened into fanatical obsession. This tragic complex, whether we place the responsibility for it on human nature or on the circumstances that brought Childers to Ireland, takes rank among the causes of the friction that was to cut the Delegation in two.

Lloyd George seems to have a vivid and not ungenerous recollection of Erskine Childers, "his slight figure, his kindly, refined and intellectual countenance, his calm and courteous demeanour." His mind "imaginative" and "well trained," his will "tenacious." "Brave and resolute he was undoubtedly, but unhappily for himself also rigid and fanatical."[1] Certainly Erskine Childers was as determined that Ireland should preserve the Republic as Lloyd George was that she should not. He was perfectly prepared to place his slight figure across the onward march of an Empire.

The Cabinet drew up *Credentials* for the Delegation. These were ratified by the Dail on September 14th, a motion for restricting their scope being withdrawn under pressure from De Valera. In virtue of the authority vested by the Dail in the President for the purpose, the Credentials constituted the Delegates "Envoys Plentipotentiary from the elected Government of the Republic

[1] *Daily Telegraph*, December 23rd 1922.

in Ireland to negotiate and conclude with the representatives of His Britannic Majesty George V a Treaty or Treaties of association and accommodation between Ireland and the Community of Nations known as the British Commonwealth."

But before the Delegation left for London the Cabinet gave them also *Instructions* under which "the complete text of the draft Treaty" about to be signed was to be "submitted to Dublin and reply awaited." The comparison of these in a sense inconsistent documents has given rise to endless controversy.[1]

All that need here be understood are the two distinct objectives that the Dublin Cabinet had in mind. (1) To prevent the signature of any Treaty to which they had not first given their consent. (2) To secure the acceptance of the Delegates as Plenipotentiaries of the Republic, and hence, if only by implication, to secure the recognition of the Republic itself. But the resulting position of the Delegates was paradoxical, and might in skilful hands be turned against them.

[1] The main questions are (*a*) *From the Delegates' standpoint*, how far were they morally entitled (1) to sign voluntarily any Treaty at all without reference back; (2) to sign voluntarily any Treaty that failed to preserve the Republic. (*b*) *In International law*, how far were the British entitled to treat them as (1) Plenipotentiaries for all purposes; (2) Plenipotentiaries for all purposes short of surrendering the Republic. The answer in all cases will vary according to the view taken of how far the Delegates were accepted as Plenipotentiaries by the British. Griffith and Collins admitted that they were never *officially accepted* as such, though they claimed that Lloyd George had "seen" their Credentials. It is impossible to lay down binding conclusions about a whole situation which is generally held to have been *sui generis*.

## CHAPTER IV

# THE CONFLICT OF IDEAS

"Observe, however, that of man's whole terrestrial possessions and attainments, unspeakably the noblest are his Symbols, divine or divine-seeming; under which he marches and fights, with victorious assurance in this life-battle: what we can call his Realised Ideals."

THOMAS CARLYLE.

*British versus Irish proposals—Trade and Finance—Defence—The Ulster issue—Crown and Empire—The conflict mainly one of symbols—The significance of the symbols of independence—The Irish proposals for External Association—Their sinister connotation for British Imperialists—The British symbols based on an obsolete position—The relation of External Association to British political exigencies—What the scheme would have accomplished.*

WE must now compare the British terms handed to De Valera on July 20th and published on August 15th with "Draft Treaty A," the scheme brought to London by the Irish Delegates, though naturally kept to themselves.

The British proposals offered Ireland Dominion Status subject ostensibly to six, but actually to seven, qualifications. Four of these qualifications were concerned with defence; a trade clause insisted on freedom of trade between the two countries, and a financial clause that Ireland should assume liability for a share of the British National Debt and War Pensions. The seventh qualification lay in an insistence that "the powers and privileges" belonging to the Ulster Parliament and Government under the Act of 1920 could not without her consent be "abrogated or diminished."

The Irish draft proposals joined issue all along the line. There were five heads of conflict: (1) Trade; (2) Finance; (3) Defence; (4) Ulster; (5) Crown and Empire. But of these, Trade and Finance, though the decisions were sure to affect vitally national prospects, were never likely by themselves to cause a breakdown. The Irish trade clause was still to be drafted by the Minister for Economic Affairs, and the finance clause by the Minister for Finance, Michael Collins. The former would aim at some arrangement fostering the growth of Irish industry without jeopardising overmuch the flow of cross-Channel trade. The latter would emphasise the necessity for taking into account, when a financial balance was struck, Ireland's counter-claim on the score of huge overtaxation throughout the nineteenth century. It was desired, however, to leave these and various matters of secondary importance—navigation, submarine cables, communications, etc., to special joint committees.

Defence was far more integral to the main course of the struggle. Yet even here it is hard to believe that the British claims, when toned down to the limit of inoffensive phrasing, could in any circumstances have provided an occasion for forcing a renewal of the war. From the beginning Ireland had always believed and undertaken to prove that her independence was in no way incompatible with the security of England. She was the more ready to believe that her independence was not subtracted from by the conditions which England, on behalf of that security, claimed.[1]

This is not to say that Ireland failed to fight the issue stubbornly or that the work of Collins, and Childers too, lacked results. The July proposals claimed (1) that the Royal Navy should control the seas around Ireland and Great Britain; (2) that it should have all the facilities essential for naval purposes both in peace and war in the Irish harbours and on the Irish coast; (3) that it should do this work alone, *i.e.* that Ireland should have no navy; (4) that the Irish military force should be strictly "territorial"; (5) that in order to assist the world movement towards disarmament its numbers should be proportionate to those of the British army; (6) that Great Britain should have all facilities for the development of air defence and (7) of civil communication by air; (8) that voluntary recruitment for the British forces should be permitted throughout Ireland. A hope was also expressed that Ireland would

[1] Ireland was concerned, of course, to prove that the conditions demanded were really unnecessary, but in face of a plain negation from the British War Office and Admiralty there were facts likely to render her less stubborn under this head than, say, under Crown and Empire. In the first place, it was thought that Britain might give way over symbols and prestige but not on an issue that touched security directly. Again, while it might have proved well-nigh impossible to maintain a British Government in a rebellious Ireland, it should not have proved a matter of any great difficulty in the last resort to retain the defence facilities in question. And then it seemed probable to some, and possible to all, that for several years at least certain of the British conditions might prove positively beneficial to Ireland by saving her expenditure that she could ill afford. Finally, the dearest objectives in this sphere were conceded from the very beginning with the withdrawal from Ireland of the British army and the British-controlled police. Childers, however, with relentless logic, continued to see in the restrictions imposed by the British terms a contradiction of true independence.

come to contribute voluntarily to the expenses of Imperial defence.

Of these eight propositions (they appeared as four clauses) eventually three were more or less abandoned and not a single one was to emerge intact. Yet on the whole they form the basis of Clauses 6 and 7 of the Treaty, while the Irish defence proposals of Draft Treaty A might as well have never been. The Irish Article Five had begun, "Ireland accepts and the British Commonwealth guarantees the perpetual neutrality of Ireland and the integrity and inviolability of Irish territory." It had gone on to prohibit Ireland from any international action—for example, any compact, inconsistent with the position assigned her—and had imposed on her the duty of repelling with force "any abuse of her neutral position or any attempt to use her territory for warlike purposes." It does not seem that British politicians or experts ever considered seriously the practicability of these suggestions.

It was the two remaining issues, National Status and Ulster,[1] that presented possibilities of insoluble conflict. The Ulster situation was curious. In this one case both sides were agreed on the ideal solution—severance of Ulster from the United Kingdom and incorporation in a united Ireland—but neither side separately, nor even both in concert, could move towards this consummation without a third party's consent. The British Cabinet (and the average Englishman) was just as convinced that it was common sense that North and South should be one as that Ireland should accept Dominion Status. But the path was barred alike by sentiment and pledges. The latter were incomparably the stronger force. Ulster could now claim that she had only accepted the Act of the previous year—the Partition Act—as a last and greatest sacrifice and on the explicit understanding that, unwelcome as it was to her, it at least made her safe for ever. In these circumstances no responsible body of British opinion and certainly no British Government would dream of incorporating her with the South by force.

Nor was Sinn Fein in any better case. They could accept no settlement as final which did not end Partition, nor could they recognise the separate nationhood of Ulster. Yet even so, their own history and outlook made the use of force unthinkable, and on August 10th De Valera had made this plain. "We do not con-

[1] The word "Ulster" should, strictly speaking, only be used of the nine counties, Antrim, Down, Armagh, Londonderry, Fermanagh, Tyrone, Monaghan, Cavan, and Donegal. But for the sake of convenience we make constant use of it when the Six Counties or Northern Ireland would be more accurate. We believe that no ambiguity will be caused by our use of the term.

template the use of force. If your government (the British government) stands aside we can effect a complete reconciliation. We agree with you that no common action can be secured by force."

"If your government stands aside." It was to be the whole burden of the Sinn Fein contention at Downing Street, that until Britain would stand aside, Ulster would never come round to a reasonable way of thinking. But suppose Britain did stand aside and Ulster still remained adamant—what then? And, in any case, how could Britain, in honour, cease supporting Ulster until she knew that Ulster was ready to think in terms of a reconciliation with Sinn Fein? Yet on the Sinn Fein hypothesis, so long as Britain supported Ulster, Ulster would show no change of heart.

Ulster then was strongly placed. She might be subjected to moral suasion and economic pressure but no force would be used on her. It was hard so see how Sinn Fein was ever going to persuade Britain "to stand aside from behind her." Ulster's policy must be to stand on existing agreements and steer clear of fresh bargaining. But over one thing she must be very careful. Two of her six counties, Fermanagh and Tyrone, contained Catholic and presumably Sinn Fein majorities. There must be no talk of plebiscites or of adjusting the Ulster frontier in accordance with the wishes of the inhabitants. High among the "existing powers and privileges" must come the existing area.

This is to rationalise standpoints that only gradually became straightened out. The attitude attributed to Ulster was held by the Orange leaders and in fact prevailed. But throughout the negotiations neither Sinn Fein nor Lloyd George despaired of a victory for contrary counsels, and many still believe that the Treaty would have after all brought in the North *if* it had been accepted by a united South. The sequence for us is that the negotiations began with Sinn Fein pressing the suggestion that Britain should stand aside; that Britain turned the suggestion down, but came herself to assume the task of breaking down Ulster's recalcitrance; that her attempt failing, she formulated schemes apparently calculated to bring about the same purpose and establish without coercion the "essential unity" of Ireland; that her schemes were accepted in the Treaty.

The Ulster issue played a confusing part throughout the negotiations. Griffith had set his heart on securing "essential unity," dearer always to him, as many others than the Republic; and if he had not felt that he had secured "essential unity," he would have refused to sign the Treaty of December as he had previously voted against the terms of July. So too would Collins.

But Ulster was not the main issue, as can be seen from the negligible time spent in the Dail debate over the Ulster provisions of the Treaty. Ulster indeed will come to concern our story less as an area or a people than as a strange abstract factor in tactics, its importance derived from its reactions on the central conflict. Sinn Fein, seeing that British liberal and world opinion was likely to be against her in seeking a Republic, and with her in seeking a united Ireland, planned early that it should be on the latter head that the break, if break there must be, should come. The plan was justifiable and ingenious, but the retaliation it provoked was crushing.

It is time to turn to "Crown and Empire."

As late as June 21st the British Government was still insisting on the subordinate Parliament of the Act of 1920 and refusing autonomy to that subordinate Parliament even in its own internal finance. But on July 20th she had made an offer that purported to be one of Dominion Status, an offer that went farther than any previously made to Ireland and whose liberality, Lloyd George was justified in protesting, the sense of the world acclaimed. Yet Ireland, whose representatives were enthusiastic in 1914 at the thought of a subordinate Parliament, had turned down this new and princely concession with alacrity.

Now it is true that the events of 1914 to 1919 had placed the vast mass of the South behind the demand for an independent Republic, and those of 1921 had but confirmed them in their faith. It is true that the new Dail on August 15th had unanimously sworn allegiance to the Republic of Ireland. But the ideal of an *isolated* Republic, if it had ever existed among Irish thinkers, was dead—its fate sealed by the decision to seek in conference how "the association of Ireland with the British Commonwealth could best be reconciled with Irish national aspirations." What then was the magical difference between their own proposals and Dominion Status, so patent and absolute that Dominion Status was unanimously rejected in July, was fought against from then to December, was only then accepted under threat of immediate and terrible war; that even so the distinction cut the Dail into halves, led to civil war, embittered ever since the political life of the country? For there is no denying that the difference in practical powers between the Irish scheme and Dominion Status as enjoyed, for instance, by Canada, was always small, was always likely to vanish and has apparently vanished to-day.

Here where the main battle was fought we enter a field of

psychology and symbols; of phrases—"Dominion Status," "Allegiance to the Crown," "Common Citizenship," and the like —phrases provocative of perennial controversy among constitutional lawyers and no less of passionate loyalties and antipathies in the minds of delegates and peoples.

No doubt it would be dragging in subsequent knowledge unduly to treat the struggle as having been concerned *solely* with symbols. In 1921 the Dominions, for all their signature of the Peace Treaties and membership of the League of Nations, had not yet achieved their present independence in foreign affairs,[1] nor had their internal freedom yet been regularised or placed beyond dispute. Erskine Childers and others passionately believed that geographical propinquity would prevent the acquisition by Ireland of those beneficent conventions under which, in the case of the other Dominions, the strict legal position had been rendered obsolete and true autonomy obtained. But such fears (understandable though over-pessimistic as they proved) were not the root-cause of opposition to a Dominion Status. That cause was simply this—that to accept Dominion Status, or more accurately to accept as a definition of Ireland's status the symbolism of a British Dominion, would be to renounce from motives of fear, though under a compact that would always be called voluntary, a declared independence sustained for two years in arms.

And was not this to renounce for the first time in Irish history all hopes of undoing the conquest? To deny the whole Irish rebel tradition? To accept what every Irish leader had refused? To set a boundary to the march of a nation, and hence to degrade and debase its citizens for ever? Was it not to resume in fresh and final humiliation the psychology and character of a subject people? What could it leave of Irish sense of citizenship, Irish love of country or Irish self-respect?

The status aimed at by the Irish Delegates throughout the course of the subsequent negotiations in London is defined in the recital and in the first five clauses of the Draft Treaty taken to London. The essential points are these—(1) Great Britain and the Dominions shall recognise Ireland as a sovereign independent state. (2) Great Britain renounces all claim to govern or legislate for Ireland. (3) Ireland agrees to become an "External Associate" of the Commonwealth. In this capacity Ireland's status shall be not less than that of the "sovereign partner states" of the Commonwealth. She shall be separately represented at the Imperial Con-

[1] See Appendix 7.

ference. In later drafts it is explained that Ireland is to be associated with the British for matters of common concern, which are to include defence, peace and war, and perhaps political as distinct from commercial treaties. (4) Irish citizens and citizens of the British Commonwealth shall enjoy reciprocal rights, *i.e.* Irish citizens shall enjoy the privileges of British citizenship and vice versa.

The principle which was developed in various minds right up to the end of November had germinated in De Valera's brain. Exactly when, is not clear, though he was in a position to explain its main outlines to Barton on the latter's release in July. Its object was threefold, to reassure England,[1] to save her face, and to satisfy Irish national aspirations. On the first score it would guarantee that in foreign policy, the only sphere where Irish antagonism could damage England, Ireland's freedom to go her own way would be as limited as that of the Dominions. On the second, it would refute the sneer that England had been forced by violence to let Ireland sever all connection with the Empire. On the third score it would make it plain that in all affairs within her borders—the sphere which she cared about—Ireland's freedom of action was to be complete and unfettered; that in curtailing her range of action in the relatively unimportant foreign sphere Ireland was acting voluntarily[2] and foregoing rights in exchange for accruing advantages; that the resulting position left Ireland an independence unchallengeable in the eyes of the world. And the scheme provided a framework consistent with and making possible the retention of the Republic—the symbol of separation and independence.

The practical position accorded to Ireland under External Association differed little as already explained from that under Dominion Status. But Ireland would not have been a Dominion nor "within the Empire." There would have been no allegiance to the Crown. Irishmen would not have been British subjects. There would have been "reciprocal" but no "common" citizenship.

[1] A consideration only less vital was the reassurance of Ulster and the loyalist minority in the South. Special safeguards were planned for Ulster, while the retention of a close connection with Britain, including provision for "reciprocal citizenship" would, it was hoped, appeal to loyalist sentiment in the North and South alike. Compare De Valera's letter to Lloyd George of August 10th. "A certain treaty of free Association with the British Commonwealth we would have been ready to recommend had we an assurance that the entry of a nation as a whole into such Association would secure for it the allegiance of the present dissenting minority, to meet whose sentiment alone this step could be contemplated."

[2] The voluntary aspect of any compromise reached after recent hostilities was bound to be slightly unreal. No claim to terminate unilaterally at will the Treaty of Association was ever put forward. Presumably it would have been left in the position of any other international treaty.

Now to Englishmen the existing Imperial symbolism, with the Crown as the supreme symbol of unity, was vital to the spirit of co-operation and hence to the continuance of the Commonwealth. For the ties of blood and the course of history have reared round the forms under which British constitutional law conveys the ideas of unity and free partnership, many mellowing associations, and the generous imaginative interpretation that looks beyond the words. But Lloyd George, writing of that "bond of union which is represented by a common fealty to the Sovereign," admits that it is "not easy to interpret the potency of the invisible bond" (or, he might have added, the freedom and equality it accords) "to those who are brought up to venerate other systems." And the reason is plain. Taken literally, the British symbols would completely mislead an impartial stranger to the system, expressing as they do a British domination over the Dominions, and a subordination of the Dominions to Britain, that have long since passed away. Still more would the British symbols seem incompatible with freedom and equality to Irishmen, since for Irishmen would be gathered round the British Crown associations of sheer tyranny.

As the negotiations progress we shall find the Irish Delegates making certain concessions. At the beginning they are as anxious to emphasise, over-emphasise perhaps, with their symbols the independence accorded under the practical position proposed, as the British are anxious to overstress the element of union. Gradually they come to agree to recognise the Crown as head in the foreign sphere, where Ireland is to act in concert with the Commonwealth. But any arrangement which would involve allegiance (*i.e.* subordination in matters domestic, as well as in matters external, to the British monarch), or the presence of the King in the legislature (*i.e.* the Royal Veto), or common citizenship making Irishmen into British subjects, is resisted to the end. Above all they could countenance no arrangement that made Ireland a British Dominion, with its suggestion that Irishmen were "Britain's children" by origin, enjoying their freedom only so long as Britain suffered them to do so. Nor could they contemplate the abandonment of the Republic, the symbol that their freedom was substantially complete.

There was nothing indeed theoretically impossible about a Republic not associated with, but actually a member of the Empire, *i.e.* a Dominion. This arrangement was, however, never seriously put forward by either party, and throughout the choice will lie between an Externally Associated Republic and a Dominion within the Empire. The proposals for the former preserved in all their subsequent development their underlying principle, and represented no less than Dominion Status a coherently worked out relationship. But their language was repugnant to British minds; it suggested imperfect loyalty; and *prima facie* British statesmen were no doubt correct in judging that they would totally fail to reassure the British people. And in the special circumstances of the day they were *prima facie* just as inadequate to save the face of Britain before the world. Grant Dominion Status, and Ireland would still be in the position eventually achieved by conquered rebels like the Boers. Grant External Association, and Ireland could have been represented as having fought her way out of the Empire, and having achieved what the British Government had a hundred times pledged themselves never in any circumstances to tolerate—a Republic.

On the whole matter some will conclude that the difference between an External Association and Dominion Status was negligible, and that it was stark insanity for Irish leaders to provoke a renewal of the war for the sake of such a shadow. But let them remember that England was striving to impose on Ireland alien symbols. Ireland was merely seeking the right to choose her own. Let them ask themselves too whether those who contended that the difference between the two proposals was merely a shadow might not be expected to surrender this shadow to those who considered the difference worth dying for; whether the Irish symbolism did not go far nearer than the British to expressing the reality proposed; and whether it was not far more likely to have brought a final settlement.

## CHAPTER V

# INDEPENDENCE THROUGH DIFFERENT EYES

"Be ye all of one mind."
St. Peter.

*External Association and the Dublin Cabinet—Griffith—De Valera—Collins—Cosgrave—Griffith and Collins sent over with a scheme not emanating from them.*

How deeply rooted among the various sections in the Dublin Cabinet, and the corresponding elements in the country, was the preference for External Association over Dominion Status? Republican controversialists allege that Griffith had never cared for the ideal of a Republic, and that Collins had despaired of a Republic by June, but that on the "rock of the Republic" De Valera and those who afterwards opposed the Treaty had stood firm throughout. Extreme supporters of the Treaty retort that all were really "in the same boat," since all, De Valera and Griffith alike, had realised by the beginning of the negotiations that the Republic would have to be renounced and Dominion Status accepted. Close investigation leads to neither scathing conclusion. Let us take the members of the Cabinet in turn.

Brugha and Stack never loved External Association, but they tolerated and accepted it. From first to last they were ready to fight rather than abandon the Republic or accept incorporation in the Empire.

On the other wing Griffith, the operative founder of Sinn Fein, had for years before 1916 recommended a dual monarchy under which Ireland would have her separate "Lords and Commons," but George V and his heirs would be Kings of Ireland in identically the same way as they were Kings of England. As late as 1917 he had agreed to the Sinn Fein "Republican" constitution only on the insertion of a provision that once the Republic had been recognised the people should be free to choose their own form of government. Collating these facts and the remarks credited to him by Stack we shall conclude something like this. Griffith was a statesman who throughout weighed against one another three elements in the situation. (1) Any personal conviction of his own that the Republic was the only true expression of Irish independence. (2) The supposed feeling of the people that such was the case, and the necessity of satisfying that feeling if only to avert civil war. (3) The damage England could and would inflict on Ireland if the demand for a Republic was persisted in. The first element weighed relatively little with him all along. The second influenced him mightily and was behind all his efforts for External Association in Downing Street. But in the last resort the first and second elements counted with him for less than the third. No doubt he would have struck a different balance if, like some of his colleagues, he had been a more passionate Republican or a less passionate opponent of war.

De Valera had many times exhibited a great flair for preserving harmony. It was so in 1917 when Brugha and Griffith came together under his leadership. It was so now when he conceived External Association not only as a bridge between Ireland and England but as common ground on which all sections of the National movement could if necessary take their stand and fight. But though infinitely ingenious and adaptable in modifying details towards compromise, he would die rather than surrender where he reckoned a principle was involved. The difference between External Association and the isolated Republic was one of detail. For explicit internal autonomy, declared independence, and the Republic itself, were all preserved in the first scheme as well as in the second. The climb-down from External Association to Dominion Status was for him, as for that matter it was for the British, one of principle. There is no evidence to show, and there is no reason to believe, that he ever considered it for a moment.

His opponents have diligently combed his utterances of the period to refute the claim that he stood firm "on the rock of the Republic."[1] Yet his language, admittedly ambiguous at times, can be explained easily enough. "I am not a doctrinaire Republican," he said in the Dail; but at that time he was explaining that he had no doctrinaire attachment to Republicanism as an internal form of government. On various other occasions he is supposed to have claimed that he "did more than any man to batter down the walls of a Republic"; to have begged Griffith "to get him out of the strait-jacket of the Republic"; and to have agreed, when Griffith protested that he could not bring back the Republic, that "neither you nor any man can do that." Whether or not one accepts these anecdotes (or for that matter one told by P. S. O'Hegarty in *The Victory of Sinn Fein*, to suggest that De Valera had invented External Association to bring Brugha and Stack into line and did not intend to take a final stand on it) they can all

[1] This phrase was attributed to De Valera, wrongly it appears.

be explained by simply keeping in mind that in each case De Valera was referring to the isolated, not the associated, Republic. It is possible that after the Treaty and especially after the failure of *Document No. 2*[1] he tended to use language that minimised the extent of his pre-Treaty concessions. But then could one expect a leader who in the course of negotiations had gone to the furthest point consistent with national honour, to revive a National movement from that precarious and uninspiring position? And so he may have reverted occasionally to the language of isolation, and tended to overlook past divergences from the isolationist policy.

Barton appreciated De Valera's attitude and came to develop one very similar. So too outside the Cabinet did Childers. But to Collins and Cosgrave, as good Republicans as any, the difference between External Association and Dominion Status was important but hardly fundamental, and they never grasped that it was fundamental to De Valera. Hence many of the misunderstandings that followed. At this time, however, neither had emerged with a political attitude on the nature of the settlement with England. Collins, the brains of the military movement, Sinn Fein's most active executant, the one rival to De Valera in the loyalties accorded him and far more than De Valera with his hands on the vital strings—Collins could clearly transform the situation if he came down on any side. But Collins's friends are unanimous that up till now he had not had time for "the political end." As his reluctance to join the Delegation showed, he had been diffidently anxious to leave the settlement to others.

He loved the Republic, and his relentless prosecution of its cause in arms had made men think of him as militarist and extremist. But he was no fanatic. He was at once too warm-hearted, too concerned with men and women in the present, too determined to find some immediate way of assisting them. Nor for all his rare acuteness and far from negligible cultivation was he a man with much taste for, or experience of, the world of symbols or abstractions. Nor was he the man, once the idea of practical association was accepted, to draw distinctions of life and death between one definition and another. On the personal side, now especially that the war was suspended, he was drawn more and more into sympathy with Griffith. They had the same conception of an Ireland free from British occupation, British penetration and British laws; the same concern for practical

[1] A document on the lines of External Association put forward by De Valera *after the Treaty* in an attempt to secure national unity.

construction. Collins more than any man in the Irish Delegation was to come to the negotiations with the ordinary Irish outlook and the open mind. No man was to be so much influenced by the actual course that the negotiations ran.

Cosgrave had not at this time revealed himself what Mr. Churchill afterwards found him, "a chief of higher quality than any who had yet appeared." But long before October he was inclined to act with Griffith and Collins, with each of whom he shared important qualities. During the next few months in Dublin his mind, working independently to that of Collins, was to reach the same conclusions.

The Irish Delegates then were proceeding to London with a novel and complicated scheme of External Association, which should renounce Ireland's claim to isolation but preserve what was judged essential of the power and symbols of independence. The scheme, if it were ever to have any chance of acceptance would require advocacy whole-hearted and brilliant, and patent readiness to face war if it were turned down. De Valera who had originated it was remaining in Dublin. Childers who had done much to develop it was only Secretary. The two leaders of the Delegation were as loyal Irishmen as ever breathed, in different ways most effective advocates, and could be relied on to do all in their power to further External Association. But as Griffith protested afterwards in the Dail, the scheme "did not emanate from us."

## CHAPTER VI

# THE CHOSEN REPRESENTATIVES

"I had rather have
Such men my friends than enemies."
SHAKESPEARE: *Julius Cæsar.*

I: *The Irish arrive in London—The meeting in Downing Street.* II: *The British Delegates—The Big Four—Their coadjutors.* III: *The Irish Delegates—Griffith and Collins—Duggan and Gavan Duffy—Barton.* IV: *The Secretaries—Tom Jones—Lionel Curtis—The principles of the Round Table—Lionel Curtis and Erskine Childers—John Chartres.* V: *The circumstances of the two Delegations.*

## I

THE Irish Delegation were given a tremendous reception when they arrived at Euston on the evening of Saturday, October 8th, and made their way through thronged streets to one of the houses taken for them—22 Hans Place. Two full staffs of servants had been brought from Ireland, and the party was completed by a host of secretaries, expert advisers, and typists. A Sunday paper detected a touch of the "quaint humour really natural to the occasion in the cabful of cooks with their implements of office that brought up the rear." A judicial Daily reckoned the four young typists as "good-looking as most Dublin girls," and found "the mother of the whole party" in Mrs. Folkard, the "matronly" cook.

Outside the Delegates and the two leading secretaries, Childers and John Chartres, the most notable figures were Desmond Fitzgerald, Minister of Publicity, Dermot O'Hegarty, Secretary to the Cabinet, and one of the Assistant Secretaries to the Delegation, and Professor Smiddy, Economic Adviser. Desmond Fitzgerald enjoyed already a unique position among British and foreign journalists, with his youth, his looks, his combination of literary grace and wit with ferocious activity and endurance, of gaiety with fixed resolve. Dermot O'Hegarty, the "civil servant of the revolution," the man perpetually behind the scenes, could conceal from few who met him the gifts that were to make possible the

Irish constitutional achievements at the Imperial Conference of 1926. Professor Smiddy was to do the Irish Free State credit at Washington as their first diplomatic representative.

Michael Collins, however, for whom the cries had been loudest, did not reach London until Monday morning, the day before the Conference was due to begin. He slipped quietly to 15 Cadogan Gardens, where he stayed throughout, accompanied by his famous bodyguard.

"How did you get to Hans Place this morning without being discovered?" asked a reporter.

"I always," replied Collins, "watch the other fellow instead of letting him watch me."

But "this big, good-humoured Irishman with the soft yet decisive voice" proved to have "another side." His face grew stern as he said "with something like emotion": "The *Daily Express* was the newspaper that called me a murderer."

"We had neither the desire nor the intention to be unfair to you," said the well-meaning reporter.

The day of October 10th was spent in preliminary arrangement between the secretaries, Tom Jones and Sir Edward Grigg on the one hand, Erskine Childers and John Chartres on the other. The English showed a desire to exclude stenographers, and only to allow long-hand notes: the Irish consented, while thrusting on their opponents the responsibility for the suggestion.

The Conference began with a Plenary Session at eleven o'clock on Tuesday, October 11th, half-hysterical crowds cheering both teams impartially as they drew up at 10 Downing Street. Lloyd George adroitly solved an initial difficulty of introduction. It was very doubtful whether the Irish Delegates would consent to shake hands with Sir Hamar Greenwood, Chief Secretary for Ireland, on whom the publics of both countries were agreed in fixing official responsibility for the Black-and-Tans, and whose gallant attempts to defend his agents had destroyed Irish reliance on his declarations. Nor was enthusiasm expected among the English for shaking hands with Michael Collins. Lloyd George, however, greeted the Irish Delegation at the door, shook hands with them warmly and led them to their places along one side of the table. Across it he effected introductions to the English drawn up on the other side. The seating was as below, the secretaries sitting a little behind their principals, and taking no part in the discussions.

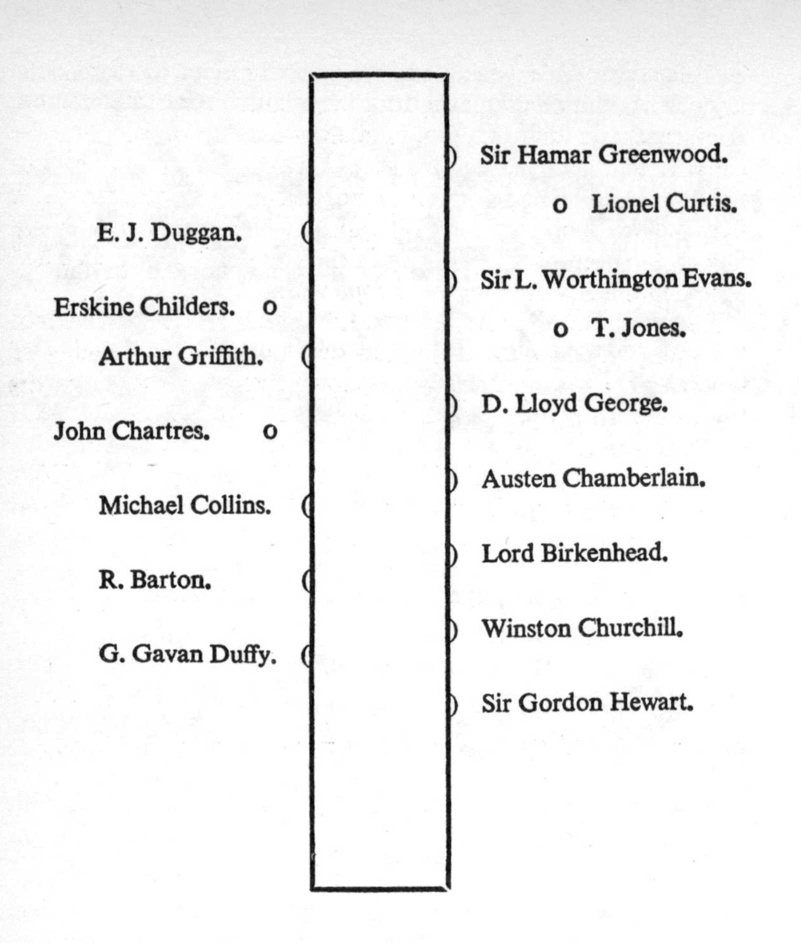


## II

England has seldom been so rich in political personality as she was just at that time. Any one of her leading quartet could have played Prime Minister with distinction. To-day the greatest of all is dead: two sponsor attitudes whose vogue has passed or is not yet; only Sir Austen Chamberlain retains his old authority, and he has yielded office to younger men. In 1921 they were well adapted to represent before their untried adversaries everything most overwhelming in the power and resources of England.

Lloyd George was admirably suited for the twin tasks of hardening his heart against the Irish and of bending them to his will. Externally, he had so much in common with them, internally so little. A radical, brought up by a village cobbler, a friend of small nations if his speeches about the war and the peace were to be believed, a Welsh-speaking Celt, he could talk to perfection the jargon of Nationalist aspiration yet could remain far more unsympathetic than an Englishman would have been to the demand that such aspirations should find expression in political freedom. And he had a power of magnetism, of getting people to like and trust him personally, against which only a De Valera had so far been proof. Nothing in their previous experience had prepared the Irish Delegates to cope with it.

He could, too, be very terrible. Like some others sprung from the lower middle-classes, he had developed in his hey-day of power a strong authoritarian vein, showing itself in a new approach towards both people and ideas. It is plain from Lord Riddell's diary how much the war and the aftermath had accentuated this strain, so that by 1921 even his secretary Kerr, a gifted, sophisticated hero-worshipper, was finding him "a real autocrat." Conscious that he owed everything to merit and his own exertions, he could play the bully without compunction. Accustomed too long at the head of an empire to exploit every device towards an end indisputably just, he could by now, once his mind was made up, brook no argument, nor could he recognise even sincerity in anyone who took a different line from him. He believed in the paramount necessity of settling the Irish question, and he was out at all costs to obtain a settlement. But the feelings of the Irish people were only one element in the problem. There were, after all, only three million or so Southern Irish, fewer than the British casualties in the Great War. Still less could he deal in fastidiousness or chivalry towards individuals. Personal embarrassment, even personal injury, he could not hesitate to inflict, if they served to end this conflict of centuries.

And then he was a politician, not a philanthropist or international philosopher. After a certain point his own ideals would become irrelevant, and the sole question— what would Parliament stand? His own reputation was endangered any way by negotiations. It would be blackened inevitably by the consequences of a further recourse to war, but it would be destroyed once and for all by any surrender that Parliament judged one of principle, by permission, say, for Ireland to retain her Republic.

Altogether, a formidable fellow, as the Irish soon perceived. Yet till all was over they never recognised the two most deadly aspects of his art. The power apparently to commit himself, yet leave himself by inspired prevision a single way of escape; and the power, so decisive on the last day of all, to get accepted his own statement of any problem, his own relative emphasis on the various elements in any situation. His negotiating genius lay partly, perhaps largely, in the fact that it kept itself concealed.

Austen Chamberlain was the perfect British Parliamentarian; a phenomenon inspiring awe. In a Conference where all would strive to express themselves in solemn yet graceful parliamentary language, to combine candour and force with taste and courtesy, he who had lisped since early manhood in ministerial accents, whose courtesy was as spontaneous as his dignity, and both as perfect as proverbial, he of all men was likely to suffer least restraint, to be stimulated even by this atmosphere of imposed forms. And his father had abandoned Liberalism rather than yield Ireland a subordinate legislature. His own political career had been much absorbed in the continuance of the same struggle. In sharing in the offer of Dominion Status and coming into conference at all, he was taking a course "fundamentally divergent from the whole tradition and even character of his party."[1] With him, an Irish Republic, associated or otherwise, could scarce do other than contradict a vital principle. And when principle was touched, he would yield to no Irishman in devotion.

At this time Lord Birkenhead still loomed in Irish Nationalists' imagination as a sinister, even satanic power. Carson's galloper in 1914, he had more recently been foremost in the public reiteration that the rebels must be crushed by force. The South thought of him as a materialist, with what political altruism he possessed used up in fierce allegiance to the British Crown; full of contempt for what was small, and callousness towards what was suffering; as one likely to pay scant attention to the plea for special treatment of what he probably regarded as a disloyal and treacherous sect.

And there could be no doubting that if he wished to assert an unwelcome authority, he possessed every requisite gift. The first advocate of the day, an academic authority on the British Constitution, the author of a standard work on international law, and these last two years a great constructive jurist, he could hardly fail to tower above Duggan and Gavan Duffy. Nor was there anything to reassure in his frontal combination of offensive weapons; the patronage, the nonchalant impromptu exposition, the world-famous repartee. Nor in the Herculean physique which dwarfed all the Irishmen except Collins.

The event proved that his opponents had underestimated, not indeed his gifts, but his humanity. Throughout the two months of negotiations they continued to marvel at his unfailing aptitude

[1] Winston Churchill.

for debating retort, for legal exegesis, for instantaneous drafting. And there was no question, as with Lloyd George, of his being their special ally. He was nothing if not a British patriot throughout. But he gave them credit for being patriots, too, and as such he always treated them. They were aware of his might, but they admired and trusted him. "It was not the least of Birkenhead's services," as Sir Austen Chamberlain has written, "that he did enter into Michael Collins's mind, won his sympathy and secured his confidence. The very fact that to him life was a gallant adventure created a link between him and Michael Collins without which we might never have reached agreement."[1] Even those Irishmen who afterwards had only mournful memories of the Conference were glad that Birkenhead had been present.

What a team it must have been that could relegate to fourth place in its councils Winston Churchill; a national figure since his twenties, an orator on a scale as grand as Birkenhead, a historian destined to surpass all others over the period from 1914 onwards, and to forge unforgettable phrases to describe this very Conference. For all his Home Rule past and his pre-War experiences of an Ulster mob, he least of them all was likely to entertain kindly feelings towards Sinn Fein.

Like the others he was fired by dreams of the sweep and glory of Britain, but unlike them he had been reared in an aristocratic atmosphere which precluded the least fellow-feeling for the uprise of a race suppressed. Unlike them again he was not only thoroughly familiar with the technical requirements of defence but prepared if necessary to give them precedence over those of politics. Propounding the theory that "integral communities like human beings are dominated by the instinct of self-preservation," he admired the qualities bred by war. But it must be warfare waged on the recognised heroic lines. Himself retaining the instinct of a soldier, a lover of the King's uniform and a friend to all who wore it, such a man contemplated with mingled shame and disgust the methods by which England had been forced to treat. To the Irishmen responsible he could be no friend.[2]

[1] *Daily Telegraph*, March 29th 1932.

[2] He could have said with Chamberlain that Michael Collins's code of honour was not his, and that "between him and me there could be no real sympathy and perhaps only partial understanding." It is true that he credits Collins with regret that Ireland had not been able to adopt more orthodox military methods. Still, even so, Collins, "the man whose hands had touched the springs of terrible deeds," always ranks below Cosgrave, "the chieftain of higher quality than any who had yet appeared."

In the discussions that preceded Lloyd George's invitation in June, Churchill's personal preference had been for "beating them first," if necessary

Soberly considered, the aspect of the Big Four was not encouraging. Lloyd George had once been a minor martyr on behalf of the Boers fighting for freedom; later a radical reformer at home; more recently in the Great War the chief instrument of British Imperial achievement. Still nominally Liberal, he was now the dominating yet embarrassed leader of a Coalition basically Conservative. Winston Churchill, the other nominal Liberal, had been brought up a Tory. But, discouraged by Balfour and differing on the one issue of Free Trade, he had left the party where every tradition-bred impulse should have retained him. The Conservatives, remembering as much as anything against him his Home Rule speeches before the War, had ejected him from responsible office at the 1915 Coalition. They would watch him and Lloyd George very carefully and suspiciously now.

The two Unionists, Austen Chamberlain and Lord Birkenhead, were in danger of being tarred with this same brush. Both till recently could point to the most respectable antecedents. The former had proved worthy of a father who had left the Radical party and subordinated his desire for social transformation to smashing the first Home Rule Bill; a father who had finished the founder of the new Imperialism. The latter before the War had been no whit behind Sir Edward Carson in his incitements to armed resistance if Home Rule were imposed on Ulster. But both of them had bowed to the inevitable, sponsored the Act of 1920, shared in the even more suspect offer of July, and were now sitting down in conference to discuss it with pledged Republicans. Already they had alienated many loyal and strenuous Conservatives, and many warm friends.

Sinn Fein's demand was to be allowed to secede from the Empire. Even from an idealistic standpoint a disposition to consider it seriously would have been improbable in Lloyd George or Winston Churchill; such a disposition would have been inconceivable in Chamberlain and Birkenhead, who in permitting the violation of the sanctity of the Union had already sacrificed one prime political conviction. But the Big Four were anything but

by the execution of hostages. But he was shrewd enough to realise that public opinion forbade this course and he was one of the strongest in urging a Dominion offer first.

Churchill's own services to Ireland did not come until 1922, when as Colonial Secretary he piloted the Irish Free State Agreement through a restless House of Commons, a magnificent parliamentary feat. Yet even at that time his overbearing language caused embarrassment to the Free State Government, and resentment throughout Southern Ireland. In Ireland he remains the British Imperialist and militarist *par excellence*. But no man living has written with more imagination of this whole phase of Ireland's history, nor interpreted more stirringly the drama of the Treaty's signing.

free agents. All four were sincerely anxious to bring about an Irish settlement without further bloodshed. All of them were prepared to run grave risks with their own reputations and careers for such an object. But not one of them was individually quite secure, not one of them could try any experiment and rely upon personal prestige and abstract justice to put it over. They spoke continually of the difficulty of carrying even a Dominion settlement through their own Party Conventions. And after all, the House of Commons had been selected to hang the Kaiser and squeeze Germany until the pips squeaked. It was full, in Mr. Baldwin's words, "of hard-faced men who looked as if they had done well out of the War." No worse House could be imagined for Ireland's purpose. In one respect only its very Chauvinism recommended it. Any settlement it agreed to would be one by which England would abide.

The remaining three members were little more than the inevitable supplements. There was the Chief Secretary for Ireland, Sir Hamar Greenwood, to-day Lord Greenwood and Chairman of the A.B.C. Him we have met before. There was the Conservative Secretary for War, Sir Laming Worthington-Evans, formerly a financial solicitor and at that time a helpful party politician. He was ready in the Treaty debates to rout about the House of Commons Library and return a few minutes later with an account, peremptorily acquired from Anson, of the origin of the Oath of Allegiance. He was ready a few years later to expound to the House of Commons, at an hour or two's notice, the Government's policy for unifying the Currency and Bank Note Issue. To sit with them on constitutional topics was the Attorney-General, Sir Gordon Hewart, the present Lord Chief Justice. His mellifluous oratory and the charming literary style with which the *New Despotism* has since familiarised the public lay latent during the negotiations. He played a well-meaning part in one important Sub-Conference. An ungrateful little sequel rewarded him.

Of these only Sir Hamar Greenwood will be remembered in Ireland, and of him few Irishmen will have much to say that had not better after this length of time be left unsaid. Disinterested Englishmen regret the Black-and-Tans and apologise for them. There is little point now in allocating official responsibility for their crimes. No doubt Greenwood showed courage in ever taking on a thankless and dangerous task.[1] No doubt he conceived it his duty to stand up for his men. But even here "his superabundant

[1] For a tribute to Greenwood's courage see *The Aftermath*, p. 310. Also Riddell's *Diary, passim.*

energy so often carried him beyond the boundaries of fact that he became as one crying in the wilderness" (General Macready). For almost worse in their effects than the atrocities by Crown agents were the explanations of them in the House of Commons. The truth would have shocked the world more at the moment, but would have stamped on the Irish mind a less lasting belief in the honour of British governments.

## III

The Irish Delegation was weakened by the absence of De Valera, the living symbol of the Republic, and the least impressionable man on earth. But Griffith and Collins were splendid representatives, far out of the common run of men. Different in most things, they were united, as Austen Chamberlain instantly perceived, by their passionate love of Ireland. And they had also two other characteristics in common. They were both men of enormous physical strength and vitality, and they were both extremely quick and shrewd in a deal. Of Collins, still only thirty-one, tall of stature, deep of chest, loose-limbed, and with buoyant elastic gait, in every way a magnificent specimen of manhood just matured, it could readily be believed that he had been the leader not long before in every Gaelic sport. Griffith eighteen years older, "small, quiet, drab" (Austen Chamberlain), with the air of a "tired scholar" (Churchill), did not strike one as an athlete, yet he was a powerful swimmer, a long-distance cyclist, an astonishing rope-climber. A ram in body and mind, George Moore had called him, noticing his tremendous shoulder development. And all the controversies, and they were many and dangerous, that life had brought him, had not induced him to carry firearms. A social editor had once impugned the honour of a lady and Griffith had thrashed him with his own hands. A rough had molested him in the street and Griffith had knocked him out with ease.

In sub-committees on details Collins, the younger, the more assimilative intellect, proved a mainstay. Sub-committees were set up on financial relations, naval and air defence and observance of the Truce. Collins was a member of them all, and on the first two the only Irish representative. British experts were amazed at the rapidity of his technical grasp. They forgot that this former clerk from the Post-Office and Guaranty Trust, this present "gunman," had raised a year before a loan of three hundred and eighty thousand pounds in face of furious proscription, and that he had for several years been doing work almost unaided that in England would have occupied handsome staffs in a variety of Government departments.

But in the Plenary Conference when the supreme issue was joined it was Griffith to whom the Irish looked. Except where precise data were available or where his spirit was moved, Collins was liable to overtrustfulness. At heart he always retained a doubt of his own qualifications for politics. Arthur Griffith was retarded by no doubt, no credulity, and as little self-consciousness as De Valera. Lloyd George would gather up all his authority and emphasise in portentous terms the seriousness of some Irish breach of the Truce. There would seem to be no answer, but Griffith, without any chance to prepare, yet quite imperturbably, would soon in short flat sentences cancel the effect of the preceding oratory.

No other man in Ireland, and few outside it, could have challenged Lloyd George on his own terms and conceded not one inch of ground in these semi-public interchanges. If the greater experience of the British in the end brought them an advantage, if the negotiating genius of Lloyd George eventually came into its own, it was in the long-distance strategy and not in particular debates.

For the rest Griffith impressed the British[1] with his studiousness, his silence, his fidelity. Collins with his flamboyance. Both with their courage. Griffith was "the writer who had studied deeply European history and the polity of states, with the face of a thinker and the air of a tired scholar worn out by too much burning of midnight oil. He was that unique figure—a silent Irishman. He hardly ever said a word, but no word that issued from his lips would he ever unsay. A man of laconic utterance, he answered in monosyllables when most men would have considered an oratorical deliverance to be demanded by the occasion. But his yea was yea, and his nay meant nay."[2]

Collins was the "figure with swaggering gait, loud voiced and with noisy laughter[3] that seemed to belong to the open spaces and the rough life of frontier settlements and mining camps."[4] "A handsome young Irishman," says Lloyd George. "None could mistake his nationality. Irish through and through, in every respect a contrast to his taciturn neighbour, vivacious, buoyant,

[1] See articles by Lloyd George and Chamberlain, *Daily Telegraph*, December 23rd, 1922 and March 29th, 1932 respectively, and p. 305 of *The Aftermath*.

[2] Churchill.

[3] It has been protested that Collins had a soft Cork accent, and the quiet South of Ireland way of talking, and that in other respects the description does not give a fair picture of him.

[4] Chamberlain.

highly strung, gay, impulsive, but passing readily to grimness and back again to gaiety, full of fascination and charm—but also of dangerous fire. That was Michael Collins, one of the most courageous leaders ever produced by a valiant race."

Winston Churchill dismisses the other Delegates as "overshadowed by the two leaders." This, however, is to do far less than justice to the men or to the part they played. They had been elected we know as likely "to work in well" with their leaders Griffith and Collins, and they had ample credentials for the task.

Duggan was a solicitor and Gavan Duffy had been one before he was called to the Bar, but there the likeness ended. Duggan, "a sober resolute man" (Winston Churchill), the son of a peasant, had sacrificed hardly won opportunities in the cause of Irish freedom. He had played his part in the Post-Office in 1916 and been duly imprisoned. He had been imprisoned again in 1920 and only released at the Truce. General Macready, while hardly fair to the cause for which he was working, gives a vivid illustration of his efficiency as I.R.A. Director of Intelligence. All would admit his value to Ireland, his popularity and his dash, and his qualifications to represent the ordinary mind of the movement. Thick-set and rubicund, he would have passed for a political pundit but for something jolly and human in his eye.

Gavan Duffy's father had begun life as one of the organisers of the Young Ireland Movement in the 1840's. He had ended it at home once more, as Sir Charles Gavan Duffy, K.C.M.G., ex-Prime Minister of Victoria. Gavan Duffy himself, after an education at Stonyhurst and in France, had acquired a considerable practice in London which he had jeopardised in 1916 by coming forward to act as Casement's solicitor. When the Dail was established in January 1919 he played the chief part in drawing up the Declaration of Independence, and acted for a time as Secretary to the Executive Council. Later he went as Dail envoy to Paris, and on the strength of this work had been nominated a Delegate by De Valera and Barton; Collins originally preferring Duggan. Compact and trim, with rimless eye-glasses and close-cut beard, Gavan Duffy looked what he was, an Irishman of refinement and cosmopolitan culture. With his neat appearance and formal manner went a mind acute and logical but prone to concentrate its emphasis on precision and legality. It was no bad thing that a delegation whose methods might verge on the slipshod and happy-go-lucky should carry with them such a corrective. The pity of it was that Gavan Duffy's position did not carry that weight at or away from the conference table that his talents warranted and at times his attitude demanded.

Gavan Duffy was more sensitive and highly strung than his colleagues. Yet that he could rise to fine heights of courage was shown by what he did for Casement and other prisoners in 1916, by his defence in the Dail of the memory of Erskine Childers, and his expressed abhorrence of the executions of that time. And when pressed to recant on a matter of principle there was no one, even in that company, more stubborn. He was the last to consent to sign the Treaty.

Barton's story was more curious, and yet so natural that the wonder is that he did not find more comrades on his road. He was the only man in either Delegation of the country gentleman type. A Protestant, a large landowner in Wicklow, educated at Christ Church, he had already passed from Unionism to Nationalism by the time he left Oxford. Like his cousin Childers, however, he accepted a commission in the War, and it was as a British officer in charge of prisoners after the 1916 Rising that he underwent the experiences which decided him to join Sinn Fein. Profoundly moved by the faith and the stoicism of the prisoners, he came to see them as the representatives of the new spirit in the country and to reckon it a crime to resist their movement further. From 1918 he was a convinced Republican.

With the establishment of the Dail Cabinet in January 1919 he had been appointed Director of Agriculture, in which capacity he had won golden opinions by his organisation of a most successful Land Bank. Arrested for a speech containing threats of unspecified retribution if his own completely innocent election agent were not released, he escaped from Mountjoy Gaol—an unprecedented feat—and for ten months was "on the run" in the closest intimacy with Collins. Re-arrested[1] in the spring of 1920, he was removed to Portland Convict Prison, where his hardships did not stop at those laid down in the regulations.

Released at the Truce, for which he himself and Duggan made the final arrangements with Macready, Barton resumed his position in the Cabinet as Director of Agriculture and in the new Cabinet became Minister for Economic Affairs, well fitted for the position by agricultural achievements of his own and by lifelong study of the possibilities of Irish industrialism. But, liked and respected by all, he had been inevitably set somewhat apart by

[1] Through the merest accident. Collins had information that No. 44, where Barton was sleeping, would not be raided. But one of the 4's happened to be partially rubbed off the fanlight and the British mistook the house for No. 4, which they had instructions to raid.

differences of circumstance. His imprisonment had accentuated the distinction and snapped even the thread of his intimacy with Collins, though the mutual affection remained. In consequence, he was sadly out of touch with the crucial psychological developments.

On the surface, it is true, the plans for the negotiations seemed clear enough. The official policy was to put forward this scheme of External Association—a perfect godsend which left no trace of British authority over Irish affairs, compromised, if at all, only in the foreign sphere, and preserved the Republic of Ireland. That during the last fifteen months of bloodshed and destruction, there might have been growing up in the minds of some who, like Collins, were bearing the brunt of the war, a half-formed conditional preparedness to forgo in certain conceivable contingencies the Republic, and accept membership of the Empire—this was a circumstance of which Barton had inevitably no inkling. He continued to imagine that the renunciation of the Republic was still unanimously regarded, as it was when he was imprisoned, as a dishonour to which death was without hesitation to be preferred. Nor did he begin to plumb the depths of the antagonism between Collins and Brugha nor realise how already it was cutting the Cabinet into halves, and drawing Griffith and Collins into private counsel. If he had, he would have used his vote and every atom of his influence to bring De Valera to London and so restore the unity which was already hanging by a thread.

And if it was left to him to save the Republic, and if his spirit, intelligence, and utter disinterestedness seemed to fit him peculiarly for the task, his isolation made his gifts of no avail. Education and final adherence to a Republic aligned him with Gavan Duffy, but Gavan Duffy was not a Cabinet Minister and special affinity was lacking. Childers, his great friend, could co-operate, but only from the outside. Barton, come to London as economic expert, would find it his function to thwart his leaders' plans. He would have to act in ignorance of the determining undercurrents, and when ultimate responsibility was reached, quite alone. Before him lay confusion and embarrassment, beyond them the tragedy of dilemma.

## IV

The secretaries were worthy of the principals they had been chosen to serve. The Plenary Conferences were attended on the English side by Tom Jones and Lionel Curtis (once by Sir Edward Grigg); on the Irish by Erskine Childers and John Chartres, once by Dermot O'Hegarty. No one should ever speak, perhaps no one has ever spoken, of Tom Jones without cordiality and respect. Here is the true happy warrior, the man who has had to fight his way up almost from the bottom and yet has always found time to fight the battles of others first. A man of the people, an intellectual, a philanthropist with all he has ever possessed—his labour. Born in a Welsh mining village, son of a one-time grocer's assistant, at fourteen he had been working as a clerk in a steelworks, yet somehow he had found his way to Glasgow University, and through the bounty of Lord Russell to a research scholarship at the London School of Economics. Later he had been travelling Barrington Lecturer up and down the whole of Ireland and Professor of Economics at Belfast. Turning from academic paths to those of social inquiry and reform, and from these to the Civil Service with the War, he had become by 1921 Assistant Secretary to the Cabinet, in which capacity he remained, till his retirement, the close personal confidant of each succeeding Prime Minister.

His activities at this time were constant, and sustained to the last day of the Conference. He soon won the confidence of the Irish Delegates. He was able to exhibit his knowledge and love of a Celtic language; to talk to them of Thomas Davis, his own boyhood's hero, of work and holidays spent in Ireland, of holidays he hoped to spend there again. With his own membership of a small nationality, his lowly origin and modest estimate of his own abilities, he was able to sympathise with any awe or disgust they may have felt at the pomp and majesty of the British. Best of all, he was able to impress on them that many of his own feelings and sympathies were shared by Lloyd George himself; that in a different sense from the rest of the Delegation and in face of overwhelming difficulties from colleagues, Parliament, press and public, Lloyd George was their friend.

Let there be no misunderstanding here or suspicion of irony. With a man like Tom Jones there can be no question of insincerity. But after all he was a Civil Servant acting for and under a revered master, and himself believing that Ireland would find her highest destiny within the Empire. For all his genuine love of Ireland, his sympathy for her Delegates and his desire to see them fairly treated, he was a subtle if unsuspecting instrument in the hands of their most dangerous antagonist. He was an unforeseen menace to the Republican cause. Yet in Ireland he will always be remembered with gratitude and affection.

Lionel Curtis and Sir Edward Grigg were of a different kidney. Curtis had fought through the Boer War and he, Grigg and Kerr had all been members of the Oxford Kindergarten, with whose help Milner had laid the foundations of the new South Africa. The same group had founded the *Round Table* quarterly in 1910 to press the cause of closer Empire unity, and by 1916 Curtis had evolved a complete Federal Constitution for the Empire with a central legislature, executive and judiciary.[1] For the next five years he was concerned with the great experiment of Dyarchy, with inventing it, with its adoption by Mr. Montagu and Lord Chelmsford, and with its embodiment in the Government of India Act of 1919.

Before 1921 Curtis, himself of Anglo-Irish antecedents, had had little time to spare for Ireland. Still, in "The Commonwealth of Nations," the name he invented for the Empire, he had devoted a luminous hundred pages to Ireland's history in the eighteenth century. He had stressed there the evils that flowed from the absence of government by consent, and still more those resulting from the 1782 arrangement which provided no means of settling differences between England and Ireland save the patronage of a common Crown. In March 1921, however, Curtis and Dove, editor of the *Round Table*, visited Ireland and between them produced in the June number of their review as fair a summary of recent Irish history as anyone could wish.

But as usual Curtis must draw a moral from his historical studies, and as usual it was one which could be linked to what he called first principles. It appeared that the great defect of the Irish people was and had ever been their lack of moral discipline. And no wonder, for they had never been entrusted with the responsibility of governing themselves. To cure this disease of character, to mitigate the menace to civilisation which they at present constituted, they must be given responsibility, a double dose if possible, the responsibility in fact of a Dominion.

Kerr was Lloyd George's secretary until April 1921. Grigg, another disciple of Curtis, succeeded him. An advance copy of Curtis's article was not slow in reaching the Prime Minister and certainly played its part in eliciting the invitation to De Valera. From now on Curtis was as inevitably cast for the rôle of broad constitutional adviser as Tom Jones for that of personal go-between. Meanwhile Grigg, a gallant soldier and still more intrepid draftsman, hovered expectantly in ante-rooms, his mind aglow with prospects of Empire preservation along lines of Liberal compromise.

"The Round Table combination," said Lloyd George to Lord

[1] See *The Problem of The Commonwealth*, still the best exposition of the Federal argument applied to the Empire.

Riddell on October 23rd, 1921, "is perhaps the most powerful in the country," and it might be thought lucky for Ireland to find so near the seat of power an influence so obviously on the side of the angels. Had they not helped to set on its feet and start again a South Africa stricken low after Vereeniging? Had they not gone far and incurred bitter obloquy in conferring self-government on India? Had not their voices been raised these last fifteen years on behalf of complete equality between the Mother country and the Dominions? Were they not even now pressing an Irish solution in advance of average British opinion? Was not their journal openly contemplating the concession of fiscal autonomy? And yet Ireland has never responded to the overtures and schemes of the Round Table combination. She has shown no readiness to be fitted into their framework in accordance with their first principles.

Of what after all do these first principles consist? "The goal of all human activity is a growth in the sense of duty which men feel to each other."[1] (2) "That growth is a product of freedom and order, two different aspects of the same condition."[1] So far so good. Two fine thoughts finely expressed. But from them derive others less congenial.

(3) War, argue Curtis and his colleagues, is the greatest enemy of order, and hence, under another aspect, of freedom. And between areas diverse enough to demand local autonomy there is only one way to prevent war—by linking them in federal union. Hence the hope of the future reveals itself in a world of ever-expanding federations, eventually coalescing into one. Hence "the real contribution of Americans to the cause of freedom was the effective union of all their states in one greater commonwealth and the victory of the North in the Civil War."[2]

(4) But it is the British Commonwealth and no other whose high and unique destiny it is to point the way to the super-state embracing all humanity, and eventually to lead all nations within the fold. And (5) the claim of the British Commonwealth now is in its nature as absolute as will be that of the World Commonwealth hereafter. "Allegiance can no more be rendered by one citizen to two Commonwealths than homage can be paid by one subject to two Kings. The people of Britain and those of the Dominions have yet to decide whether it is to this mighty Commonwealth as a whole or merely to the territory in which they live that their final allegiance is due."[3]

[1] Curtis, *Capital Question of China*, p. 300.
[2] Curtis, *The Commonwealth of Nations*, p. 678.
[3] *The Commonwealth of Nations*, p. 705.

So the member-states of an association must recognise that their union is for all purposes, not only for foreign affairs? So they have a right to freedom, but only to freedom *within* the British Commonwealth? So, if there be final conflict, the interests of the greater party must override those of the less? If those were his beliefs, what sympathy could Curtis feel for the Irish plan of External Association? or for the philosophy which finds no principles more primal, no conceptions more sacred than those which safeguard the right of self-determination to each nation however small?

Erskine Childers was a philosopher of this latter sort. Even Curtis was not a more ruthless adherent of intellectual principles, and there were other points of resemblance between them. They both had an Irish background. They had been at Haileybury together. They had both fought in the South African War and both had written much about South Africa. Both in the years before the War had been anxiously concerned with imperial defence and not less with everything that touched the future constitutional basis of the Empire. Both had passed from paternalism to belief in government for the governed by the governed, Childers having put forward in 1911 the very Irish solution that Curtis was urging now. Both respected the highest artistic standards and both commanded English of richness, lucidity and power. Both asked nothing, refused indeed everything for themselves.

Yet it was no accident that these two old school-fellows so alike in opportunities and attainments should now, trained almost from boyhood for this special task, be confronting one another like rival seconds for the last round of the conflict of centuries; that they should be providing a contrast every whit as symbolic as that of 1798 (once noticed by Childers himself) between two very different men, "Fitzgibbon Lord Clare standing out like a block of black granite and the slender figure of Wolfe Tone." For, given the circumstances, there were always the contrasts in the men themselves to see to it that this clash must come. Intellectually, one had worked his way to a complex code of principles, fundamental but liable to qualification when experience suggested or when expediency compelled. The other, after equal travail, had come to take his stand on a few simple manifestations of the supreme doctrine of liberty. In morals both were humanitarians. But one was by temperament on the side of the big significant forces, the other on the side of the weak, the subject, the oppressed. In spirit one was all Imperialist, the other all Irish at the last. Since that time one has gone on from strength to strength, indispensable alike to cabinets and common-rooms and wherever men meet to plan a better world. The other faced a firing-party at dawn a year later for a cause that he took to be the same as that he had represented at Downing Street. Each accepted his own fulfilment with the same resolution and faith.

The typing and household staffs responded to every call on them, Miss Lily O'Brennan in her labours epitomising them all. Of the official secretaries not yet mentioned, Fionan Lynch organised life at the two Irish Headquarters to everyone's satisfaction, while Childers was efficiently assisted by John Chartres. Chartres, a trained barrister, had served during the War in the Intelligence branch of the Ministry of Munitions, and later made a reputation by indexing and reorganising *The Times* Reference Library. But his Sinn Fein sympathies had passed unnoticed, and his last-minute selection caused surprise. Even to the Irish Delegates, some of whom knew nothing of him personally, he remained something of a mystery man throughout. Nor did his credentials as a constitutional lawyer escape criticism. When the Delegation had been originally selected, Austin Stack had been most insistent that they should employ some authority of recognised standing, a foreigner if need be, even an Englishman if a man like Lord Bryce[1] could be obtained. Later he asked Collins, on one of the latter's visits to Dublin, whether they had got anyone. "Oh," replied Collins, "we have John Chartres acting for us," but could only give as qualifications his authorship of a treatise on the Workmen's Compensation Act. However, Chartres's knowledge of procedure and of sources of information often proved useful, and so on occasion did his experience in technical drafting. At one important stage of the negotiations he suddenly emerges from the shadows with a scheme which he has silently matured.

## V

The advantages on the British side should now be appearing. First their experience, and as a team their negotiating calibre. Second their unity. Lloyd George directed both strategy and tactics. Certain limits had been set him by his Conservative colleagues, but they were such as the House of Commons would in any case have imposed. There was nothing, therefore, to offset the gain of having with him such men as Chamberlain, Birkenhead and Churchill. On the other side, Griffith and Collins worked closely together, and Duggan invariably supported them. But they had always to be referring back to President De Valera in Dublin,

[1] Bryce's family came from Ulster.

and to be carrying with them two colleagues of divergent outlook who were certainly not going to take orders from them, as Greenwood took them from Lloyd George. A minor advantage belonging to the British was their ability to fix their own times for conferences on the plea of urgent other business; the holding, too, of the Conference in London saved them such physical strains as that of the double sea-crossing to which, in the last few hours before signature, the Irish were subjected. Much more fundamental was England's possession of the "big stick," the power to do far more harm to Ireland than Ireland could ever do to her. For England a breakdown of the negotiations meant a continuing political nuisance, a considerable expenditure, a loss of Crown servants' lives less, probably, than that in an average day on the Western Front; for her Delegates, loss admittedly of reputation, possibly of office, but little physical inconvenience and no physical misery or danger.[1]

For Ireland, breakdown meant nation-wide devastation and sufferings that would certainly not fall short of and, if recent experience was any guide, would far exceed those suffered by the civil population in the last stages of the Boer War; for her Delegates (though of this more in a moment) long imprisonment for four members, and now that he was recognised, almost certain execution for Michael Collins, the fifth. Doubtful though it must be to the last whether the potential British power to hurt would ever be fully used, there was no equal distribution here of the material for terrorisation.

Yet the very fact that all her destiny hung on the outcome of the Conference yielded two assets to Ireland, one mechanical, one of the spirit. The English were pressed by much and varied administrative business, the Irish had their whole time to give to the negotiations. And they were all men who, even if their personal fortunes did depend on a settlement by consent, were beyond cavil qualified to meet this particular hazard; for they had long held their personal fortunes of small account beside their ideal. Of all of them this was true, whatever form their ideal took then or later. Duggan and Gavan Duffy had sacrificed professions, Barton had exchanged a life of prosperity for a convict cell at Portland, Griffith had for thirty years surrendered every wordly advantage to work for Irish independence. And Collins happened to be an old-fashioned hero.

[1] We reject, on the authority of *The Aftermath*, the allegation that the Prime Minister's surrender owed anything to failing nerve. The assassination of British Ministers was never seriously considered in Dublin.

## CHAPTER VII

# THE FIRST THREE PLENARY SESSIONS

"Non in dialectica placuit Deo salvum facere populum suum."

*The First Plenary Session—The preliminaries—Objections raised to British qualifications on Dominion Status—Ireland's claim to Fiscal Autonomy—Second Plenary Session—Finance—Defence—Dominion Status—The place of Royalty—Griffith pleased with the first day—De Valera anxious—Third Plenary Session—Infringements of the Truce—Barton on Trade—Griffith presses De Valera for Ulster Clause.*

### First Plenary Session, 10 Downing Street

11 a.m. Tuesday, October 11th

Lloyd George opened in grave yet friendly tones. England was anxious to make peace, but there were limitations beyond which she could not go. There were also limitations on the other side. "If these limitations prove insuperable, then the responsibility for failure will rest, not with those at the Council table, but with others."

This simple statement covered considerable finesse. It relieved the British Delegates from the necessity of arguing fundamental ethics. It presented them not as independent agents free to choose their own principles, but as faithful mandatories for others. The discussion was transferred from the sphere of morals, where it was thought that the Irish would like to concentrate it; the problem was rendered one for the practical intellect; both sides were to join in the common task of reconciling divergent positions. And the threat of force was hidden a long way back; every opportunity was to be given to Ireland to recognise that the British terms satisfied the realities of her demands, and to enter a free association freely.

Griffith replied in his cold, impassive style, each word dropping like a stone. "England's policy in the past has been to treat Ireland as a conquered and subject country. If there is a change in the policy of subordinating Ireland to English interests, then there appears to be possibility of peace." Griffith in a few words had placed Ireland on a negotiating equality. He would acquiesce in the intellectual effort of reconciliation, but only if there went with it on the British side a change of heart.

Procedure was discussed, and Lloyd George invited objections to the proposals already made by England. Griffith's choice of reply was crucial. The opportunity was patent for asserting that in no circumstances would Ireland enter the Empire. But the strategy arranged in consultation with De Valera was different. Its aim was to place first things last; to reach the great deciding issues in an atmosphere cleansed of irritating misunderstandings over detail, and of the venom of personal suspicion, while lighted by dawning recognition of the beauties of External Association. So Griffith now turned not to the offer of Dominion Status, but to six reservations by which the offer of that status was qualified. He intimated that they implied the military subordination of Ireland. Lloyd George expressed horror at the thought. "We certainly don't desire that, we seek nothing in the way of military domination of Ireland."

He set himself to assuage Irish fears on various aspects of the defence and trade proposals. Those connected with naval and air facilities were governed by no sort of desire to make them a kind of base for control over Irish affairs; they were dictated only by vital considerations of British security. Aerodromes were essential to protect British merchant shipping against submarines, but "We are not really thinking of aerodromes except in so far as they are necessary for naval defence." Again, access to Irish ports by the British Navy was necessary, not for commercial, but for defence purposes, submarines being the especial danger. "Coastal defence is what we really care about." "Our people might starve." "Purely defensive rights." "Not offensive in regard to yourselves," were phrases used. He added, "Beyond these limitations we cannot go."

Against his proposed guarantees ensuring the restriction of British facilities to defensive purposes, the protest was inevitably raised that England had broken treaties with Ireland in the past.

Lloyd George's reply is interesting. "You have never made a treaty with the people of this country before. Treaties in the past have been with oligarchies ruling this country."

Winston Churchill and Birkenhead both intervened, the latter the more happily. Churchill found an elaborate analogy for the Irish facilities insisted upon, in British rights at a South African naval port. Under cross-examination, however, he had to admit that the port was under South African control. Barton tried to push the dissimilarity further by recalling that South Africa need not join in a British war. Birkenhead checked him with the famous air that now as often imposed finality; "That is not conceded."

The discussion turned on trade. The War might have introduced Lloyd George to emergency duties, but he had still a warm regard for his old principles of Free Trade.

He launched into powerful deprecation of tariff controversies, "wars between the two Democracies," as influences destructive of that peace which England so greatly desires. And Ireland would suffer most. For England was after all Ireland's only market, whereas England could obtain her food-stuffs from other countries. Birkenhead emphasised that "Nothing is intended to prevent the economic development of Ireland," and Lloyd George explained with triplicated eloquence, that Ireland would be free to give premiums, bonuses and bounties. She would be free to do anything necessary to develop the country agriculturally and industrially. Barton had come over to defend Irish trade, and he was not slow in scoring the natural hit, "If we are dependent on you, why do you fear a tariff war?" Lloyd George: "There is a temptation on both sides. I want peace." Barton: "We want to be self-sufficing; our independence in the past was always restricted by you." Lloyd George: "We are not offering you 1779 terms."

The Conference adjourned from twelve thirty-five till four p.m. Some of the tension was gone from the atmosphere. Fundamentals were still a long way off, but there was no impression, so far at least, of difficulties beyond adjustment.

### Second Plenary Session, 10 Downing Street

4 p.m. Same day

Lloyd George began cheerfully. Their feeling was that the objections made to the six British conditions by the Irish representatives in the morning could be allayed with a little clearing up of the position held by each side—on the economic question, for instance. Would the Irish prefer to suggest amendments themselves? Griffith said yes, they would like to submit a re-draft. This was agreed to.

Griffith now raised the question of finance. Lloyd George proposed a sub-committee, and Collins at once insisted that it must have an open reference—the whole ground of liability past and present to be discussed. Lloyd George told them that the "real question" was that of war debt, but he was not allowed to take Ireland's liability for the war as admitted. Nor did the Irish Delegates fail to let him see that in their eyes the real question was not how much Ireland owed England, but which country was in debt to the other. Finally a sub-committee was agreed upon. Reference was to be completely open, and the Irish counter-claim could be raised. The acceptance of the possibility that such counter-claim might prove to be valid was a nice little achievement for the Irish. Lloyd George gave the sub-committee his blessing; "Something fair is wanted to both countries."

Defence produced some rather rambling exchanges. Griffith tried to work in together an illustration of the special inconvenience to which Ireland would be subjected under the British naval facilities with an argument (along the lines of Draft Treaty A) for an Ireland permanently neutralised, her neutrality, if possible, guaranteed by England. The grounds that Griffith chose for attacking the naval facilities were that they made such a neutrality impossible. For what country at war with England would count as neutral an Ireland that rendered such vital assistance to her enemy? Griffith assured the British that Irish neutrality would be a great advantage to England; there would be no danger of her violating it, for once free she would be hostile no longer.

Lloyd George, in various replies, tried to disabuse the Irish of three distinct ideas. (1) That the actual facilities demanded were intended as defences against a hostile Ireland or against an enemy allowed to land there. Lloyd George explained that England's requirements were for *defensive* facilities, anti-submarine, etc.[1] (2) That Ireland as a Dominion could be permitted to call herself neutral. She could have the same position as Canada and Australia. "England could not hypothecate Ireland's resources—and could not force Ireland to hypothecate them." But "to repudiate British wars means leaving the Empire. . . . Neutrality repudiates association." (3) That a theoretical neutrality guaranteed any real security. He pointed to Belgium's violation and spoke of the overwhelming necessity of winning a war. "In war guarantees of neutrality vanish, vanish. War with the United States is a horrible thought—but there are other countries."

After Birkenhead's "that is not conceded" of the morning, it was encouraging to hear Lloyd George admitting that there was no obligation on a Dominion to lend active assistance in a British war. Otherwise his attitude, franker than would have been expected

[1] He suggested and secured agreement for a committee on defence at which British experts, Lord Beatty among them, could explain the absolute necessity for the facilities in question.

and deafer to normal idealism, suggested no loophole through which a provision for neutrality might slip. He now went on to expound, in language which even in 1921 would hardly have satisfied Dominion jurists, his conception of how the Empire was organised for foreign relationships. The Dominions had the right to have a "voice" in foreign relations, but "conduct" of them remained with Britain. Distance made a difficulty, but Ireland was near. She would have a voice like the Dominions "and the same voice as we have." When, however, he came once again to his desire that Ireland on equal terms should enter a free league freely, Griffith laconically interrupted, "We have no free choice if the alternative is war."

Dominion Status was spoken of in several aspects. Gavan Duffy, conscientiously determined to let no air of gathering goodwill obscure deep contrasts of sentiment, raised the possibility of future elections of Governors-General. Lloyd George gently turned him down: "Royalty," he said, "is, after all, very useful. They are getting to realise that in the Dominions. Dominions are always consulted about Governors. I don't think they will ask for elections. If you have an elected Governor, you are getting away from the conception of the King." And Churchill added that following Dominion precedents it would be the Irish Ministers upon whose advice the Irish Governor-General would act.

An agreed statement of what exactly Dominion Status did involve had clearly become imperative, and Lloyd George suggested that Curtis and Childers should draw one up together. But the Irish were understandably loth to commit themselves at this stage to an estimate of their opponents' scheme. The piquant idea was dropped, Curtis was instructed to draw up a statement alone, and a museum piece was lost to posterity. Before the end a committee on observance of the Truce (including care of prisoners) was added to those on defence and financial relations. The full Conference was to reassemble on Thursday.

The day had shown the British anxious to accommodate differences on finance and trade, but one's main impression, reading the record to-day, is of their blank rejection of neutrality and blank insistence on facilities for their own defence. Griffith did not ignore the obstacle in his evening letter to De Valera; "This question of naval defence *re* the coasts of Ireland is a fixed idea of theirs," he wrote. "They believe it vital to their lives." No doubt, however, he was delighted to find no such debating disparity between the two teams as had been feared, and his prevailing mood was optimistic.

"The meeting of to-day has left on my mind the impression that the English Government is anxious for peace. Lloyd George is a remarkably suave and astute man," and "the most difficult part has yet to be discussed;" but "on the whole we have scored to-day."

De Valera was hardly as pleased as Griffith with the way that the first day's Conference had gone. "I note," he wrote back, "that Lloyd George is just covering again the ground he covered with me. You will have to pick him up soon on this 'further than this we can't go' stunt."

### Third Plenary Session, 10 Downing Street

12 noon, Thursday, October 13th

The third session accomplished little. Its liveliest moments came early. Lloyd George and Chamberlain (who now appeared for the first time) protested that the Truce had been intended to preserve the *status quo*, and that now the Irish were using it for what would have been impossible previously, public drilling and public holding of Dail Courts. Chamberlain declared it quite impossible, especially in view of Parliamentary criticism, to allow drilling to continue organised as this was, with Press photographers and cinema operators in attendance.

The situation looked nasty for the Irish, as Griffith admitted in his report. "The Courts publicly summoned and opened were a serious matter." But a lucky circumstance presented Griffith with the kind of debating opportunity in whose use he was unrivalled. "The English forces," he retorted, "have commandeered the Victoria Hotel, Sligo, and also the Courthouse where the municipal offices were situated, all this without notice to the Liaison Officer." Poor Worthington-Evans, Secretary of State for War, was left to explain this violation of the Truce. He supposed that "troops were probably going into billets for the winter," but he was not allowed to escape so lightly. Collins, Griffith and Duggan each read him a short lecture. "He was making strategic moves"— "This throwing out of elected representatives"—" It was the worst way of getting accommodation." General Macready was called in —very stiff to attention, very respectful, very unlike the Olympian who glitters from every page of the *Annals* of his *Active Life*. He denied strategic moves, but admitted that the seizure of public offices was unfortunate, and promised to telegraph for further details. Meanwhile the Irish peccadilloes had sunk into the background. They were referred back to the Truce Committee.

The rest of the morning was taken up with Trade, Barton putting the case for full fiscal autonomy. Lloyd George's own figures were used to show that it would constitute no danger to England. But any restrictions on it would make mock of Ireland's status of nominal equality with England, and make it impossible for Ireland to build up her industrial life in face of highly organised British competition, often dependent on low-paid labour.

Lloyd George hit back effectively against the plea of inequality by pointing out that England's autonomy would be as much restricted as Ireland's. But he lost his way—something seemed wrong with his brief—when he tried to show that tariffs were not necessary for Irish industrial development.

COLLINS: "English boots are dumped below cost in Ballina. We must protect ourselves against dumping."

LLOYD GEORGE: "Your real protection is cheap labour. Lord Pirrie has proved the advantage of cheaper labour in Belfast where there is neither coal nor iron."

BARTON: "Our railwaymen will not accept your wages."

LLOYD GEORGE: "Surprising, but that is exceptional. Your cost of living is lower, and Irish workers accept wages that Englishmen would not look at."

BARTON: "The cost of living in Ireland is higher, and the kind of cheap labour that you speak of is of little value for industries like spinning, etc."

Lloyd George, however, spent most of his time trying to prove that free trade between the two countries should be looked upon not as an irritating restriction but a protective boon which they ought to think themselves lucky to procure. And Churchill went so far as to express doubt whether under the British proposals England was not giving up too much. Which efforts to save Ireland from herself drew from the incorrigible Gavan Duffy: "If the benefit to us is so great why impose it upon us as a condition precedent?"

In the end Barton seemed to convince the English that Ireland had no aggressive trade intention nor desired to penalise England in any way. Chamberlain opined that it might be possible to find a formula to prevent England strangling Irish industries in their cradle.

LLOYD GEORGE: "We will promise to look into that."

Three sessions had passed and the Irish had possibly enlarged the area of potential agreement. They had certainly spun out time while External Association could be perfected in London and the clause containing their Ulster proposals arrive from Ireland. But Griffith was quite as aware as De Valera that further delay would soon begin to look suspiciously like acquiescence in the principle of the British terms. "Our tactics have been successful up to the present," he wrote, "but unless we can get in our Treaty proposals by Monday the initiative will pass to them. If we cannot have the Ulster and other omitted clauses by ten o'clock Monday at the latest, we must fight them on ground of their own choosing."

## CHAPTER VIII

# THE FOURTH AND FIFTH SESSIONS

"Time elaborately thrown away."
YOUNG: *Love of Fame.*

*The Fourth Session—Griffith denounces Partition—Lloyd George ready to be helpful—He views idea of Boundary Commission sympathetically—Lloyd George's first impression of the Irish Delegates—Fifth Session—Griffith equipped with Ulster Clause—Further wrangles over Truce—Griffith insists British must undo Partition—Lloyd George less forthcoming with Boundary Commission—The position left open.*

### FOURTH PLENARY SESSION, 10 DOWNING STREET

11 o'clock, Friday, October 14th

THIS day was to prove a Fabian triumph for Griffith. It began rather drearily with the usual difficulties over infringements of the Truce. Then Sinn Fein's worst fears were realised and Ulster came up. As Griffith wrote to De Valera: "We could not defer it further as only it and the question of the Crown remained for the moment outstanding." But the "Ulster Clause"[1] was not expected from Dublin for another two days, and in the meanwhile Griffith was quite uncertain how their Ulster proposals stood. Yet the British were "anxious for him to suggest something." He was quite magnificent in the breach.

He began an elaborate, not to say prolix, exposition of the unnaturalness of Partition. He set himself especially to disillusion the

[1] Containing the official Irish policy towards Ulster.

English of the idea that Ulster was a separate nation which could be set on an equality with the rest of Ireland. Ulster was far more like an English county, say Yorkshire. The present position was as if Yorkshire were to set up an independent government. . . . Again, the unanimity of Ulster was ridiculously exaggerated in England. A third of the population of the six counties were Catholics, and 15 to 20 per cent. of the Protestants were Nationalists. . . . He himself, for example, had been elected by 1700 votes, though there was only a majority of 700 Catholics. . . . He went on with more and more ample figures to show how Dublin Castle had jerrymandered electoral areas to prevent the fair working of Proportional Representation. In Belfast one-fourth of the population was against the Union, yet the anti-Unionists had secured only one member out of sixteen.

All this and much more Sir Austen Chamberlain had followed with the closest attention, but with an increasingly puzzled frown. At last he felt compelled to intervene. "Excuse me, Mr. Griffith, this is all very interesting, but I'm afraid that I do not quite understand what exactly it is all leading up to." "It is all perfectly clear to me," said Griffith, loftily, and he proceeded in the same strain as before. He confessed afterwards that he would have dearly liked to lean over and say confidentially, "Mr. Chamberlain, I have no more idea than you have."[1] But it is unlikely that Griffith was ever in much danger of succumbing to this temptation.

Some of the figures he quoted from memory had next day to be corrected, but at the time the British swallowed them like lambs. According to him, the British Delegates were "remarkably ignorant of the facts—this is not play-acting though they tried that also. Their knowledge geographically and statistically of the province is very poor."

Lloyd George stopped him later on in the meeting when Griffith took the British proposals to mean an increase of Ulster's powers. Lloyd George explained that, on the contrary, under these proposals the higher powers would, just as at present, be reserved to the British Government. This might involve a Customs barrier between North and South. Was that practicable? Here was a trap. A denunciation of such a barrier might have opened the way for the British, if Partition became inevitable, to refuse fiscal autonomy to Southern Ireland. Griffith was quite equal to the occasion. "Yes," he said, "it was practicable but we do not want that. Ulster would never be able to stand against a Customs barrier." And he went back to arguing that Ulster was not a separate nation economically

[1] Beasley, *Michael Collins*, Vol. II, p. 303.

or politically; "They are our countrymen in the North-East, though they hold different views."

Lloyd George remained very urbane, aiming always to find ways round recognised stumbling-blocks. He kept expressing his conviction that the best way to bring Ulster in was to woo her sweetly: "Sir Edward Carson is confident that if no coercion was used Ulster would come in." Griffith insisted that there was no Irish intention of *coercing* Ulster, but England was standing behind her, was not giving her opportunity of free choice. Lloyd George retorted that otherwise there would be civil war. Griffith worked off an eloquent tirade about the origin of all the Ulster riots lying in the activities of Belfast politicians, and in the ambition of Belfast capitalists to keep labour disunited.

Then Gavan Duffy and Collins took up the tale, each stressing that Partition was not a natural fact but an artificial difficulty created by the Act of 1920. Gavan Duffy's contribution was as usual barbed in venom. "England having set up a Northern Parliament in violation of the Treaty of the Union, and without any Irish votes in its favour, is now attempting to take advantage of her own wrongdoing. There would be no difficulty if England would stand aside."

The rest of the discussion was revealing. Lloyd George, while continuing to urge that the best hope of ending Partition was to let it pass away gradually as had happened in Canada, South Africa and Australia, admitted that English opinion would be glad if Ulster would come in with the rest of Ireland. It was impossible of course to let Ulster be coerced, and he was pleased to find that Mr. De Valera agreed that force was out of the question; "But we promise you," he said, "to stand aside and any efforts to induce Ulster to unite with the rest of Ireland will have our benevolent neutrality."

Collins and Griffith responded to this helpful spirit. Collins thought there might be "a Boundary Commission or local option whatever you may call it." And Griffith apparently inclined favourably to this idea, with the observation that "if the majority of the North-East are not to be coerced they in turn must not coerce others." Lloyd George let slip the pregnant words, "That is fair, if applied all round, for example in North Cavan."

The meeting ended with everybody reaffirming their own standpoints. Once more Griffith accused England of creating the trouble; she had divided that she might govern (phrase of tragic ironical omen for every Irishman present). Chamberlain referred to the difficulties of the British Government. The whole political future of those coming into the Conference was involved. And Lloyd George quite agreed with him.

It had been a trying morning for Griffith, and lacking the Ulster clause, he had done well not to give himself away. Both sides had yielded a little; at least there was a hint of something less than the expected irreconcilability of viewpoint. It was pleasant for the Irish to find their opponents so thoroughly disliking Partition, so obviously anxious to collaborate in bringing it to an end. This aspect seems to have struck Griffith with some force. "They are I think willing to go any distance short of using force against Ulster. They want to save their face." It was certainly more than had been expected of a Delegation containing Chamberlain and Birkenhead, who had been understood in the old days to regard Partition as natural and inevitable.

On the other hand, England had half disposed of the danger that the Irish Delegation might refuse even to discuss a settlement that did not bring the whole of Ulster directly or indirectly under Dublin.

Over the week Griffith had served his country well, but his delaying tactics, misunderstood by the British, had hardly enhanced his reputation with them. This Sunday Lloyd George talked over the Conference with Lord Riddell.[1] "Honestly he could not say that much progress had been made. His experience with De Valera had been repeated, he could get nothing definite." He went on to pass unflattering comments which he was very soon to retract, "The Delegates are impossible people, they come to the point, but would not come to decisions. He really could not say why. He could not say whether they did not want to do so or whether they were afraid. Arthur Griffith was no doubt the leader, but unfortunately he had no power of expression. It was difficult to understand what he said. He spoke rather like ——, a clever incoherent Welshman. On the other hand, Collins was undoubtedly a considerable person." (A fortnight later Griffith had become "a pretty considerable person" and Collins had lapsed into "quite a different sort of person, one with a simple sort of mind such as is often found in a great military commander.") Lloyd George referred also to secret advices, stating that there was a schism in the ranks of Sinn Fein. "The moderate section wanted a settlement whereas the gunmen did not." He thought that "during the next fortnight the Irish Conference would come to an end one way or the other."

[1] Riddell, *Diary*, pp. 328–329.

## Fifth Plenary Session, 10 Downing Street

### 3.30 p.m. Monday, October 17th

Before the next meeting Griffith had heard three times from De Valera. A report of a speech by General Tudor to the R.I.C. was passed on by the President, no doubt entertained by this "exposure" of his plans and prospects. "We have information that the reason why De Valera is not going to London is that he wished to remain to see how things are going on at home. He is fed up, but has his bit made and intends to clear out." More significant was De Valera's warm approval of a strong bid for the "neutrality agreement which would make such a clean sweep of the whole business"; his reminder that "our main propositions are External Association and neutrality in the main Treaty, and the Ulster clause on the Ulster and constitutional question"; and his anticipation that the "battle royal on the main Treaty will take place in the coming week." Above all, he forwarded the Ulster clause itself.

The Six Counties were to be asked to surrender the 1920 arrangement and be represented directly and exclusively in a Dublin Parliament like any other part of Ireland. If they, or any substantial part of them, declined this offer, the recusant area was to be allowed to retain the 1920 subordinate Parliament, but the overriding powers and the representation in the overriding Parliament would be transferred from the Imperial Parliament to the one to be established at Dublin. Safeguards for Ulster were to be arrived at by agreement with the South.

The clause explained the Sinn Fein objective along anticipated lines. But it threw no light on the manner in which the terms should be put up to Ulster, or by what declaration of British policy they should be accompanied; nor on what steps were to be taken in the last resort if Ulster rejected the terms. And judging by Friday's experience it was these questions that would occupy most attention at the present stage.

So it proved on Monday. It was *how* Ulster was to be approached, and what was to be done *if* she proved recalcitrant that captured all the attention at a session where, in Griffith's words, "matters were now getting more lively"; but first came the familiar preliminary squabble over alleged breakage of the Truce.

It was the turn of the Irish to be able to take the offensive. Griffith read a circular issued from British G.H.Q., intended, he said, to give the military and police the idea that the negotiations would not last long, and that when they broke down they must be prepared for a remorseless "hunting down of rebels." Lloyd George handed the document to Worthington-Evans, saying that they must hear Sir Nevil Macready on the subject and would have an answer tomorrow. Evans could only murmur that "for the moment I don't know that it was issued." Michael Collins: "*We* know. You can't issue these documents without my knowledge." Evans failed to see a breach of the Truce in the document as far as he had read. But Collins was not to be baulked. He recalled a case where the British had refused to take seriously the circulation for police purposes of a photograph of himself and, more recently, where a British agent, clearly by no accident, had come to watch him at Mass.

Lloyd George said that he had to contemplate a possible breakdown of the Truce and consider what must be done in that event; but Duggan pointed out that "to note the movements of men on the opposite side was to break an article of the Truce," and Collins proudly declared, "We prefer to take risks rather than break our word." One can understand his irritation, not to mention his patriotic anxiety. Without perfect incognito his most daring exploits, and indeed his continued survival the last two years, would surely have been impossible. Once he had escaped the Black-and-Tans by slipping into a cinema and dry-shaving off his moustache with a razor that he happened to be carrying. On this occasion, as on so many other, he had mingled with his pursuers and joined most zealously in the search. Much of this advantage had already gone with his coming into the open, and more of it was going every day that the negotiations lasted.

Lloyd George turned the flank of the attack and converted all these complaints into an argument for an early end to the Conference. Chamberlain repeated once more what was true in every case, but especially so in his, that "my position is getting more difficult every day." And Griffith agreed with him. "No doubt an early decision would be the best thing."

Griffith now returned by request to Ulster. He opened as elaborately as on the Friday, but this time with carefully prepared maps on the table, figures in his head, and the Ulster clause in his pocket. One of his maps showed that in the whole province of Ulster five counties had Catholic majorities, and only four Protestant. Even in the four Protestant counties, Antrim, Down, Armagh and Derry, there were strong Catholic areas. In Armagh and Derry there were so many anti-Unionist Protestants that if these two counties were left free to vote "they would vote themselves out of Partition." Lloyd George cut across the avalanche: "What do you propose about Ulster? What is your proposition?"

Griffith did not lay on the table the Ulster clause, with its alternative offers to Ulster of either direct representation in the Dublin Parliament or reduced representation there coupled with a subordinate Parliament of their own. Instead he requested that the British Government should stand aside and let them "make Ulster a fair proposal. We can probably come to an agreement with them if you will stand aside." In the contingency not provided for in the Ulster clause, that of Ulster refusing to come in even if England stood aside, Griffith repeated his Friday's claim that those in the Six Counties should be allowed to choose freely whether they would be in North or South.

Something like the Boundary Commission tentatively discussed on Friday was cropping up again, but Lloyd George seemed to have been thinking the matter over. "Suppose," he asked, "the whole of Ulster were to be the area for this local option," *i.e.* suppose the whole nine counties of Ulster were to give a decision binding them collectively for or against Partition?

Griffith did not like the idea at all. If the vote proved in favour of Partition, still larger areas than at present would come under an Ulster Government, to which those areas were bitterly opposed. Poor law areas would be the best units for local option.[1]

Proceedings got rather out of hand under strenuous Irish denunciations of the part played by the English in establishing Partition, and of the iniquity of expecting Catholic areas in any circumstances to remain under the Belfast Government. Contradiction superseded controversy.

COLLINS: "The Northern Parliament is not serious."

LLOYD GEORGE: "It will function to-morrow."

GRIFFITH: "It will never function. Our people will never consent to remain subject to it."

DUGGAN: "Everybody in Ireland knows that."

The Irish refused, however, to take a pessimistic view; they repeated that if England would only stand aside they could prevent the question arising of Ulster's "opting out." Lloyd George could hardly have been more anxious to be helpful. "We will take no steps and we will undertake to sanction any arrangements you make with them," but he did not see how the Southern Irish "could get out of this Six-County arrangement, except by dealing direct with Ulster." Here Griffith, who had previously insisted on the British standing aside, must have seemed to his opponents some-

[1] Behind Lloyd George's suggestion seemed to lie the idea that a vote over the whole nine counties would give each part of Ireland a sporting chance, to the South to end Partition, and to the North to add three counties to its territory.

thing less than reasonable. "No," he insisted, "it is you who have made the position and you must repair it."

Finally, Lloyd George brought Griffith back to the question of what in the last resort he would prefer, the maintenance of the *status quo* (six counties) or local option for the province as a whole (nine or none). Griffith refused to impale himself on either horn of the dilemma. "The only way is to have option by units." Birkenhead did not care for this style of reply. "I should have liked to have an answer to the Prime Minister's question." Lloyd George intervened hastily and pacifically, "Well, we see your point of view." Birkenhead was not to be put off: "Local option on the basis of constituencies would not work. Believe me it is not practical. It must be either the Six-County area, or option for the whole of Ulster."

LLOYD GEORGE: "Well, we cannot carry it further at present."

How then, after two long conferences on Ulster, did the matter stand with the three prime questions: (1) The terms to be offered Ulster; (2) The manner of the offer; (3) The steps to be taken if Ulster refused? The first question, the Irish answer to which was contained in the Ulster clause, had hardly been touched on, Griffith being content to mention that his side had a "fair proposal in their mind." On the second and third questions, which went so closely together, the Irish attitude was not quite clear. Was the "fair proposal" to be put up by themselves, or by the British Government? And if the worst came to the worst, were they or were they not prepared to see four Orange counties or their equivalent opt out from under the all-Ireland Parliament? But there was nothing ambiguous about one thing. Their resolve that the British Government, authors of the twin crimes of Partition and of placing two Catholic counties under Protestant domination, should use all its influence to recommend to Ulster proposals agreed on with Sinn Fein; and should make it plain to Ulster that the alternative to acceptance was the loss at least of her preponderatingly Catholic area.

The British, on the other hand, were ready, even anxious to support an arrangement which brought Partition to an end. But they had no more intention than had Sinn Fein of coercing Ulster and, awed by the sanctity of the Act of 1920, they still jibbed even at approaching her with bribes or threats.

And suppose Ulster dug her toes in? Lloyd George was making a good deal of play with this vote "in or out" over the whole nine counties of the old province. But not much could come of it. The choice must lie between three courses: (1) Forcible incorporation of Ulster with the South; (2) Subtraction from Ulster of the two Catholic counties or their equivalent; (3) Support for Ulster in retention of all her existing area. The first was ruled out by all parties, the third seemed hardly just to the South. The second would probably be accepted by Sinn Fein, but was it in keeping with the Act of 1920? Did not Ulster's area fall among those "existing powers and privileges" which Lloyd George had promised in July were not to be abrogated without her consent? The British had seemed to think so on Monday, but there was still on record Lloyd George's response of Friday to the first mention of a Boundary Commission: "That is fair, if applied all round." That way lay hope for Sinn Fein—hope in any case of saving something from the wreck, hope, if things fell fortunately, of persuading Ulster that it was not worth while to stand outside.

CHAPTER IX

# THE PRESIDENT'S MESSAGE TO THE POPE AND THE SIXTH SESSION

"Fire in each eye, and papers in each hand,
They rave, recite, and madden round the land."
POPE: *Epistle to Dr. Arbuthnot.*

*The Message—Sixth Session—Lloyd George's indictment—Griffith's defence—Oration by Churchill—The Irish to reply on Monday—The rival interpretations of the Truce.*

So far all had been plain sailing, if in no obvious direction. The course of negotiation, hastened by no favouring breezes, had been threatened by no fatal storms. Suddenly an incident outside the Conference raised an issue which those inside had combined to let rest in abeyance, and bade fair to wreck the settlement for which they had begun to hope.

Extracts from three telegrams and from one leading article give the episode its English perspective.

*Pope Benedict XV to His Majesty King George V*

"We rejoice at the resumption of the Anglo-Irish negotiations and pray to the Lord with all our heart that He may bless them and grant to Your Majesty the great joy and imperishable glory of bringing to an end the agelong dissension."

*His Majesty King George V to Pope Benedict XV*

"I have received the message of your Holiness with much pleasure and with all my heart I join in your prayer that the Conference ... may achieve a permanent settlement of the troubles in Ireland, and may initiate a new era of peace and happiness for my people."

*President De Valera to Pope Benedict XV*

"The people of Ireland have read the message sent by your Holiness to the King of Great Britain, and appreciate the kindly interest in their welfare and the paternal regard which suggested it. I tender ... gratitude. They are confident that the ambiguities in the reply sent in the name of King George will not mislead you into believing that the troubles are in Ireland, or that the people of Ireland owe allegiance to the British King. The independence of Ireland has been formally proclaimed.... The trouble is between England and Ireland and its source that the rulers of Britain have endeavoured to impose their will upon Ireland. We long to be at peace and in friendship with the people of Britain, as with other peoples; but the same constancy through persecution and martyrdom that has proved the reality of our people's attachment to the Faith of their Fathers, proves the reality of their attachment to their national freedom and no consideration will ever induce them to abandon it."

"*The Times*" (*Leading Article, October* 21*st*)

"Mr. De Valera has sent a telegram to the Pope. Towards the Pope himself it is an act of impertinence; and towards the King it is unmannerly to the point of churlishness. What value can attach to Mr. De Valera's assurance that 'we long to be at peace and in friendship with the people of Britain' when he deliberately flouts the settled convictions of the British people upon the only terms on which peace and friendship between the British and Irish peoples are possible?"

The manner of De Valera's intervention was not relished by Griffith or Collins and jarred on many English sympathisers with Ireland, and yet it was not untypical of De Valera, whose courtesy his worst enemies have usually conceded. What other method was open to him, striving as he was to build up in men's minds a conception of Irish independence to which their reason inclined them, but behind which their mental habits lagged? Even those Englishmen who most ardently sponsored the claims of Ireland to choose her own Government, half-consciously thought of Irishmen as subjects of the King, and of the King as in some sense the common father. "By this message," as De Valera wrote to Griffith, "the Vatican recognised the struggle between Ireland and England as purely a domestic one, for King George, and by implication pronounced judgment against us." (That the struggle was not *domestic* but *international* was the essence of the Irish claim.) "The British reply took the misrepresentation a step further, treating the dispute as one between warring factions in Ireland." Etiquette is usually on the side of conservatism, and De Valera more than once felt compelled to free himself from its limitations. But it was Griffith who had to meet the British on Friday.

### Sixth Plenary Session, 10 Downing Street

12 o'clock, Friday, October 21st

Lloyd George was ominously calm. "I wonder, Mr. Griffith, have you any preliminary questions which you would be anxious to raise before we proceed with the business." Duggan scratched up a complaint about the continued occupation of the municipal offices in Sligo. A promise was given to look into it, a pause, and Lloyd George began a slow portentous indictment.

"I am sorry, but I have two or three preliminary questions of the gravest character to raise. The first is that we have unmistakable proof that during the period of the Truce advantage has been taken of the Truce to accumulate destructive materials for the manufacture of bombs and arms." The German police had seized a ship with arms destined for Ireland, and in England a serious conspiracy had come to light for the manufacture of bombs and other destructive weapons. One man had been arrested at Cardiff and proved to be in communication with high Irish officials. "The [next] matter of which we have to complain is the publication of Mr. De Valera's telegram to his Holiness the Pope—that very grave and defiant message from the head of your Government. The document deals with the very issues in controversy. It is challenging, defiant and, if I may say so, ill-conditioned; it will make our task almost impossible."

He began to repeat himself as he enumerated the Irish offences, but he was able to add to the list. "The Secretary of State for the Colonies has brought to my notice a formidable document presented by Mr. Michael Collins which challenges the whole position (De Valera had just 'challenged the very issues'), in matters vital to our country and to the security of our shores against attack in the future." "I think," interrupted Collins, "it safeguarded your security." But Lloyd George swept on. "You realise the risks we are taking in this Conference—the political risks; in fact it is not an exaggeration to say"—the Irish affected unconcern—"that the risks we have taken place the life of the Government in issue." The Irish breathed again and perhaps Michael Collins smiled. Then came the operative sentences: "We must know exactly what your attitude is on the vital issues raised in our letters. We must know whether allegiance to the King is to be finally repudiated by you, whether the conecting link of the Crown is to be snapped, whether you are prepared to be associated like the other Dominions in the community of nations known as the British Empire, and whether you are prepared in principle to accept our right to take the necessary measures effectually to prevent attacks on our very life and to give us all the necessary facilities for that purpose—not by a Treaty which can be cancelled, but as a fundamental part of the central agreement between us." He would give the Irish time to prepare their answers to these questions. They could have till the afternoon or till Monday if they wished.

Here was a pretty kettle of fish for Griffith. It was bad enough to have to justify a telegram to the Pope which he himself thought a grave mistake. It was a cruel mortification to see the whole atmosphere of benevolent inquiry and mutual instruction swept away, and one of blunt ultimatum substituted. But what on earth was this new conspiracy? It was not his province; for all he knew half the Irish National leaders might be seriously involved. But, as usual, he was equal to the occasion, first finding a general principle to cover a particular enormity; then basing on a particular weakness a general counter-attack; finally playing for time.

"First with regard to the question of the Truce, and the importation of war-like material which you complain of; my conception is that the Truce does not mean that your military forces should prepare during the period of the Truce, and that we should not. We have done nothing since the Truce which was not being done before the Truce.

"With regard to President De Valera's message I must demur to the view that it was defiant and insulting. Mr. De Valera only stated public facts. I should say that the message was called for by the phrase in King George's letter in which he refers to troubles in Ireland. This would be taken to mean a fight between Irishmen. The trouble is not a trouble in Ireland, but is one between Ireland and Great Britain."

He refused to take a pessimistic view of the position reached in the negotiations. "So far we have begun by seeing how far we could find points of agreement. If we could reduce our points of disagreement to a small number we could probably find a means of getting over the main difficulty. We had intended on Monday to hand in our written proposals. Between those and yours we could see if we could arrive at a solution." He probed automatically the tender spot. "We do not know the exact position, we do not know how you stand with regard to Ulster—whether you are going to throw in your influence to keep things as they are." Outstanding differences of opinion over Defence and Trade he did not regard as insoluble. "I had proposed if that course commends itself to you and your colleagues to submit our proposals to you on Monday."

Collins burst in to defend the Irish attitude on Defence, and refute Churchill's description of his document as "formidable." It could only be formidable if it interfered with British security, and he would like to know why this should be asserted of it. He recalled as in favour of his own and against the British proposals that Sir Laming Worthington-Evans had admitted in the Defence Committee that the British proposals conferred on Ireland an inferior status. Collins drew the inference that England could never find a friend or ally in an Ireland thus degraded.

The business of answer was left to Winston Churchill, principal British representative on the Defence Committee. He had hitherto played little part in the Plenary Sessions. He now orated at length, and with a wealth of illustration.

"I must say that the document was one of marked ability, but it was a reasoned and deliberate refusal of every article which we had made out for the defence of our security from the military and naval standpoints. Use of forts, aerodromes, facilities for recruiting, prohibition of Irish Navy, all had been turned down. Instead the alternative was put up of a guaranteed Irish neutrality. The Irish representatives promised to provide effective machinery for defending their neutrality, including the building of small craft, mine-layers and the like." He himself, with the help of Admirals Beatty and Brock, had tried hard to explain that to accept these propositions would be "to endanger our very life. . . ."

Churchill's points amounted to three: (1) That England could not be sure that Ireland, with the best will in the world, would be able to preserve her neutrality, prevent for example the harbouring in her ports of German submarines; (2) That England could not in fact rely upon the existence of Irish goodwill; (3) That even supposing its faithful and effective maintenance, "the position of absolute neutrality would have been a great difficulty to Britain in the late War. We could not have used your ports as bases from which to defend ourselves against submarine attack." This last was in response to Collins, who made repeated attempts to win acceptance for his previous point: namely, that England would be more safeguarded by a friendly and neutral Ireland than by an Ireland resentful and in spirit hostile as she had been in the last War.

Collins, however, kept returning to the benefits of a friendly Ireland, at times begging the question somewhat disingenuously. "Don't you agree that if neutrality is a greater safeguard to you than anything else, it would be a most valuable thing to you?" At last Chamberlain transferred the controversy to constitutional fundamentals. "But neutrality means that you would be outside the Empire?" Gavan Duffy argued pertinaciously that whatever the status finally agreed on for Ireland it need not be influenced by neutrality which was independent of status. He introduced analogies from the Belgian Congo and from Luxembourg, but Chamberlain remained sceptical alike of the utility of such an arrangement and of its compatibility with Dominion Status. The discussion petered out, but not before Griffith had insisted that under the British July terms Ireland was not in fact receiving Dominion Status as alleged. "All the Dominions can have an army, and a navy if they wish to. It is not a question of our building a navy, but it is the question of our having the right to build it. In this you are putting us in an inferior position to the Dominions." Lloyd George's answer was suggestive. "We began like this with all our Dominions and we subsequently invited them to undertake these responsibilities; we shall ask you to go through the same process."

We see here the germ of the idea developed later in Clause 6 of the Treaty, that Ireland would find herself as privileged as the other Dominions when she proved herself as loyal and innocuous as they.

The British Delegation then withdrew for consultation. On return Lloyd George expressed pleasure that the Irish were presenting a document on Monday. It was essential that it should define the Irish attitude on (1) Allegiance to the King; (2) Entry "freely and of her own accord within the Empire"; (3) Concession of the necessary facilities to secure the "immunity of [British] shores from attack by sea." Lloyd George added that he could not accept Griffith's interpretation of the Truce, that it enabled Ireland to do everything that had been done before.

Griffith refused to let the Conference adjourn without resisting any notion that the Irish admitted themselves in the wrong over the Cardiff incident. This kind of thing followed:

GRIFFITH: "We do not accept your statement regarding preparations for attacks on civilians."

BIRKENHEAD: "Is it proper in accordance with the terms of the Truce to employ agents in England?"

COLLINS: "We would like to know the real facts."

BIRKENHEAD: "I have had some experience of these matters and I predict that the very able legal advice which you will get will not attempt to put the facts in issue."

COLLINS: "I do not accept your facts any more than you accept our statement."

LLOYD GEORGE (*disgusted at the threatened interference with the settlement he had set his heart on*): "I do not understand why you do these things. You lose public opinion."

GRIFFITH: "If we have to fight we have to prepare"; an answer strangely comparable to one four days earlier by Lloyd George himself, resented by the Irishmen at the time.[1]

[1] The foregoing discussion proved once again what widely different interpretations could be placed on the terms of the Truce, Griffith being informed for the first time of the British view that, since the British on their side were not sending in fresh "troops and cannon," Ireland was not entitled to import arms. Lloyd George was inclined to talk without distinction of two separate things: (*a*) What was technically permitted by the Truce terms and (*b*) what was advisible in view of public opinion. The main points were: (1) That the Truce terms were ambiguous and indulgent; (2) that from a military point of view the British were prepared to wink at a great deal, but that politically they felt compelled to take action against any flagrant violation of the sense in which the British public understood the terms.

## CHAPTER X

# THE FIRST IRISH PROPOSALS, THE LAST PLENARY SESSION AND ITS SEQUEL

"The obstinate enthusiasm of the Commonwealth men was very remarkable."

DR. JOHNSON: *Life of Milton.*

*The first Irish proposals—A discreet document—Arrangements for Sub-Conference—The Seventh and last Plenary Session—External Association discussed—The first Sub-Conference—De Valera worried by its tendency—A storm blows over.*

GENERAL TUDOR had predicted that the moment the Conference opened, Lloyd George would ask the Irish, "Do you waive your claim to a Republic?" Tudor had been proved wrong, and for ten days the Delegates had joined in the removal of subsidiary disagreements. Yet now Lloyd George had asked for satisfactory answers to three questions. "Will you pay allegiance to the Crown? Will you accept membership of the Empire? Will you give us the naval facilities necessary for our defence?" The Irish were faced with the dilemma anticipated by Tudor. It was unthinkable that they should surrender, yet war waited close on a straightforward negative. The time had come for External Association as sketched in their Draft Treaty A.

The Irish proposals, the first that Sinn Fein had ever submitted to England, were as discreet in their omissions as in what they included. They tried to put the case for Ireland's association with the Commonwealth in a way a little different from the rest of the Dominions, without defining the Irish status in constitutional forms too surprisingly in conflict with established British phraseology, or too jarring on conventional British susceptibilities.

The tone, however, was declaratory, even didactic. "If Irish national aspirations are to be reconciled with the British Community of Nations, British statesmanship must keep the fact constantly before its mind, that Ireland is no Colony or Dependency but an ancient and spirited Nation." "Misdescription may often be honest in intention but . . ." "The claim of Ireland is not Dominion Status, but if it were"—and the point is well developed —"your proposals would not confer that status." "You desire to safeguard the security of your Empire. Ireland is resolved to achieve her freedom. We offer you proposals for a Treaty which will ensure the realisation of these ends."

Now comes the vital clause. "On the one hand Ireland will consent to adhere for all purposes of common agreed concern to the League of Sovereign States associated and known as the British Commonwealth of Nations. On the other, Ireland calls upon Great Britain to renounce all claims to authority over Ireland and Irish affairs." There was no mention here of a Republic, nor express rejection of allegiance to the Crown or membership of the Empire. But was it conceivable that the language of either allegiance or membership of the Empire could be found reconcilable with the renunciation by Great Britain of all authority over Ireland and Irish affairs? There follows the clause that one would have expected to reassert the claim to guaranteed neutrality. Collins, however, had had the word "neutral" altered to "free," without apparently much change in the meaning.[1]

The proposals pass on to suggest conventions on trade, commercial air facilities, reciprocity of civic rights, etc., etc. Barton had tried to get inserted a specific claim for complete fiscal autonomy with a trade convention giving England most favoured nation treatment. But as throughout, his zeal for fiscal autonomy outran that of his colleagues. "One other matter" was said to remain. "A matter domestic to ourselves, but which British policy in Ireland has rendered an obstacle to peace and amity between the two nations." Great Britain is asked to stand aside and leave the decision to the two parts of Ireland. Failure, if the British Government stands aside, is thought unlikely, but if it occurs, "Freedom of choice must be given to the electorates within the area."

The type and purpose of this reply are intelligible at a casual glance. It is true that of the three British questions the first (Crown) had not been answered at all, and the second and third (Empire and

[1] "We propose that Ireland shall be recognised as a Free State, that the British Government shall recognise Ireland's freedom and integrity, and that the League of Nations and the United States of America shall be invited to join in that guarantee. Ireland, on her part, will bind herself to enter into no contract and to take no action, nor permit any action to be taken inconsistent with the obligation of preserving her freedom and integrity."

The significance of "freedom" in this special context as opposed to "neutrality" would appear to be twofold. On the one hand, it would be made clear once for all that England had no right of occupation in time of war. On the other hand, some scope would apparently be left Ireland to join in a war; she would not therefore, from a military point of view, be completely sterilised as she would be under neutrality. This conception of "freedom" was thoroughly in accord with Collins's notion that England would get far more assistance, passive and perhaps even active, from an Ireland untied, than from one compelled by imposed Treaty to afford in all circumstances defence facilities to Britain.

Defence) had been dealt with in a way that the British Delegates could hardly accept. Yet in all three cases there was such an atmosphere of new ground broken and new possibilities laid bare, that it would be hardly open to Lloyd George to turn the whole thing down without full investigation of its underlying intentions. In effect the Irish were saying, "You recognise Irish nationhood, but regret that certain hard realities affecting your security prevent your granting us the separation we claim. Very well, we will grant you all the realities which you would get from us under full Dominion Status. But where we can't give way is over certain symbols, certain phrases,[1] which are indispensable to our nationhood, but which you will agree are of no value whatever to your security. We feel sure that on reflection you will recognise that it would be absurd to press for them." The British might have retorted that certain very real naval facilities were being denied them, but then no one thought that the Conference would break down on naval facilities. On Status, which was the only issue on which Ireland would fight to the last, the onus of proving the wisdom of insisting on a particular phraseology seemed to have been thrust on the British.

At least that is how the matter would have stood if the argument had really been between two parties of equal strength with no Parliaments behind them. As it was, there could be no immediate question of Lloyd George accepting the Irish terms, and advantage gained in documentary debate could only be conceived as an advantage in the eyes of the world should the negotiations break down. Ireland therefore had postponed a smash. She got very good at this in two months of negotiations. It is possible that it would have paid her to have staged a break herself at one of these propitious moments when war could scarcely have followed. But she could never be quite sure whether war would come or not, and if it came she had so much more to suffer from it than England.

All this time Duggan had been performing much important liaison work, and had been thrown a good deal into touch with Cope. On Monday morning he transmitted to his colleagues a request that Griffith and Collins should meet Lloyd George and Chamberlain for "ten minutes' private conference," either before or after the full Conference that afternoon. Barton and Gavan Duffy were rather dismayed, but could find no real ground for objection, and at the end of the Plenary Session took place the "ten minutes' private conference." The Irish were given to under-

[1] The Irish Delegates would not have used this language or judged it adequate to express their aspirations.

stand that Lloyd George's desire to split up the Conference was due to his difficulty with certain of his supporters, apparently Worthington-Evans and Greenwood. To those who had witnessed their treatment at the Plenary Session it was news that the Prime Minister cared a fig for the opinions of either. Two other considerations surely weighed more with Lloyd George; the desire to reduce the size of a Conference whose extensiveness had hitherto clogged the functioning of the personal touch; and the determination to exclude Childers, whom the British credited with fanatical opposition to any Dominion settlement.

At a meeting of the Dail Cabinet on December 3rd we shall find Cathal Brugha raising provocatively the circumstances under which the Delegation was split up and ascribing to the British a choice of "the two weakest members of the team." But if only two Irishmen were to be present they would naturally be the leaders Griffith and Collins. And Brugha was rightly called upon to withdraw his statement. There was one sense, however, in which the British might consider Griffith and Collins "the weakest." Being the leaders, and therefore more responsible, they might be expected to be more anxious for a settlement and therefore more amenable to compromise. Griffith, moreover, was reckoned a less intransigent Republican than the rest.

## The Seventh Plenary Session, 10 Downing Street

### 5 p.m. Monday, October 24th

Now at last the records give us Griffith setting forth External Association. We get, too, Lloyd George's public reaction to the first intimation he had received from the Irish of the existence of such a plan.

Lloyd George: "The stage is critical and we cannot much longer prolong discussions on these questions. I am going to ask you for an explanation of your document as you have asked us to explain ours. Take the word 'adhere' ('Ireland will consent to adhere for all purposes of agreed concern to . . . the Commonwealth'). Does that mean if all other conditions are satisfied you are prepared to come inside the Empire as New Zealand, Canada?"

Griffith: "That is not quite our idea of association."

The significance of this reply will not be missed. The "official" Irish view was that the distinction between External Association preserving the Republic, and inclusion in the Empire surrendering it, was fundamental to national independence, and hence to national honour, civic spirit and Irish self-respect. But it was held no less that the distinction did not affect English security, and it was the official strategy not to disturb the British unduly with the magnitude of the gap between the two schemes, but gradually to educate them to a realisation of the advantages of the Irish plan as satisfying Ireland and doing England no harm. Hence Griffith, who pressed this strategy to extreme lengths, replies when he is asked if the Irish are prepared to come inside the Empire, "That is not *quite* our idea of association." (Italics ours.)

Lloyd George was entitled to jump to the conclusion that he had nearly got the Irish in.

LLOYD GEORGE: "Association is not the position of Canada and Australia. What is the distinction between association and coming inside the Empire?"

GRIFFITH: "We should be associated with you—outside that a free people." This was in accordance with the underlying Irish conception. He then added incautiously: "*They* are bound by the link of the Crown."

Lloyd George was on to him in a flash. "By 'adhere,' you don't accept the link of the Crown?"

GRIFFITH (in a desperate effort to evade this particular metaphor, gave away further ground):[1] "We will accept the Crown as head of the association."

LLOYD GEORGE (suspiciously): "As allies?"

GRIFFITH: "Something more; permanent allies, not temporary."

LLOYD GEORGE: "Yes, but not as members of the same Empire."

GRIFFITH: "Not as members, but in points of common concern, we should take the decision of the Imperial Conference."

LLOYD GEORGE: "Common concern? What do you mean by that?"

GRIFFITH: "War and peace, for example. Large matters." He explained that he was not at present ready to define the matters of common concern exactly. An agreed list would have to be included in the Treaty. "The defence of our country and yours is a matter of common concern"—although this was qualified a moment later—"it *might* affect our situation if you were at war." (Italics ours.) An attack on Australia would not necessarily be a matter of common

[1] Neither in Draft Treaty A, nor in the Irish proposals just presented, was there any suggestion of this qualified acceptance of the Crown. But already it had been discovered by the Irish Delegation—the credit must go largely to Chartres—that some recognition of the Crown was not incompatible with the theory of External Association, and from now onwards steady progress was made in fitting such recognition into the original scheme.

concern, though it could become so perhaps if conducted by a great naval Power.

It did not appear that Griffith had worked out with any precision this side of his thesis, and Lloyd George brought him abruptly to the plain man's way of looking at it. "To put it bluntly, will you be British subjects or foreigners? You must be either one or the other."

Griffith had a good reply ready. He developed the Irish conception of "reciprocal citizenship" whose practical effects would come to pretty much the same as those of the "common citizenship" demanded by the British. "We should be Irish, and you would be British, and each would have equal rights as citizens in the country of the other."

Birkenhead accomplished a service in a different sphere by at last bringing into direct conflict the English claims for naval facilities and the Irish for neutrality. "If Ireland granted to England the defence facilities which the English naval advisers declare to be indispensable, no country would be willing to recognise Irish neutrality." Griffith and Collins wriggled frantically, but to no purpose. Finally Birkenhead swept them off the board. "You mean that it might not pay another country to declare war against you? Nevertheless, neutrality is reduced to a shadow—a meaningless trophy which would give you nothing. There is nothing in it." In their hearts the Irish had always recognised that Defence touched Ireland's honour least and British security in British eyes most. They had hoped to convince England that a friendly neutral Ireland was better than any imposed facilities. It was not to be.

GRIFFITH: "We accept the principle that your security should be looked after, though the working out of details might be very difficult."

Not much more was likely to be heard of the Irish claim to neutrality; Britain had won on Defence.

LLOYD GEORGE: "I think we must confer among ourselves."

The British then retired, and after twenty minutes took place the "conversation" previously arranged between Lloyd George, Chamberlain, Griffith and Collins.

Both sides appeared to have done well. Griffith had put up External Association, not his scheme, but the one he was pledged to forward. It had been discussed, and it had not been ruled out as impossible. It was hardly credible that De Valera could have presented it in a form so unexceptionable to Englishmen.

Lloyd George, on the other hand, could feel that he was already almost safe. It was true that the Irish had reached a point at which they would try to stick. But after all how much separated that point from the Dominion goal to which he was hurrying them along? There was nothing of the De Valera Republicanism here—"Dominion membership is not quite our idea of association." "We would accept the Crown as head of the association." Permanent allies, too, not temporary.

This Griffith is really very sensible. And Collins is very influential in Ireland. We shall get along in fine style when we have those two alone—away from that impossible Childers. The silly fellow ought to read *The Times* Leader of, wasn't it, August 17th? "There are reserves of political thought into which English logic practical and theoretical refuses to be led. In the English mind any ground for controversy simply does not exist." But there is no arguing with a fanatic.

The first Sub-Conference at once quickened the pace. As Griffith wrote in the evening, "The British talked freely—Chamberlain frankly. The burden of their story was that on the Crown they must fight. It was the only link of Empire they possessed."

Again and again they tried to get Griffith to accept the Crown provided agreement was reached on other points. But he told them that he had no authority. "If we came to an agreement on all other points I could recommend some form of association with the Crown." Conversation ranged over the Irish document. The British refused to consider an Irish freedom guaranteed by the United States and the League, and just as firmly, an Elective Head. Always they kept returning to the impossibility of peace except on acceptance of the Crown. Griffith told them that the only possibility of Ireland considering association of any kind was in exchange for "essential unity," a concession, as he put it, to Ulster. Finally, it was agreed to continue on the basis of settling all other points, leaving the Crown till last.

Griffith had provisionally satisfied the British that it was worth their while going on with the Conference, continuing to risk their reputations, and turning their immediate attention to Ulster. He had done so by conditionally agreeing to recommend some form of "Association with the Crown"—which might mean anything or nothing. For by now the clash between External Association and Dominion Status had taken on two aspects: (1) Association with, versus membership of, the British Commonwealth; (2) A limited recognition of, versus allegiance to, the British Crown. "*Association with the Crown*" covered any part of either aspect that anybody chose to read into it. It was a fine ambiguous phrase, and behind it the struggle over Ulster might begin.

October 24th, the day of the first Sub-Conference, distinguishes the end of the first phase of the negotiations, but its events brought a curious sequel. An interlude in the negotiations—indispensable, bearing in mind later controversies, to a comprehension of the attitudes of the various Irish leaders at this stage.

De Valera had read with concern the account of the meeting of the 24th, and Griffith's letter had deepened his anxiety. What was this reference in the minutes to "recognition of the Crown as head of the association?" External Association as it had left Dublin had found no place for the Crown. "We're all here at one," wrote De Valera, "that there can be no question of our asking the Irish people to enter into an arrangement which would make them subject to the Crown, or demand from them allegiance to the King. *If war is the alternative we can only face it*,[1] and I think that the sooner the other side is made to recognise it, the better." He offered to come over to London himself, though loth to go unless the situation imperatively demanded it.

The first paragraph of this letter created a scene at 22 Hans Place. Griffith said he would go home unless the Cabinet left their hands free. Collins was in a towering passion. He declared that those in Dublin were trying to put him in the wrong and get him "to do the dirty work for them." He seemed to fear that he was being led into a trap by Brugha and Stack; that he was to be committed to a compromise and discredited. Duggan was also very angry.

A letter of reply was drawn up and signed by all the Delegates, stating Griffith's view in somewhat moderated language. Strong resentment is expressed at "this interference with our powers." "The responsibility, if this interference breaks the very slight possibility there is of settlement, will not and must not rest on the Plenipotentiaries." The powers given under the instructions admittedly laid down the necessity of reference back to Dublin before decisions on the main issues, but imposed no limits on the fullest freedom of discussion. This freedom, the President, without constitutional authority, was now trying to impair. Finally, the particular warning in his letter ignored the implications of the very scheme they had been instructed to propound. "Obviously, any form of association necessitates discussion of recognition in some

[1] Our italics.

form or another of the head of the association." They would very much like the President to come to London if it were possible to do so privately, but otherwise counselled him not to come unless they sent him an urgent message.

De Valera was surprised at the way his warning had been taken. "There is obviously," he wrote back at once, "a misunderstanding. There can be no question of tying the hands of the Plenipotentiaries beyond the extent to which they were tied by their original instructions. These memos of mine, except I explicitly state otherwise, are nothing more than an attempt to keep you in touch with the views of the Cabinet in Dublin."

And so the storm blew over. The Delegates had established the necessity for the widest possible freedom in their discussions with the British; they had recognised the binding force of their instructions, and the duty imposed of referring back to Dublin before coming to major decisions; they had recorded, and it seemed won, acceptance for the view that External Association involved some form of association with the Crown. But more significant was the declaration in De Valera's first letter. Even if he seemed to climb down somewhat in his second letter, that declaration was never withdrawn, nor was it ever disputed by the Delegates. "If war is the only alternative" to becoming British subjects and rendering allegiance to the British Crown (to membership, that is to say, of the British Empire,) "we can only face it."

CHAPTER XI

# THE NEGOTIATIONS AFTER OCTOBER 24TH

"Beware! Beware!
His flashing eyes, his floating hair!
Weave a circle round him thrice."
COLERIDGE.

*The central controversy—The place of Ulster in the negotiations—The Sinn Fein strategy—The break, if break there must be, to come on Ulster—Lloyd George's reply.*

UP till October 24th, characters had been sized up, positions stated, points of view exchanged; but no moves that mattered had been made on either side. From now on, however, every step counts, has consequences, leads to others, is irrevocable. To grasp the extraordinary intricacy of the rest of the negotiations we require some appreciation of the plans of the two parties, plans not, of course, strictly adhered to, yet underlying the main strategy.

On Defence, Trade and Finance, it always appeared probable that agreement would be reached. National Status and Ulster stood on a different footing. Under the first head Ireland's resistance was compounded of such elements as these: (1) You are not offering us even the legal forms of Dominion Status. (2) Even if you were, we could not rely on their permitting us the same effective freedom as they give to the Dominions. So near is Ireland to England and so bitter the suspicion between the two countries. (3) Above all, even effective Dominion Status would not satisfy Irish national aspirations.

This third difficulty, by far the greatest stumbling-block, was one of symbols (although most people in both countries would have rejected this description as inadequate to and belittling the conflict). The Irish were determined to retain a symbolism of independence. The new symbolism to be tolerable had to be compatible with two ideas, interwoven but distinguishable. (1) The idea of Ireland being a separate nation which had agreed for certain purposes to make a Treaty with England; and (2) the idea that even under this Treaty England should have no control, real or nominal, over Irish internal affairs. Of separation in both these senses, the Republic had been adopted by the people of Ireland and remained as the positive symbol. And it was agreed by both sides that it was impossible to be at once a Republic and a member of, or inside, the British Empire.[1]

[1] Short of entering the Empire, Ireland was ready to go a long way in the direction of association. But apart from the fact of Dominion membership, there were three special aspects of any probable Dominion scheme which jarred on deep-seated Irish feeling. (1) Any proposal for a Governor-General or "royal" veto would obviously bring the British King into the Irish legislature, and give him just that authority over Irish internal affairs which it was one of the two main Irish objectives to avert. (2) Any arrangement that involved "allegiance" to the Crown would imply submission to the British King *in all matters*, including once again Irish internal affairs. According to British lawyers such allegiance to the Crown would automatically arise under Dominion Status. (3) Any Oath of loyalty to the King would be bad, but one that explicitly imposed allegiance would be unthinkable, for even if entry into the Empire already technically involved the duty of allegiance, the Oath (besides by its unnecessary explicitness aggravating the sore) would be taken to convey a moral as distinct from a legal obligation of obedience and fidelity to the Crown, precluding any *future* right of resistance or secession against England's will. Although therefore, of no legal significance, although only "the symbol of a symbolism," the Oath became the centre of the fiercest controversy, and among the Irish Delegates the importance of getting it

Lloyd George was anxious, desperately anxious for a settlement. But there was a fixed limit to his range of concession. Almost any settlement which brought Ireland into the Empire was an achievement; a settlement which did not was far worse than no settlement at all. What methods he would have found if there had been no Ulster is guesswork. The existence of an Ulster problem raised a wood covering his own flank and his enemies'. It made the operations more complicated and more dangerous, but it offered more varied and provocative scope.

The Irish had realised early that the Ulster question, on the face of it an unmixed curse, provided tactical compensations. For here, as was not the case with National Status, both parties were agreed on the ideal solution. We find Lloyd George expressing the wish that all Ireland might be voluntarily united. Ulster must not of course be coerced, but if only Ulster could be persuaded—well, the Irish spectre was hardly likely to be otherwise laid. Sir Austen Chamberlain and Lord Birkenhead assented apparently to a proposition that, while not inconsistent with their previous utterances, demanded from them considerable imaginative generosity in the cause of Irish peace. Here then was a consummation desired by both parties to the Conference, but blocked by a third outside it.

Just as important were the probable reactions of British liberal opinion and general world opinion to the different issues on which the Conference might break down. (1) If Sinn Fein had refused unconditionally to come into the Empire, such opinion might have been solid against her; (2) If Sinn Fein refused to go more than a certain distance until the British had tried to persuade Ulster into what they, the British, admittedly believed the reasonable course, opinion would be sympathetic to Sinn Fein; (3) If Sinn Fein and England reached provisional agreement, and Ulster stood in the way of the solution agreed on, world opinion would be against Ulster, and no less against England if England, in these circumstances, recommenced war on Sinn Fein.

Sinn Fein's original policy had been to try to get England to stand aside and let the two parties in Ireland settle the Ulster affair themselves. The Fourth and Fifth Conferences had shown the hopelessness of this demand. The first few Sub-Conferences revealed, as we shall see, a readiness in the British to try to induce Ulster to come into a three-handed conference, on the basis of

phrased inoffensively obscured at times the unbridgeable gulf that was to arise between them on the issue that in the last resort must be supreme: "Was Ireland to be a British Dominion or an Externally Associated Republic?"

certain proposals believed to be agreeable to Sinn Fein. From October 24th to November 25th the chance apparently persisted that Craig might be led to consider a conference on these terms. And the Sinn Fein policy was drawn up accordingly.

They had three strings to their bow: (1) That Ulster would be persuaded to accept terms providing in some sense for the unity of Ireland; (2) That the British, thwarted by Ulster, would offer Sinn Fein large concessions in atonement for a failure admittedly regrettable; (3) That Britain, unable to persuade Ulster, would yet not make Sinn Fein a suitable offer; that the negotiations would break down and public opinion, attributing the break to the recalcitrance not of Sinn Fein but of Ulster, would make impossible a British renewal of war on Sinn Fein. Through everything that follows the Sinn Fein Delegation must be presumed to have all these possible outcomes in mind, especially (1) and (3). At one moment there would seem a chance of unity, the finest outcome of all; at another they would be fighting desperately to make sure of the "break on Ulster." While all the Irish Delegates would have made great sacrifices to preserve the "essential unity" of Ireland, it is probable that Collins and Griffith, who sat for Ulster as well as for Southern constituencies, would put up the greatest fight, and pay the greatest price.

The plan was ingenious, but it suffered from certain defects. The concessions by the Irish made in the first place before ever the British consented to approach Ulster at all, might, besides themselves being considerable, have to be such as would inevitably convey the hint of greater ones to come. Whatever happened then over Ulster, Sinn Fein would have given the impression that, after all, their demand for a Republic (unlike the British demand, that they should come within the Empire), was not absolute but liable to be bartered away in certain contingencies. Their bargaining position would be that much weakened. Secondly, the British might find a way of appearing to achieve, without actually achieving, Irish unity, and all the Irish sacrifices would have been made for a chimera.

Lloyd George, in fact, turned the tactics of the Irish Delegation against themselves on ground of their own choosing. There was hardly a day (from October 24th) when he was not making progress in one of two directions. Either he was extracting more provisional concessions from Sinn Fein to induce them to continue with Craig, or he was working out proposals which, even if he failed with Craig, would give Ireland no excuse for a break. No one would question the genuineness of his desire to bring Ulster into a united Ireland. But he was always faced with a possibility, soon a probability, that Craig would not consent.

His game, indeed, was far harder to play than that of the Sinn Feiners, who could adopt one set of tactics, and await with equanimity any one of three dénouements. Lloyd George had two desirable outcomes in mind. But too strong a push towards a settlement that included unity (the most desirable outcome) might ruin any chance of the other outcome, a Dominion settlement with the South at least. For if he brought really heavy pressure on Craig and Craig still refused, he himself would be committed to that view of Ulster as obscurantist which the Sinn Feiners were so anxious to establish. And it would then be impossible to handle the big stick against Sinn Fein.

Lloyd George's policy was therefore: (1) to secure handsome provisional concessions from Griffith; (2) to try with all his might to persuade Craig to come in, while taking care not to get lined up against Craig and alongside Sinn Fein; (3) in the event of Craig's refusal, somehow to find a scheme to persuade Sinn Fein that he had secured the "essential unity" of Ireland.

The negotiations that follow can be reviewed in four phases. From October 24th to November 3rd we have Lloyd George's extraction of provisional concessions from Sinn Fein. From November 5th (his first meeting with Craig) till November 17th (the Liverpool Conference) we have on the one hand his invitations to Craig, on the other his persuasion of Sinn Fein, more especially Griffith, that he is winning them the "essential unity" of Ireland. From November 16th (when new British proposals were presented) we have the third phase; Lloyd George is still in communication with Craig, but Sinn Fein now begin to bear anew the brunt of his assault. Sinn Fein proposals for External Association are discussed and rejected. The British consider the possibility of revising the Oath and of guaranteeing Ireland not only the law of the Dominions, but their practice and constitutional usage as well. The fourth phase begins with the presentation of the final British draft on December 1st. Its features are the Cabinet Meeting in Dublin on December 3rd and the last two days of negotiations in London, December 4th and 5th.

## CHAPTER XII

# A PRICE PAID AND A POSITION WON

"A politician . . . finds that there is a great difference between the effect of written words, which are perused and re-perused . . . and the effect of spoken words which . . . vibrate for a single moment on the ear."

MACAULAY.

*A Sub-Conference on Ulster—An exchange of notes—The Irish accept Crown as Head for certain purposes of proposed Association—Sunday, October 30th, meeting at Churchill's house—Monday, October 31st, Diehard Vote of Censure defeated—Tuesday, November 1st, Barton and Gavan Duffy attack Griffith's draft letter to Lloyd George—Wednesday, November 2nd, Griffith eventually dispatches revised letter after long arguments with members of both Delegations—Thursday, November 3rd, Griffith's letter rewarded by prospects of pressure on Ulster—Griffith elated—Lloyd George's appraisement of the situation.*

THE first phase opened auspiciously for Ireland. On October 26th Griffith and Collins saw Chamberlain and Hewart in Sub-Conference on Ulster. The latter pair were well intentioned but rather helpless. "We are committed to the Six-County area—what can we do?" "The people must at least have freedom of choice," replied the Irish. The British did not deny the wisdom but they did the practicability of this.

At last, however, with every precaution against committing themselves, every emphasis on their absence of authority and on the fact that they were just exploring various solutions, the British allowed a new proposal to peep out. "Suppose the Six-County area remained as at present, but that its subordinate Parliament came under the all-Ireland Parliament?" This, if not quite the Ulster clause (which would have brought Fermanagh and Tyrone under the all-Ireland Parliament directly) signified the first readiness that the British had shown to move seriously for a radical alteration of the Act of 1920. The symptom whetted Irish appetites and enhanced their confidence in their tactics. But Griffith and Collins concealed their interest. "While," wrote Griffith, "we did not hold out any hope that it might be a basis, we, between ourselves, thought that it might be a possible basis." In the end he told Chamberlain and Hewart that "no Irishman could even discuss an association with the British Crown until the 'essential unity' of Ireland was agreed to by the parties"; brave words to be falsified unwittingly within a month.

The turn of the month was to witness hectic days. Sinn Fein had been granted one tempting glimpse of Ulster. To secure another, she was to find herself lured away still further from her base. But first came a sharp exchange of official notes. It led to nothing, neither side throwing their statement into the form of a definitive draft, and it need not detain us long, except to notice on the Irish side one new concession and one fresh confirmation of the distance they were prepared to go.

"The Crown," said the British, "is the symbol of all that keeps the nations of the Empire together. It is the keystone of the arch in law as well as in sentiment." And again, "The Crown is the symbol of a common citizenship which makes all subjects of the King one in international law. No man can be a subject of two States. He must either be a subject or an alien, and the question no more admits of an equivocal answer than whether he is alive or dead. The essence of common citizenship is that all who enjoy it are at peace or at war together in respect of any foreign State. It is not compatible with neutrality in any form."[1]

[1] The British document suggests on the face of it an examination of the feasibility of previous Irish proposals and a rejection on constitutional grounds. But if we go closer it proves to be nothing of the kind. It strives indeed to link together as part of the indissoluble logic of the Constitution several distinct ideas. The Crown, common citizenship, the idea that all citizens of the Mother Country and of the Dominions are British subjects and subjects of the King, the idea that they are all automatically at peace or war together—who rejects one of these rejects, it is argued, all. But in the first place, this legal or constitutional argument bristles with controversial dogma whose correspondence with the situation even in 1921 was fully open to question. And in the second place, the Irish were quite content to hear that all the British conceptions mentioned were linked together. For to them all these conceptions were equally repellent. They themselves wanted to graft on to the Empire an Ireland related under a completely different set of terms. And the British document did nothing to dispute the practicability of the Irish symbolism, or give reasons for believing that their own was superior. What the document did, and did effectively, was to show that the connection of the various ideas, Crown, common citizenship, etc., was very strong in the minds of ordinary Englishmen, and to add the old reminder that of the two sets of symbolism the British was the only one that it was open to Ireland to choose.

The British document strives to give the impression that it would be *constitutionally impossible* for Irishmen to combine the *practical* advantages of common citizenship with "exclusion from the British Empire." But there was no constitutional reason given for this view, nor why the Irish plan of "reciprocal citizenship" should not have been tried. On the other hand, it is

The Irish reply was brief, propagandist, and suitable for publication supposing the negotiations broke down. Though the achievement of the unimpaired unity of Ireland is emphasised as a condition precedent to any Treaty of Association, and fiscal autonomy coupled with a trade convention is reasserted, the main British questions are unashamedly begged. No mention is made of common citizenship or of allegiance to the Crown. But concessions on defence, previously foreshadowed, are made actual and the first surrender of the negotiations manifest. "We accept the principle that the naval and air defence of the Irish coasts would be a matter of common concern to the British Commonwealth. We are accordingly prepared to agree that the British Government should have such coastal facilities." The facilities are to be granted under licence, subject to the condition of no armed occupation or political control, and only until such time as the Irish shall be able to provide for their own defence. And further, they are only to be "such as may be agreed to be necessary." But—and this is the point—for the first time the British claim to facilities is accepted in principle. In principle the facilities are conceded.

The only other notable clause is the last. "The Irish Delegates are prepared to recommend that the elected Government of a free and undivided Ireland, secured in absolute and unfettered possession of all legislative and executive authority, should for the purposes of the association recognise the Crown as symbol and accepted head of the combination of signatory states." So at last the "Chartres Crown"[1] has become embodied in formal proposition. Ireland is to recognise the Crown as accepted head of the combination. *But only for the purposes of the association*, in matters, that is, of common concern. When the clause reached De Valera it worried him. "We are not quite certain," he wrote, "what exactly the last three lines may involve, and accordingly refrain from making any comment. You know the view here."[2] Later he, too, came to appreciate the merits of the "Chartres Crown," a marvellous

perfectly possible to appreciate the standpoint of British sentiment which said, "Why should Irishmen get all the advantages of association and reciprocal citizenship if they can't show sufficient spirit of sympathy to adopt common forms and call themselves British citizens?" This attitude prevails widely to-day, even among those who are ready to leave Ireland absolutely free choice between leaving or staying in the Empire. "She must stay right in or go right out," they say, still thinking of the coherence of their ancient symbolism.

In one case only did the British constitutional claims depart from the symbolic sphere. Ireland's right to be neutral was once more strenuously denied.

[1] See footnote, p. 147.

[2] From the letter of October 25th that created the scene in Hans Place.

device for keeping within the bounds of External Association and yet saving the British face. But the British kept on stolidly demanding allegiance for all purposes, not recognition only for some.

Griffith and Collins had seen Lloyd George and Birkenhead before they presented the Irish proposals. If Ireland would accept the Crown (in *some* sense) the British let it be understood that they would send for Craig: "*i.e.* force Ulster in as I understand," wrote Griffith to De Valera in sanguine mood. A much more important talk, some would say the most important in the whole negotiations, took place on Sunday, October 30th.

This day and the week that followed belonged to Griffith. With some help from Collins and some encouragement from Duggan, but hampered, almost hamstrung, by Barton and Gavan Duffy, he came through a series of manœuvres of superlative ingenuity and coherence. By Thursday night he would be thinking that he had gained much and yielded little. He would be instilling this belief into De Valera, who would be writing back to him in warm congratulation. Yet in so far as the negotiations are to be thought of as a gradual surrender of the Republic before a mixture of *force majeure* and diplomatic finesse, the days from October 30th to November 2nd, especially the first of them, can be said to have sealed its fate.

At 9.30 on the evening of Sunday, October 30th, Griffith first saw Lloyd George alone. The meeting was at Churchill's house. Lloyd George was arranging his speech against the Die-hard Vote of Censure which was to be brought forward the next evening in the House of Commons. The Irish memorandum, he told Griffith, had been so worded that he did not know where he stood. Griffith replied that the British document was obviously couched for publication in the event of a breakdown. The Irish had replied in the same strain. Lloyd George then came down to business. The Crown, *Free Partnership* (Griffith's italics in writing to De Valera) with the Empire, and naval facilities—these were vital matters. "If I would give him personal assurances on these matters," wrote Griffith to De Valera, "he would go down to smite the Die-hards, and would fight on the Ulster matter to secure 'essential unity.' "

On the Crown, Griffith gave him the assurance that the Irish Delegates would be prepared to recommend its recognition provided that they were satisfied on the other points at issue. The formula expressing this recognition was postponed till later. On the Empire, "the formula defending the association of Ireland with the Empire was left over." The discussions on Defence and

Trade were not productive. Under Ulster, Lloyd George said that he could carry a Six-County Parliament subordinate to a National, *i.e.* Irish, Parliament. Alternatively, he said he would try to carry a plan for a new boundary, or a vote by Ulster as a single unit on inclusion or exclusion, "but he was not hopeful of doing so."[1]

Later Griffith was joined by Collins, and Lloyd George by Birkenhead. The two sentences in which Griffith sums up to De Valera the result of the evening's conversations are as important as anything in their correspondence. "They indicated that if they were certain of real goodwill on our side they would take risks and fight. We parted on the understanding that they would go strongly against the Die-hard attack and go strongly for peace with Ireland" in the debate. Griffith then had satisfied the British. How he had done so will appear when the events of the next few days have been chronicled. At what cost we will speculate later.

On October 31st the Die-hard Vote of Censure was proposed with spirited bitterness by Gretton and Gywnne, sternly resisted by Lloyd George, and crushingly defeated at the division. Late on the evening of the next day, Tuesday, November 1st, Griffith presented to the Irish Delegation a draft of a letter that he proposed to send to Lloyd George, in compliance with the latter's request for some documentary evidence to show at the great Unionist Party gathering at Liverpool on the 17th. Griffith was anxious that the letter should be personal from himself. After all, the interview with Lloyd George, and the undertaking to write the letter had both been personal. Moreover he was most anxious to shield Collins from attacks (Brugha and Stack would leap into everybody's mind) on the score of compromise.

The letter took the form of a recapitulation of the assurances given Lloyd George at Churchill's house. The two crucial clauses ran—"provided I was satisfied on every point" (including the "essential unity" of Ireland), "I was prepared to recommend recognition of the Crown, the formula in which this recognition was to be couched to be arrived at at a later stage. I similarly agreed to recommend free partnership with the British Commonwealth,

[1] Of these three plans for meeting the Ulster difficulty, the one which Lloyd George "could carry" was apparently the one least disagreeable to Sinn Fein. But it fell short of their Ulster clause in so far as it placed Fermanagh and Tyrone under an Ulster legislature, though admittedly the latter would be subject to Dublin. Sinn Fein had therefore to be convinced of its special merits. The fact, for example, that it could be carried through the British Parliament.

the formula defining the partnership to be arrived at in a later discussion."

But for the first time Griffith found his authority contested. Barton and Gavan Duffy strongly opposed the sending of a personal letter, and objected just as vehemently to its tone. Childers, though with some diffidence as not a Delegate, supported them. Collins and Duggan took little part. The meeting dispersed without reaching an agreement, but not until Griffith had used some very steep language towards Duffy. Barton, Duffy and Childers met afterwards and decided that in no circumstances would they permit this letter to be sent as personal from Griffith, or with its contents in their existing form.

Next morning Gavan Duffy was early astir, and by 9 o'clock, when the Delegates met, had drafted an elaborate memorandum. It began with a most energetic protest against the terms of the proposed letter. "I would urge you very strongly not to send to Mr. Lloyd George the letter of which you have shown us the rough draft. The main effect of the letter must be to undermine the stand we have taken. We had, in our last memorandum, very carefully limited the recognition of the British Crown that we would recommend; your letter abandons this for a form of words which, by its very omissions, will be used by Mr. Lloyd George as indicating your willingness to sponsor allegiance by the Irish people to the British Crown."

Plenty of other passages in the memorandum vindicate Gavan Duffy from any charge of being blind to the direction in which the negotiations were moving. "Lloyd George's memoranda have all been as stiff as possible, the climbing down has all been on our side. He wants another letter from you I am convinced, not merely for Sir James Craig, but to use against Ireland in Washington or here when it suits him. I want to see a settlement, which I am persuaded we can get on non-allegiance lines, explored to the uttermost, before our Chairman even suggests that he is prepared to go further. Until such a settlement has been discussed, and our proposals criticised in writing by the other side, we cannot say that we have explored that avenue."

He ends with a forcible protest against the letter, if it is to go at all, going as personal from Griffith. The reason he gives is that in any case all the other members of the Delegation would he held responsible for it wherever it was read. More potent with him, as with Barton and Childers, was the fear of any move likely to accentuate the splitting of the Delegation into two halves; one, their own half, left ignorant and powerless, the other swept forward by Griffith in a scheme of tactics highly dangerous and liable to misconstruction, with no guarantee of a Republican goal. But to Griffith, engrossed like Lloyd George in the business of somehow obtaining a settlement which Ireland could reasonably accept, Gavan Duffy's objections seemed at once logic-chopping and naïve. Diplomacy was a complicated game in which teams should support leaders. For the moment it was his, Griffith's, function to take Lloyd George on alone.

Nevertheless, he gave way this time. He could hardly break his promise to Lloyd George and not send the letter at all. But he agreed that it should go as from the whole Delegation; he agreed also to insert one very important qualification in the sentence dealing with the Crown. "I was, on the same condition," he now wrote, "prepared to recommend that Ireland should consent to *a* recognition of the Crown *as head of the proposed Association of Free States.*" In the circumstances, the change was considerable. It substituted for the notion of a recognition of the Crown *in undefined terms* mutually acceptable to both countries, a recognition *on the lines of the Irish proposal of the 29th* (which it virtually reproduced). From the English point of view, this was External Association once again raising its hydra head.

This same day, Wednesday, November 2nd, Griffith and Collins saw Lord Birkenhead at 12 o'clock, and Lloyd George, Birkenhead and, ultimately, Chamberlain, at 6.45. Lloyd George and Birkenhead were at extraordinary pains to get Griffith's letter altered in its Crown and Empire passages. They insisted that they wanted the letter as an answer to the arguments of the Craig party. (Their difficulty with Craig was real enough, but came in, none the less, exceedingly useful for tactical purposes. Griffith could be faced with it in no spirit of trickery, and yet be screwed to the limit.)

Birkenhead made no headway in the morning. When Griffith and Collins arrived at his room at the House of Lords their "Empire clause" committed Ireland to free partnership *with* the British Commonwealth under a formula to be later arranged. Birkenhead asked if Griffith could not change this to free partnership *within* the British Commonwealth. "I stated," reported Griffith, "it could not be done," for free partnership *within* the British Commonwealth could only mean one thing—partnership with the Dominions as a Dominion. At lunch time the clause was still intact, but Birkenhead had persuaded Griffith and Collins to meet himself and Lloyd George at 10 Downing Street at 6.45 p.m.

The evening discussion lasted two hours. Six or seven alterations were suggested—two were accepted by the Irish, one declined, and the rest disposed of by redrafting. The ease with which on one point they rose superior makes one marvel at the ease with which on another they fell victim to a humorously sly dialectic. The Irish had agreed to recommend a recognition of the Crown (in a certain capacity). In a draft of their own letter now placed before them by the British, they found that this "a" had been omitted, and that they were asked to recommend simply "recognition." They saw at once the significance of the change. If they accepted, they would have been implicitly driven from their own novel and peculiar brand of recognition to the ordinary British recognition, in which was included, no doubt, Allegiance. They pierced this stratagem and scouted it.

But the next one tricked them properly. Griffith was recommending free partnership with the British Commonwealth. Birkenhead had tried for free partnership within the British Commonwealth and been refused. Why not, the British now suggested, "Free partnership *with* the other States associated within the British Commonwealth." This looked all right to the Irish. After all their partnership would still be "with," *i.e.* from outside, the British Commonwealth. "I accepted this," reported Griffith, "as it did not alter the essence of the formula." Later, after a good deal of trouble, he secured the assent of the whole Delegation to the letter in its newest form. It was dispatched to Downing Street at 11 o'clock, that night. Griffith sent a copy to De Valera next day, through whom it would pass to the Cabinet in Dublin. Not one of all these seems to have disputed Griffith's contention that the change in the "Empire clause" "did not alter the essence of the formula."

But did it not indeed? "Free partnership with the other States associated within the British Commonwealth." It is possible to read this as meaning "Free partnership *from without* with the other States of the Association, all of which happen to be associated within the British Commonwealth?" Surely not. If not, it must mean that Ireland is to accept free partnership with the States which, *like Ireland*, are associated *within* the British Commonwealth. Everyone who believes himself capable of interpreting non-technical phraseology must judge for himself whether here there is even ambiguity. For our part, we can see no sense in the clause, unless it be a promise by Griffith, provided he be satisfied on other points including "essential unity," to recommend Ireland's inclusion within the Empire as a partner like the other Dominions.[1]

This point seems of significance no less striking because it must not be exaggerated. Griffith clearly did not realise that the clause could bear the interpretation that to us seems inescapable. He was trying to be clever, to shake hands across the boundary line, and he was pulled over without noticing it. In a sense, no doubt, he was completely uncompromised by his letter; for although it could be widely exhibited, it could hardly be held over his head under threat of publication, or used in any other way to force him to implement his pledge. Yet it was by manœuvres such as these that the Irish position was gradually undermined.

The next morning, Thursday, November 3rd, seemed to bring the Irish the first-fruits of their concessions. Griffith and Collins saw Birkenhead at 11 o'clock at the House of Lords. Immediately afterwards Griffith recorded the three main points that emerged:

(1) That the British highly appreciated "the letter of November 2nd as a document upon which they could deal with Craig."

(2) That before Craig was sent for they wished to see Bonar Law and Carson and dissuade them from opposition.

(3) That if Ulster proved unreasonable they would resign rather than use force against Sinn Fein.

Griffith's letter to De Valera of this day, November 3rd, is the most jubilant of the series. After describing faithfully and fully events that we have seen taking place in London, it goes on to review the future in a passage whose prophecies we shall be able to estimate at their true value as the next few days unfold themselves. Let the record up to November 3rd end on a note of Irish triumph. "They are satisfied to face the Ulster question on it (*i.e.* on Griffith's letter to Lloyd George) and assure us that if Ulster proves unreasonable *they are prepared to resign* rather than use force against us. In such an event no English Government is capable of formation on a war policy against Ireland."

[1] "I was prepared," ran the final version, "to recommend a free partnership with the other States associated within the British Commonwealth." The paragraph concludes, "I was prepared to recommend that Ireland should assent to a recognition of the Crown as head of the proposed Association of Free States." This sentence has changed places with its predecessor, and in its present position there is no indication whether the Association in question is to be of External or Dominion character. The letter goes on to emphasise and deepen a concession of the 29th envisaging the grant of naval facilities "pending an agreement similar to those made to the Dominions providing for the assumption by Ireland of her own coastal defence." All concessions are left conditional on the achievement of "essential unity."

Meanwhile Lloyd George was giving Lord Riddell his own impressions of what the Irish would surrender and what they would insist on in return.[1] Already, on October 30th, before the conversations of that evening he confided: "It looks as if the Sinn Feiners would accept the Sovereignty of the King; they will agree to remain part of the British Empire, and will also agree to give us the facilities we want for the Navy." The Delegates were said to be very angry about De Valera's message to the Pope emphasising the Irish claim for independence. Lloyd George is sure that they "want to settle." By the 3rd he is prophesying with still greater certainty: "Sinn Fein are prepared to accept allegiance to the Crown and to agree that Ireland shall remain part of the Empire."

If he is too sanguine here, he is under no illusions about the Sinn Fein attachment to "essential unity." On the 30th "they will demand Fermanagh and Tyrone, and that the Customs and Excise, etc., and the Post-Office shall be controlled by an over-riding Parliament." And on the 3rd their entry into the Empire is to be "subject to Tyrone and Fermanagh being joined to Southern Ireland, or at any rate to a plebiscite, and subject also to Irish fiscal, postal, telegraphic arrangements being delegated to a central Parliament, to be elected on the basis of population. On the 30th, and by implication on the 3rd, he doubts whether they would be prepared to give way on the points mentioned. "The prospect is very awkward."

His own purposes are still more interesting. Unfortunately they are not very coherent. On the 30th he seems personally war-like, but doubtful of the high-principled support he deserves; "the Ulster people will never agree, and the question will then arise whether the English people are prepared to fight in order to support them.... There is no doubt that in principle the country is hardening against the Sinn Feiners, but the point is whether people are prepared to give effect to their principles." But by the 3rd he seems mellowed by contact with the potential enemy (this although, or because, Bonar Law has come out as the advocate of Ulster). "I am not," he now tells Lord Riddell, "going to continue the Irish war if a settlement is possible. I shall resign, and the King will have to send for someone else." He goes on to explain the Irish terms as above. "If the matter can be settled on these lines I am not prepared to continue civil war."

Was Griffith right then in thinking that on November 3rd Lloyd George intended to resign if Ulster refused to accept an overriding Parliament at Dublin? It seems so from Lord Riddell's *Diary*

[1] See Riddell, *Diary*, pp. 330–332.

(where Lloyd George appears to recognise the justice of the Sinn Fein claim to Fermanagh and Tyrone *as well*). But a month later Ulster is being allowed to reject an all-Ireland Parliament,[1] and Sinn Fein threatened with immediate war if she does not accept the result. Is it credible that on November 3rd Lloyd George was really so sympathetic to the overriding Dublin Parliament that if this Parliament proved impossible of achievement he would have refused to make war on the South? Did he really change his mind completely between November 3rd and December 5th? Was it ever really touch and go whether he would resign?

## CHAPTER XIII

# THE POSITION UNDERMINED

"Then with a kind compassionating look,
And sighs, bespeaking pity ere he spoke,
Few words he said."

DRYDEN.

*The British apparently entangled—Their contingent pledge of resignation—Craig sees Lloyd George, Saturday, November 5th—Jones adumbrates to Griffith plan for Boundary Commission—De Valera congratulates Griffith—Jones now imbues Griffith with desire that Lloyd George should not be forced to resign—The Boundary Commission a way of avoiding this—Griffith accepts it as a tactical manœuvre—Lloyd George released from pledge to bring about all-Ireland Parliament or resign.*

GRIFFITH had written on the 3rd to De Valera about his famous letter to Lloyd George. "They are satisfied to face the Ulster question on it and assure me that if Ulster proves unreasonable they are prepared to resign rather than use force against us." He envisaged in such circumstances no possibility of an English Government being formed with a war policy against Ireland. Then he continues:

"The tactical course I have followed has been to throw the question of Ulster against the question of association and the

[1] It is true that, if she did so, she would be faced with a Boundary Commission, but the latter, not even involving a plebiscite, was destined to be of no use whatever to the South.

Crown. This is now the position: the British Government is up against Ulster and we, for the moment, are standing aside. If they secure Ulster's consent we shall have gained 'essential unity' and the difficulty we shall be up against will be the formula of association and recognition. *You will observe my wording, which they accept, is consistent with External Association and external recognition.*"[1]

Meanwhile, the British leaders were awkwardly, even critically placed. For it was as likely as not that Ulster would refuse to come in, and if that happened they were pledged to resign rather than use force against Sinn Fein. We shall now see them begin to work their way out of this entanglement.

Craig saw Lloyd George on Saturday, November 5th, as expected, and again on November 7th.

On the 8th, Tom Jones came round to see Griffith and Collins at the Grosvenor Hotel. Convincingly woe-begone, he little seemed to realise the silver lining that the Irish would find in his tidings, or in what a hopeful light Griffith would feel able to present them to De Valera.

"Craig," said Jones, "is standing pat." He refused to come under any all-Ireland Parliament, he refused to change the Six-County area. Lloyd George was going to see the Ulster Government on Thursday, and propose to them that they should accept the Six-County area under an all-Ireland Parliament. If they refused, he would go down to the House of Commons, announce his resignation, and retire altogether from public life. Birkenhead and Chamberlain, so Jones guessed, would also resign. There would be no dissolution. Instead, Bonar Law would form a militarist Government against Ireland!

Jones then became infinitely sympathetic and anxious to avert from the Ireland of which he was so fond the horrors of this alternative régime. He had a scheme in his mind. Suppose the Twenty-Six Counties of the South were to be given all the new powers under discussion, and suppose Ulster were to be not only restricted to its existing powers, but also submitted to a *Boundary Commission set up to "delimit" her area*? How would that strike the Irish Delegates?

"The arrangement," in Griffith's understanding "would give us most of Tyrone and Fermanagh and part of Armagh, Londonderry, Down, etc.", but he would give Jones no definite opinion on the matter. It was, as he saw the situation, "their look-out for

[1] Our italics.

the moment"; and he concludes to De Valera, "he is to see us again tomorrow. It is partly bluff, but not wholly. It is possible that the Conference may end with this week. If so, all policy dictates it should end on the note of Ulster being impossibilist in order to throw the Dominions against her."

So, disappointing as was Craig's refusal judged by ideal standards, events were moving happily along their next best course. Lloyd George was still pledged to resign if he could not induce the Ulster Cabinet to be more reasonable than Craig. And supposing he resigned. Griffith had foretold in his letter of the 3rd that "no British Government was capable of formation on a war policy against Ireland." It is true that he now admitted Jones's threat of Bonar Law militarism not to be wholly bluff. But if the Coalition Cabinet was overthrown on the Ulster issue, the inevitable confusion and conflict in England would leave Ireland pretty safe.

Above all, "it was England's look-out for the moment." This Boundary Commission of Jones's, a plan which Lloyd George had been very doubtful about on October 30th, and which did not seem to have his authority even now, called for no immediate decision or reaction. Lloyd George was committed to his attempt to bring Ulster under an all-Ireland Parliament. Whether he succeeded or failed, Ireland would have cause for congratulation.

The above seems a fair reconstruction of Griffith's mental attitude immediately after his talk with Jones. Four days later he had made startling and secret concessions, which could hardly have been forced from him if he had continued to read the situation as he did when he wrote to De Valera. Yet it was not that the essential elements had changed. Only that Lloyd George had, by the 12th, rammed home a tiny advantage for which—the slowest of us can see it now—Jones had opened the door on the 8th. If Griffith had flatly turned down the very discussion of a Boundary Commission, Lloyd George would have found his powers taxed to the uttermost to liquidate his contingent pledge of resignation. But Griffith, always predisposed to silence, thought it was not his turn to speak.

De Valera had not written to Griffith since October 30th. He now replied to all letters up to and including that of the 8th. From the beginning, he said, he had been of the opinion that the break should come on Ulster provided "that Ulster could not go out with the cry, 'Attachment to the Empire and loyalty to the Throne!' " And provided, which was always the difficulty, that the fundamental national claim was not prejudiced. "There can be no doubt whatever that the Delegation has managed to do this admirably." Opinion among the Cabinet in Dublin was unanimous that if a break came Ulster would be condemned by the public opinion of England, Ireland and the world.

But he tempered congratulation with warning. If he failed to see the full verbal implications of the Griffith letter, he was under no illusion about its tendency. "The danger now is that we shall be tempted, in order to put them more hopelessly in the wrong, to make further advances on our side. I think, as far as the Crown-Empire connection is concerned, we should not budge a single inch from the point to which the negotiations have now led us." No allusion is made to Jones, or to the Boundary Commission. Griffith had made this issue seem secondary to the one whose climax was at hand.

On the same day, Wednesday, November 9th, Jones again called at the Grosvenor Hotel and was received by Griffith and Duggan. Craig's attitude he described as "non possumus." He had become far more intractable as a result of certain interviews in London. But Lloyd George was holding a meeting of his whole Cabinet the next day (the 10th), and if he secured their support he would be in a strong position to fight Craig and his backers. This "strong position" against Craig was proving singularly elusive, and the Irish could have been forgiven a comment to that effect. But Jones was holding their attention fast. Lloyd George desired to play a second card against Craig if the latter refused to accept a subordinate Parliament. This would take the form of a Boundary Commission "to delimit Ulster," "so as to give us," in Griffith's words, "the districts in which we are now a majority"—the same plan, in fact, as Jones had had in his own mind the previous day. Did the Irish think that Ulster would accept this delimitation (combined, of course, with restriction to their present partition and powers)? "No," said Griffith. "I quite agree," said Jones.

He outlined a special argument for the new move. If Ulster's obduracy led to Lloyd George's resignation, Bonar Law would probably come in and try Crown Colony Government on the South for a couple of months. But he, Jones, was anxious to prevent this at all costs, and therefore to keep Lloyd George from resigning. Now, if a Boundary Commission were mooted and if, as seemed probable, Ulster refused it, Lloyd George would be able to raise a most telling cry that Ulster was, in truth, impossibilist. Instead of resigning as a man who had failed to solve the Irish question, he could then remain in office as the one man in the least likely to snatch a solution from a hopeless impasse.

All along Jones had represented Lloyd George to Sinn Fein as their "friend." He had additional excuse for doing so now in the sudden re-emergence during the last few days of Bonar Law, hated traditionally in the South and himself supposed to reciprocate the abstract hatred in a sick Canadian-Ulster brain. And Jones laid it on just right. He did not pretend that Bonar Law's policy would last for long. If he had done so he might have frightened the Irish off their tactics (tactics which Lloyd George had fully penetrated and was determined to keep in motion against themselves). He simply emphasised the difference between two months of military government by Bonar Law and a continuance in power of their "friend," reinforced in his good offices by public condemnation of Ulster.

The Boundary Commission, then, was a "tactical" manœuvre to deprive Ulster of support in England by showing people that she had now passed beyond all reason and justice and was trying to coerce areas anxious to come under the South. "Would the Irish Delegates stand behind such a proposal?" Griffith answered with, as he thought, circumspection. "We said that it would be their proposal, not ours, and we would not therefore be bound by it, *but we realised its value as a tactical manœuvre and if Lloyd George made it we would not queer his position.*"[1] Jones was satisfied with this. What had he accomplished? What, rather, had he not?

If we compare Griffith's attitude here with that when he wrote the letter of the 3rd before Craig's refusal to consider an all-Ireland Parliament and before the two visits of Jones, we gauge at once the ravages effected by Jones's diplomacy. On the 3rd Griffith had contemplated with equanimity the results of a resignation of the Lloyd George Government on the "all-Ireland Parliament" issue. He had stated without qualification that "No English government is capable of formation on a war policy against Ireland." But on the 9th, under Jones's tuition, we find him obviously impressed with the paramount urgency of Lloyd George continuing in power; we find him prepared, half consciously, to modify his plans for that end.

Indeed, he was already as good as reconciled to the Boundary Commission as an alternative to the all-Ireland Parliament—a probable two counties against a certain six. He wrote of it, it is true, and thought of it still as a tactical manœuvre and not as something which would one day actually operate. But if you accept some policy as a tactical manœuvre, you almost certainly

[1] Our italics.

accept it in fact without this qualification. You cannot withdraw acceptance when its original tactical purpose seems lost. For all his care in refraining from putting his party behind the scheme for a Boundary Commission, Griffith had agreed "not to queer Lloyd George's pitch." *By doing so, he had released Lloyd George from his obligation to secure an all-Ireland Parliament or resign.* Lloyd George was making light of the grip which had cost Griffith so much to fasten on him.

## CHAPTER XIV

# THE POSITION DISSIPATED

"Into the very closet and retreat
Of England's Minister."
THOMAS HARDY: *The Dynasts.*

*The Lloyd George–Craig correspondence—Griffith sees Jones on the 11th—Griffith still optimistic—November 12th, Griffith sees Lloyd George at 25 Park Lane—British proposals for Ulster put into writing—"Break on Ulster" vitiated.*

CRAIG had been joined by his Ministers at the Constitutional Club, Northumberland Avenue, and to all outward appearance was resting there, calm and inert. On Thursday, November 10th, Lloyd George, after a full Cabinet meeting, wrote him a long, persuasive letter. A solemn correspondence ensued and was published after the Treaty. In the result it was completely sterile. But the dates and general purport of the various letters are worth mentioning as are a few of their salient features.

Lloyd George wrote to Craig on the 10th,[1] asking the Ulster Government to come into conference, and explaining the settlement towards which the British Government had been working.

Craig wrote back on the 11th expressing the opinion that any discussion would be fruitless unless the British Government withdrew the proposals for an all-Ireland Parliament. As an alternative, tolerable, though far from attractive, he suggested that the Six Counties should be set up on the same basis and with the same powers as the proposed Southern Irish area, even if this meant that they lost their representatives in the Imperial Parlia-

[1] He had seen him alone on the 5th and 7th.

ment. In other words, though the phrase is not used, he suggested that Ulster, no less than the South, should be made a Dominion.

On November 14th, Lloyd George wrote back to Craig refusing the Ulster proposal, hoping that Ulster would not persist in making preliminary conditions, and issuing a pressing invitation to come into, at any rate, personal consultation with himself. Craig replied on the 17th (Thursday) in general terms as uncompromising as before, but expressed a readiness to meet Lloyd George any time after the following Monday, November 21st. Within twenty-four hours Craig went down with influenza, and the meeting with Lloyd George did not eventually take place till Friday, November 25th. Craig returned to Ulster, and on the 29th made a short agreed statement at the opening of the new session of the Ulster Parliament. "By Tuesday next, either negotiations will have broken down, or the Prime Minister will send me new proposals for consideration by the Cabinet. In the meantime the rights of Ulster will be in no way sacrificed or compromised."

From these dates it is clear, and other sources confirm our knowledge, that while Lloyd George never relaxed his efforts to win over Ulster, he was faced from the 11th onwards with a strong probability that she would refuse to come into conference, and would afterwards contest whatever concessions at the expense of her 1920 position were made to Sinn Fein in the Treaty. The outcome of Lloyd George's despair of progress in the Ulster direction appears in the presentation of British terms to the Sinn Fein Delegates on the 16th (the day before the Ulster reply to the second invitation was received). In short, from the 11th onwards, Lloyd George employed the other prong of his policy, and bent all his energies to securing a settlement with Sinn Fein direct and alone. But Ulster, although he had apparently failed in his blandishments in her direction, had indirectly been very useful to him in the last three weeks, and was to become still more so in the days that followed. For the very existence of Ulster had kept Sinn Fein moving forward along the course he desired.

Cheered perhaps by De Valera's congratulations of the 9th, Griffith wrote back on the 11th, contentedly, even gaily. His foreboding of the 9th seemed to have evaporated. There is no talk now of the menace of Bonar Law, or of the need to accept a Boundary Commission as a tactical manœuvre against him.

He had just met Jones at the Grosvenor, and reports complacently the latter's account of Lloyd George's first letter to Craig; "Sinn Fein had contingently undertaken to recommend agreements on Association, the Crown, Defence," etc.[1] "Then had followed," Jones told Griffith, "the proposals for an all-Ireland Parliament." Jones showed Griffith a first reply just received from the Ulster Cabinet. "So long as the suggestion of the Government contains a reference to the establishment of an all-Ireland Parliament, they feel it would be impossible for them to meet in conference on the subject." (Griffith.)

The detailed reply (Craig's first letter in the correspondence above) was to follow in the evening. "Lloyd George evidently believed," wrote Griffith, "that the Ulsterites are being gingered up, possibly by Bonar Law, in the hope of snatching an anti-Conference verdict at the National Unionist Conference at Liverpool next week." But Chamberlain was to go down there and come out strongly for settlement. He had considerably influenced the "outer Cabinet" the previous night by declaring "that the Sinn Fein Delegates were straightforward, honourable men" whose word he was ready to take after his own experience of speaking with them.

Griffith's beginning had been cryptic: "The Crown and Empire can only come up on the Ulster basis. It is their move and they don't know it." But his ending was plain enough: "The Ulster crowd are in the pit that they digged for us, and if we keep them there we will have England and the Dominions out against them in the next week or two."

Meanwhile the Unionist chiefs were far from happy about the Liverpool Conference. They were leaving nothing to chance. Sir Archibald Salvidge was reckoned the dominating figure in Liverpool politics. His influence might win firm decision there on Thursday. This afternoon (Friday 11th) Lord Birkenhead wired to him, "I think it indispensable that you should come to London to-night," and the next day Chamberlain appealed to him afresh. "It is very important that I and all the others should see you Monday"; but Salvidge had too bad a cold to travel to London,

[1] Lloyd George had really written to Craig in terms more definite than these. He had envisaged a settlement whose first principle involved Ireland in explicit allegiance to the Throne and membership of the Empire. Griffith did not see the Lloyd George letter till next day (November 12th). When a few days later it was shown to his colleagues, a wretched scene ensued. Barton and Gavan Duffy called for instant repudiation of any such Dominion settlement; Griffith, who prevailed, insisted that "though our goal is not Dominion Home Rule, we must explore their avenues if we expect them to explore ours."

though by Sunday (13th) he was well enough to go out to Knowsley for an "indecisive" and "unhappy" afternoon.[1]

If there had been no 12th of November there might have been no Treaty. Whether the day's work is to be deplored or rejoiced over will naturally depend on how one regards the Treaty and what one calculates would have been the consequences if the negotiations had broken down. But from the standpoint of objective history the significance of the day is beyond argument. This makes it the more unfortunate that for once our material is not quite satisfying, so that we are forced to introduce into our narrative an element of speculative reconstruction.

Griffith, it is true, described this day in his longest letter to De Valera; but here our difficulty begins. For Griffith's letter is largely concerned with an interview between himself and Lloyd George, and of this interview another, and not at first sight identical, description is available in an account by Sir Austen Chamberlain. This latter version is based on Sir Austen's personal recollection of how Lloyd George described his (Lloyd George's) interview with Griffith immediately after it had occurred. It is unnecessary to dwell on the unchallenged probity of Griffith and Chamberlain; almost as superfluous to stress the meticulous accuracy peculiarly characteristic of both their minds. It becomes therefore our task to reconcile these two different versions; to reconcile them, moreover, in some manner that renders intelligible the consequences of what happened this day.

The first part of Griffith's letter gives us no trouble. He had, he wrote, seen Jones in the morning at 22 Hans Place, and Lloyd George in the afternoon. (The place of meeting was the house of Sir Philip Sassoon, 25 Park Lane.) Lloyd George had given him a hurried reading of the letters to and from Craig of the 10th and 11th. Griffith gathered that all members of the British Cabinet except Lloyd George were simply astounded at his proposal, after four pages of frantic professions of loyalty, that Ulster should be made a Dominion and should pay none except voluntary contributions to England. Even Bonar Law was reputed to be "a bit knocked out" by it.

Lloyd George was sending a further reply to Ulster, "refusing their Dominion proposal, but offering to create an all-Ireland Parliament, Ulster to have the right to vote itself out within

[1] For these and other quotations and pieces of confidential information regarding the activities of Sir Archibald Salvidge, see *Salvidge of Liverpool*, by S. Salvidge, Sir Archibald's son.

twelve months; but if it did, a Boundary Commission to be set up to delimit the area, and the part that remained after the Commission had acted to be subject to equal financial burdens with England."[1]

"Lloyd George intimated that this would be their last word to Ulster. If Ulster refused, as he believed she would, he would fight, summon Parliament, appeal to it against Ulster, dissolve, or pass an Act establishing the all-Ireland Parliament." Now what does this really amount to? Surely that if Ulster refused both the two alternatives now offered, the all-Ireland Parliament and the Boundary Commission, Lloyd George would proceed without the consent of Ulster to set up an all-Ireland Parliament, option out of which, on Ulster's part, would involve a Boundary Commission delimiting her area.[2] And surely this is another way of saying that if, as seemed likely, Ulster did in fact opt out and the Boundary Commission were set up, Sinn Fein would find what she had accepted, *as a tactical manœuvre only*, becoming actualised as a concrete solution. Let us study closely Griffith's own account of how he met this danger.

> "I told him it was his proposal, not ours. He agreed, but he said that when they were fighting next Thursday with the Die-hards and 'Ulster' in front, they were lost if we cut the ground away behind them by repudiating the proposal.
>
> "I said we would not do that, if he meant that he thought we would come out in public decrying it. It was his own proposal. If the Ulstermen accepted it, we would have to discuss it with him in the privacy of the Conference. *I could not guarantee its acceptance, as, of course, my colleagues knew nothing of it yet. But I would guarantee that while he was fighting the 'Ulster' crowd we would not help them by repudiating him.*" (Our italics.)

With this outcome to the interview Griffith was quite content. He had got it fixed in his mind that Lloyd George was thoroughly satisfied with Sinn Fein and thoroughly dissatisfied with Ulster; and that the trouble that was evidently brewing was going to fall on Ulster's head. His letter ends in the familiar happy strain. "This satisfied him. They are to send this letter on Monday.

[1] When it came to the point the threat of a Boundary Commission was not mentioned to Ulster at this stage, on the grounds that to do so would be to accumulate sympathy for Ulster at the Liverpool Conference on the 17th.

[2] Lloyd George's proposal as described by Griffith, can be read in a way more favourable to Sinn Fein, viz. that if Ulster refused both alternatives, one of them, the all-Ireland Parliament with no option out, would be imposed on her. But the context renders this reading unlikely.

Birkenhead, Chamberlain, and Derby will go to the Liverpool Unionist Conference and if the Ulstermen refuse, start it on Ulster. Until after that there is not likely to be much development. Before I left I told him that as I was helping him over the 'Ulster' difficulty, he should help us over the 'Crown and Empire,' when it came up."

According to himself, then, Griffith had indeed given an undertaking this Saturday, November 12th, but one that committed him no further, except that it was more direct and formal, than the assurance he had given on November 9th to Jones. They realised, he had then told Jones, "the value of the Boundary Commission as a tactical manœuvre, and if Lloyd George made it they would not queer his position." Surely he was making no further concession now by guaranteeing not to repudiate (*i.e.* not to come out in public decrying) Lloyd George "while he was fighting the Ulster crowd"? It was in this light that Griffith regarded the happenings of November 12th, and that his colleagues, who relied on him absolutely for their information, were bound to regard them. In his eyes, and consequently in theirs, the break on Ulster was still safe, and three weeks later we find him and them trying to stage it in the last hours of the Conference.

But if we turn from Griffith's account of his interview with Lloyd George to that given by Sir Austen Chamberlain, we shall suspect at once that the break on Ulster was from November 12th onwards closed to Sinn Fein. Chamberlain enters the story when, on that Saturday afternoon, he is summoned to 25 Park Lane, and finds there Lloyd George. Lloyd George tells him of the talk he has just had with Griffith.

His first task had been to impress Griffith at once with the gravity of the situation and the opportunity contained in it. The fate of the negotiations, he had said, hung on the efforts of Chamberlain and Birkenhead at the Liverpool Unionist Conference the coming Thursday.[1] If they succeeded in their mission, Die-hard opposition would be checkmated, England would not support Ulster in an unreasonable attitude, and the road to settlement would be clear at last.

But he had no intention of asking them to embark on an enterprise which, even if ultimate settlement resulted, might smash their political careers, unless he felt sure that he could rely on Griffith not to let him down.

He was going to offer Ulster two alternatives. An all-Ireland

[1] Cp. Griffith's letter: "This meeting on Thursday is a critical one for the Unionist leaders," etc. etc.

Parliament which they had already refused, or a Boundary Commission to adjust the Ulster boundary, as closely as possible in accordance with the wishes of the population. If they refused both, nevertheless he would proceed with the second. He would be much criticised for doing so, and there would come a crisis which he could only survive if he could represent his scheme as the one compromise acceptable to Southern Ireland.

He must be able, therefore, before sending Chamberlain and Birkenhead to Liverpool, to know that Griffith would lend the scheme his personal support—he did not expect and did not at the moment require the backing of the others. Indeed he did not want active sponsorship from Griffith; all he wanted was an assurance that if he confronted Ulster with the alternatives described, Griffith would not afterwards repudiate him, and break off the negotiations on the score of the Ulster clauses.

And Griffith had agreed to do what he was asked. He had promised "not to let Lloyd George down" on the British Ulster proposals; to find in them, that is to say, no cause for breaking off the negotiations. In effect, understood Chamberlain, Griffith's promise excluded any further possibility of a break coming on the Ulster head.

Moreover in order that there might be no misunderstanding of what the British Ulster terms actually were, Lloyd George had given instructions to Tom Jones to draw up a rough summary of the agreement reached. This was how matters stood when Chamberlain reached Park Lane.

But Lloyd George himself was in a hurry to leave for the week-end. Would Chamberlain mind checking the document when Tom Jones had drawn it up? The precaution was wise, for Jones, sharpest of secretaries to trap and render into formal draft exact shades of loosely expressed compromise, this once had missed perfection. However, with Chamberlain's help, the plan to which Griffith had become committed passed into memorandum form.

Sometime about 7 p.m. the next day, Sunday, November 13th, Jones showed Griffith the paper. Griffith briefly indicated his assent to its proposals.

What exactly did Griffith's acceptance of this paper involve? The paper itself ran as follows:

"*If Ulster did not see her way to accept immediately the principle of a Parliament of all Ireland* . . .[1] she would continue to exercise

[1] The omitted extract runs: "Coupled with the retention by the Parliament of Northern Ireland of the powers conferred upon it by the Act of 1920 and

through her own Parliament all her present rights; she would continue to be represented in the British Parliament, and she would continue subject to British taxation, except in so far as already modified by the Act of 1920. In this case, however, *it would be necessary to revise the boundary of Northern Ireland. This might be done by a Boundary Commission* which would be directed to adjust the line both by inclusion and exclusion so as to make the boundary conform as closely as possible to the wishes of the population."

Now it should be recognised that these proposals are nothing more than an elaborate statement of the plan of which Griffith had for some days been hearing from Jones, the plan described to the Dublin Cabinet in his letters of the 8th and the 9th. They are the terms which the Dublin Cabinet would understand him to be referring to in his letter of the 12th. There is no conflict therefore over the *nature* of the terms in which Griffith in some sense acquiesced.

But there are two patent differences between Chamberlain and Griffith; one an explicit difference, one implied; one concerned with Griffith's attitude to the British terms, one with the physical form in which those terms were presented. First, then, in Chamberlain's version Griffith promises "not to let Lloyd George down." And this is understood to mean that Griffith will not find cause in the British Ulster terms for a break, that he will accept them in fact as a concrete solution. According to Griffith himself, however, he does no more than promise not to repudiate Lloyd George "while he is fighting the Ulster crowd"; he accepts the British terms as a tactical manœuvre only.

And second, in Chamberlain's account Griffith is shown the terms in writing and gives assent to them in their written form. In Griffith's account there is no mention of any document.

What is the explanation of these two differences? The second must be decided in Chamberlain's favour and can be so decided without in the least reflecting on Griffith. It seems certain (from what happened on the last day of the Conference) that on November 12th Griffith did in fact acquiesce in some sense in *written* proposals. But that he should not have mentioned this fact to De Valera, or apparently to any of his colleagues, need cause no surprise, and is certainly no evidence whatever of any intentional

such other safeguards as have already been suggested in my letter of the 10th November—we should then propose to create such Parliament for all Ireland, but to allow Ulster the right within a specified time on an address to the throne carried in both Houses of the Ulster Parliament, to elect to remain subject to the Imperial Parliament for all the reserved services. In this case..."

concealment. For as explained above, the British terms were the same as those he had already described in the Dublin Cabinet, and it would seem to him quite unimportant that he had seen them written down.

But the second divergence (that bearing on the question of what Griffith actually said in relation to these terms) is harder to understand. Everyone is entitled to their own explanation. But for judgment, this piece of fore-knowledge is necessary: when Lloyd George used Griffith's pledge against Griffith in the last hour of the Conference, he was able to treat it as containing a promise "not to let himself (Lloyd George) down," and as precluding a Sinn Fein break on Ulster. And after a certain amount of trouble he was able to get Griffith (apparently acquiescent in this interpretation) to abandon the Ulster break. That is a known fact. In supplement we must introduce our theory.

Our theory is simply this: that on November 12th Griffith gave some kind of assent to the British Ulster proposals in language, or in a manner, that could afterwards be used to imply a much more far-reaching undertaking than Griffith conceived of at the time. For, whatever Griffith meant by the pledge when he gave it, Chamberlain understood it in the wider sense from the first, and we shall find him acting on that wider interpretation when he jeopardises his political future at Liverpool. (Indeed, it is certain that from the 12th onwards, all the British leaders acted on the assumption that if agreement could be reached on the other disputed points, Ulster would present no difficulty.) It will become very difficult therefore for Griffith to deny the wider interpretation when he is faced with it on December 5th, unless he is absolutely certain that on November 12th he made his meaning absolutely clear. And such certainty is just what he may not be able to feel.

For this point occurs to us. Griffith had explained his attitude towards the Boundary Commission in interviews with Jones on November 8th and 9th. But the 12th was the first day that he discussed the matter with Lloyd George. Is it not possible that he credited Lloyd George with already knowing his attitude pretty fully, and that he himself was at no great pains to elaborate what he thought Lloyd George already knew? Is it not possible that when he wrote to Dublin on the 12th he believed that he had left the exact impression described in his Report, but that later he could be made to feel that he had been much less explicit on the 12th than he should have been? Is it not likely that consequently he felt himself in fairness prevented from denying the interpretation that Lloyd George placed on his words?

If this be the truth then the existence of the document shown Griffith by Jones would be decisive. It is true that, even if Griffith had mentioned it to his colleagues, it is not certain that they would have scented danger. For, if Griffith's promise had involved no more than he and they thought, the fact that it referred to written terms might not have worried them. But in practice, if not in logic, the existence of a document made things so very much more definite. There, down on paper, were the terms in which Griffith had acquiesced. Where, on the other hand, were these qualifications which he believed he had made? The binding force of the terms would henceforth be very great, that of the qualifications henceforth very little.[1]

No misunderstanding must be allowed to arise from our account of Griffith's doings this day. No one with any knowledge of his character needs telling that he concealed nothing, and would never under any pressure have concealed anything from his colleagues, that he judged of material importance. In his report of the meeting of December 4th he described with no shadow of embarrassment the first occasion on which the British attempted to make use of his undertaking.[2] What is also worth noticing is that when the full facts about the undertaking came to light on December 5th, when it was made to play a crucial part in the Conferences of that day, and later when the records of that day's meeting were circulated, not the faintest suggestion was ever raised, even by the most bitter critics, that in giving the undertaking Griffith had acted unwisely—much less improperly. We, however, concerned only with tactical analysis, must record the

[1] Two alternative theories suggest themselves both premising that Griffith's account of the interview of the 12th was unquestionably correct and the account given to Chamberlain wrong. 1. That on December 5th, by which time the whole face of negotiations had changed, Griffith failed to recollect exactly what he had promised three weeks earlier; that by that time a distinction between accepting the Boundary Commission as a tactical manœuvre only and accepting it as a concrete solution—a distinction intricate enough in all conscience—had become somehow obscured in his mind. 2. That on December 5th Griffith came to feel that to break on Ulster at that stage would be violating even the limited pledge that he reported in his letter of the 12th; to feel, in other words, that since Lloyd George was still negotiating with Craig, to break on Ulster would be "to repudiate Lloyd George while he was fighting the Ulster crowd"—the one thing that he, Griffith, had without question foresworn. Neither of these versions is impossible, but that in the text seems far more likely to be true.

[2] Cf. Griffith's report of the Conference of December 4th: "Turning to our proposal I said that we did not take any responsibility for the Ulster proposals. They were theirs, not ours. They agreed but said that if Ulster refused them, they intended, nevertheless, to go on with them. I had said I would not let them down on them as against Craig. I confirmed this. I had given them my personal assurances but we were not responsible for putting them forward and could not be placed in such a position. They agreed."

opinion that the plan of accepting the Boundary Commission as a tactical manœuvre only, a plan always infinitely precarious, was finally stultified by Griffith's acceptance of the document of November 12th.

For, whatever our particular theories and reconstructions, our knowledge of what is to come compels us to lay down as historical fact, that henceforth it will be possible, when the crux comes, for Lloyd George to persuade Griffith that he is precluded by a solemn promise, given on November 12th, from bringing about the break on Ulster. And Griffith will not realise, and his colleagues will not have the chance of realising, that this blow is about to fall.

It remains to consider the wider aspects of the acceptance of the document, and in doing so to summarise the negotiations up to this point. Griffith from October 30th onwards had carried the Delegation with him in accepting or appearing to accept important sacrifices on Crown and Empire conditionally on the "essential unity" of Ireland being secured. This "essential unity" had at first taken the form of an all-Ireland Parliament, which Lloyd George had promised to secure or resign. Either dénouement would have been equally acceptable to Sinn Fein. Suddenly (see letter of the 9th) Griffith began to be impressed with the dangers rather than the attractions of a Lloyd George resignation. His prime desire was still to see an all-Ireland Parliament, but failing that (and by the 11th he knew that Ulster had refused once already), he wanted or must be supposed to have wanted to see a breakdown of the negotiations which yet left Lloyd George in power. To make this possible the Boundary Commission was accepted as a tactical manœuvre. But now a new stumbling-block arose. Lloyd George, to whose survival in office Griffith had come to pin his faith, refused to proceed with the Boundary Commission unless his assurances were very definite that "he would not be let down." And Griffith, in the strength of his desire to see the Boundary Commission used as a tactical manœuvre, gave pledges in relation to it that could later be used to persuade him that he had accepted it as something more. In short the Irish Delegation had indicated readiness to make great concessions on Crown, Empire and Defence in the hope of achieving either something very desirable, indeed almost beyond their dreams (an all-Ireland Parliament), or else a complete breakdown on a selected issue. The dream was fading, while the breakdown was being averted by the very diplomacy intended to bring it on. Only the concessions remained.

They had had Lloyd George in safe keeping as long as he was pledged to resign if he failed to push through an all-Ireland Parliament.

But he had wormed away from their hold; in a moment he would be turning round on them and it would be they, pulled down from their seats into the arena, who would be struggling for life. Responsibility, greater or less, for his escape, rests with all those on the Irish side who were privy to the gradual emergence, though it were for tactical purposes only, between the 8th and the 12th of the Boundary Commission as an alternative to the all-Ireland Parliament. Most of all, however, with Griffith, the man bearing the heaviest burden and occupying the post of greatest difficulty, for his acceptance of the document of November 12th. Save for that acceptance, when the crisis came the Delegation could have justifiably denied that they were committed to the Boundary Commission, even if Craig's consent to it had by that time been secured. And without Craig's consent to it they could have scoffed at its pretensions to achieve the "essential unity" of Ireland.

## CHAPTER XV

# THE SHIFT AGAINST THE SOUTH

"Because the good old rule
Sufficeth them, the simple plan,
That they should take who have the power,
And they should keep who can."

WORDSWORTH.

*Fresh British proposals—Decline in the Sinn Fein position—Rout of Die-hards at Liverpool Conference—Irish once more counter Dominion terms with External Association—Some Irish concessions on Defence.*

WE must not allow our reading of what follows to be too deeply coloured by our knowledge of the Park Lane promise, or by our easily-come-by suspicion that the break on Ulster is already doomed. It would be a fundamental mistake to think that at any time to the last hour or two of the negotiations Griffith realised that the chance of a break on Ulster had gone. If henceforth the structure of the Irish policy is subject to a fundamental flaw, it is one concealed from him no less than from his colleagues. From now on, however, strains which are eventually to find it out begin to be exerted against Sinn Fein.

The week just ended had brought good tidings to Dublin. Griffith had written on Friday the 11th, "The Ulster crowd are in the pit they digged for us," and on Saturday 12th, "If the Ulstermen refuse, they" (Chamberlain, Birkenhead and Derby) "will start it on Ulster; until after that there is not likely to be much development." The letters of the 15th, 16th and 18th suggest to us now a sudden turning of the tables, too staggering to be comprehended easily. Griffith writes on the 15th: "Lloyd George proposes to hand us a draft Treaty and leave it to us for our consideration for a couple of days. If agreement is reached on the Treaty, it is to be signed by us and by them—Parliament to be called together and a ratifying Act adopted." And he adds with apparent nonchalance, "The Treaty draft will of course probably raise crucial questions."

So it is Sinn Fein, not Ulster who are to be faced with crucial questions in the next few days? Where is the "pit" in which "Ulster was imprisoned" on the 11th, or "the starting it on Ulster," and "until then not much development" of the 12th?

On the 16th, the British draft duly arrived, its appointments lacking something of the customary Whitehall finish. It bore no official caption, address, or signature, and Childers, who had more than once irritated Griffith by meticulous attention to minutiæ, commented severely on the omission to De Valera. Birkenhead asked Griffith to come and see him in the evening (Lloyd George having retired to Bournemouth for a couple of days' rest), and he judged from Griffith's manner that he had not been greatly perturbed by the British terms. As a matter of fact, Griffith had spent a busy day reassuring the leaders of the Southern Unionists about land purchase, Second Chambers, double income-tax and educational and religious safeguards. When he wrote to De Valera in the evening, he had "only just read the thing over." The Irish Delegates were to meet for a full discussion the next day: he had had time, however, to reach a tentative conclusion. "Our reply on Friday should be, I think, that it won't do but that we'll have in an alternative Treaty proposal on Saturday or Monday."

One might think from Griffith's letter that there was something ambiguous, something that required analysing and measuring about the British document. Such was far from being true of its primary controversial propositions.

The Ulster arrangements were on the principles sketched by Griffith, and reported by him to De Valera on the 12th. Ulster was in theory to start under the jurisdiction of the new State, but the powers of the Parliament and Government of Northern Ireland would not be exercisable for twelve months, and between the end of the six and the twelve months Ulster could opt out and in effect retain the position and relation to the United Kingdom now possessed under the Act of 1920. If, however, she exercised this option, "a Commission shall be appointed to determine in accordance with the wishes of the inhabitants the boundaries between Northern Ireland and the rest of Ireland. And the boundary shall be such as may be determined by such a Commission."

The wording, or rather the omission of words in these draft terms of reference for the Commission are of exceptional significance. Wishes of the inhabitants alone are to decide. *There is no mention of the economic and geographic considerations that four years later were to prove decisive in losing the Irish Free State every atom of anticipated benefit.*

On Defence, Trade, and Finance, the old demands for facilities, for free cross-Channel trade and for Irish liability for a share of the National Debt were all in evidence. Yet for the first time the possibility of an Irish Naval Force one day coming into existence is envisaged, and the trade restriction is "not to be construed as preventing the imposition of Customs duties designed to prevent dumping or other unfair competition."

There was plenty here to gratify and encourage, but the first two all-important clauses were as flatly uncompromising as the equivalent passages in the terms of July. They seemed to place Ireland firmly and unequivocably inside the Empire. What hope did they give to those who felt that death was preferable to the dishonour of Empire membership? Still, there were certain notable omissions. There was no Oath, no mention of Allegiance, none of the Crown; Ireland was not even labelled a Dominion, merely assured of the status of one. Was there not room here for a definition of status along Republican lines? The real position of Canada in relation to the Imperial Parliament and Government need be no bar. For was not that in fact complete independence, save in matters of common concern in which Ireland, too, was ready to accept some measure of restriction? Could not therefore a counter document be submitted to the British rejecting no single one of these claims, yet proclaiming and emphasising a symbolism which would make all the difference to Ireland?

Reason this way though they might, it seems incredible to us now that the Irish leaders both in London and Ireland should not have recognised in these terms a British resolve unshaken and unshakable by argument that Ireland should come into the Empire; that they should not have begun to lay definite and detailed plans against a situation that one would have thought looked certain to arise when this basic British demand should be pushed to the point of war.

The terms of De Valera's reply to Griffith are worth studying for his precise reaction to the formal insistence on Ireland's entry into the Empire. He suggests that while it would be possible to follow the British procedure and submit an unsigned draft, yet "there has been so much beating about the bush already that I think we should now get down to definite business and send them as far as possible our final word."

And it should not be overlooked that he still maintains that the "exact line" on the main questions would best be presented by the draft Treaty prepared before the negotiations began, "modified somewhat to meet the exact position."

Griffith wrote again on the 18th, one passage in his letter concealing mild comedy. He relates his discovery, after a talk with Lloyd George and Birkenhead, that the British document was "not after all a Treaty draft," but contained "tentative suggestions only." What had really happened, unknown to Griffith, was that Lloyd George had reached Bournemouth before going through the document carefully; to discover to his horror that important safeguards offered to induce Ulster to come into an all-Ireland Parliament had somehow been omitted. Feverish telephoning ensued between himself, Jones, and the official draftsman. Eventually, it was decided to present it as indicating the British attitude on certain vital points, but as palpably not complete. The Irish, however, were not likely to cavil at this derogation from the document's status. It enabled Griffith to suggest to De Valera a reply with a similar document, not with a Treaty draft.

Passages more striking bear witness to the decline in the Irish position since the Saturday preceding: "The crucial question, Crown and Empire, must be next week. If Ulster gets us to break on them she will have re-won the game. The seriousness of the position will be realised by members of the Cabinet, and I trust they will give us their best weighed suggestions."

The day before, November 17th, the great Liverpool Conference had come off at last. To expound at length the internal stresses which through all this time bade fair to split the Conservative party would take us too far afield, and in any case, they have been dramatically elaborated by Mr. Stanley Salvidge in his absorbing life of his father. On his narrative and on the contemporary press we rely for a few outstanding instances. Gretton was to move the main resolution calling for the "condemnation of the long-continued ascendancy of crime and rebellion in Ireland"—a vote of censure on the British Government for negotiating with Sinn Fein at all. Salvidge, traditional champion of the Orange interest in Belfast, debated all Sunday (November 13th) with Lord Derby, his own son, and his own conscience; then decided, so long as Ulster was safeguarded, to use his influence for peace. By Tuesday morning the daily papers were featuring with head-lines his statement that "he would decidedly refuse while the negotiations were in progress to be identified with a revolt which would help neither Ulster nor the Unionist party." But already on Monday afternoon Birkenhead, "obviously under the impression that Salvidge was entirely hostile," had telegraphed to him from London: "*Whitehall—O.H.M.S. Absolute priority*. Am making special and secret journey to see you. Arriving Adelphi Hotel 9.30 to-night—leave communication there whether you are well enough to come and see me to-morrow morning about 10.30—if you are not I must come to Hoylake but I do not wish to do so. B.'.

The visit was kept successfully secret at a time when every member of the Irish Conference was dogged by journalists morning and night. Next morning Birkenhead received Salvidge in his bedroom thus: "Give me twenty minutes. Don't say a word. You could not come to the Cabinet so the Cabinet or at least its representative has had to come to you. Under a bond of secrecy which I ask you to give I am going to take you briefly through the inside story of the Irish Conference. . . ." These things and much else must be studied in Mr. Salvidge's pages. But one or two quotations are essential. "If Ulster declined to co-operate in Dominion Home Rule there would," said Birkenhead, "be no coercion. But at least in her own interest she should consider it and get the best terms possible. He would not agree to any settlement which did not preserve the supremacy of the Crown, that did not keep Ireland within the Empire, that did not leave the British navy the sole guardian of the shores and seas of Great Britain and Ireland, or that required Ulster's consent by duress. He could assure me that such a settlement was almost reached. It only required the impetus of a successful vote at the Liverpool Conference to carry it on to fruition."

Salvidge could see that Birkenhead "believed in the settlement more than he had ever believed in anything." He produced the morning papers with his own friendly announcement. But Birkenhead insisted that what Salvidge had in mind "did not go far enough." The Conservative Delegates "must have a clear mandate from the Party Conference for continuing the Irish negotiations." They themselves, however, were not coming to the Liverpool debate. "They held other men's secrets as well as their own. It is too dangerous for them to be cross-examined at such a gathering." Salvidge objected that he must have at least Worthington-Evans present. This point conceded, he agreed to do all that lay in his power.

The meeting concluded on a note of sentiment that does justice to Birkenhead's memory. "He said he realised it was a pretty tough job for me. He was returning to London but I had to go on living with people it might take years to see that what we were doing was the right thing for all the interests concerned. However, it was destiny, I could not avoid it, it had come to me. And even if it finished us both it would prove not a bad sort of finish. . . . He had to go then to catch his train. He went straight out to a waiting taxi with his coat collar up and his hat pulled down over his eyes."

After these romantic preliminaries the actual Conference comes almost as an anti-climax, though it is hard to imagine a day of more passionate outpouring or suspense felt more keenly at the time. Lord Farnham in a notable speech impressed the minds of all with the sufferings of the Southern Loyalists; General Prescott Decie won loud applause with an amiable reference to "parlance with the murder junta," and Colonel Gretton moved his vote of censure as bitterly as ever and rather more effectively. But Salvidge, Derby and Worthington-Evans always carried the bigger guns, and when it came to the vote an overwhelming majority supported the Salvidge amendment: "That this Conference expresses its earnest hope that consistently with the supremacy of the Crown, the security of the Empire and the pledges given to Ulster and the safeguarding of the interests of the minority in the South of Ireland, a solution of the Irish difficulties may be found in the Conference now in progress which will bring peace to Great Britain and Ireland, and strength to the Empire."

Chamberlain had been waiting out at Knowsley for the result, unable, till it was known, to determine finally his speech for that night's mass meeting at the Sun Hall. Now proceeding thither, he rose under the inspiration of the afternoon's decision to superb heights of oratory. In the finest speech of his life he scattered and silenced the Die-hards; and henceforth, for a few weeks at least, the Irish Conference could proceed without regard to their attentions. But the time had gone by when that prayed-for consummation could arouse much enthusiasm among Sinn Fein.

On Tuesday, November 22nd, the Irish Delegates met to consider a suitable reply to the British terms. A draft had been prepared by Erskine Childers, Barton and Gavan Duffy, principally by Erskine Childers. But owing to the animosity which Griffith had shown to proposals put forward by Childers it was decided to let Griffith, Collins and Duggan suppose that it emanated from Barton.

Discussion within the Delegation changed several essential features—its title, for instance. Toned down from "Heads of an Agreement" to "Memorandum by the Irish Representatives," it now committed its authors less compromisingly to precise concessions, less heroically to the stand on principle. Divided, however, unlike the documents of October 24th and 29th, into systematic definite clauses, it constituted even in its final modulated form the first detailed exposition of what in practice Ireland could accept.

The first three clauses defining Ireland's future status reproduced the root ideas of the previous proposals, and indeed of the draft Treaty originally brought to London. Legislative and Executive authority in Ireland were to have an exclusively Irish derivation, but Ireland was to be associated with the British Commonwealth "for purposes of common concern," enjoying in such an association rights equal to those of a Dominion, and in respect of the common purposes recognising the Crown "as the symbol and accepted head of the association." This recognition of the Crown had not been envisaged in the original draft Treaty, but it had been foreshadowed by Griffith in the last Plenary Session of October 24th, adumbrated in the propagandist proposals of the 29th, and referred to explicitly in the Griffith letter of November 2nd. From the Irish point of view, its inclusion now represented no new surrender; yet might not its appearance in black and white do something to introduce the British to the merits, now for the first time fully exposed, of External Association?

There was little about Ulster. The proposals were put forward "on the assumption that the 'essential unity' of Ireland was secured," and suggestions were made for persuading Ulster to accept a legislature subordinate to Dublin. None, however, for meeting the situation should Ulster refuse to come in. Trade and

Finance were pretty well as they had been all along, though an agreement was proposed under which certain selected commodities could be treated "on the basis of free trade." Under Defence, however, one could detect real concessions, considerable indeed compared with those of the draft Treaty, though anticipated perhaps in the document of October 29th and the letter of November 2nd.

The interval of waiting for the British reply was filled in with an unhappy disturbance. Barton, Gavan Duffy and Childers had continually maintained that all the concessions were being made on the Irish side. To prove this contention, which not unnaturally had caused resentment and dispute, Childers drew up a memorandum running point by point over the proposals of the 22nd in their final amended form. It must be confessed that the Chairman would not have been human who swallowed with equanimity a memorandum whose manifest ability would render it all the more infuriating. "Ireland's full claim," began Childers, "is for a Republic, unfettered by any obligation or restriction whatever." He concluded that "out of the ten paragraphs of the proposals Nos. 1 and 7 are the only ones which do not make concessions from this position."

Griffith read the document and was furious. He accused Childers of working against a settlement. Childers, a man of personality as concentrated as Griffith's, demanded the accusation in writing. Griffith indicated regret for what he had said. But henceforth there could be little more pretence that the Delegation was a band of friends, and no chance left of tolerably close co-operation.

Childers, the old Committee Clerk of the House of Commons, was prone to a formalism, strange to Ireland and, in the eyes of Griffith, ridiculous. The story is told of how Childers, in the best Whitehall tradition, would stamp "secret" on memoranda from, say, economic advisers in Dublin, and how Griffith could hardly bear the sight of the stamp. It has been said, and not by enemies of Griffith, that behind these trifling exasperations lay a genuine and growing suspicion that Childers was no honest friend of Ireland. Be that as it may, there is no doubt that Griffith saw in Childers, with his rigid limits on the verbal scope of the bargaining, an obstacle not much less menacing than the British themselves to a satisfactory settlement—that settlement to hopes of which Griffith had dedicated his life and surrendered all fortune, and which, once infinitely far off, seemed, but for Childers, certain to mature now. Put together the long wrangle over the Griffith letter of November 2nd, the scene at Hans Place when Lloyd George's first letter to Craig first reached Sinn Fein,[1] and now this last outburst over the Childers memorandum; recollect, too, the fact that it was thought necessary to substitute Barton's for Childers's name as author of the last proposals, and we shall get some picture of the level to which relations within the Delegation had sunk.

Barton and Duffy had more than once seriously considered resigning their posts. In the end, however, they had decided that Duffy should go over to Dublin and try to secure an instruction from the Cabinet that the sub-conference method must cease, and full conference be resumed. Not that they had any idea that Griffith and Collins were contemplating acceptance of Dominion terms. What they felt was that Griffith and Collins were easier going than they were, and were steadily getting the worst of it. They objected, too, to the tactics their side was pursuing. Lloyd George was being given the impression that if he proceeded strongly against Ulster, he could rely on a Dominion settlement, whereas Griffith surely knew that such a settlement was out of the question. And Barton once went so far as to tell Griffith that these tactics were not fair. Duffy, however, failed to impress the Cabinet in Dublin with their forebodings. His mission was a complete failure.

His position and Barton's became in consequence unenviable. They saw courses adopted which they despised and feared. But they were always in a minority, and they had been originally selected as likely to "work in well with Griffith and Collins." With the rejection of Duffy's warning their main positive function was frustrated. Barton fought on to win the fiscal autonomy—a vital triumph. In relation, however, to the main drift of the struggle, the pair lingered, embarrassed, Cassandra-like, inevitable victims of the tragedy which eventually overtook them on the evening of the 5th. It is true that they could have cut the knot by resigning, but to have done so was to present England with a heaven-sent opportunity for driving home the wedge, and to discredit their country in its first international trial. They would have felt no option if they had had any idea that Griffith and Collins would even consider a Dominion solution. But in the case of Griffith, their realisation only came after November 22nd, and gradually, and in the case of Collins, not till the hour of travail following Lloyd George's final ultimatum.

Of course, there was another side to all this. Griffith and Collins

[1] See footnote, p. 173.

might argue that they were the leaders; that the others were there to render them expert assistance, Barton on trade, Gavan Duffy on constitutional law and over points of drafting; that these two, and still more Childers, had no business to develop counter-policies of their own, to constitute themselves a kind of watch committee with, it was suspected, independent reports to Dublin, and generally to devote their energies to criticism rather than supplementary construction. Griffith and Collins could argue, too, that they themselves, and to some extent Duggan, were the only men who so far had been able to establish anything that could be called negotiating relations. That it was easy enough to take-up a magnificent static attitude and say "no" to everything; but settlement implied compromise, compromise exchange, and exchange exploration this way and that of countless combinations. That risks had to be taken to circumvent an enemy immune to frontal assaults; that what the Delegation required was help in taking them successfully, not complaints that they were being taken at all. Add to this a natural irritation that it should be Barton, Gavan Duffy and Childers who should take the strong self-righteous line in the privacy of the Delegation sitting-room, while it was they themselves, Griffith and Collins, who alone up to this point had made any real impression on the British.

## CHAPTER XVI

# EXTERNAL ASSOCIATION ON THE TABLE

"Only we still retain
The name and all the additions of the king;
The sway, revenue, execution of the rest,
. . . be yours."

SHAKESPEARE: *King Lear*.

*Deadlock for a time—Sub-Conferences on Wednesday, 23rd, and Thursday, 24th November—Chartres on External Recognition of the Crown—The conflict reduced to one of symbols——Birkenhead adamant—Irish proposals to be formulated in writing.*

THE Irish document piqued and disappointed Lloyd George. It struck him as a flat and definite refusal of the only arrangement, Dominion Status, which it was possible for England to consider.

He sent for Jones and asked him his opinion. Jones, who was more intimately in touch than his chief with stresses internal to the Irish Delegation, thought that the document showed signs of distinct advance in spirit. He cited the recognition of the Crown, and the open mind shown on the whole question of defence facilities.

Lloyd George now imposed on him a delicate mission; to present the Irish Delegates with an effective ultimatum, yet see to it that on no account were negotiations broken off. Jones knew that now, as on so many occasions hereabouts, he would receive unstinted censure if he allowed the Irish Delegation to pack up and go. On the other hand, it had been made equally clear to him that any excess of encouragement of the Irish would lead to his instant repudiation by Lloyd George.

The Irish proposals had been handed in at 12 noon. Jones rang up Griffith at 1 o'clock, and with a fine show of haste, was round at Hans Place at 1.15. Lloyd George, he said, was in despair about the document; Birkenhead and Chamberlain also considered it quite impossible. It did not accept the Crown and the Empire. It brought them back to where they were six weeks ago, and treated all the discussions since then as though they had never been. Lloyd George's only idea of a reply to it was a letter ending the negotiations, but Jones was desperately anxious to find some way of warding off this disaster. Could not Griffith withdraw the document, or at least substitute for it some more conciliatory statement? Griffith replied that the document could not be withdrawn or supplanted. He argued the case for the proposals *seriatim*. On Crown and Empire they had indicated a method of association which was favourable to both sides. On Defence, the British Admiralty had put forward contradictory claims whose emergence in coherent shape the Irish were sympathetically awaiting.

Deadlock was complete on the face of things, but between the two men, both intent on keeping the negotiations alive, a bridge was not likely to fail. Jones mentioned that Lloyd George had asked for specific safeguards for Ulster, and that there was no reference to them in the Irish Treaty. Griffith pointed out that the draft agreed to extend safeguards when Ulster should have stated her requirements. Jones admitted that Lloyd George had misunderstood this part. There might be other misunderstandings. Could not Griffith and Collins meet Lloyd George and Birkenhead and see if the ambiguities could be cleared up?

Collins now happened to arrive at Hans Place, and Griffith asked him to come in. During the conversation Griffith suggested that the British Government was trying to get a blank cheque from them, which would be playing Craig's game. "Jones," he wrote afterwards, "was taken aback at this view, which he denied." The rest of the interview assumed the form that one would have thought would by now have become thoroughly familiar, not to say ominous, to Griffith. Yet his suspicions did not seem to have been aroused. He wrote that: "The British hoped to meet Craig on Thursday under an agreement with us that would enable them to defy him and his backers. Owing to the crux over the Crown and Empire, they felt their position weakened, if not gone." To which there would seem to have been a simple answer: "You have already extracted from us very considerable concessions on the plea of strengthening you against Craig. You have said repeatedly that the latest advance on our part was all that you required for your purpose. You are now attempting to make us travel the whole way before Ulster moves an inch." Griffith may have talked to Jones somewhat in this sense, but in his heart he does not seem to have realised the danger and, from his point of view, the unfairness of the British change.

The next sentence in Griffith's letter is one to mark. He has just referred to the "crux" over Crown and Empire, and he continues: "In view of your letter of October 25th, I cannot discuss the alternative with them." The concluding passages explain his meaning. He mentions that a meeting has been arranged for the next day between Lloyd George, Birkenhead and possibly Chamberlain, and Griffith, Collins and Barton (the last a noteworthy addition). "We shall urge the acceptability of the arrangement *re* association we have proposed, but I have little hope of any good result." Griffith is obviously trying to explain to De Valera that a settlement can be reached, but not unless Ireland assents to come into the Empire and pay allegiance to the Crown. Are we wrong in reading further an implied entreaty to let the Delegation at least discuss a settlement on those lines? Is it not permissible to find a hint in Griffith's language of his having by that time reached a personal conclusion that such a solution should in all the circumstances be accepted?

The meeting of November 23rd was inconclusive. "On the Crown," reported Griffith, "they had no alternative, they must fight. We put up our counter proposal briefly, but they declared it impossible." On Defence, Trade and Ulster, progress was made in clearing away misunderstandings. For example, the right to occupy all or any of the Irish ports would only operate as a right in the event of war and not as the Irish had imagined under peace conditions. Lloyd George, returning from a private consultation with his colleagues, intimated that before he met Craig he must know where he stood on fundamentals. "If he had to fight on fundamentals, there was no help for it, but it would be a tragedy if we broke up on any verbal or technical misunderstandings." All this time he had been acting towards Ulster on the basis of the Griffith letter of November 2nd. Griffith and Collins had seen Lord Birkenhead before that letter was finally dispatched. He suggested that these three should meet again.

The proposal was not so innocent as it looked. It meant little else than the elimination of Barton, the spearhead in British eyes of the De Valera-Childers faction. Nor was Birkenhead behind Lloyd George in guile. He expressed a hope that Griffith and Collins would bring with them a constitutional lawyer, and declared himself satisfied when Griffith agreed to bring with them Mr. Chartres. While the British were absent, Birkenhead had discovered that Griffith would be likely to pass over Childers and pitch on Chartres. He had learned, too, a good deal about Chartres's experience and attainments. His inquiries had confirmed his self-confidence—as well they might.

Expert indexer of *The Times* Library, formidable, even deadly antagonist in a controversy over Workmen's Compensation, it was unlikely that in knowledge of any branch of constitutional law Chartres would make much headway against a British Lord Chancellor who, in the constitutional field, was known to carry a professorial erudition at his finger-tips.

These disparities and those of dialectics apart, Birkenhead's massive authority, relaxing at times into a mild, almost fatherly benediction, could be relied upon to ward off serious inroads on the British attitude of "non-possumus." Yet the fact of the debate could subsequently substantiate a British announcement that after full and fair technical controversy the legal impossibility of External Association had been demonstrated once for all.

When the next day arrived, however, each side had added to its forces. The Irish included Gavan Duffy, an unwelcome visitor from the intransigent camp. Birkenhead brought Sir Gordon Hewart, the Attorney-General, whose rather curious status in the British Delegation (he was to act with the others when constitutional questions were discussed) conferred on him some of the chilly glamour of an impartial expert from outside. Whereas Birkenhead was admittedly partisan.

The subject for discussion was the position of the Crown under the proposed Treaty of Association.[1] Chartres spoke of the importance of agreement on the realities of the new relationship before attempting to discover a formula based on those facts. In matters of common concern, Ireland would be prepared to recognise the Crown as head of the aggregate of States. But on purely Irish affairs she must be absolutely independent. To Hewart's question whether it was proposed not merely that the Crown should not in practice function in Ireland, but that it should be made impossible for it to do so, Chartres replied that within Ireland the Crown should have no existence whatever.

Lord Birkenhead was most accommodating. On the realities it soon appeared that there was no difference between him and the Irish. Ireland, he said, would possess the status of Canada. No interference in Ireland was intended. He even went so far as to suggest that it could be expressed on the face of the Treaty that the Crown should not act in Ireland except on the advice of Irish Ministers.[2] Your status, he repeated, "would be that of Canada," and when Chartres sarcastically quoted "as nearly as may be," Birkenhead said that those words could go out if any great point was made of them.

Chartres now turned himself to explaining why it was that a royal symbolism, not in fact involving any material interference with their internal freedom, was yet offensive to, and intolerable for Irishmen. "We must deal with the existing fact that in Ireland there is the greatest distrust of the British Government." Ireland would quite fail to be convinced that Lloyd George was sincere in offering Ireland "control of every nerve and fibre of her national life" if at the same time it was proposed to set up a royal veto, however much it was alleged that the latter would not be allowed to function.

Lord Birkenhead did not meet this objection directly. He emphasised instead the British way of looking at the Crown. In Ireland it would be no more than a symbol, just as it was no more than a symbol in Canada. (In other words, it would have no power to influence Ireland's fortunes against her will.) Yet its utility in binding together in voluntary union the various members of the

[1] For what follows we rely largely on the only full account in existence, that drawn up by Chartres after the meeting. That account did not pass unchallenged at the time, but the criticisms levelled at it do not invalidate it for our purposes. See Appendix 3.

[2] This provision was not in fact included in the Treaty. Irish gains during the last days of the negotiations (see November 29th) presumably made it seem unnecessary, but the claim was not officially admitted by the British till the Imperial Conferences of 1926 and 1930.

Commonwealth was immense. "Symbols might be very important." Gavin Duffy now interposed, urging two vital reasons for placing Ireland in a different position towards the Crown from that of the Colonies. First in the case of the Colonies, but not in Ireland's, the Crown symbolised a unity based on something real, the tie of blood. Secondly, the Crown was the executive authority in the colonies, a position Ireland could never accept. Geographical reasons alone linked the Crown too closely to Downing Street for Ireland ever to accept it as impartial.

The last point was bringing the Irish case back to the practical danger to Ireland inherent in the Crown. It was not likely to impress Lord Birkenhead, who had already expressed himself perfectly ready to remove all doubts on this material plane. Chartres cut through the finely drawn hypotheses, accepted for the moment Birkenhead's declaration that the Crown would be impotent in practice, and argued strongly that the whole vital discussion over Ireland's future was proceeding on a mere technicality. Lord Birkenhead did not contradict him, but said that the British people attached the greatest importance to the symbol of the Crown.

The issue was now at last, perhaps for the first time in the negotiations, fairly stated and fully faced. Chartres had explained that the Irish people insisted on a symbolism tolerable to themselves. Birkenhead had retorted that the British people also had their symbolism which they would never allow Ireland to repudiate.

The moment was ripe for an Irish leader, heavy-armed with debating weapons, to push the argument home: to refuse to allow Birkenhead simply to say that the British people would not stand this or that: to make him disclose their reasons for insisting on Allegiance, at least as fully as the Irish had disclosed theirs for resisting it, and to make him produce his own justification in logic and morals for the British attitude. Once Birkenhead had been forced to describe his difficulties, there would have been some chance of proposing alternative schemes to overcome them.

If Griffith had been arguing the Irish case, he might have done something to make Birkenhead expose his hand. But in the nature of things, such slashing offensive courses were not for Chartres or anyone in his position. He tried instead to interest Birkenhead in a scheme under which the Irish legislature should evidence their acceptance by voting annually a contribution to the King personally, to form part of the civil list. Birkenhead knew the answer to this: "It would be a fine gesture and would undoubtedly make a very great impression on the British people, but it would not meet the great difficulty."

The rest of the discussion was mainly occupied with vigorous orations from Collins, Griffith and Gavan Duffy. Collins argued that Ireland was offering a great concession to British sentiment for the sake of a real peace. Then Griffith took up the tale in a classical statement of the advantages of External Association. Never afterwards should either Irish party have argued that he failed to devote his energies to pleading it. But the moment when he could have caught up Birkenhead had passed; the British position had gone on record, its reasonableness unquestioned.

Still, Griffith made a bold showing: "Surely this corner can be turned; are we to resume war on a mere technicality? We met on the basis that each held his own position. We have moved nearer to one another. For external affairs, such as peace and war and defence, Ireland will recognise the British Crown in the way we have explained, while for internal affairs she will retain the Republic." A fragment of dialogue that followed was destined to make history. Griffith: "You may prefer to translate 'Saorstat Eireann' by 'Free State' (instead of Republic). We shall not quarrel with your translation." Lord Birkenhead: "The title, Free State, can go into the Treaty."

"The Irish proposals," concluded Griffith, "are a *via media* between two apparently irreconcilable positions. They preserve the honour and interests of both peoples, and satisfy the pride of both. They could end the struggle of centuries."

Hewart, who had hitherto cut no great figure, assured the Irish Delegates (so Chartres relates) that they must not suppose that the British Government was contemplating the alternative of war. Birkenhead, however, at once removed any impression of tenderness. On all other issues there was substantial agreement, but this issue (allegiance to the Crown) was vital. Behind these words lay war as the alternative to settlement. Gavan Duffy and Griffith made final appeals. Birkenhead requested that the Irish proposals for recognition of the Crown should be formulated in writing. This was agreed to.

## CHAPTER XVII

# NOVEMBER 25TH TO DECEMBER 2ND

"Slip past, slip fast,
Uncounted hours from first to last,
Many hours till the last is past
  Many hours dwindling to one—
One hour whose die is cast,
  One last hour gone."

CHRISTINA ROSSETTI.

*A visit to Dublin—A new Irish document—No real concessions—Monday, November 28th, Chequers—Tuesday, November 29th, Sub-Conference—Important Irish gains—Attendant embarrassments—Thursday, December 1st, British final draft—Small revisions—Last financial controversies—The Irish leave for Dublin.*

WE can move a little faster now. Lloyd George had seen Craig on the 24th after the "Chartres–Hewart Conference," but the outcome, largely negative, was not to appear till November 29th. Meanwhile the Irish had undertaken to prepare and submit a formula expressing the limited sense in which they were ready to recognise the Crown. A consultation in Dublin was indicated and thither the Delegation repaired. Collins had returned almost every week-end, but it was Griffith's first visit during the negotiations.

At a Cabinet Meeting in Dublin on Friday, November 25th, two decisions were unanimously approved. (1) That Ireland should recognise the British Crown for the purposes of association, as symbol and accepted head of the combination of associated States; (2) that an annual sum be voluntarily voted to the civil list. In each case the unanimity represented an advance towards compromise. Ideas originating with Chartres and developed in London were now stamped with the assent not only of De Valera and Cosgrave but of Brugha and Stack. But since the first of the ideas in question had been common property among the Delegation in London for a month at least, and had been touched on in discussions with the British for almost as long, while both ideas together had only the previous day been found utterly inadequate by Birkenhead and Hewart, it cannot be said that the Delegation returned to London much richer in expedients than when they left.

On Monday 28th they handed in a memorandum yet once more expressing and justifying their conception of External Association. The proposals were followed by a note, the whole being signed by Griffith as Chairman, but described as a "memorandum by the Irish Delegates." The note, though brief, strikes one as about the ablest document that emanated from Hans Place. Yet the arguments it relied on were always such as laid themselves open to an effective answer. Briefly, it contended that allegiance to the Crown, acknowledgment even of the existence of the Crown within Ireland, would in practice for geographical and historical reasons deny Ireland that freedom which admittedly the Dominions possessed. "The Crown thousands of miles away would never menace the Dominions with its powers. The Crown close at hand would prove a constant menace of this kind."[1]

The Irish contention that while in theory the Crown in Ireland would be identical with the Crown in the Dominions, yet in fact it would retain powers in Ireland that in the Dominions had long been obsolete, expressed a general suspicion which Childers more than anyone inspired. Years spent in studying the Irish policies of England had forced on him the conclusion that whatever the reason, lay it in history, geography or the whole ideology of Imperialism, England could not be trusted to behave towards Ireland with reasonable fairness or honour. It seemed to him that if the Irish accepted Dominion Status they would be entrusting England through the Crown or Imperial Parliament with powers that legally entitled her to treat Ireland as a subordinate, but which it was hoped that England, following her conduct towards the Dominions, would forbearingly render nominal. Now it was the essence of Childers's argument that there was neither the same temptation nor the same opportunity in the case of the Dominions as in that of Ireland to use the legal powers up to the hilt. England's forbearance towards the Dominions was inevitable and cost her nothing. Towards Ireland, it would involve considerable voluntary sacrifice. To ensure the continuance for all time of this sacrifice Childers reckoned it madness to rely on the development in directions favourable to Ireland of an unwritten British Constitu-

[1] A last paragraph emphasises the immense concession represented by Ireland's recognition of the Crown in any capacity whatever. Its opening words, "We offer a solution that is practicable and honourable," were afterwards used by opponents of the Treaty to show that External Association had indeed been the official plan.

tion, whose authoritative interpretation would always rest in the hands of British jurists.

These were not the only grounds on which Childers was ready to resist to the death—no figure of speech—the status of a Dominion. He was just as strong, stronger even, on the national degradation of a surrender under duress of the symbols of a declared independence. But the special argument just explained, appealing to his own intellectual imagination and Griffith's forensic gifts, was always likely to be pushed forward in discussions with the British to the neglect of the other more elemental conviction.

Childers now presented to the Delegation a memorandum entitled "Law and Fact in Canada and Ireland," outlining with masterly compression of learning the position of Canada, first in strict constitutional law, and then in actual fact.

In Law: Canada is a subordinate dependency.

In Fact: Canada is by the full admission of British statesmen equal in status to Great Britain and as free as Great Britain.

In Law: The British Parliament can make laws for Canada.

In Fact: Canada alone can legislate for Canada.

In Law: The British Government can veto Canadian Bills.

In Fact: It cannot.

In Law: The Crown has supreme authority in Canada.

In Fact: The Crown has no authority in Canada. It signifies sentiment only.

In Law: There is an Oath of Allegiance to the Crown in Canada.

In Fact: The Canadian owes obedience to his own constitution only.

In Law: The Governor-General is the nominee of the British Cabinet only.

In Fact: He is the joint nominee of the Canadian and British Cabinets.

This document should be borne in mind in reflecting on the Irish reaction to certain British concessions now at hand. It is true that Childers had begun the memorandum by asserting (1) that what with restrictions on Defence and Trade Ireland was not even on paper being offered full Dominion rights, and (2) that in any case Dominion Status was inappropriate to an Ireland that was "not a colony but an ancient and spirited nation with an inherent claim to independence." Nevertheless, the burden of the memorandum seemed to be that the *chief reason* why Ireland could not accept the British terms was because in her case unlike Canada's the law would be the fact, and the nominal subordination be real.

On the evening of Monday 28th, Griffith was asked to come down to Chequers to discuss his latest proposals. He agreed to come and bring Duggan, but following the rule adhered to throughout by his party he declined to accept hospitality. The meeting after dinner with Lloyd George, Birkenhead and a newcomer, Sir Robert Horne, Chancellor of the Exchequer, was short but momentous. Lloyd George, confronted for the fourth time (October 24th, October 29th, November 22nd, November 28th) with a document declining Allegiance, fell back on his habitual formula. "The document is impossible. Any British Government that attempted to propose to the British people the abrogation of the Crown would be smashed to atoms." Griffith replied as placidly as ever that they had no authority to deal on any other basis than the exclusion of the Crown from purely Irish affairs. The discussion then became general.

Suddenly the British hold on the rope loosened; the Irish went sprawling on their backs. They found themselves offered the chance of inserting in the Treaty "any phrase they liked which would ensure that the position of the Crown in Ireland should be no more in practice than it was in Canada or in any other Dominion." On the face of it here was a concession which alone made worth while these long racking negotiations. The bogey reared by Childers in which they had all believed was effectively scotched at last, was to be outlawed in the printed text.

But the next moment showed the Irish the embarrassments of the new gift. For what was now to prevent acceptance of the British terms? As Griffith wrote next day to De Valera: "With this offer they knocked out my argument on the document they sent in—that the Crown in the Dominions was merely a symbol but that in Ireland it would be a reality." For so much of the opposition to Dominion Status had been concentrated behind the plea that such status would not be the real thing in the case of Ireland. It was pretty hard to be called upon at this stage to find a completely new set of reasons for opposition.

Yet the gain, whatever its tactical inconveniences, was in itself a capital achievement. According to the promise given this day, Ireland in the Treaty receives not only the law of Canada, but in addition her practice and constitutional usage. If during the last ten years Childers has proved a false prophet and Ireland so far from being denied constitutional advantages accruing to the other Dominions, has actually led the way in Dominion constitutional advance, the credit must go to the splendid persistence of Griffith, and of Childers himself.

The concession, again, while dismissing the leading overt argument for resistance, had added to the attractions of Dominion Status. The British hastened to illustrate the range of independence it conferred. The elective head would be the Premier. The nominal head, the King's representative, would be only appointed in consultation with the Irish ministry. No one would ever be appointed to whom the Irish ministry offered any objection. They guaranteed that he would have no power, be in fact merely a symbol.

They went further, and on one matter to which the Irish had kept doggedly recurring, held out the possibility not only of equation but of progress beyond the other Dominions. "The Oath of Allegiance," reported Griffith, "was an immense difficulty with them, but they would try to modify it if that would help us."

Griffith and Duggan drove back to London through the night fortified with the first two substantial successes won by their team. Sterilisation of the Crown! Modification of the Oath! The collapse of the argument hitherto most relied on against Dominion Status assumed subsidiary proportions.

The next day, Tuesday, November 29th, Griffith, Collins and Duggan met Lloyd George, Chamberlain and Birkenhead at 10 Downing Street. Barton and Gavan Duffy after their brief emergence in the previous week were again being left behind. Little more was done than confirm the conversation of the previous evening and arrange the end of the programme. The British offered to put a phrase in the Treaty ensuring them that the Crown should have no more authority in Ireland than in Canada. They produced a form of oath different from the one subscribed to by members of Dominion Parliaments. The Irish refused it, but there was in no sense a deadlock. The Irish stated their case under Defence and Trade.

What took place in arranging the programme is described by Griffith thus; the final sentence is peculiarly interesting. "They proposed to send their final proposals to Craig and ourselves on Tuesday (December 6th). We objected. We should see them beforehand. They agreed to send us them on Thursday evening (December 1st) but formally to hand them to us on Tuesday."

Now on the same day Craig was making a statement in the Ulster Parliament, a statement agreed upon by Lloyd George at their last meeting (on November 24th). "By Tuesday next (November 29th) either negotiations will have broken down or the Prime Minister will send me new proposals for consideration by the Cabinet. In the meantime the rights of Ulster will be in no way sacrificed or compromised."

It seems clear then that Lloyd George's plan when he saw Craig on Thursday 24th, and the one that he would still have preferred on Tuesday 29th, was to send his final proposals to Craig at the same time as he sent them to Griffith. The Irish Delegates thought that they were obtaining an advantage in seeing the proposals before Craig saw them. But actually they did themselves a disservice by this policy. For without it they would have been in the same position as was De Valera towards the terms handed him in July. There would have been no ultimatum. There would have been plenty of time to discuss the terms in Dublin and reach a decision there.

Wednesday passed without incident. On Thursday arrived the "final" British proposals. "I enclose," wrote Lloyd George in an accompanying letter, "a draft of the Treaty which we are prepared to submit for the approval of Parliament." The incidents from now till the signature of the Treaty may be set out in schedule.

*Thursday, December 1st.*—Griffith and Collins see Lloyd George, Chamberlain, Churchill, Birkenhead.

*Friday, December 2nd.*—(*a*) Griffith travels by day to Ireland.
(*b*) Collins and Childers discuss Ulster financial arrangements with Lloyd George, Horne, Curtis, Hawtrey, etc.
(*c*) Collins and residue of Irish Delegation cross by night to Dublin carrying British terms.

*Saturday, December 3rd.*—Meeting in Dublin of Irish Cabinet and Delegation.

*Sunday, December 4th.*—(*a*) Irish Delegates prepare counter-proposals.
(*b*) Irish counter-proposals rejected by British.
(*c*) Lloyd George, through Jones, tries to get Collins to come and see him.

*Monday, December 5th.*—9.30 a.m. Collins sees Lloyd George.
10.20 ? a.m. Lloyd George sees the King.
12 noon. British Cabinet Meeting.

3 p.m. to 8 p.m. approx. Griffith, Collins, Barton meet Lloyd George, Birkenhead, Chamberlain, Churchill.
9 p.m. to 11.15 p.m. Final discussion at Hans Place.
11.20 p.m. Conference resumed.

*Tuesday, December 6th.*—2.20 a.m. Treaty signed.

The document presented on Thursday, December 1st was to undergo many alterations; its chief economic provision was to be scrapped; but it remained the "final draft" in the sense that no further document was submitted from the British side; its amended text was to emerge five days later as the Treaty. Compared with the British terms of the 16th, it reflected the concessions mooted at Chequers. The grant of Canadian practice was to supplement that of Canadian law, and the Oath, while it still imposed allegiance to the Crown, did so now only in view of the Crown's capacity "as head of the State and the Empire," and it put Ireland easily first.[1] By the time it reaches the Dublin Cabinet on Saturday, December 3rd, certain alterations will have been engineered by Griffith and Collins on December 1st and by Collins and Childers on December 2nd.

The changes of the 1st were minor save for one new inspiring pledge. Clause 6 had ordained that the coastal defence of Ireland was to be undertaken "exclusively by His Majesty's Imperial forces *until an arrangement has been made* (our italics) between the British and Irish Governments whereby the Irish Free State undertakes her own coastal defence." There had been no promise that an arrangement of this kind would ever be reached or approached. An amendment, if it did not ensure, at least extended a reasonable hope of change within a definite period. "The foregoing provisions of the Article shall be reviewed at a conference of representatives of the British and Irish Governments at the expiration of ten years."

The revisions incorporated, the British draft reached Griffith at 1 a.m. (Friday, December 2nd). By 8.30 he was *en route* for Ireland. Collins stayed behind for a last tussle over financial safeguards for Ulster. At 11.30 a.m., accompanied by Childers, he met Sir Robert Horne and Curtis at the Treasury. He refused a clause suggested by Horne, and promised to return at 5 o'clock, with one of his own. This time he came alone to confront Lloyd George, Horne, R. G. Hawtrey of the Treasury (already competent to dazzle and befog beyond the common run of economists), and British Government draftsmen. His clause was not accepted, nor

[1] For details see Appendix 4A.

could he accept the proposal eventually handed in by the British. Not till the following Monday was an agreement reached, Ulster and the Free State being then left to come to a financial arrangement between themselves.

This day, Friday, therefore, had no direct influence whatever on subsequent events, yet it would have been pleasant to have lingered over its discussions. They showed Collins at his versatile best. How many clerks trained in the lower walks of the Stock Exchange and the Guaranty Trust could have held their own in financial interchange with two ex-Chancellors of the Exchequer, and the most bewildering of contemporary economists? Collins was immensely indebted to Childers, steeped in the financial lore of Anglo-Irish relationship since the days of the *Framework of Home Rule*, and at the end of this day's discussion Collins warmly acknowledged the debt. Yet the other side had Curtis, a recognised authority on the relations financial and otherwise of associated or federalised communities. And all day it fell to Collins to play the responsible, the statesman's part. He came away at night with a clause that, unsatisfactory, was yet an improvement, and with the feeling that in the last resort England for once at least would leave an Irish question in Irish hands.

Collins, Gavan Duffy and Childers caught the night train from Euston to complete the gathering of the Irish forces at next day's meeting in Dublin. Collins was in fine spirits on the train. There was the Oath to be dealt with. There was fiscal autonomy to be secured, and an independent army. But, these things accomplished —the possibilities were tremendous.

Saturday dawned, day of challenge and critical decision for Ireland. It ran its painful, feverish course. It ended with the challenge half met, with several decisions taken, but, for reasons understandable in the case of each individual, with one conceivable emergency left unprovided for, one most vital decision ignored.

CHAPTER XVIII

# THE CABINET MEETING IN DUBLIN, SATURDAY, DECEMBER 3RD

"Vain wisdom all, and false philosophy."
MILTON: *Paradise Lost.*

*The Cabinet and the Delegation—Views on the British draft—Opinion divided—Griffith, Collins, Duggan—Barton, Gavan Duffy, Childers—A scene with Brugha—The Cabinet left alone—De Valera and Brugha—Full session resumed—Griffith reassures the Cabinet—An Oath of loyalty to External Association agreed on—Irish amendments to British draft—An incomplete Mandate.*

ELEVEN a.m. saw gathered at the Mansion House, Dublin, the seven members of the Cabinet—De Valera, Griffith, Brugha, Stack, Collins, Barton and Cosgrave; the Delegates outside the Cabinet, Duggan and Gavan Duffy; Erskine Childers, Secretary to the Delegation; and Kevin O'Higgins, Assistant Minister for Local Government, who was accustomed to attend, though not to vote, at Cabinet meetings.

For the seven vital hours that were to follow, it would be impossible to conceive a worse preparation than that which had befallen Collins, Gavan Duffy and Childers. At 3.30 that morning, their boat had collided with a schooner off the North Stack. Four only of the schooner's crew had been saved.[1] They had been taken aboard the mail-boat and conveyed back to Holyhead, and it was not till 10.15 a.m. that the Irish Delegation landed at Kingstown. Childers's case was typical. He had worked till 2.30 a.m. the night before, he had spent Friday in ceaseless technical exertion; he slept no wink all Friday night. They were a desperately tired and haggard little party when they arrived at the Mansion House.[2]

The opinions of the Delegates and their Secretary were at once taken whether the British draft, which represented in theory, final

[1] The Irish party showed up prominently, reassuring the passengers, at a moment of some alarm. "I have been in tighter corners than this," said Michael Collins.

[2] For comments on the final draft and for our authorities for this day's meeting see Appendix 4. O'Murchadha, Assistant Secretary to the Cabinet, took some unofficial notes, whose value has been much disputed.

terms, should be accepted or rejected. Griffith spoke strongly in favour of acceptance. He refused to break on the question of the Crown, giving as one reason that to do so would be to hand to Ulster the position from which she had been driven. He emphasised his conviction now and repeatedly throughout the day that these were substantially the best terms that could be wrung from Britain.

Barton disputed the last point hotly. He felt sure that England's last word had *not* been reached, and that she would *not* declare war on the question of Allegiance. As they stood, the terms would not even give Dominion Status, nor any guarantee in the matter of Ulster. He would vote against acceptance. Gavan Duffy was just as definite as Barton against the Treaty. He, too, believed that England was bluffing. The Irish proposals, with small reservations on Defence, could be obtained. He put forward a new suggestion, that the Treaty be rejected by the Dail, and the amended draft be sent back to London with reinforced authority.

On the other side were Duggan and, so it would appear, Collins. Duggan agreed with Griffith. The Treaty was England's last word, and he refused to take the responsibility for saying "No." Collins's attitude was more obscure. He had been in high spirits starting back from London the previous evening, but back in the atmosphere of the Cabinet with two deadly opponents at his elbow, with something of the future gulf revealed and something of the future bitterness casting its shadow, his buoyancy and spirits flagged. His volubility dried up, and it is as reticent, morose even, that he is remembered during these next few days.

Stack's notes, written a year later, recall that "Mr. Collins did not speak strongly in favour of the document at all." But there is no discounting the emphasis of O'Murchadha's contemporary record that "Mr. Collins was in substantial agreement with Messrs. Griffith and Duggan. The non-acceptance of the Treaty would be a gamble as England could arrange a war in Ireland within a week. With pressure further concessions could be obtained on Trade and Defence. He would recommend the Dail to go to the country on the Treaty, but he would recommend non-acceptance of the Oath."

One point at least is clear. What was troubling Collins essentially was the Oath of Allegiance in its present form. Another conclusion seems reasonable: that those around him read into his words intentions appropriate to their own several outlooks. It must, one would think now, have been obvious that he had come, by this time, to set peace above External Association. But it is not quite certain whether, on this point, even in his own mind he had yet reached a completely final conclusion, and it must be remembered that the hostility of Brugha and Stack made it impossible for him, if he was to retain his influence with the Army, to run ahead of middle opinion.

Finally, the opinion of Childers was elicited. Here there was no likelihood of ambiguity. Any settlement reckless of the Republic was, of course, anathema; but on this Saturday, he, a specialist of world renown on matters military and naval, concentrated mainly on the humiliating character of the Defence provisions before them. Clause 7 dragged Ireland automatically into every British war, while Clause 6 deprived Ireland of the right even to her own coastal defence, and accordingly of all National Status.

The discussion became general and rambled round the central persistent dilemma. Then the Trade clauses excited a long argument. Barton was the champion of complete fiscal autonomy. The others saw less hope of it. Griffith mentioned compensations from free trade on both sides. Next day in London it was found impossible to achieve agreed recollection of what had been decided.

But most of the onslaught was directed against Griffith's refusal to "break on the question of the Crown." Eventually, Brugha could contain himself no longer. "In reply," relates O'Murchadha,[1] "to a question by the Minister for Defence as to who was responsible for the splitting of the Delegation so that two members (Messrs. Griffith and Collins) did most of the work, and so that the other members were not in possession of full information, it was stated that the British Government was responsible for the arrangement, but that it had the approval of the whole Delegation. *The Minister of Defence here remarked that the British Government selected its men.* On the motion of Mr. Griffith, this remark was withdrawn."

Brugha's own account given in the Treaty Debate robs the original comment of some of its offensiveness. "I said, 'Yes, the British Government selected their men.' In saying this I did not mean to cast any reflection on the honour of these men; but before these men were selected at all, I told them what I thought of their ideals of freedom. I said at the Cabinet Meeting on that fateful Saturday: 'Yes, they selected their men.' My meaning was this: because they knew they were the two weakest men we had in the team; and Lloyd George and his friends pretty soon discovered that; and that is how they came to select them out of the five." At the time Griffith closed the incident with dignity. But now

[1] Assistant Secretary to the Cabinet. See footnote, p. 206, and Appendix 4 B.

the gap between the two parties was widening before the eyes of all.

The Cabinet were left to debate alone. The President gave it as his opinion that the Treaty could not be accepted in its present form. He personally could not "subscribe to the Oath of Allegiance nor could he sign any document which would give North-East Ulster power to vote itself out of the Irish State." He might understand Griffith giving up independence for National unity, but "you have got neither this nor that." With modifications, however, "it might be accepted honourably, and he would like to see the Delegates go back and secure peace if possible. He believed that the Delegates had done their utmost and that it now remained to them to show that if the document was not amended, they were prepared to face the consequences—war or no war. He would deal with the present document exactly as with that of the July 20th—say it could not be accepted, and put up counter proposals. He took his stand upon the last Irish proposals which meant external connection with the Crown." Brugha was in perfect agreement with the President, except for his dislike of the latest version of External Association, under which, it will be remembered, the King was to be recognised as head of the association. For him, as for the President, the British document quite failed to guarantee the "essential unity" of Ireland.

Griffith continued to argue and plead. "He did not like the document, but he did not think it dishonourable." It would practically recognise the Republic, and the first allegiance would be to Ireland. He then made the point, of which so much was to be heard in the Treaty debate. "If it were rejected the people would be entitled to know what the alternative was. The country would not fight on the question of Allegiance and there would be a split." He made a curious suggestion. "He would not recommend the Government to accept, but would say that the Plenipotentiaries should sign and leave it to the President and Dail to reject."

The afternoon wore on. The Plenary Meeting was resumed. Griffith stuck to his guns, determined to sign. Barton appealed eloquently to De Valera to join the Delegation in London. Was it fair to force Griffith, resolutely set against plunging the country into war, to pursue terms whose achievement demanded a readiness to face war, if the worst came to the worst? Nothing came of it. Griffith was adamant in declining to take the responsibility for "breaking with the Crown." When as many concessions as possible had been conceded, and when it was accepted by Craig, he would go before the Dail. "The Dail was the body to decide for or against war."

Suddenly Brugha turned to him, saying, "Don't you realise that if you sign this thing, you will split Ireland from top to bottom?" The force of this seemed to strike Griffith, and he said, "I suppose that's so. I'll tell you what I'll do. I'll go back to London. I'll not sign that document, but I'll bring it back and submit it to the Dail and, if necessary, to the people."[1] That was quite satisfactory to everybody. There was felt to be no necessity now for "substitute Delegates" to go over and break off the negotiations. De Valera, in particular, abandoned the idea of going over himself, assured now that nothing would be signed which committed Ireland to Allegiance, or inclusion within the Empire.

In view of the controversies that subsequently raged round this incident, it is as well to see exactly what was decided. Griffith had been urging that the Delegation should sign, that the Government, should, if they wished, reject, but that, in any case, the Dail should (as was inevitable if the Treaty was to be ratified), have the final say in accepting or rejecting. Brugha, with tragic prescience, urged that this course (which was in the end adopted) would, by dividing the leaders, split Ireland from end to end. Griffith saw the force of this and agreed, if confronted with the threat of war, to refer the document, *without signature*, back to the Dail, whose decision would presumably be adopted by a united Cabinet. One possibility (probability it seems to us now) was overlooked. That the right to a reference back would be denied by the British, and war threatened unless the Delegates signed then and there in London.

The air was now cleared of the threat of signature without reference back to Dublin, and at last an attempt was made to evolve amendments which there was some chance of the British accepting. The Oath took up most of the time. Cathal Brugha objected to any form of oath. "Of course," he said, "if the British wanted an oath from us to respect whatever Treaty was made, we might give it provided they swear to us in return." De Valera also wanted to know where lay the need for any oath of any kind. Collins said it was to be "sugar coating" to enable the English people to swallow the Treaty. De Valera had been reiterating the principle of External Association. In his next remark he still had it in mind. "Well," he said, "if it be really necessary and if we get

[1] This was the pledge usually and apparently rightly referred to as the one not to sign any document involving allegiance to the Crown or inclusion within the Empire. See Appendix 5. The above account of how it was given is from Stack.

all else we want, what harm would there be if we had an oath something like this," and he spoke these words: "I do solemnly swear true faith and allegiance to the Constitution of the Irish Free State, to the Treaty of Association, and to recognise the King of Great Britain as Head of the Association."[1]

It was evening now. There were only minutes left if the Delegates were to cross back to London that night, and the possibility of postponing return in the interests of clear and cool decision was not entertained. Instead, four decisions were hastily come to; they are recorded by O'Murchadha thus:

(1) Delegates to carry out their original instructions with same powers.

(2) Delegation to return and say that Cabinet won't accept Oath of Allegiance if not amended, and to face the consequences assuming that England will declare war.

(3) Decided unanimously that present Oath of Allegiance could not be subscribed to.

(4) Mr. Griffith to inform Mr. Lloyd George that the document could not be signed, and to state that it was now a matter for the Dail. (He was to try and see that the break came on Ulster.)

A question, asked by Childers after these decisions had been reached, should be read along with them. Did the alteration insisted on in the Oath include alteration in Clauses 1 to 3 of the final draft? (These were clauses conferring Dominion Status and, by implication, turning down External Association.) "Yes," said De Valera, without contradiction, and Childers was satisfied. But next day it was with some difficulty that he recalled this question and answer to the mind of Griffith and Collins. They had quite sincerely professed no recollection that the Cabinet had

[1] O'Murchadha substitutes "Head of the Associated States" for "Head of the Association," but de Valera made it plain afterwards that "Association" was what he must have said. Not only was it the phrase that had been in previous Irish drafts, but it was the phrase that would be consistent with the idea that the King would be connected with Ireland only for the purposes for which Ireland would act in concert with the other Associates: Consistent also with the idea that the King's relationship to Ireland would remain external throughout. "Head of the Associated States" would, on the other hand, have suggested that the King would be head of Ireland for all, including domestic, purposes.

Next day in London opinion was divided about what the President had actually said: Griffith, Collins and Duggan plumping for "Associated States" and Barton for "Association." Barton had actually taken down De Valera's words, but in the hurry he had had to abbreviate the last word into "Assoc." So he could throw no decisive light. He gave way to the majority and "Associated States" appeared in the last Irish terms presented to the British.

given any further mandate for pressing External Association.

The Cabinet meeting ended with two last hurried decisions. By a majority vote the Delegation was empowered to meet Sir James Craig, if so desired, and it was agreed that the President should not join the Delegation at this stage of the negotiations. Barton, Gavan Duffy and Childers dashed off to North Wall. Tim Healy and Sir Horace Plunkett happened to be travelling the same way. But Griffith, Collins and Duggan took the mail from Kingstown. So far had fellowship been severed.

What mandate did the Delegates carry away from Dublin? Let us strip the question of its intolerable burden of over-ingenious justification and technical plea. How far, when he left Dublin, should a reasonable member of the Irish Delegation have considered himself entitled to sign in London without reference back to Dublin (*a*) any Treaty at all; (*b*) any Treaty involving surrender of the Externally Associated Republic?

"In spite of our original instructions," he might have reasoned to himself, "they will not quarrel with the mere fact of our signing a Treaty without referring back to them. In fact, they will be delighted if the Treaty is on the lines they desire. But how far are we allowed to diverge from the ideal in the attempt to secure immediate settlement? What are the minimum alterations that we must effect in the British draft? We must get the Oath of Allegiance changed; we must get it purged of explicit allegiance to the Crown—that is understood. But what of Dominion Status? Must we get rid of that, too, at all costs, and have the Associated Republic restored? I thought I heard the President give a decision to that effect, and there was that promise of Griffith's not to sign anything involving allegiance to the Crown. Yes, I don't see how we can possibly sign ourselves into the Empire without referring back to Dublin. If the worst comes to the worst, we must leave the Dail the decision between Dominion Status and war. But there are two better outcomes than that to hope for. (1) That the British accept a Republic. Hardly likely. (2) That we stage the breakdown on the Ulster issue. There should be a good chance of our bringing that off, and then this question of Dominion Status or war would not arise."

So might our friend arrive at a fair definition of his mandate. But he would be ignoring, like the authors of his mandate, one possibility. Suppose it becomes, or appears to become, impossible alike to break on Ulster and to transfer the decision to the Dail? How will Griffith reconcile his promise not to sign any document involving allegiance with his avowal that he would not break on the Crown? Will the mandate have any meaning left to it if it proves to have failed to provide for the one circumstance which will now be overriding all others? Will it any longer be a guide, or exercise any longer authority?[1]

CHAPTER XIX

## SUNDAY, DECEMBER 4TH, IN LONDON

"Rightly to be great
Is not to stir without great argument,
But greatly to find quarrel in a straw,
When honour's at the stake."
SHAKESPEARE: *Hamlet.*

*Irish proposals drawn up—Serious conflict of opinion—Collins stays behind—Griffith attempts the break on Ulster—The British horrified by the Irish terms—The Ulster break frustrated—Gavan Duffy lets the cat out of the bag—The negotiations apparently concluded—Lloyd George resolves to try to see Collins.*

"WE went away," said Michael Collins, "with a document which none of us would sign. It must have been obvious that, in the meantime, a document arose which we thought we could sign." There arose, too, he might have added, circumstances to make mincemeat of the plan of resistance.

The Republican wing were early astir, and by lunchtime had drafted a memorandum for presentation to the British, under the heading: "Amendments by the Irish Representatives to the proposed Articles of Agreement." Clinging to External Association, and including the Oath tentatively indicated by the President, it embodied to the best of their recollection the decisions reached by the Cabinet the previous day.

Its authors did not meet their colleagues till three o'clock, although a meeting with the British had been fixed for five.

[1] After the Treaty, both sides overstated their cases. Griffith and Collins, trying to minimise the duress involved in signature, claimed that even apart from the ultimatum there was no moral obligation that prevented signing. Their opponents argued that, ultimatum or no, the Delegates' mandate, when they left Dublin, obviously permitted no course but blank refusal to sign.

Griffith, Collins and Duggan, disgusted, one may guess, with the position in which the Dublin Cabinet had left them, had drawn up no proposals of their own. But they protested strongly against certain features of the "Republican" handiwork.

Collins had no recollection of the Cabinet having insisted, yet once more, on External Association along with modification of the Oath. Childers, however, recalled the answer he had obtained on this specific point, and Collins eventually gave way. A long wrangle followed on the Trade clause. Under the final draft, it will be remembered, "no protective Customs duties were to be imposed between the two countries except to stop dumping or other unfair competition." Now all were agreed in claiming the additional right "to take measures for the encouragement of infant industries and for the economic development of Ireland." Barton, who himself had never wavered in demanding that full fiscal autonomy should be established from the beginning, insisted that the Cabinet had stood out for such full autonomy after ten years at the latest, but he gave way when even Gavan Duffy failed to support him. Finally, after various other alterations, an agreed document was achieved.

Of the five familiar questions, Ulster, Trade, Finance, Defence and National Status, Ulster was not mentioned, though it was understood that the document was put forward on condition that the "essential unity" of Ireland was secured. Trade was dealt with as described above; tariffs could be used to encourage infant industries, but full fiscal autonomy was to be restricted, not for ten years only, but indefinitely. Finance, in effect, was left over to the Commission which for some time both sides had recognised as inevitable. On Defence there were signs of a weakening, despite all the exertions of Childers. Still, a bold front was maintained. The British demand for facilities specific in peace, undefined in war, was at last conceded, but only "for five years, pending the establishment of Irish Coastal Defence Forces." With this phrase was coupled an express Irish obligation of providing for her own defence by sea, land and air. The result was to deny even for the immediate future that *exclusive* right of Britain, asserted in the final draft, to carry on the coastal defence of Ireland; and where the final draft had merely indicated hopes, to lay down as operative policy that England should have no share whatever in Irish coastal defence when five years should have elapsed.

But it was improbable that the British Ministers would get as far as these refinements. The first five clauses would sufficiently shock and dismay them. For there could be no two opinions about it; here was External Association once again. It is true that an oath had been added during the week-end, and an annual contribution to the King's revenue since the last full-dress proposals of November 22nd. True, too, that in the remaining clauses there was no positive phrase incapable of acceptance. (Was not the first clause—"The legislative, executive and judicial authority of Ireland shall be derived exclusively from the elected representatives of the Irish people" later to emerge almost intact as Clause 2 of the Constitution of the Irish Free State?) But the omissions were all too glaring. No Dominion Status, no Allegiance, nothing explicit or implicit to disestablish the Republic. Its omissions alone would damn the document unless the British collapsed.

Of the document in its final form Collins was afterwards able to say in the Dail, "We went away (from Dublin) with certain impressions in our minds, and we did our best faithfully to transmit these impressions to paper in the memorandum we handed in to the British Delegation." And Duggan said, "We put up the proposals that the Cabinet said we should put up. They were turned down, and had been, two or three times previously. We told the Cabinet that they would be turned down, but we carried out these instructions."

Yet at the deciding moment, when the presentation of the document was being considered, a moment when, if ever, failure to combine was lamentable and fatal, the Delegation could not manage to agree. Griffith, Collins and Duggan refused to present the document to the British, saying that it was for those who wanted to break to present it. It was only when Barton and Gavan Duffy accepted the challenge, and were preparing to go, that Griffith realised the absurdity and danger of the little party setting off alone and presenting to the British the schism in all its nakedness. He consented after all to act as their leader. Collins, however, was adamant in refusing to accompany the Delegation.

At five o'clock the Irish party arrived at 10 Downing Street to find awaiting them Lloyd George, Chamberlain, Birkenhead and Horne. The serious business was prefaced by a discussion of certain pledges given on November 16th by Griffith to the Southern Unionists. Lloyd George apologised for misunderstanding Griffith on a previous occasion, and was quite satisfied with an assurance that the Southern Unionists would be catered for in the Lower Chamber by Proportional Representation, and in the Upper by some scheme to be arranged between Griffith and themselves.

Griffith now turned to the Irish proposals, and for two hours or so his comrades marvelled at and inwardly applauded one of his greatest efforts in debate. Considering that a few moments before he had been flatly refusing to come at all, his force and conviction were astonishing. Determined, at all costs, not to break on any point connected with the Crown, he began on Ulster, and all the time he kept fighting his way back to it. The Irish, he said, did not take any responsibility for the Ulster proposals. They came from the other side and belonged there. The British agreed, but said that they intended to go on with them, even if Ulster refused, and recalled Griffith's promise not to let them down "as against Craig."[1] Griffith confirmed the fact of his promise, but emphasised that neither he nor anyone on the Irish side could be responsible for putting forward, with no guarantee of acceptance by Craig, proposals that might well involve Partition. The British saw the point of Griffith's argument.

Griffith pressed home his attempt to effect a break on Ulster. He had written the British a letter, he said, in which he conditionally accepted association with the Crown in exchange for "essential unity." It was Craig's turn now. He should write them a letter accepting "essential unity." And Griffith expanded the contention. The British unconcernedly let the waves beat over them. Craig, they said, would not write such a letter, for he was going to refuse the proposals. Nevertheless, they repeated, they would go ahead with them.

In view of his promise of the 12th, how could Griffith protest further? He had to turn instead to the Irish amendments, on the lines of which he declared the Dublin Cabinet ready to recommend the Dail to ratify a treaty. Various questions were asked in elucidation of particular points, and for some time Lloyd George and Chamberlain engaged Barton on Trade. The British then withdrew for discussion among themselves.

When after about ten minutes they returned Lloyd George made a long solemn statement. The amendments, he said, were a complete going back upon the discussions of the last week. They had offered Ireland the chance to become a willing member of the Empire like other nations—the Boers, for example—who had fought with equal gallantry. The amendments, however, constituted a refusal to enter the Empire and accept the common bond of the Crown. They were but the same proposals which had been already discussed and rejected. The British might have accepted a change in the Oath, but the document just presented was a refusal

[1] The reference was, of course, to the Park Lane undertaking of November 12th. And see page 180, note 2.

of the fundamental conditions. Or so it seemed to the Cabinet. On such a grave matter they felt it right to confirm their impression.

There was an embarrassing penetration about the British criticisms, but Griffith gamely persevered, pointing out the mention of the King's name in the Oath as evidence of an effort to meet British susceptibilities. A general discussion followed, Barton arguing that what was needed was a permanent peace based on goodwill, and that this was what Ireland was offering; Gavan Duffy, that for all purposes essential to the British the proposals provided the necessary connection. Griffith tried, as he put it later to De Valera, "to work back on Ulster. They were asking us to give up our best ground without a guarantee that Craig would accept the unity of the Irish nation. There was nothing tangible in our hand. How could Ireland trust the faith of the British Government?"

The British replied with a new temptation, fresh evidence it seemed of the genuineness of their offer. If the Irish signed the Treaty, "they would immediately call Parliament together and pass the ratifying Act before Christmas. They would hand over Dublin Castle and withdraw their troops from the country."

Yet once more the discussion reverted and circled, the British declaring that their own Dominions would denounce them if they even considered the Irish terms. No English Government could entertain them. Back went Griffith to Ulster, but he could not, he explained afterwards, "get it into its proper place." The British talked of their difficulty and the Irish of theirs. The Irish said that they had tried their best to find a *via media*, and the British asked them what was the difficulty about coming into the Empire with a standing like that of Canada.

The irrepressible Gavan Duffy was all too ready with an answer. "We should be as closely associated with you in all large matters as the Dominions, and in the matter of Defence still more so; but our difficulty is coming into the Empire."

Here at last the Irish claim had slipped out of the bag. If Duffy had said that his side could on no account give up a Republic, the effect could have been no more electrical. Chamberlain jumped up, "That ends it," he cried. The other Ministers were on their feet immediately—it looked as if the situation had been prepared against—they closed the conversation and undertook to send round next day copies of their proposals. The Irish promised to send a formal rejection, and the British replied that when they received it they would inform Craig that the negotiations had broken down.

Possibly through Cope, who had inevitably spent Saturday in Dublin, the British had understood before the meeting that the final draft had been turned down by a narrow majority in the Dublin Cabinet. But they had hardly bargained for the reappearance of External Association barely diluted, still less for the flat refusal to come within the Empire.

The supposed progress of the last month seemed illusory and the end of negotiations to have been reached. "Most unsatisfactory" was how one of those present recorded his impressions of the afternoon. But from Lloyd George the occasion seemed but to call forth latent resources. Griffith, he could guess by this time, was no willing party to the intransigence. And where was Collins? He himself was seeing the King at ten next morning, and the Cabinet at twelve to decide on steps consequent on a final breakdown. If only he could see Collins before he saw the King! Jones was summoned and departed hot foot on the trail.

Meanwhile the Irish Delegates were driving home, conscious that in the one unquestionable task set them by Dublin, that of seeing that the break, if break there must be, came on Ulster, they had ignominiously failed. Barton congratulated Griffith on the way he had kept fighting back on to the Ulster issue, but Griffith was in no mood to let himself be soothed. He turned on Gavan Duffy, the proximate occasion of the catastrophe, and he rent him.

# Part Four

## THE BRITISH PRESS ON THE CRISIS

*The Times* (Monday, December 5th).—"The main fact of the moment is that negotiators who have shown themselves resolute in the endeavour to reach a settlement have not yet given up the task. . . . The negotiations are not broken off."

*Daily Telegraph* (Monday, December 5th).—"The outlook is authoritatively spoken of as 'very grave' . . . although it is officially stated that there has been no breakdown of negotiations."

*Daily Mail* (Monday, December 5th).—"The situation is more difficult perhaps than at any time during the Conference, but there is no reason yet for despairing of success."

*Daily Chronicle* (Monday, December 5th).—"GRAVE IRISH OUTLOOK.—Little Hope of Settlement now Entertained."

*Daily Herald* (Monday, December 5th).—"SINN FEIN'S ANSWER: DARK OUTLOOK.—Mr. De Valera in a speech yesterday used words which warned Ireland to be prepared for the worst."

*Daily Express* (Monday, December 5th).—"IRISH CONFERENCE FAILS.—Sinn Fein's refusal . . . insensate."

*Manchester Guardian* (Monday, December 5th).—"As for entering on a new war with men of our own speech and partly of our own blood, the thing would be inhuman and intolerable. . . . There is surely no grounds for precipitating a crisis or thinking in terms of an ultimatum."

*Morning Post* (Monday, December 5th).—"Even if the rebel junta have actually consented to the last ignoble expedient suggested to them, can the result bring peace to Ireland?"

*The Times* (Tuesday, December 6th[1]).—"It is indeed unthinkable that, if the negotiations break down, any of those who have sat so long together in conference should lightly contemplate conditions under which they would be plunged into active enmity: yet, if once the counsels of the extremists in either camp prevailed, such conditions might become inevitable."

*Evening Standard* (Monday, December 5th[1]).—Late Night Special.—"Both the Government and the Sinn Fein leaders are undesirous of breaking the Truce, nor do I think, speaking on the best authority, that it will come to an end.

*Daily Chronicle*[2] (Tuesday, December 6th[1]).—"IRISH CRISIS.—Chances of Getting Round It.—If the negotiators prove still unable to sign a compact, let them adjourn their negotiation for a fixed period of weeks."

*Daily Herald* (Tuesday, December 6th[1]).—"The Irish people will never agree to those terms. They stand for freedom and friendship; the British Government stands for forced allegiance and truckling to the Ulster capitalists. So it is inevitable that Mr. Lloyd George and his Government will have to confess failure. He will not, however, be allowed to resume the war, instead he must be compelled to resign and recommend a General Election.

---

[1] Written before the signing of the Treaty.
[2] Lloyd George's semi-official organ at this time.

## CHAPTER I

# MONDAY MORNING AND MICHAEL COLLINS

"IAGO: O you are well tuned now!"
SHAKESPEARE: *Othello.*

*Collins persuaded to see Lloyd George alone—"Essential Unity"—Collins satisfied on Boundary Commission—Oath of Allegiance—Defence—Trade—Negotiations tentatively re-opened—Collins's attitude to settlement—His original reluctance to come over—His outlook essentially practical—His "stepping-stone" position—His preference for bilateral amendment of the Treaty—How far would Statute of Westminster have satisfied him?—His vision of a League of Free States—His attachment to External Association—His optimism about the future of Dominion Status—His reluctance to impose a solution on his country—His new confidence that the Treaty would give "Essential Unity"—What Lloyd George had accomplished—Barton's reasons for agreeing to re-enter Conference.*

JONES saw Griffith at 10 p.m. and begged him to persuade Collins to see Lloyd George alone. Griffith, however, made little headway, and all in 22 Hans Place retired to bed (Collins slept at 15 Cadogan Gardens) with no interview arranged. But they were not to be allowed much rest. In the early hours of the morning the telephone bell rang in Hans Place, and shortly afterwards Jones appeared to make a final appeal. Griffith undertook to try Collins once more. When the time came, he put in everything he knew, and Collins yielded at last. It had been a near thing. Jones had suggested the interview for 9.15 a.m., but in Collins's own words, "As I had not made up my mind until after speaking with Mr. Griffith this morning, I did not see Lloyd George until 9.30."[1]

Collins had his points set out under four heads:

(1) "Essential Unity" of Ireland—an answer from Craig one way or the other imperative.

[1] Collins described the interview in a full Memorandum written immediately on his return to Hans Place.

(2) Oath of Allegiance.

(3) Defence; coastal defence, especially.

(4) Trade—restrictions on fiscal autonomy.

But Lloyd George took the offensive. He was meeting his Cabinet, he explained, at twelve to inform them that the Conference had broken down as a result of the interview of last night. Ignoring the question of Allegiance, except to intimate that he was willing to consider any form of oath in the attempt to meet Irish sentiment, he emphasised that the break was definitely on the question "within or without" the Empire. Collins turned the blow aside by saying that he would like to express his opinion on the British document.

He said he was "perfectly dissatisfied as regards the position of the North-East," and he pressed on Lloyd George the necessity of a reply from Craig, whether accepting or rejecting. Now come the crucial sentences in his record: "*Mr. Lloyd George remarked that I myself pointed out on a previous occasion that the North would be forced economically to come in.* I said that the position was so serious, owing to certain recent happenings, that for my part I was anxious to secure a definite reply from Craig and his colleagues, and that I was as agreeable to a reply rejecting as accepting. *In view of the former we would save Tyrone and Fermanagh, parts of Derry, Armagh and Down by the Boundary Commission*, and thus avoid such things as the raid on the Tyrone County Council and the ejection of the staff. Mr. Lloyd George expressed the view that this might be put to Craig."

Contemporary evidence leaves no room for doubt that this conversation about Ulster influenced Collins profoundly. Up to this point he was, as he put it himself, "perfectly dissatisfied as regards the position of the North-East," and far from ready therefore to make any sacrifices of principle or prestige for the Treaty as a whole. After his talk he came back to Hans Place convinced that there was a splendid chance of the unity of Ireland being secured. But what fresh offer had Lloyd George made to him? It is hard to see any in the exchanges just reported. Lloyd George reminded Collins how he (Collins) had said on a previous occasion that after the Boundary Commission had done its work, the North would be forced economically to come in. And Collins had said to Lloyd George, apparently without contradiction, that under the Boundary Commission the Free State would gain two counties and parts of three others. Collins had then gone on to plead, not for a change in the Ulster clauses, but for a definite answer from Craig. And that was all.

Yet we know that Collins got an impression from his talk, a new or greatly strengthened impression, that Ireland, under the Boundary Commission, was intended to gain "large territories"; and that Ulster, reduced to an uneconomic unit, would probably be "forced in" before long.

Collins now explained to Lloyd George the need for a modification of the Oath.[1] Lloyd George was friendly, but placed the issue in its British perspective. Clauses 1 and 2 (the Dominion clauses) of the final draft were the substance; a definite understanding had to be reached on them first; then the form of the Oath could be discussed.

Defence came next. Clause 6 of the final draft provided that to begin with, at any rate, the defence by sea of Great Britain and Ireland should be undertaken exclusively by His Majesty's Imperial Forces. Collins objected to that "exclusively." It implied that Ireland was to take no measures for raising even "a coastal defence force." Lloyd George interposed that there could be no question of Irish submarines. Collins explained that he resented the assertion that Ireland could build *nothing*. The second part of the same clause had provided for joint review at the end of ten years. Collins thought that he could find agreement if the Review Conference definitely meant the transfer to the Irish Government of the responsibility for coastal defence.

From this claim, never destined to be granted in its entirety, he passed finally to Trade, emphasising that it was the fetters in Clauses 9 and 10 to which he objected. "Lloyd George suggested that if there were complete freedom on one side there should also be complete freedom on the other"; that is to say, Britain should be as free as Ireland to impose tariffs on the other's goods. Collins said that this would meet his view, as for that matter would the proposal put forward by the Irish on November 22nd, that a free list should be agreed on first, but that after that each side should have carte blanche to impose what duties it chose. "Lloyd George," records Collins, "made notes of all the objections as expressed above, and suggested that if we thought fit he would meet us at two o'clock to-day." Collins let the appointment stand tentatively.

Lloyd George, as one would expect, rounded off the conversation with a last temptation. Could not Collins, and through him

[1] It was apparently at this stage that Collins handed Lloyd George a new form of oath which a legal friend had suggested to him. Lord Birkenhead produced it approvingly at the afternoon Conference and it passed almost intact into the Treaty.

his colleagues, accept Clauses 1 and 2, bringing Ireland within the Empire? These once accepted, he would be in a position to hold up any British action until the Irish had, if they desired to do so, submitted the matter to Dail Eireann and the country. "I left at that," says Collins, "saying that unless I sent word to the contrary, some members of the Delegation would meet him at two o'clock."

So contact was re-established and the situation transformed. The previous evening two months' negotiation seemed to have gone for nothing, and the Irish to be adamant, more adamant even than at the very beginning, in their refusal to come inside the Empire. Yet here on three occasions during the interview Lloyd George had put up to Collins that Clauses 1 and 2, the Dominion clauses, were the substance, and on no occasion had Collins protested. Collins had argued Ulster, Oath, Defence and Trade, but never Status. He had never pressed or, it would appear, even mentioned, External Association. Here, in fact, was Lloyd George making it clear to Collins that further negotiation could only serve a useful purpose if conducted on an Empire basis; and here was Collins leaving behind him a strong impression that he would do all in his power to bring his colleagues to a conference on these lines, and that he would probably prove successful. How explain this outcome of an interview on which Collins had been so reluctant to embark?

In Collins's case it is futile to speculate what settlement, if the responsibility had been his alone, he would have accepted in July or even October. There are casual sayings attributed to him—Stack's recollection, for instance, that the July terms seemed to him "a great advance." There is a quite unsupported allegation that the I.R.B. of which he was the guiding spirit had by June or July already come to an agreement among themselves not to fight against Dominion terms. But those who knew Collins best are agreed that up till the Truce and indeed up till the time when, against his wishes, he was appointed a Delegate, he had not considered politics seriously. He was a fighting-man and an organiser of resistance. It was for others to see what could be made of his labours.

De Valera said in the Dail in August "I am not a doctrinaire Republican." This was true if he meant that he was prepared for a compromise that abandoned the isolated Republic. But he was a doctrinaire Republican in the sense that he was prepared to die—and call on others to die—rather than abandon what seemed to him the essential elements of independence as expressed under External

Association. Collins was a doctrinaire Republican in neither sense. He came to London passionately attached to the Republic to which he had sworn faithfulness, but with a mind completely open upon what form of settlement would be acceptable, and what could be obtained. For some form of settlement, however, he became as he studied and meditated only less anxious than Griffith. And this for two reasons, one fundamental and psychological, one peculiar to the problem.

Mr. Liam O'Flaherty, in his book *The Martyr*, has put into the mouth of a Free State officer called Tyson, an exaggerated yet suggestive distinction between two types of Irishmen, the Conquerors and the Martyrs. The contrast should not be mistaken for one between those who care for results and those who do not. It lies rather between those who believe that nothing succeeds like success and those who believe that nothing succeeds like heroic failure with intact ideals. Ireland, locked in secular struggle with a materially overwhelming adversary, had relied in the past on gallant defeat to rouse her own people and to influence in her favour opinion in England and the world at large. The astounding triumph of the Easter Rising, negligible as a military adventure, had lent peculiar sanction to this "blood sacrifice" procedure.

But Michael Collins was of a different outlook. He stood for the new Ireland, the Ireland which aimed to succeed, not by eliciting sympathy, but by compelling respect. He had set himself out to inconvenience and intimidate the British Government in Ireland. He had defied them to do their worst, and he had succeeded to the point of securing an offer undreamt of in, say, July 1919, when Lloyd George had said to Sir Henry Wilson about Dominion Home Rule, "I absolutely agree that it is all pure nonsense." Collins's present anxiety was to consolidate the Irish position, and for this purpose to make full use of a moment when Irish resistance was at its peak, and England's international embarrassment extreme. He would have been happy to go on fighting "until the surviving soldiers of the Republic dug themselves into the Aran Islands, fighting to the last,"[1] if those had been his instructions. But charged with negotiation, his native inclination was all towards a successful arrangement.

This inherent tendency was lent application by a set of ideas which he developed at an early stage of the negotiations and which came to be described as his "stepping-stone" attitude. Collins never accepted the Treaty as a final settlement nor did he

[1] Extract from speech of Alexander McCabe at Private Session of Dail Eireann, August 1921, as recollected by Stack.

merely qualify acceptance with such a phrase as that used by Griffith: "It is no more a final settlement than we are the final generation on the face of the earth." There is no doubting that Collins meant to see to it that, in his own lifetime, whatever settlement was reached was greatly expanded in Ireland's favour. As he said in a famous sentence during the Treaty debate: "The Treaty gives us freedom, not the ultimate freedom that all nations desire and develop to, but the freedom to achieve it."

To write thus is perhaps to disturb many English friends of Ireland, who will feel that this account conflicts with their notion of Collins as an honourable man prepared to stand by his bond. But they need have no uneasiness. They must not misunderstand the different aspects under which the Treaty appeared to the two countries. A large though hardly a predominant section of English opinion may have thought the Treaty inexpedient and even ignominious. But no reasonable support was forthcoming for the view that England was giving up, under pressure, her rights. In Ireland it was otherwise. Not a man in the National Movement but denied any right of England to interfere in Ireland at all; not a man, for or against the Treaty, but regarded it when it was first signed as withholding certain rights that belonged in some sense to Ireland. Not a man but would have felt that Ireland was morally justified in insisting on its amendment at the earliest possible moment.

Collins, however, was fully aware of the disadvantages—loss of national repute, perhaps, among them—that would always attend any amendment to which England did not give voluntary consent. When he persuaded his extremists of the I.R.B. to vote for the Treaty (the I.R.B. turned the scale), with talk of what could be done in five years' time, he had in mind the kind of development that has actually come to pass. The Treaty status would prove dynamic; it would grow and become enriched along with the general status of the Dominions; before 1935 the position would be reached in which it would have become incredible that any Dominion wishing to leave the Empire could be restrained by force.

But was Collins convinced that Ireland's ultimate destiny would take her outside the Commonwealth? There is no proof that he was. He was not content, and would never have been content, with Ireland's position as guaranteed by the Dominion Status of 1921; but the prodigious developments that have culminated in the Statute of Westminster, in which his successors have played such great part and to which his own decision to accept the Treaty paved the way—we cannot take it on ourselves to say that these developments would have left him still dissatisfied.

What is not open to doubt is the powerful influence exerted on Collins's mind by the gradual revelation to him during the Armistice of the possibilities inherent in Dominion Status. Nor was it a question of London influence or British influence at all. He conducted his studies himself, relying on friends to introduce him to the leading and latest authorities. It was not a year since Duncan Hall's brilliant anticipation of a Dominion Autonomy on which the next ten years were to set the official seal. Josiah Wedgwood had recently returned from a tour of the Dominions with a tale of "The bond that there is no bond"; and Berriedale Keith was beginning to pile up that amazing corpus of Dominion constitutional exposition to which each passing year brings up-to-date addition. These Collins read and pondered, and drew from them lessons very different from those drawn by Childers, the Dominions expert of the Delegation—or indeed by the authors themselves.

Collins conceived the theory that the British Empire was evolving into a higher form of organisation, a League of Free States. These views he expressed in a remarkable memorandum "*On the Wider International Aspects of an Anglo-Irish Settlement.*" It was presented to the British in supplement of the official proposals for External Association on November 28th. "A new era is dawning, not for Ireland only, but for the whole world. . . . The problem of associating autonomous communities can only be solved by recognising the complete independence of the several countries associated. . . . Into such a league might not America be ready to enter?" Collins, in short, saw a universal league of equal nations arising in the not-too-distant future from the ashes of the British Commonwealth.

With such conceptions the proposals for External Association were well in tune, and Collins for a long time was most reluctant to abandon the idea that Ireland, while recognising the Crown as symbolic head of the League, should, for domestic purposes, retain complete independence and her own elective head. Nevertheless, the hope that the Empire was in any case loosening its ties was a powerful inducement to accept in the ultimate extremity Dominion Status during a period of transition.[1]

He was guided in the same direction by his whole attitude to the question of symbols. In regard to these he was what is usually called

[1] To him acceptance of the Treaty would not mean renouncing pressure towards the Association of Free States just described. And in fact he will be found the day *after* the Treaty publicly reproducing much of the thought and language of the Memorandum of November 28th.

a realist. They mattered to him but they did not enshrine the national soul nor did their surrender involve national degradation. "The Irish struggle," he wrote soon after the Treaty, "has always been for freedom—freedom from English occupation, from English interference, from English domination, not for freedom with any particular label attached to it," and while his feeling for the old symbols was deep and genuine there was something before which it would yield—a practical chance of "restoring Ireland." Before that chance indeed "names, formulas, figureheads" would pale into insignificance, as would such questions as whether Ireland "was to be called Saorstat or Poblacht." It seems certain that by the middle of November Collins was considering a Dominion settlement of some kind very seriously, and that by the time that the Dublin Cabinet met on December 3rd he would not personally have refused such a settlement if the sole responsibility had been his.

But there was a reason why he should not make these views plain. For Collins had another side; he was a good comrade, he was loth to impose solutions on his fellow-countrymen. De Valera and Griffith were no doubt just as sound democrats in the sense that they would embrace no policy that did not seem to them likely to prove acceptable in the long-run to the nation. But in the short-run they would be prepared to stand on some doctrine, be it separation or be it peace with England, for which their own efforts had to manufacture the immediate majority. Collins, while accustomed in the military or other executive sphere to act with audacious self-reliance, had not in 1921 acquired the confidence of a democratic leader who determines policy. It was one thing then for Collins to overcome personal distaste for entering the Empire, another to agree to that entry in face of strong and perhaps majority opposition at home. And it is not unfair to add that, with Brugha and Stack supposedly against him, he had no intention of forfeiting under charge of treachery his control of the military machine, on which, if war was to be resumed, the country would once more rely for its life.

We can understand, then, his failure to speak up very definitely at the Cabinet Meeting on Saturday; his hope on the Sunday that the Cabinet had given no mandate for presenting External Association once more; his refusal, when convinced that the mandate had been given, to press the proposals himself; his reluctance, however, to meet Lloyd George alone. He was disgusted at what seemed the unrealistic attitude of his friends in the Cabinet and the Delegation, but with all the horrors of a split before him, he was in no mood to go beyond their decision or to do other than stand by it to the end. Before his interview with Lloyd George he had resigned himself to the duty of war.

Lloyd George accomplished three purposes in his morning conversation with Collins. He satisfied himself that Collins was not personally in favour of rejecting Dominion Status if war were the alternative. He had had a shrewd idea of this before, and Cope had no doubt posted him in the deliberations of the Dublin Cabinet. But the fact that Collins had argued Ulster, Oath, Defence, and Trade, without ever mentioning Status, was final reassuring evidence. Secondly, Lloyd George was able to impress Collins favourably with his own attitude on the four points that Collins raised, and most of all on Ulster. De Valera had complained on Saturday that he could understand Griffith abandoning independence for National unity, but he was getting neither this nor that. Collins left Downing Street convinced in his own mind as he had not been before that, when the consequences of the Boundary Commission had worked themselves out, Ulster would be forced for economic reasons to join the South. So National unity was safe.

In the face of the old British terms he had been willing to discount, in the interests of Cabinet unity, his personal readiness to settle, but did not these new prospects justify him in acceding to his own best instinct? Might they not in any case be sufficient, if they were brought back to Dublin, to secure the very unity desired? Collins himself did not envisage at this time the ultimatum of the afternoon. He would be thinking in terms of a fresh British offer and a reference back. By making the tentative appointment for two o'clock he was not, of course, promising to sign. But, and here comes in Lloyd George's third successfully accomplished purpose, he was leaving on Lloyd George the strong impression that in the last resort he would accept the British terms, even if presented under the form of an ultimatum that permitted no reference back. Lloyd George's morning achievement, then, lay not in persuading some Irish Delegates to come round and see him in the afternoon. They could hardly, in any case, have refused to send representatives. What he had done was to persuade Collins to come; a Collins impregnated with a sense of new gains that would not be on offer long and must be won quickly if at all; a Collins who, if Lloyd George was any judge of men, would not now judge it in the national interest to resist an ultimatum.[1]

A long argument followed Collins's return to Hans Place. Griffith

[1] For Lloyd George's further movements on the morning of December 5th. see Appendix 6.

and Collins were determined that Barton, the third Cabinet Minister and the leader of the "Republican" element, should accompany them to Downing Street. Barton was most unwilling. The British had insisted on Dominion membership, and he understood that there was no intention of yielding to them. What could possibly be the point of another meeting? Griffith, however, was doggedly patient. He recalled the instructions of the Cabinet, that if a break came they must at all costs see that it came on Ulster. In this they had failed lamentably the previous day. At last Barton agreed to go with Griffith and Collins, in the hope of assisting to transfer the break from Status to Ulster.

## CHAPTER II

## THREE O'CLOCK TO NINE O'CLOCK

> "Time flies, death urges, knells call, heaven invites,
> Hell threatens."
>
> YOUNG: *Night Thoughts.*

*The participants—The atmosphere—Griffith's Park Lane undertaking harped on—Irish amendments invited—A tactful Oath of Allegiance—Finance, Defence, Trade—The British withdraw—The last resort of the Irish—Lloyd George hunts for a letter—No more break on Ulster—Fiscal Autonomy conceded—The Ultimatum—Griffith agrees to sign—The Ultimatum elaborated—A last amendment—Ireland's answer required by ten o'clock—The Irish accept the Ultimatum as absolute.*

IT was three o'clock, an hour later than originally suggested, when the last Conference began. On the one side Lloyd George, Chamberlain, Birkenhead and Churchill. On the other, Griffith, Collins and Barton. Three of the former have since published accounts of the hours that followed: Lloyd George in the *Daily Telegraph* of December 23rd 1922, Chamberlain in the same paper of March 29th 1932, and Winston Churchill in one of the most famous chapters of *The Aftermath*. For Irish sources we have a long, at times verbatim, minute, written by Barton next day at the request of Griffith, and a much shorter note written by Griffith himself. Barton also described the proceedings in a brief speech on the Treaty. Neither Lloyd George nor Churchill allows pedantry over details to interfere with impressionistic effect, but on essentials the various accounts harmonise remarkably, and on the only point which has given rise to serious controversy, whether or not Lloyd George threatened Ireland with immediate war, they display agreeable unanimity.[1]

Let us turn for our atmosphere first of all to the measured melodrama of Mr. Churchill. "After two months of futilities and rigmarole, unutterably wearied Ministers faced the Irish delegation themselves in actual desperation, and knowing well that death stood at their elbows." Lloyd George takes more trouble over the background. He recalls "a dreary December evening when on one side of the Cabinet table in 10 Downing Street sat four representatives of Great Britain, and on the other, five (*sic*) Irish leaders. It was the famous room wherein British Cabinets have for generations forged their Irish policies. Coercion and concession alike issued from that chamber. Pitt's Act of Union, Gladstone's Home Rule, etc., etc. . . . and now came the final Treaty of peace. Would it be signed? It was an anxious moment charged with destiny for the two great races who confronted each other at that green table. Associated with me on this occasion were Mr. Austen Chamberlain . . . Lord Birkenhead . . . Mr. Winston Churchill . . . Sir Gordon Hewart, the man who had risen on the pinions of a powerful intelligence to the height of Lord Chief Justice of England. My recollection is that the other two British Delegates, Sir Laming Worthington-Evans and Sir Hamar Greenwood, were stricken with illness and were unable to be present."[2]

From the first moment the clouds of impending war hovered over the Council Chamber, and weighed down the spirits of all. It was realised by both parties that the Ulster Parliament was to meet the next day, and Lloyd George had promised Sir James Craig that he should know the result of the Conference before the Session opened. Yet no ultimatum had been issued, nor had any question of an ultimatum arisen. Ways of escape, or at least postponement, still dangled before Irish eyes.

[1] Chamberlain and Churchill describe the threat of immediate war at some length. Lloyd George does not mention it directly, but his account hardly makes sense except on the supposition that it was delivered.

[2] The above account contains several mistakes: Three, not five, Irish Delegates were present. Sir Gordon Hewart did not attend. If he had attended, he would have made five, not four, Englishmen. Worthington-Evans and Greenwood appear to have been absent, not for the reason given, but for the same reason as Hewart, Gavan Duffy and Duggan—that they were not invited to what was technically a Sub-Conference. Winston Churchill is just as large-minded over small things, times of the day, for example; he changes ten o'clock to "nine," and 11.20 p.m. to "long past midnight," etc.

Lloyd George at once directed discussion to the Ulster issue, and it absorbed all the early stages of the Conference. For this was the one question which it remained for Lloyd George to clear up. He could not risk the Conference breaking down, with the Sinn Fein Delegates left to tell the world that a settlement had been frustrated by Ulster intransigence, backed by English indulgence or intrigue. He informed the Irish, therefore, that he must know once and for all where they stood as regards the Ulster proposals. Could they deny that the Ulster proposals in the document now before them (it was still the final draft as laid before the Dublin Cabinet on the Saturday) were exactly those to which Arthur Griffith had agreed and on which he had undertaken not to let Lloyd George down?

There may have been justice in Lloyd George's claim when one remembers Griffith's Park Lane pledge, but it was only gradually that Griffith realised his full predicament. He still clung to the argument that while he of course stood by his undertaking, and was satisfied with the Ulster proposals, yet he could not be expected to agree to the earlier Articles in the document until he knew whether Craig would accept the Treaty. In other words, he could not be expected to sacrifice the Republic, the symbol of independence, unless he was at least certain of getting in exchange the "essential unity" of Ireland.[1]

Lloyd George and Chamberlain denounced such a proposition as inadmissible, unreasonable, and contrary to the undertaking not to let Lloyd George down. Chamberlain went further. It will be remembered that it was to protect him and Birkenhead from a fruitless sacrifice at the Unionist Conference on November 17th, that Griffith's undertaking had originally been given. With all the earnestness at his command, and there would be no play-acting from him, he reminded Griffith that "without that undertaking not to let us down" he and Lord Birkenhead would never have assumed an attitude of friendship to Sinn Fein, and staked thereon their political future.

Thoroughly irritated by these continual references to an undertaking that as far as he knew had no relevance, Michael Collins burst in tempestuously. Every proposal put forward from the Irish

[1] It was not always clear what reaction Griffith and Collins thought it reasonable to insist on from Craig before signing the Treaty. Was it only some reply from Craig that they wanted? or was it a reply accepting the choice of alternatives, subordinate Parliament versus Boundary Commission? or was it a reply accepting a subordinate Parliament? On the whole the second represented their demand, the notion being that if Craig refused to choose either alternative he might somehow manage to nullify this part of the Treaty entirely and, as actually happened, finish up with his powers, his relation to the South and his territory all unchanged.

side had been conditional on the "essential unity" of Ireland being secured. If Craig refused to come in under an all-Ireland Parliament, and still more if he refused to have anything to do with the Treaty, the "Irish position" (the Republic) would have been lost, and "essential unity" not won.

Lloyd George became excited: shaking his papers in the air he declared that the Irish were deliberately trying to bring about a break on Ulster because their Cabinet in Ireland had refused to come inside the Empire. A shrewd dig this, though Griffith gave no sign of its having gone home. Lloyd George, piqued understandably at the occurrence of the very situation which the Park Lane episode had been specially designed to avert, stormed on and on about broken pledges.

The argument became circular, and the main considerations recurrent. Griffith declared his adherence to his undertaking, but argued that it was not unreasonable to require a reply from Craig. Lloyd George retorted that this *was* letting him down, because Craig could only give one of two replies. He could either accept the Parliament subordinate to Dublin or he could refuse. In the latter case the British would proceed, whether Craig liked it or not, with the Boundary Commission. In his undertaking of November 12th Griffith had shown himself agreeable to either outcome. He could have no further complaint.

Lloyd George overlooked or ignored the possibility that a complete refusal by Craig to take his part in setting up the Boundary Commission might postpone the operation of, and eventually sterilise, that part of the Treaty altogether. This danger would have provided a perfectly genuine ground for Sinn Fein resistance until Craig's decision was received, and of course an admirable occasion for a tactical break on Ulster. For the moment, however, Lloyd George eased his pressure. He and his colleagues, he said, must withdraw to consider the matter amongst themselves, but first he would like to hear what further objections the Irish had to the proposals. In reply to a question from Griffith, he added that the first three clauses (the Dominion and Governor-General clauses) were indispensable.

The tension relaxed and the heat left the discussion, as changes now great now small were suggested in the Oath, and in the Defence and Trade clauses. It was Griffith who raised the alteration of the oath. Birkenhead, intervening for the first time, said that Mr. Collins had handed in that morning a form of oath on which it appeared that he, Mr. Collins, had been working. He himself had made some small alterations in it, and he now produced it as amended. With one small alteration now ("British Commonwealth of Nations" for "the British Empire"), and one at the evening Session ("do swear" for "swear"), it passed into the Treaty, a result reflecting credit on the common sense of the English, especially Birkenhead, and on the ingenuity of the Irish, especially Collins.

The Oath in the final draft had contained "true faith and allegiance to the Constitution of the Irish Free State, the British Commonwealth and the King as Head of the State and the Empire"; the Treaty Oath retains "faith and allegiance" but only to "the Constitution of the Irish Free State as by law established." It concludes "I will be *faithful* to His Majesty King George V, his Heirs and Successors by law, in virtue of the common citizenship of Ireland with Great Britain, and her adherence to and membership of the group of nations forming the British Commonwealth of Nations." The story that Birkenhead described this Oath as the "greatest prevarication in history" has been authoritatively denied. The Oath remains, however, a monument of tenderness for every possible susceptibility, and it might well have provoked him, if not to indiscretion, at least to a sardonic smile. Unfortunately the Irish are constitutionally suspicious of ambiguity and are not easily appeased by it. And so it was to go hard with this most tactful of oaths.[1]

Finance was lightly touched on, the Irish continuing their effort to remove from Clause 5 any trace of a presumption that when the final balance was struck, net liability would fall on Ireland. Defence provoked more realistic conflict, the Irish linking together their objection against coastal defence for the next ten years being undertaken *exclusively* by His Majesty's Forces, and their complaint at the absence of positive assurance that when the ten years were up, coastal defence or a share in it would pass without ques-

[1] Imposing, as has already been explained, no legal obligation, its exact significance need not hold us back long. It is clear, however, that Englishmen can read into it a promise (1) to preserve the Irish Free State, and by implication to keep at arms-length the Republic; (2) to keep Ireland on a basis of common citizenship, whatever that may mean, with England, and within the same Commonwealth; also, perhaps, as De Valera feared, (3) to pay a kind of indirect allegiance to the Crown through allegiance to the Constitution of the Irish Free State of which the King is head.

Irishmen, on the other hand, can (1) not only resist this last claim and deny that allegiance to the Crown or other British Institution is anywhere contained, but (2) can deduce an allegiance to Ireland prior to and overriding all other obligations; an allegiance to Ireland permitting a breach of faithfulness to the British Royal Family and to the connection with the British Commonwealth, if the continuance of such faithfulness or connection should ever come into conflict with Irish interests.

tion into Irish hands. They argued at great length that the word "exclusively" robbed them not only of the abstract right to build, but also of the power of making preparations and proving themselves qualified to carry on coastal defence themselves: while as the clause stood at present the Review Conference at the end of ten years would not be of the slightest use to them if the British should not happen to want to reconsider the subject.

Churchill led for the British, and he, Collins and Barton became involved in a lengthy recapitulation of arguments that, by now, either side could have repeated by heart. Churchill was at no pains to disclaim the rôle ascribed to him in Ireland of supreme tyrannical militarist, nor to disguise his refusal to let the British Navy, bulwark of Empire and civilisation, be curbed by the pretensions, however creditable, and in the political sphere irresistible, of a puny peasant state. If Ireland, he proclaimed, were permitted any Navy, it would be impossible to get the Treaty through Parliament. The English people would believe that the Irish were going to build ships which, in war, might be used against them. The possibility of Irish submarine and Irish mine-layers ready and eager to attack British food-ships would be argued from every angle. Still the Irish clung to their position; "exclusively" must go; it ought indeed to be explicitly stated that Ireland should be required to build one or more ships for her own coastal protection. This last was absolutely refused, but the notion of Ireland being allowed to build something was at last conceded. A phrase was inserted that the exclusive undertaking of Irish coastal defence by His Majesty's Forces was not "to prevent the construction or maintenance of such vessels as are necessary for the protection of the Revenue and the Fisheries." But the last word rested with Churchill; he not only definitely opposed any provision that Ireland should have a real Navy of her own *now*, but said that if he had the opportunity he would oppose it five years later.

After this last announcement, destined to look rather strange within the hour, Collins took up the Trade clause, and hammered away at Lloyd George's half acceptance that morning of the idea of freedom on both sides. The British then withdrew.

After all these weeks, the moment had come to Griffith, Collins, and Barton, when a big decision could be deferred no longer. They took counsel and arrived at two determining resolves. If the British insisted on an immediate answer, they would break off negotiations, declining to sign, or reject the terms pending a decision from Craig. Secondly, whatever the exact nature of the predicament,

Griffith's last card should be to demand reference to the Dominion Premiers.

The door opened and Birkenhead entered, but no one followed him in. All he had come for was to take away notes of the particular amendments desired. Eventually Chamberlain, Birkenhead and Churchill reappeared and resumed the Conference, but it was another ten minutes or so before Lloyd George rejoined them.

Tragedy and romance attended every turn of the negotiations; farce had just enlivened the private British discussion. Lloyd George was genuinely surprised and mortified at this persistence of Griffith in his struggle to secure a break on Ulster: he had thought that he would only have to mention the Park Lane undertaking to knock down all that rhodomontade like a house of cards. But he had underrated the deep adamantine firmness of Griffith's character, the fixity with which, especially after Saturday's Cabinet, he was concentrating himself on this one outlet from the dilemma of war against England or civil war in Ireland. Still, Lloyd George could pull himself together as well as any man. Griffith, he calculated, for all his shrewdness and wisdom, lacked experience across a table. It should not prove impossible to hustle him over the last stage. But where on earth was that paper? It had been shown to Griffith on November 13th, but no one knew where it had got to now; a frantic search ensued, Downing Street was searched, the Prime Minister was searched, his old clothes were searched. Eventually an insignificant pocket cast up an envelope and a piece of paper. A copy of the paper was typed out and the Prime Minister was ready.

Now it was full steam ahead. Smash Griffith's attempt to break on Ulster, extend a few concessions, represent them as open for a few hours only, demand an immediate verdict on Dominion Status, win over one man, Griffith probably, press on him an ultimatum with immediate war the alternative to refusal, paint war in all its horrors, and fasten on the Delegation, man by man, the responsibility for imposing it on Ireland.

Meanwhile Churchill was proving unexpectedly generous over Defence, though he gave away little that mattered. The Irish prospects at the end of five years were, on the face of things, considerably improved by his agreeing to add to the provision for the Conference at the end of that time the phrase, "With a view to the undertaking by Ireland of a *share* in her own coastal defence."[1] He

[1] It is doubtful how far this proviso brought net gain to the Irish side, for the phrase "share in coastal defence" tended to rule out the possibility that *all* coastal defence would be eventually ceded.

then elucidated the meaning of the Care and Maintenance Parties insisted on in the Annex. The reference to Admiralty property and rights at Berehaven did not mean that the British would demand compensation if at any time the docks, etc., passed to Ireland. Birkenhead, superbly nonchalant as ever in his exposition of constitutional niceties, explained that if the docks were handed over to the Crown Representative in Ireland, the Crown could not demand payment from the Crown.

By this time Lloyd George had returned, and he now reapplied himself to Griffith. In his hand he brandished an envelope from which what seemed to be a letter half obtruded. He reminded Griffith that the paper had been shown him by Tom Jones on November 13th and that he had agreed to its contents. Barton was thoroughly mystified—he could remember no letter save the one of November 2nd, and so it seemed was Collins. "What is this letter?" Barton whispered to Collins. The relations between these two, real friends for all the gulf that separated their circumstances, were very strained these last days. Collins growled back at him: "I don't know what the hell it is."

Independently Lloyd George put him to the test. "Do you mean to tell me, Mr. Collins, that you never learnt of this document from Mr. Griffith?" Collins gave no sign. It was obvious that he had had no definite knowledge of it; to the British it remained possible that he had gathered from Griffith that some such compact had been entered into.

Lloyd George put back the envelope in his pocket and Chamberlain passed across the table a copy of its contents. It ran as follows:

"If Ulster did not see her way to accept immediately the principle of a Parliament of all Ireland . . .[1] she would continue to exercise through her own Parliament all her present rights; she would continue to be represented in the British Parliament, and she would continue subject to British taxation except in so far as already modified by the Act of 1920. In this case, however, *it would be necessary to revise the boundary of Northern Ireland. This might be done by a Boundary Commission* which could be directed to adjust the line both by inclusion and exclusion so as to make the

[1] The omitted extract runs: "Coupled with the retention by the Parliament of Northern Ireland of the powers conferred upon it by the Act of 1920 and such other safeguards as have already been suggested in my letter of the November 10th—we should then propose to create such Parliament for all Ireland, but to allow Ulster the right within a specified time on an address to the throne carried in both Houses of the Ulster Parliament, to elect to remain subject to the Imperial Parliament for all the reserved services. In this case..."

boundary conform as closely as possible to the wishes of the population."

Now there was no definite promise here that Griffith would assent to the terms mentioned *before* Craig had consented or had even replied. But Lloyd George knew by now a good deal about Griffith. He knew, for example, Griffith's passionate self-respect, and his abnormal sensitiveness to any charge that involved his own or his country's honour. He cared nothing in the ordinary way for whether people liked or disliked him, but all through the negotiations he had set himself, as Chairman of the Delegation, to see that Ireland on her first appearance in the intercourse of nations made a worthy showing, and to dissipate any doubt that sprang from the years of her "grim uprising." So now "Lloyd George appealed to Arthur Griffith, reminding him that he had undertaken that if we consented to such a provision for Ulster as we now offered to him he would not let us down. Griffith answered simply, 'I said I would not let you down on that, and I won't.' " Thus runs Chamberlain's summary. But it appears that Griffith's full response was more volcanic. Shaking his pencil across the table he repudiated with staggering emphasis the charge that he was breaking faith. "I have never let a man down in my whole life and I never will." And then came his simple agreement to abandon all attempt to bring about the break on Ulster.

Again the discussion was resumed, and ranged over many points. It had already become evident that the messenger (Mr. Geoffrey Shakespeare) would be unable to catch the boat-train for his journey to Belfast. A special train was now ordered to be waiting at Euston and a destroyer at Holyhead. But the elimination of the possibility of a break on Ulster had clarified the issues in just the way that the Irish had fought so hard to avoid. On to the scales Lloyd George now pushed a concession which meant much to Griffith, more to Collins, and most of all to Barton. One does not know whether to admire more the self-control which kept it back till now—for surrender on this point had been considered as early as April—or the artistry which produced it at the exact moment when men's minds were wobbling to decision. The concession was full fiscal autonomy.

With the likelihood of "essential unity" demonstrated on the last morning, with the chance of an agreeable oath extended on the last afternoon, and with fiscal autonomy now emerging in the last minutes, no one could accuse any Delegates who signed of consenting to the same terms as had been rejected in Dublin. Lloyd

George knew how to add gravity to the moment, to assume the air of one surrendering principles and running counter to life-long convictions. He himself "had been the strongest of the British Delegation in favour of compulsory free trade on both sides. But he was not going to let his personal feelings . . ." In short, he was prepared to agree provisionally that there should be freedom on both sides to impose any tariffs either country liked. This offer not to stand open, not to go forth to the world as an arrangement in itself satisfactory to the British Delegation, but to be understood as a last sacrifice in the effort to persuade Ireland into voluntary membership of the British Commonwealth of Nations. The offer was to be conditional on Irish signature of the other Articles of Agreement.

Everything possible had been done to placate Irish opinion and sentiment, and to impress the Irish Delegation with the opportunity that attended immediate acceptance. But the issue was now stripped of all subsidiary benefits and obstacles. At last it was narrowed down to this: would Ireland accept inclusion within the Empire, or would she rather face war? It had been insisted all day that the messenger must leave that night for Belfast if Sir James Craig was to know the result of the negotiations in accordance with the Prime Minister's promise. But no ultimatum had yet been launched; Griffith strove desperately, in his own words, "to get them to put it back for a week, to get back to the Dail"; but "I could not get it done." The Prime Minister's promise to Craig was absolute.

Lloyd George recognised his hour. He stated bluntly "the British could concede no more and debate no further. The Irish Delegates must settle now. They must sign the agreement for a Treaty or else quit . . . and both sides would be free to resume whatever warfare they could wage against each other."[1] It was the end of all dreams.

The Irishmen, in Mr. Churchill's recollection, "gulped down the ultimatum phlegmatically"; but it would be hard to know which of them was undergoing the most tormenting conflict. Griffith in particular had promised to sign no document involving allegiance to the Crown. But against that he had declined all along to break on the Crown. He was bound to violate one undertaking or the other, and in that sense could take his choice between them. He chose peace with a settlement that he personally was satisfied with, and that he believed would recommend itself to the vast majority of his countrymen. In his own words: "I said, 'Provided

[1] Winston Churchill.

we came to an agreement on other points, I would accept inclusion in the Empire on the basis of the Free State. They then asked whether I spoke for myself or the Delegation. I said I spoke for myself.' "[1]

Winston Churchill has immortalised the scene. "Mr. Griffith said, speaking in his soft voice and with his modest manner, 'I will give the answer of the Irish Delegation at nine to-night; but Mr. Prime Minister, I personally will sign this agreement and recommend it to my countrymen.' 'Do I understand, Mr. Griffith, that though everyone else refuses, you will nevertheless agree to sign?' 'Yes, that is so, Mr. Prime Minister,' replied this little quiet man of great heart and great purpose." "A braver man than Arthur Griffith," says Sir Austen Chamberlain, "I have never met." No armchair critic of negotiations can ever soil that epitaph.

Griffith refused to let his personal acceptance spell the end of his comrades' struggle. His colleagues, he said, were in quite a different position from himself. They were not parties to the promise not to let Lloyd George down, and it was not fair to demand acceptance from them before Craig replied. Lloyd George would have none of this tomfoolery, this resurrection of the break on Ulster. Again and again he tried to put the question of acceptance or rejection directly or indirectly to Collins and Barton, and each time Griffith prevented him.

At last he grew impatient. He had always, he said, taken it that Arthur Griffith spoke for the whole Delegation, and that all of them were Plenipotentiaries. It was now a matter of peace or war and each of them must now make up his own mind. "Every Delegate must sign the document and undertake to recommend it, or there can be no agreement. We as a body have hazarded our political future (the familiar pompous phrase, and yet it was to prove true enough); you must do likewise and take the same risks."

Showman to the end, he then produced two letters and held them, one in either hand. "I have to communicate with Sir James Craig to-night. Here are the alternative letters which I have prepared, one enclosing Articles of Agreement reached by His Majesty's Government and yourselves, and the other saying that the Sinn Fein representatives refuse to come within the Empire. If I send this letter it is war, and war within three days. Which letter am I to send?[2] Whichever letter you choose travels by special train to Holyhead, and by destroyer to Belfast. The train is waiting with

[1] Extract from Griffith's official letter to De Valera.

[2] The above sentences are quoted verbatim from Sir Austen Chamberlain. Those that follow are based on Irish notes.

steam up at Euston. Mr. Shakespeare is ready. If he is to reach Sir James Craig in time we must know your answer by ten p.m. to-night. You can have until then, but no longer, to decide whether you will give peace or war to your country."

He concluded with a passionate appeal to them to think again before they rejected so generous a settlement. Towards the end he particularly addressed himself to Barton. He knew well enough where lay the centre of recalcitrance, and as about Griffith, so about Barton, he knew several crucial things: his separation from the movement during his fifteen months in prison, his uncertainty of how the real feeling lay in Dublin, his consequent reluctance to take a strong line on his own, especially seeing that the leadership had been entrusted to Griffith and Collins. He told Barton that those who were not for peace must take the full responsibility for the war that would immediately follow refusal to sign the Articles of Agreement. "The English Prime Minister with all the solemnity and the power of conviction that he alone of all men I ever met can impart by word and gesture—the vehicles by which one man oppresses and impresses the mind of another—declared that the signature and recommendation of every member of our Delegation was necessary or war would follow immediately."

The quotation just given from Barton's speech in the Dail a fortnight later ruefully attests the impression made. No one has ever gainsaid Lloyd George's pre-eminence in this particular field. Arguing little, applying rather to conversation the arts of the platform, himself determining the emphasis which all should accord to each consideration, he impregnated his opponents' minds with five reflections to oust all others. That it was impossible to postpone an answer to Craig. That there was nothing unreasonable in asking the Irish for an answer without giving them the chance to refer back to Dublin. That immediate and terrible war would in fact follow refusal. That the responsibility of choice rested on each of them; and hence that the responsibility for war would rest with any Irishman who refused to sign.

Griffith undertook to give the Irish reply by ten o'clock. It was already after eight, but there was still one Irish amendment to be haggled over. Under the existing draft, Craig need not make his choice for twelve months, between an all-Ireland Parliament and a Boundary Commission. The long transition period would provoke uncertainty in the Free State and danger to the minority in the North. Lloyd George consented to shorten it, withdrew at Collins's request the British Delegation while the Irish settled on a period, and returning, accepted a proposed period of a month.

The Conference adjourned till ten o'clock. "Michael Collins rose looking as though he was going to shoot someone, preferably himself. In all my life," says Winston Churchill, "I have never seen so much pain and suffering in restraint."

Mr. Churchill goes on: "We then went off and drummed our heels, and had some food and discussed plans of campaign. No one expected that anyone but Griffith would agree, and what validity would his solitary signature possess?" Birkenhead considered things to be going so badly that, having to speak in Birmingham next day, "he had prepared a speech on the old Anti-Home Rule lines demanding National support for the suppression of the gunmen."[1] Whether Lloyd George was equally pessimistic we cannot tell. What is certain is that on the British side there was nothing to be done, on the Irish, everything still to be decided.

The Irish Delegation had hardly started the drive back to Hans Place when Collins gave out that he meant to sign. Barton was thunderstruck. That Collins would accept a settlement disestablishing the Republic had simply never occurred to him—a fact of significance showing how deep by this time was the rift. But soon Hans Place was reached, the five Delegates and Childers assembled, and the last tragic wrangle began between the six men chosen by Ireland to represent her in her greatest crisis; all worthy in character and attainments of their position, all ready to die for her, but all by now overtired, overstrained, and hopelessly at variance. There was no more beating about the bush. It was simply a Dominion and certain peace versus a Republic in some form and apparently certain war.

The discussion that followed puzzles us by the expedients overlooked. Griffith had insisted up to the last at Downing Street that Collins and Barton could not be expected to give their decision until Craig's answer was known. He had attributed his own signature to the private Park Lane obligation. But Lloyd George's final rhetoric seemed to have stamped on all minds the impression that that cock would not fight. Nothing more was attempted with it.

Again the terms of the Lloyd George ultimatum—immediate signature or war—were accepted as curiously irrevocable. To begin with, this rigmarole about Craig "having to know by next day" was accepted like a law of nature. Lloyd George, it is true, had promised to let him know by Tuesday, but he had after all been kept waiting five or six months since negotiations opened in June. To have waited another day, or another week for that

[1] Vide *Salvidge of Liverpool*, p. 224.

matter, should have imposed little strain on a patience and good humour justly renowned; in any case his temper and convenience could hardly be set against the whole future of both parts of Ireland. It is hardly credible that if Lloyd George had seen any desirable result that delay would have promoted he would have been prevented from pursuing it by fear of being behindhand with Sir James. If the Irish had simply refused to accept the message to Craig as negating the chance of a reference back to the Dail, England and the world must have sympathised with them, and Lloyd George could hardly have persisted.

But of course Lloyd George was entitled to gain a tactical advantage out of the circumstance of the promise and to use it for all it was worth. The two letters, Shakespeare in waiting, the special train with steam up at Euston, the destroyer at Holyhead, were capital turns. Supposing that Sir James must know by Tuesday, a telephone message next morning could have conveyed the essential news; but it would have been worse diplomacy and worse technique.

Finally, the Irish allowed themselves to be pushed rather softly into the shoes of Plenipotentiaries.

The British had never, until now, officially treated them as such. And what of those instructions given them in October and confirmed two days before? Suppose these had been produced with their insistence that before signature "any draft Treaty must be submitted to Dublin and reply awaited"—how could the British have refused to let them refer the decision back? How could they have gone on threatening to make war unless they got their answer within two hours? But in actual fact none of the Irish Delegates bethought themselves of their instructions at all. Even the unwearying Childers nodded this once. The one way out, so obvious now, occurred to no one at the time. Even more obvious is the question, never, so far as we know, answered, nor even asked in public: why was no use made of the telephone to Dublin? Lloyd George, if he had cast no other spell, had obsessed each Delegate with a sense of inescapable personal responsibility. He had conjured Dublin off the map.

## CHAPTER III

# THE SIGNING

"NAPOLÉON (*aside to his Minister*): My God, it was touch and go that time, Talleyrand!"

THOMAS HARDY: *The Dynasts.*

*The last argument—Barton and Gavan Duffy consent—The return to Downing Street—Agreement at last—The signature—The seven survivors—Benefits conferred by the Treaty—The final scene.*

FROM 9 till 11.15 the argument raged, now painful, now pathetic. Duggan joined Griffith and Collins in wishing to sign; Gavan Duffy joined Barton in condemning any such betrayal of the Republic. The five responsibilities (Childers, of course, had no vote) concentrated and lodged on Barton. If he signed, Gavan Duffy could hardly stand out. On the other hand, conversion of Gavan Duffy, who was not in the Cabinet, would not necessarily involve conversion of Barton, who was.

Griffith and Collins did not mince their words. Lloyd George had pictured Irish homes laid waste and the youth of Ireland butchered. They left Barton in no doubt on whom future generations would fix the blame. For every drop of blood shed in Ireland he, and he alone, would be responsible. But Barton's dilemma lay deeper than they knew. War embraced by a united Ireland he was ready to face. But supposing he brought war on a country whose chief Plenipotentiaries had already thrown in their hands? How many men would be found to sustain it at all? What chance would they have? What good would they do? Was it for him, a technical expert, outside the movement these last fifteen months of the struggle, to renew by single fiat a war repudiated by the soldier who had hitherto done most to wage it? With Collins seeking peace, what sort of claim had he, Barton, to decide that war was the people's will?

Over against and for a long time quelling these anxieties stood his oath to the Republic, to him "the most sacred bond on earth." An hour of torture passed and it was time for those who meant to sign to be setting out for Downing Street. Griffith, Collins, and Duggan had put on hats and coats and had reached the landing when Barton caught them up and pulled them back. The same thing happened a second and again a third time. At last Barton obtained consent for a private conversation with Childers. He came back with the suggestion that, if signature there must be, it should be accompanied with the explicit reservation that it was being performed under duress. The idea presented advantages at first, but it did not survive long. All attempts to tone down the sharpness of the decision had now failed.

About this time the citizens of Dublin were beginning to remember the meaning of war. Austin Stack was leaving an opera at the Gaiety Theatre. "I found Gearoid O'Sullivan and Sean O'Murthaille waiting for me. The latest news from London, Gearoid said, was to the effect that negotiations were off and the Plenipotentiaries returning. He added that the Auxiliaries seemed to be at work already, as they were all about the city armed and interfering with people. He warned me not to stay at my usual quarters that night. I said that I'd take the chance as it was too late to look up another place. And so home I went to bed."

Back in Hans Place Barton was still clinging precariously to the Republic; it really seemed as if the end had come, and that Lloyd George would be shortly receiving three of the Delegation with the news that the other two refused to sign. Suddenly Duggan broke down; his mind went back to Richmond Barracks and Kilmainham Gaol, "to that morning in Mountjoy when I saw the hangman who was to hang our young lads there." He lived again his conversations with some of those who had been executed for Ireland from 1916 to 1921. He poured out an appeal to Barton not to cast away the chance for which these simple martyrs had died, and plunge once more in blood the country they had loved so well. Unsophisticated, from the heart, utterly unlike the fierce preceding exhortations, it touched some chord in Barton, not far from breakdown himself. The claims of living humanity overcame those of abstract nationhood; he agreed to come round to Downing Street and sign the Treaty. Gavan Duffy's position was now impossible. Some minutes later he too waived his objections.

Eleven o'clock passed at Downing Street. The British began to doubt whether they would see the Irish again. The suspense had a curious effect on them. "The day," says Sir Austen Chamberlain, "had been one of unrelieved strain. The tension reached its height during the long wait for the return of the Irish Delegation in the evening. But there is a limit to human endurance. The reaction came. I recall that as we waited our talk was of the merriest, and the room rang with laughter."

Then came a message to say that the Irish Delegates were on their way. When they marched in "it was clear from their faces that they had come to a great decision after a prolonged struggle. As before, they were superficially very calm and quiet. There was a long pause, or there seemed to be; then Mr. Griffith said: 'Mr. Prime Minister, the Delegation is willing to sign the agreements, but there are a few points of drafting which perhaps it would be convenient if I mentioned at once.' Thus by the easiest of gestures, he carried the whole matter into the region of minor details. Soon we were talking busily about verbal corrections and holding firmly to these lest worse should befall."[1]

An attempt was made to remove Clause 3 imposing a "King's Representative in Ireland." The request was refused, but the word "Governor-General" disappeared, it being left to the Irish to choose a title, though Chamberlain made it plain that he must not be called President. Up till now the Military Defence Force permitted to Ireland had borne the prefix "local"; Collins demanded and secured the word's removal—his instinct told him that this would mean a good deal to the country. The Financial clause was modified once more in yet another Irish effort to leave open the question which country was on balance in debt to the other. The Irish now urged that Clause 9 forbidding restrictions "on the flow of transport trade and commerce" between the two countries should have disappeared with Clause 8, which had forbidden protective duties. Lloyd George explained that the purpose of Clause 9 was to prevent the boycotting of British shipping. Birkenhead admitted its ambiguity now that Clause 8 had gone, and promptly re-drafted it in a form satisfactory to all.

Collins raised two more points. The provision for the Ulster Militia should be fitted into the clause under which the two parts of Ireland were to arrange between them safeguards for Ulster. This was agreed to. Then he wanted to know how the Southern Ireland Parliament, referred to in Clauses 15 and 17, was to be summoned. Birkenhead, with as little hesitation as before, drafted a memorandum explaining that the Parliament would be summoned by the Provisional Government of Ireland, to which the British Government would transfer the necessary powers. The fiction of British constitutional continuity was thus preserved.

The Prime Minister thereupon asked whether, if these changes were accepted by the British Government, the Irish representatives would sign as a Delegation, and recommend the agreement with their united strength to the Dail. This time Griffith replied in the

[1] Churchill.

name of them all that they would. "Then," said the Prime Minister, "we accept."

It was now one o'clock, but an hour and twenty minutes had still to pass while the stenographers copied "the draft so disfigured with corrections, interpolations, and additions, each of which represented so many hours of hammering discussion."[1] Of this period Lloyd George and Churchill retain only the happiest recollections. One remembers the time being occupied by "a friendly chat full of cheerful goodwill"; the other noticed "a profound change that had taken place in the spirit and atmosphere now that we had become allies and associates in a common cause, the cause of the Irish Treaty and of peace between two races and two islands." But on others the convivial element made less impression, and any hilarity that occurred Sir Austen Chamberlain's earlier analysis would seem sufficient to explain.

Two copies of the final text were brought in, their titles by some accident not complete. Articles of Agreement they were headed. Not till next day were the words "For a Treaty" added to the English copy, and by that time the Irish copy was on its way to Dublin. But this night the voices of the precisians were silent. The moment blurred petty inspection. All seven who were present signed.

They were a diminished band from the seventeen who had been in attendance at the opening sessions, and though the other Delegates signed later and the Secretaries could never have signed, it is not perhaps over-fanciful to see something appropriate in the presences and the absences, and in the directions in which the two months' ordeal had thinned out the ranks. The Treaty was the most serious attempt in history to reconcile England and Ireland. Sir Hamar Greenwood, last representative of the old Castle régime, could be spared. It mocked and terminated the struggles of gallant, up-and-down Unionism. It was no place for Sir Laming Worthington-Evans or the thousands who had fought the fight with him. It owed little to first principles, there had been nothing smooth or genial about its birth, the rich rejoiced more than the poor: Lionel Curtis, Edward Grigg, and Tom Jones were just as well away. Sir Gordon Hewart and John Chartres, the constitutional advisers, were missing, and it proved impossible to work one of its clauses. It was austere; there was no Duggan. It was rich in ambiguity; there was no Gavan Duffy: in compromise; there was no Childers.

Yet with all its faults it bore from its earliest moments the

[1] Lloyd George.

marks to make it never to be forgotten. Lloyd George had seen the vision, and the Treaty will always, and rightly, be associated with his name. But it was Chamberlain who certificated it to the public conscience, and Birkenhead to the public mind. Churchill, with the written and the spoken word, clothed it with flesh and blood, and gave it its chance to gather strength in the imaginations of men. All four had fallen from office within a year—this night's work their heaviest offence.

It bore, too, the signatures of the two greatest Irishmen who ever died for Ireland, perhaps the two greatest men in all history who ever died to keep so hard-wrung a pledge. It bore the signature of Robert Barton in melancholy memorial of the circumstances under which it was signed. Truly it paid tribute to the genius and the grandeur of two ancient neighbouring races, and not less to the sacrifices and the human lives that it cost to bring them even this measure of peace.

To both countries it spelt overwhelming immediate benefits. To England relief immeasurable from an unending political distraction and an age-long sense of shame. Never again would more British Ministries fall on Irish than on English issues. Never again would Englishmen feel that there was one subject to be passed over in talking to their truest friends abroad. Ireland had graduated from a plague-spot into a polity. She was taken out of English politics. The news was too good to be true.

To Ireland it brought common sense, physical emancipation—its lighter burdens, its solid fruits. Dublin Castle would yield up her grim accumulated secrets. The hand of the British legislator, British administrator, and British judge would lie no more heavy on Ireland; the British military and the British police would patrol her paths no more. Lloyd George could salute an Ireland "free within her boundaries to marshal her own resources, direct her own forces, and guide her own destinies." And Griffith could, with equal justice claim: they had got Saorstat na hEireann recognised; they had brought back the flag; they had brought back Ireland a status of equality with England; they had secured the evacuation of Ireland after seven hundred years. They had got a chance for the first time to live their lives in their own way, in their own country, and for the first time take their place among the nations of Europe.

All previous British schemes for Ireland had been by way of Imperial Bills and Acts, establishing subordinate governments. Such had been the Act of 1914, such the Partition Act of 1920, which, six months before the Treaty, the British had refused to amend. But the Treaty, no one doubted, was, in every broad sense, an international instrument. The parties to it were, on the one side, the Ministers of the most powerful and the most elevated Empire that the world has yet seen; on the other, the representatives of Dail Eireann, an Assembly elected and acclaimed by the overwhelming majority of the Irish people, and with some title to the *de facto* government of Ireland; but unrecognised by any foreign country, and unimpressively portrayed in British law as a proscribed society in armed rebellion against the Crown.

A year before, the British Prime Minister had seen in "the whole of this nationality a sham and a fraud." He had described their military organisation as a "small body of assassins, a real murder gang, dominating the country and terrorising it." Eight months before, he was likening a meeting with Michael Collins to one with Kelly, the Phœnix Park murderer. Now he found Collins "one of the most courageous leaders ever produced by a valiant race"— fit comrade for the great task of ending the conflict of centuries.

It was well that it should be so; the world had to master a whole new outlook towards Ireland; it was fortunate if it could re-orientate itself overnight through reconsidering the character of Collins. He had been the first leader on a national scale to place himself, and draw in the mass of the people, behind the policy of armed resistance. He had been the first to see to it that there were no more unattended funerals, "no more lonely scaffolds" for his men. What finer teacher than he of the lesson that to kill in defence of Ireland was no better and no worse than to kill in defence of England; was war not murder, brutal but not brutish, horrible but not crime? All that, he could hope, was over. He could lay down his arms and he could say and feel, "If we wish to make our nation a free and a great and a good nation, we can do so now."

There is no question that the British carried off gracefully the last scene of all. It will be remembered that when the negotiations began Lloyd George had obviated any necessity for a general handshaking by leading the Irish Delegates to the far side of a conference table and introducing them to his colleagues across it. For two months intercourse had officially preserved that distance. Now, when all had signed, "as the Irishmen rose to leave, the British Ministers, upon a strong impulse, walked round and for the first time shook hands."[1] They expressed their hope that the two Delegations "might together have laid the foundations of a

[1] Churchill.

permanent understanding and lasting friendship between the two peoples."[1]

Outside in the lobby, Mr. Lloyd George tells us, "sat a man who had used all the resources of an ingenious and well-trained mind, backed by a tenacious will, to wreck every endeavour to reach agreement, Mr. Erskine Childers. At every crucial point in the negotiations he played a sinister part. When we walked out of the room where we had sat for hours together, worn with toil and anxious labour, but all happy that our great task of reconciliation had been achieved, we met Mr. Erskine Childers outside, sullen with disappointment and compressed wrath at what he conceived to be the surrender of principles he had fought for. . . . I never saw him after that morning. . . . Erskine Childers was shot at dawn for rebellion against the liberties he had helped to win."

That is Lloyd George's memory. To Erskine Childers the abiding image of these last few wretched hours was Churchill, striding up and down the lobby lowering and triumphant, all heavy jowl and huge cigar projecting like the bowsprit of a ship. The very type of overbearing British militarism.

And so after two months of controversy face to face, the Irish had accepted that Imperial bond of union which in Lloyd George's words "is represented by a common fealty to the Sovereign," and "which it is not easy to interpret to those brought up," as were the Irish, "to venerate other systems." The Irish Delegates had met wills as strong, intelligences as subtle, and diplomacy more experienced than theirs. Threats, too, more potent.

[1] Chamberlain.

## CHAPTER IV

# THE POLITICS OF FRIENDSHIP

"Condition!
What good condition can a treaty find
I' the part that is at mercy?"
SHAKESPEARE: *Coriolanus.*

*What Ireland surrendered—The physical disparity—The Irish strategy always too cautious—The break on Ulster—The only way of using it effectively—The Boundary Commission inconsistent with the break on Ulster—Even the advantages of the Boundary Commission lost—Griffith's case—How Civil War came about—How the misunderstanding originated—The British performance—Lloyd George's credit and responsibility—Three features of his diplomacy—The pledge to resign—The Boundary Commission—The Ultimatum.*

So Ireland, having refused to become a Dominion in July had agreed to become one in December. So the "Envoys Plenipotentiary from the elected Government of the Republic of Ireland," the men sent over in October to suggest a relationship to Great Britain under which the Republic could have been preserved—these men, after two months of argument, had signed a Treaty in which the Republic could have no place. They had accomplished many things, but not the one thing that would have brought peace to Ireland. Their prime objective may have all along been impossible of achievement. They had certainly failed to achieve it.

The combatants had never been fairly matched. There had never been approximate parity in their power to do one another harm. On paper External Association might seem to stand a chance; but in practice it would have been a staggering triumph if Griffith and his colleagues had got the British Ministers to accept it. In these circumstances, who are we, thirteen years afterwards, to criticise the labours of the Delegates? Who, above all, is the present writer to proclaim the "errors" of Arthur Griffith? Yet in the light of our knowledge of to-day it would be affectation to pretend that, if a Republic was indeed the goal, the ideal course was pursued towards it, or that the most fatal turns could not have been avoided by exceptional foresight combined with reasonable luck.

First, then, the Irish never made it plain to the British and the world that they stood on the rock of the Republic and would in no circumstances enter the Empire. The British, on the other hand, committed themselves immediately and unequivocally to a policy of in no circumstances allowing Ireland to stay outside. The contrast was very evident in the long Lloyd George-De Valera correspondence, in which De Valera only mentions the word "Republic" twice and then incidentally, while Lloyd George categorically denies Ireland's right of secession: "No such right can ever be acknowledged by us." It is just as marked all through the seven Plenary Sessions. Asked at once to criticise the British proposals, Griffith never approaches Crown and Empire until forced to do so in the sixth Session by Lloyd George. Submitting on October 24th official Irish proposals, he broaches indeed External Association, but with the word "Republic" still left unsaid.[1] Asked in the seventh Plenary Session whether Ireland is prepared to come inside the Empire, he replies discreetly, "That is not quite our idea of association." The point could be illustrated in a hundred different ways. The British leave no doubt about their blank refusal to consider an Ireland outside the Empire; the Irish, while asserting again and again their independence, and right to "government by consent," never demonstrate their final intention to reject all Dominion offers and to persist, come what may, in the defence of the Republic.[2]

Every kind of reason can be urged in excuse for these courses of circumspection. That they would shock and antagonise world opinion, Liberal opinion in England, and the friendly British Press; that they would lead to an instant resumption of hostilities and that it was essential for Ireland to have a breathing-space in which to re-arm. That External Association was complicated and not yet fully worked out; that, unlike any compromise, it would disillusion Irish extremists and more generally dispel Irish enthusiasm; that, contrariwise, at this stage to stand four-square on a Republic would frighten off the vast mass of non-political Irishmen. That it would be humiliating for Ireland to have pledged herself to a Republic if eventually, under pitiless warfare, she was forced to yield. Still more serious—that if such a novel

[1] It is never in fact put forward in any official document submitted to the British between October and December, though occasionally referred to in the reported discussions.

[2] De Valera went further than anybody else in declaring for independence both in his speech just before the Conference began, and in his message to the Pope. But even De Valera failed to stress the Republican aspect of the claim, and the effect of his message to the Pope was toned down by his colleagues in London. The only serious attempt in the early days to make Lloyd George realise that he was negotiating with heart-and-soul Republicans was the device of "Republican" credentials for the Delegates. But Lloyd George took these very lightly.

and unusual scheme was to get a fair chance in England, it was essential that it should be presented with caution and prevision, gradually and inoffensively.

Yet the consequences of "circumspection" suggest that all these considerations would have been better ignored. For ordinary opinion in Ireland grew used to the idea that settlement would come along Dominion lines. So did world opinion, British liberal opinion, and the opinion of the British Press. So did British Ministers. So, subconsciously perhaps, and in a much smaller degree, did Griffith and Collins. The last two results may be expanded a little. The British Ministers knew that the Irish ideal was a Republic. But they saw that, when challenged, her Delegates failed to say so. Why? Because, presumedly, they thought that to lodge such a claim meant war, and because, presumably, it was not one for which they were prepared to face war in the last resort.

And so the British began to assume that the Irish resistance to a Dominion settlement was bluff and could be smashed in extremity by an ultimatum. The Irish, on the other hand, never knew in what circumstances, if at all, and with how much reluctance, if any, the British would go to war. The Irish had shown their weakness. The British had not.

Again, the British would never in the early stages (only once, indeed, in the whole negotiations) explore the Irish scheme. The Irish were always having to explore that of their opponents. One guesses that the psychological effect must cumulatively have grown considerable.

Take all the consequences together. By December Ireland was less ready to fight for a Republic,[1] friends for such a fight were less likely to rally from outside (for the fight, by this time, had been made to seem so much more unreasonable), British Delegates were convinced that Ireland's bluff could be called, and the leading Irish Delegates had probably grown less certain of the sacredness of the issue.

So much for the general policy we have labelled "circumspect" (and for whose inception De Valera must share responsibility, though very early in the Conference he attempted to check the lengths to which Griffith was carrying it). After October 24th, more especially after October 30th, it acquired a special twist under a particular handling of the Ulster issue. It was the policy

[1] Against these psychological considerations must be set the fact that the Irish military position on the physical side had been considerably strengthened by December. See opinion of General Macready, *Annals of an Active Life*, Vol. II, p. 562.

of Sinn Fein to convince the British that they would accept a reasonable settlement under Crown and Empire if the British could secure them "essential unity" in return. In this way, reckoned Sinn Fein, either Ulster would be won or a break would come on the Ulster issue, rendering war against them impossible.

For some time the policy seemed to be succeeding. On November 3rd Griffith wrote that "if Ulster proves unreasonable they are prepared to resign rather than use force against us. In such event, no British Government is capable of formation on a war policy against Ireland"; and De Valera wrote back explaining that he had always been in favour of the break coming, if at all, on Ulster, and commenting in warm congratulation, "There can be no doubt whatever that the Delegation has managed to do this admirably." On November 3rd, too, Lloyd George was telling Riddell that if Ulster refused an all-Ireland Parliament he would resign rather than make war on the South.

That day (November 3rd) was the Irish high-water mark. Two days later Craig arrived in London, saw Lloyd George and left little doubt about the intransigence of Ulster. Lloyd George, it is true, goes on hammering away at him; Sinn Fein hopes rise higher than ever. But on November 16th the British attack is suddenly switched back on them, they are handed terms as uncompromising as ever on Crown and Empire, and now with no guarantee of "essential unity." And on the 18th the full seriousness of the position strikes Griffith. "The crucial question, Crown and Empire, must be next week. If Ulster gets us to break on them, she will have re-won the game."

The struggle to bring about the break on Ulster still persists. The Dublin Cabinet still pin their faith to it on the last Saturday and send the Delegates back with an incomplete mandate in consequence. Griffith persuades Barton to come to the last Conference to try it on once again. But when it comes to the point in Downing Street Griffith finds himself checked by a previous undertaking of his own; he is compelled to renounce the tactics. In the hours of supreme decision the break on Ulster proves useless.

Was the break on Ulster then always a will o' the wisp holding out false hopes, distracting counsel, and compelling continued concessions on the very edge of a Dominion settlement? In the event the pursuit of it certainly wrought all these evils. But were there any circumstances in which the break itself might have been achieved? It looks as if there were.

Sinn Fein would have been satisfied by either one of two outcomes: (1) The acceptance by Ulster of an over-riding Dublin Parliament; or (2) a break with England on such an issue as would have made war on the South impossible, and ultimately left Sinn Fein in undisturbed Republican rule. On November 3rd it seemed to Griffith, and even now seems to us, that one or other result was inevitable. On the 8th, however, a cloud no bigger than Jones's hand begins to darken one corner of the horizon. Jones is unofficially sounding Griffith on a Boundary Commission and Griffith is not turning it down.

Now the Boundary Commission would either be accepted by Craig or refused. If he accepted, Sinn Fein would get the equivalent of two out of Ulster's six counties.[1] If he refused, Sinn Fein would be able to raise the cry of Ulster's intransigence and break on Ulster even more reasonably than before. Jones, therefore, could make the scheme sound attractive enough. But while in a sense it kept two strings to the Sinn Fein bow, and kept the way open to both their original objectives—"essential unity" or a break—it did so in effect by renouncing the main advantages of each. For the gain of two counties was a very different thing from, a very inferior thing to, an over-riding Parliament; was not, in fact, "essential unity" at all. While the very fact of its being a compromise made it more likely that the British would push it through, whatever Craig said or did, and therefore made a break on Ulster less probable.

By tolerating the Boundary Commission the Irish must then have relaxed their hold on Lloyd George. But there still seemed a chance of a break coming "on the Boundary Commission" through Craig refusing it, and the rock-bottom safeguard if everything went wrong of large new territories at least. It needed two more disasters to crush both hopes. Somehow on December 5th Griffith found himself, or was made to feel himself, estopped by his conversations of November 12th—a day off the main track of tactics—from breaking on Ulster at all. And four years later the Boundary Commission had done its work and never added an acre to the area of the South—a result undreamt of by any Irishman who signed the Treaty. In this last case, the fault, in so far as it was Irish, must rest either on the legal intelligences of 1921 which failed to see evil lurking in Clause 12, or on those of 1925 which permitted the decision of Mr. Justice Feetham.

What Griffith ought to have done—it is easy enough to see it

[1] With the additional possibility that the loss of territory would render Ulster an uneconomic unit and eventually force her into union with the South.

now—was to preserve rigid dichotomy between the two alternative aims, and as soon as it appeared probable, as it must have done from the 8th onwards, that Craig would stand fast, to go all out for the Ulster break. Lloyd George's promise to resign if an all-Ireland Parliament proved impossible was unexpected good fortune. Griffith should have clamped him fast to it, scouted the illusion of a Bonar Law militarist régime, and stood ready to watch Lloyd George's fall with equanimity. Lloyd George might not have resigned—the palavers of the time reflect a genuine intention yet not perhaps a real likelihood—but how, if he had been kept strictly to his word, could he ever have made war on the South? On November 12th Lord Riddell reports Lord Balfour in America as saying, "acutely"; "The best plan would be to decline to coerce either Ulster or the South of Ireland."

In other words, the Republic would have been saved and the break on Ulster justified to the full.

Yet all our criticisms up till now admit of one simple retort: what, it will be objected, about the immense improvements effected by the negotiations in London upon the original British terms? What about fiscal autonomy and the new inoffensive Oath? What about the allowance for an Irish Navy and for a financial counter-claim? What about the hardly won but explicit assurance that Dominion Status would not in theory only but in fact also confer the same freedom on Ireland as on Canada? Were not these achievements the fruit of a policy of impressing British Ministers with Irish integrity and Irish desire for reasonable settlement? Is it conceivable that they would ever have been won by De Valera or by anyone out to preserve the Republic at all costs? Was not the Republic in fact doomed, whether without more war or after a return to it? Was not the only change in the underlying situation between October and December a list of advantages gained by sheer Irish skill in bargaining? Were not Griffith's tactics justified abundantly by results?

Besides, it may be argued, were there not certain respects in which the Dominion Status granted in the Treaty was actually of more benefit to Ireland than the arrangement she had striven for under External Association? The Treaty secured full fiscal autonomy; would not the final version of External Association have derogated from such autonomy? Again, were there not untold advantages in securing a position whose preservation and enhancement would be guaranteed by the self-interest and the sentiment of other dominions, rather than one which would rob

Ireland of those natural allies and leave her to defend herself as best she might, alone? Did not, finally, a settlement such as the Treaty, imposed from the British side, offer far more scope for legitimate amendment than one put forward by Ireland as a settlement "honourable" and, by implication, final?

It is possible, though not easy, to hold and develop this standpoint. It is possible, though still harder, to argue (it would be strange if the contention were true) that the fight for the Republic was conducted along lines that we with all our present knowledge could not improve on today. But what is indisputable (what we have not yet touched on) is that the circumstances in which the Delegates signed led inevitably to what was for Ireland the supreme tragedy of the period, perhaps of her whole history. The signing away in London of the symbols of national independence contrary to the wishes of a majority of the total Cabinet—here was stuff and to spare for civil war at any time, let alone a time when the whole nation, struggling heroically for freedom, hung on the verge of revolutionary hysteria.

The point is not that it was wrong to sign on Tuesday morning. Once the inaccessibility of Dublin was admitted (and here the Delegates were strangely innocent) we can presume to dictate no course better than the one actually adopted. What is hard to understand is the failure to foresee and lay plans against the emergency. It was clear that Griffith was ready to lead a party of signature; De Valera one against. It was surely not asking too much of collective statesmanship to take precautions so that whatever else ensued there should be no civil war.

Why and how the mutual understanding for this purpose was lacking should by now have emerged from these pages. Everyone will emphasise responsibility differently. It should be at least obvious that all acted as they did in what they thought the highest interests of their country, and that all were men of perspicacity, character, and courage. Under its most generalised aspect, the story is of a handful of men of widely different antecedents, linked together in brief practical intimacy for a single revolutionary purpose—the freeing of their country—with little opportunity for laying plans against the future, still less for communicating them to each other or discovering how they each severally reacted to hypothetical contingencies; a handful of men never guessing till too late what different attitudes to a Republic could split a Republican camp. England had had centuries to learn what she meant by the "integrity" of her Empire and what she would sacrifice to save it; Ireland had moved too rapidly to freedom to be unanimous as to where its essence lay. The most revealing incidents of the whole negotiations are Barton's amazement when Collins told him on the last evening that he meant to sign, and Collins's confidence till he got back to Dublin that De Valera would not repudiate the Treaty.

We must leave the Irish hopes, ruses, and failures. The British performance is less controversial. Die-hards who refer to the Treaty as a surrender would do well to transfer their scorn to the June invitation to De Valera and whatever friends he chose to bring, or to the July offer of Dominion Status. On the main issue, the Treaty negotiations proper, those from October to December, were a diplomatic triumph for Britain. And Lloyd George, Chamberlain, Birkenhead, and Churchill each played a manful and resourceful part.

Without the original consent, initiation even, of Chamberlain and Birkenhead, the path to settlement could never have been trodden. Without their firm adherence to his own person, without their prompt suppression of each incipient Conservative revolt, Lloyd George must have been driven from the path of settlement by one or other incident long before December was reached.

When Irishmen think of English politicians as self-seeking, they should honourably except Sir Austen Chamberlain and Lord Birkenhead. Each in turn saw the Prime Ministership ahead of him; each resolutely turned his gaze away from it and searched instead his own philosophy for a way of peace with Ireland.

But when every tribute has been paid to loyal and brilliant support, the Treaty remains Lloyd George's individual creation. His the major credit for such settlement as it provided, his all the responsibility for the artifices by which it was achieved. The main lines of his strategy will have become apparent. The initial insistence in public and in conference that Ireland must remain in the Empire; the seduction of Sinn Fein into advance after advance towards this position by dangled hopes of pressure on Craig with an all-Ireland Parliament as the goal; the escape from the pledge of resignation by the introduction of the Boundary Commission as an alternative route to "essential unity"; the outmanœuvring of Griffith on November 12th; the sudden pressure on the South, the last-minute temptations, the apprehension of Irish dissensions and the ultimatum which would use them to the full. The moves speak for themselves.

How far must their legacy in Ireland be one of justifiable resentment? It was too much to expect of Lloyd George that he would look a few years into the future and abjure every approach to settlement which would render settlement ephemeral. We are not concerned now with how far his ultimatum, for example, fell below standards of far-sighted statesmanship; only with the relation of his total technique to that of normal diplomacy. He can be arraigned on three counts. His general attitude to the all-Ireland Parliament; his use of the Boundary Commission; his use of the ultimatum.

On the first head a partisan will find him treacherous; a student tricky at worst. He induced the Irish concessions by promising either an all-Ireland Parliament or resignation. And it is true that he gave them neither. But he pressed Craig genuinely for a time at least, and while Ulster's obduracy was becoming established, was actually securing remission of his obligations from Sinn Fein, was practically being asked to stay in office. How far there was ever a serious chance that he would resign becomes unimportant. As the affair went he was excused from every shred of obligation to do so. No doubt he deceived Griffith in the sense of giving him an impression that he was far more on the side of the South than he was in reality, but after all the Irish tactics, though we can see now that they were beyond reproach, were at the time themselves liable to misunderstanding. Lloyd George was surely entitled to claim that to slimness he but opposed more slimness.

Our narrative has exhibited, if nothing else, the vital part played by the Boundary Commission from the day (November 8th) when Tom Jones first mentioned it, almost in passing, to Griffith. Without it the Irish would never have relaxed the hold so secure on November 3rd, and the succeeding month's negotiations would never have been. If it had not been for expectations from the Boundary Commission held out to him on the last morning, Michael Collins would never have agreed to sign and there would have been no Treaty. Collins's memorandum written immediately after his interview with Lloyd George and some hours therefore before signature of the Treaty, records what, after two months of discussion centring perhaps round this clause more than any other, the Irish believed they would get from it. ". . . We would save Tyrone and Fermanagh, parts of Derry, Armagh, and Down by the Boundary Commission. . . . Lloyd George remarked that I myself pointed out on a previous occasion that the North would be forced economically to come in." And in the end they got nothing.

"It is always difficult in the affairs of a democratic country," as has been well said of certain Articles of the Treaty of Versailles,[1] "to determine the exact point where mere inconsistency and laxity of thought merge into something like deliberate perfidy. It may so easily happen that one set of individuals give the promise and quite another act in breach of it." It happened so in this case. But the business was tortuous. The facts must be studied later and in full.[2]

The ultimatum—"Yes or no now, no consultation with Dublin"—must be distinguished from the threat of war itself. England had as much and as little right to make of war an instrument of national policy as any Empire that sees in the independence of a small community, hitherto subject, a danger to its safety or honour. The peculiar hardship of the Treaty ultimatum was not the "terrible" but the "immediate" character of its threat. Lloyd George said in effect to the Delegates: "The choice between signing away your country's independence and plunging your country into war rests with you and you alone." By so determining the responsibility he enhanced immeasurably his chances of victory beyond what they would have been if the decision had been left to the Dail. And, less disputable tragedy for Ireland, the ultimatum led directly to a split among the Irish leaders, through split to civil war, and through a civil war to thirteen years' bitterness not ended.

There is no other instance of an ultimatum of this character in the diplomatic history of modern ages. The device has been barred even by the rude standards which have governed hitherto international bargaining. Its use in the circumstances of December 5th darkens the last hours of the Conference as effectively as it squandered the efforts of two months to bring about a lasting peace. It will remain till all incidents and occasions of conflict between the two countries are forgotten, an offence against the light of nations, its author an inspired negotiator out of place in peace-making.

[1] Professor Gilbert Murray.
[2] See Epilogue, Chapter I, and Appendix 8.

# Part Five

## THE BRITISH PRESS ON THE TREATY

*Daily Telegraph* (Wednesday, December 7th).—"Wherever our tongue is spoken this news will be heard amid heartfelt joy and thankfulness. . . . This event . . . is the greatest that has happened in the internal affairs of the country for generations."

*Daily Mail* (Wednesday, December 7th).—"This plan of Irish settlement establishes clearly before the world the British love of liberty and the desire to extend it widely."

*Daily Express* (Wednesday, December 7th).—"Now for business! The settlement of the Irish question throws wide open the doors for the entry of the Boom in Trade."

*Daily News* (Wednesday, December 7th).—"God Save Ireland."

*Morning Post* (Thursday, December 8th).—"The document discloses an abandonment and betrayal of British powers and British friends in Ireland. We cannot see our way to join in the finely orchestrated chorus which greets the alleged settlement in Ireland."

*Morning Post* (November 29th, 1922).—"We regard this instrument as the most disastrous blunder ever committed by a British Government."

# THE AFTERMATH

"Peace, peace; when there is no peace."
JEREMIAH.

I: *The chorus of praise—De Valera hears something in Limerick—He gets the news from Stack—A terrible moment—The Treaty arrives—The Delegates summoned back—A full Cabinet Meeting—The split made public.* II: *From Treaty to Civil War—The inevitable steps.*

## I

THE Rubicon had been crossed and all the trumpets sounded. "Reason," said *The Times*, "has prevailed. These are indeed fitting peace terms to mark the close of an age of discontent and distrust, and the beginning of a new era of happiness and mutual understanding." "It is only by degrees," said the *Manchester Guardian*, "that we shall realise the great change that has come over British Politics by the settlement of the Irish question." The *Nation*, that almost alone in the English Press had pressed the case for a Republic, was satisfied that under the Treaty Ireland had got all she wanted: "We salute," began its leading article, "the Irish nation. It is a great thing to bring a people so gifted as the Irish into the counsels of the Commonwealth. It is a greater thing still for one country to lift the hand of oppression from another." "Well done all," said the *Daily Mail*.

The Archbishop of Canterbury offered up devout thanksgiving; His Majesty the King congratulated Mr. Lloyd George, and was himself congratulated by the President of France. Dominion Premiers replied (not as was alleged on pre-paid forms) to Lloyd George's intimations of victory with panegyrics that he himself could hardly have improved on. Sir Oswald Mosley gleaned from the result direct personal encouragement; "May those," said he, "who fought a lonely battle for this great cause in the early days of contumely and vilification be inspired by this fresh vindication of their principles, to march forward in the service of humanity and peace to the yet greater victories of the future."

No arm had been stronger in the battle than Sir John Simon's. Now that it was decided, his were the choicest phrases to express the universal prayer. "Ireland," he said, "is rich in her store of poetry and history, but the chief of her possessions and the greatest of her gifts to the world is the Irish epic that stretches from Robert Emmet, through Butt, Parnell, and Redmond, to the Irish Delegates. 'Let no man write my epitaph,' cried Robert Emmet, in the dock. 'When my country takes her place among the nations of the earth then, and not till then, let my epitaph be written.' It would be a fine gesture if Sinn Fein wrote it now."

Down in Limerick De Valera woke early on the morning of Tuesday, December 6th. He found a strange rumour—no one knew how it had come—floating over the town. An agreement had been reached in London, but its terms were unknown.

De Valera was surprised. He had assumed all along that the Delegates would carry out their instructions to the letter and sign no agreement that had not been submitted to Dublin in its final form. Still, he could imagine circumstances in which the Delegates might have risked formal rebuke for the sake of some dazzling bargain to be clinched immediately if at all. The door to External Association must have suddenly been thrown open, though with the intimation that it would not be open long. Under some lucky combination of circumstances the British must have collapsed. "I did not think they would give in so soon," he said.

It happened that he had to preside that evening at a Dante Centenary Celebration arranged by the Ministry of Fine Arts to be held at the Mansion House, Dublin. As he travelled up from Limerick his confidence of the morning changed first to vague disquiet and then to downright alarm. There was more than one indication to suggest that what had been signed would prove to be very much on the lines that the Dublin Cabinet had found impossible on the Saturday. But he could hardly believe the signs authentic.

When at last he reached the Lord Mayor's room at the Mansion House, he found Cathal Brugha and Austin Stack awaiting him. Austin Stack had already read a rough outline of the Treaty terms in the evening paper; he has left us his recollection of what followed:

"It was late when the motor arrived from Limerick. The first question the President asked was, 'Any news!' I said, 'Yes.' 'Good or bad?' 'Bad.' I was about to show him the evening paper when I decided to leave it alone until after the meeting.[1] He donned his

[1] This is incorrect. Stack showed De Valera the paper and the latter had time to glance through a summary of the first few clauses—the "Dominion" and "Oath" clauses—of the Treaty.

gown (University) and was about to lead the way into the Round Room when who should arrive but Mr. E. J. Duggan and Mr. Desmond Fitzgerald. Duggan reached the President an envelope which the President ignored. Duggan asked him to read the contents. 'What should I read it for?' 'Oh,' said Duggan, 'it is arranged that the thing be published in London and Dublin simultaneously at 8 o'clock, and it is near that hour now.' 'What,' said the President, 'to be published whether I have seen it or not—whether I approve or not?' 'Oh, well, that's the arrangement,' Duggan replied. The President took up the envelope, opened it, glanced over the contents. . . . At the moment he appeared to me to be an almost broken man.

"I should have mentioned that before De Valera opened the despatch I said to Duggan: 'Surely ye didn't make that settlement?' 'What settlement?' he asked. 'Is such and such an Oath in it?' I asked. 'Oh, yes.' 'And recognition of the Crown?' 'Oh, yes.' 'Then why did ye sign—how could ye?' 'It was war in five minutes,' he said, 'unless we signed.'

"A few minutes later we proceeded into the Round Room and I tried to listen to the different papers read on the author of the *Divine Comedy*. I half expected the President to say something to warn the people against the so-called settlement, but he never opened his mouth during the procedings save to introduce the speakers. Afterwards Cathal and myself met him in the study but little or nothing was said. We were all too full of disappointment."[1]

Next day, Wednesday, December 7th, De Valera summoned Brugha, Stack, Cosgrave and Kevin O'Higgins to a Cabinet Meeting. By now the Press of the world was ringing with congratulation to all concerned in the Treaty, but inside the Mansion House the question discussed amid infinities of despondency was how to continue the fight for the Republic. Someone even suggested that the Delegates should be arrested as traitors immediately on their return. De Valera held that was going much too far, but for a long time it looked as though the Delegates would be publicly repudiated without more ado. Cosgrave, however, interceded for them persistently: surely it was hard to condemn them without hearing what they had to say? And eventually De Valera agreed

[1] Some of the details of the above narrative are flatly denied. But the essential point, not affected by any criticisms of Stack's account, is that by the time Duggan and Fitzgerald arrived, De Valera was already overwhelmed with disappointment, and utterly sick at heart. At that moment he was in no mood for close study of the details of what he regarded as a shameful betrayal.

to let them first be heard in their defence. For this day and the next we can turn back to Stack.

"The President ordered that they be summoned back by wire for a Cabinet Meeting to take place the next day, the 8th, 'to consider the circumstances under which the Plenipotentiaries had signed the agreement in London.'[1] These or some such words appeared in the official note which he drafted for publication. Desmond Fitzgerald, who was in charge of Publicity, came into the room immediately the note had been handed him, and he said, 'This might be altered, Mr. President. It reads as if you were opposed to the settlement.' 'And that is the way I intend it to read. Publish it as it is,' the President told him. Fitzgerald said aside to me a few minutes later, 'I did not think he was against this kind of settlement before we went over to London.' I answered—'He's dead against it now anyway. That's enough.'

"The Plenipotentiaries all returned in time for Thursday's Cabinet Meeting. The attendance was complete. The President, Griffith, Brugha, Collins, Cosgrave, Barton and myself (Stack), of the Cabinet—Gavan Duffy and Duggan, Plenipotentiaries—O'Higgins—whilst Erskine Childers had also been asked to attend. The meeting lasted the whole day and late into the night. We were not unfriendly towards one another. The merits and demerits of the Agreement were gone into—but not in detail to any extent. The main thing was how they came to sign. Mr. Griffith, if I remember aright, would not admit duress by the British. Mr. Collins said if there was duress it was only the 'duress of the facts,' whatever he meant by that. But both Barton and Gavan Duffy were candid and said that they had been forced to sign. On and on dragged the discussion, the President, Cathal and myself doing our best to get the others not to press the document on the Dail. I thought Collins was seeing the trouble ahead once. I turned to him and spoke of the way the country would be divided and said imploringly, 'You have signed and undertaken to recommend the document to the Dail. Well—recommend it. Your duty stops there. You are not supposed to throw all your influence into the scale. I believe,' I added, 'if the Dail rejects this we will be in a better position than ever we were, and England will have made only a trap for herself by her action. Will you do it?' "

[1] Stack of course was writing from memory. The actual words were—"In view of the nature of the proposed Treaty with Great Britain, President De Valera has sent an urgent summons to the members of the Cabinet in London to report at once that a full Cabinet decision may be taken. The hour of meeting is fixed for 12 o'clock noon to-morrow. The date of the meeting of the Dail to which the Cabinet's decision has to be submitted has not yet been fixed."

But Michael Collins refused point-blank to dishonour his signature.

"That ended it. The meeting ended sometime too. A division was taken. Griffith, Collins, Cosgrave and Barton voting one way, and the President, Cathal and myself the other. Barton explained that he thought he was bound to vote for the document having signed it and undertaken to recommend it.

"Immediately after this meeting, the President wrote a letter to the Press,[1] explaining his position and that of Cathal Brugha and myself. This appeared on December 9th. Meantime the 'Treaty' and all the propaganda in its favour had had three days start and we never made up the handicap. The British and Irish Press carried the people off their feet in favour of the 'Treaty and Peace.'"

Stack's last comment is just. By December 9th the world had got into its head that the Treaty was an unmixed blessing for Ireland, and that it was accepted by all sane representative Irishmen as such. The jubilation that had greeted the news of signature was the measure of the irritation and abuse which De Valera stirred up against himself by his letter repudiating the Treaty. The average newspaper had of course gone much too far to change or suspend judgment without sorry loss of face. While even a man like H. W. Nevinson—and no more chivalrous or more sympathetic pen than his was ever lifted on behalf of Ireland—confessed to bewilderment and horror.

The letter itself was dignified and unexceptionable. "My friends Irishmen, you have seen in the public Press the text of the proposed Treaty with Great Britain. The terms of the agreement are in violent conflict with the wishes of the majority of the Nation as expressed freely in successive elections during the last three years. I feel it my duty to inform you immediately that I cannot recommend the acceptance of the Treaty either to Dail Eireann or the country. In this attitude I am supported by the Ministers of Home Affairs and Defence. A public session of Dail Eireann is being summoned for Wednesday next at 11 o'clock.... The great test of our people has come. Let us face it worthily without bitterness and above all without recriminations. There is a definite constitutional way of resolving our political differences...."

Holding the principles he did De Valera had no course but to write a letter of this kind. He would have been a traitor to all he

[1] The "letter to the Press" would be better described as an open letter to the Irish people.

believed in if he had held his peace. Yet no one knew better than he that after his letter things could never be the same again. For it spelt inevitably the end of that national unity, that brotherhood in quest of freedom, which had made the two years preceding not only the most revolutionary in Ireland's history, but in some ways the most glorious. "There is a definite constitutional way of resolving our differences." There may have been, but it proved impossible to find it. Dail Eireann debated the Treaty for a fortnight and agreed to it by 64 votes to 57 on January 7th. Six months later the guns of the Provisional Government were thundering against the Four Courts and Civil War had begun.

## II

The months preceding the Civil War show one great difference from those that went before the Treaty. In the earlier period we can amuse ourselves and possibly instruct posterity by criticising the crucial moves that led up to signature in the special circumstances of December 6th; we can play the game over again to our own satisfaction and triumph. But it is not so with the months of January-June 1922. Here all was inevitable, the end was in the beginning. Lofty characters and heroic souls are wound up like clockwork, and driven down predestined grooves to fatal collisions. We can offer no advice, explanations only. We can feel no superiority, only dejection.

How will the universal historian see the complicated chapter of Irish history which these six months comprised? He will see a Legislative Assembly accept a Treaty giving a far greater degree of freedom from foreign interference than any previously enjoyed, but involving the surrender of a Republic two years before established and an independence two years before declared. He will note a general agreement that the acceptance of the Treaty and the disestablishment of the Republic must be confirmed by explicit vote of the people. He will observe a General Election whose results suggest strong popular desire to acquiesce in the decision of the legislature, but conducted under such peculiar conditions that it is hard to say whether it does or does not provide a constitutional mandate for ratifying the Treaty and disestablishing the Republic.

He will see the majority treat the mandate as valid, proceed with the transition to Dominion Status, and partly under the necessities of civil order, partly under urgent representations, actual or potential, from the other Party to the Treaty, make war on a strong section of the army that clings to the Republic and repudiates the authority of the elected Government. He will see the dissentients joined for one reason or another by many men of distinction, public spirit and deliberation, who would normally have no use for revolt. He will find that their reasons can mostly be traced back to a sense of flagrant constitutional abuses in the conduct of the governing majority. But these the majority as passionately and sincerely deny.

He will conclude that the Treaty was bound to lead to armed resistance by extremists. He will entertain the possibility that any Treaty might have done likewise. But he will further conclude that this particular Treaty, signed under its own unique circumstances, was bound to do much more. He will watch it driving through the midst of the political leaders, and thence through every community, great or small, in Ireland, a deep penetrating wedge of resentment, alienation and suspicion; in such a way that from now on every motive and intention will be distorted, every act and gesture misconstrued.

Prepared now for limitless disputation and confusion, he will read without surprise of the tangle of cancelled Conventions, anomalous Pacts and ambiguous Elections, that by the middle of 1922 had so cluttered round as hopelessly to obscure the single issue—the right of the majority to rule versus the right of the minority to fight for a fuller national independence. He will see a great mass of peace-loving Republicans swept into the ranks of those in militant revolt by the conviction that the assault on the Republic, itself a lamentable sacrilege, is being conducted in a treacherous and unconstitutional form.

The universal historian will be moved to few congratulations and as little tempted to reproof. For he will feel certain that the Treaty, signed as it was, must always have divided Ireland with bitter discord, torn her with conflict between cruel exacting loyalties, and so preserved her for a space for the British Commonwealth with an economy of British lives.

# Part Six

## EPILOGUE

### CHAPTER I

### THE TREATY FULFILLED

"They shall be remembered for ever,
They shall be alive for ever,
They shall be speaking for ever,
The people shall hear them for ever."

W. B. YEATS.

*The Treaty carried out—The end of Civil War—Arthur Griffith —Michael Collins—Erskine Childers—Cosgrave and the Treaty—The constitutional advances—The debacle of the Boundary Commission—The discharge of an obligation—The Republican tradition—The Republicans realise their programme—The differences with England—The Economic War—De Valera.*

ALL that was thirteen years ago. The Treaty Party won the Civil War. They had the majority of the population on their side, though at the beginning the old I.R.A. was more evenly divided; they had artillery and the far more liberal supply of ammunition; they had the wherewithal to pay and organise a disciplined national army. They co-ordinated their purposes and pursued them in the desperate knowledge that they must win through quickly, or see themselves go under amid general disintegration and collapse.

The Republicans were decentralised, divided in counsel, and troubled in mind; those who had been through the Anglo-Irish War fought bravely, but too often a rabble, attaching itself to their ranks, mistook sabotage for military obstruction. They failed to make use of the resources open to them; they never gave De Valera, nor, in spite of all that was supposed by their opponents, Erskine Childers, effective opportunity to influence the campaign. In these circumstances, the war could have only one end.

The Four Courts surrendered after two and a half days' siege. Dublin was cleared in eight days. Throughout July one leading town after another was falling into the hands of the advancing

Free State Forces; the capture of Cork early in August marked the end of regular war. After that it was a question of rounding up guerilla bands, that split into ever smaller units. On March 23rd 1923, De Valera and Frank Aiken, the Republican Chief of Staff, called on all Republicans to cease hostilities and to dump their arms. By July the country was judged quiet enough for a General Election.[1]

Before, however, the later more heart-rending phases of the war were reached, three out of the four great figures of the revolution had fallen, and with them Erskine Childers, whose name, for twenty years a household word in England, the whole world seemed conspiring these last days to defile.

Cathal Brugha, refusing, as once before, to surrender, fell fighting at the corner of the street that now bears his name in the early days of July. Griffith, worn out by past labours and privations and present anguish, died of heart failure on August 9th. Michael Collins walked behind his coffin, revealed to an adoring populace at closer quarters than ever before. A week later he was fighting for his life not many miles from his home at Clonakilty. Soon still vaster crowds were gathering for a second funeral that will long be remembered even in the land of funerals.

On November 10th, Erskine Childers was captured at Glendalough House, County Wicklow, his boyhood home; he was found guilty of having in his possession a small automatic pistol which Collins had once given him, and on November 24th, under the provisions of a Dail resolution of six weeks earlier, he was shot at dawn.

Arthur Griffith—"the greatest intellectual force stimulating the national revival," as Childers described him—was many things. Journalist, publicist, educationist, statesman, Griffith was these and more; but above all he was a man, *vir tenax propositi.* "In one case," recalled Cosgrave, in the Dail, "a meeting to be addressed by the late President was proclaimed. At the risk of his life and leaving behind the late Commander-in-Chief as President's substitute, he set out for Sligo determined to die before he would admit the right of any person armed or unarmed to restrict liberty. . . . I bear witness to the cheerfulness with which the late President set out on that journey."

Disraeli once expressed surprise that a people with "so much genius, so much sentiment, such winning qualities" as the Irish, should be "so deficient in self-respect." Griffith in his life and

[1] The result confirmed the Treaty Party in power, but the Republican vote, with 16,000 Republicans in gaol, exceeded all anticipations.

person did most to kill that slander. Master of his own fate, he more than any man vindicated Ireland's right to be trusted with hers.

To those who remembered his life of self-denial, and who saw him after the Treaty, now President of Dail Eireann and the first man in the State, still coming into Dublin on the top of the habitual tram while all around him young "Generals" and "Commandants" tore about in military cars—to some of these may have occurred words written by Griffith as long ago as 1905 about another liberator: "Like all the truly great ones of the world, he was simple and unostentatious to the end."

Michael Collins had loomed very large to England. After all he was the first young man in living memory to disturb the Imperial counsels; the first young man on record to turn back the Imperial tide. "Mr. Collins," cried Lord Carson, on March 16th 1922, in the House of Lords, "is not only paramount over England, but he is paramount over right, paramount over wrong, paramount over logic." "Regard," said Mr. Churchill when Collins died, "will be paid by widening circles to his life and to his death." But there is no English tribute that English admirers will remember more, and none more studied and precise, than Lord Birkenhead's defence of the same speech of Collins's that led to Lord Carson's criticism just quoted. "That speech," said Lord Birkenhead, "delivered by a man without political education, is a speech which whether you examine the form of its literary expression or its judgment of affairs, no Member of this House need be ashamed of having delivered."

In Ireland he left no bitter memories. "We pay our tribute," wrote Childers at his death, "to an Irishman who, whatever his errors, worked untiringly according to his own conscience and judgment for the good of Ireland." "His death," said Kevin O'Higgins, "was the quenching of our shining lamp." "The man who won the War," Griffith called him. "He was the greatest reaper," said Mulcahy, "that this country has ever known." "He passed," says Mr. P. S. O'Hegarty, "the great test for any adult in that children loved him."

He had no illusions about what he was doing when he signed the Treaty. "I am signing my death warrant," he said. And so it proved. But if any sacrifice could propitiate the furies that torment his country it would be the sacrifice of the life of Michael Collins—so young, so human, so unique. Living, he enriched and exalted Ireland. Dying, he reduced and impoverished mankind.

As the tales of irregular destruction in the South and West reached Dublin, lying rumour credited Childers with chief responsibility, and with some fantastic plan for destroying the economic life of the nation. When he was captured, a British ex-Cabinet Minister (later he made something of amends) gloated unworthily, grotesquely. "I have seen with satisfaction," he told his constituents, "that the mischief-making, murderous renegade, Erskine Childers, has been captured. No man has done more harm or shown more genuine malice, or endeavoured to bring a greater curse upon the common people of Ireland than this strange being, actuated by a deadly and malignant hatred for the land of his birth. Such as he is may all who hate us be."

Before the Military Tribunal which condemned him to death, Childers had explained his life and life's ideals in a classical apologia, stating at the same time the Republican philosophy in enduring terms. Now he wrote to his wife from prison: "I have been told that I am to be shot to-morrow at 7. It is best so, viewing it from the biggest standpoint. I die full of intense love for Ireland. . . . I hope one day my good name will be cleared in England. I feel what —— said about my 'hatred and malice against England.' How well we know it is not true. What line I ever spoke or wrote justifies the charge? I die loving England, and passionately praying that she may change completely and finally towards Ireland."

The execution was delayed, but on the evening of November 23rd he knew that he must die next morning, and he wrote again: "The guard was relieved at eight, and the men going off all said good-bye and God bless you, and I to them. They wanted souvenirs, but I have very few, some books and some signatures. It will be the same with the present lot—in case I am unable to record it—all friendly and infinitely considerate. So we, 'Children of our Universal Mother,' touch hands, and go our ways in the very midst of the horror of this war of brothers."

And then this on the last morning: "My beloved country, God send you courage, victory and rest, and to all our people harmony and love. . . . It is 6 a.m. . . . it all seems perfectly simple and inevitable, like lying down after a long day's work."

Two hours later he was shot. He did all in his power to make the soldiers' ordeal lighter, but they were so overcome that they could hardly get through their duty.

Englishmen of distinction in all walks of life had petitioned for his reprieve, and now, amid much inevitable scurrility began to appear obituaries, critical, even contemptuous of his politics, yet conveying a sense unmistakable that here had been one of the elect. His last act before he died, said Alfred Oliphant, was to shake hands with his executioners: "How like the man." That was what those who had known him felt, and what those who had not known him came to feel. Misunderstood and misrepresented as no man in recent memory, Erskine Childers "did not die without love, for thousands loved him," and as the years pass, tens of thousands are added to those who keep his memory green.

If ever it is possible to prophesy mundane immortality for a man who has held no high-sounding office, nor given his name to any epoch-making invention, the figure of Erskine Childers seems certain to stand out always more clearly as we move onward into the future. For, with all his wanderings, his was a continuing journey, governed by no passing influences, guided to no ephemeral end. He lived and laboured, and he fought and died, under the shadow of the eternal.[1]

Of the giants only De Valera survived the hecatomb. But opposite him now rises his future secular antagonist—William Cosgrave. A small Dubliner was the new President, with a crest of fair hair and penetrating pale-blue eyes; "A chieftain," Mr. Churchill judged him, "of higher quality than any who had yet appeared; possessing," he soon perceived, "a knowledge of practical administration and State policy all his own"; possessing, he might have added, a consciousness that Ireland needed moral discipline no less than self-expression, the elements of order no less than the emblems of independence. A man possessing humour and pugnacity, marked out by nature for command.

He and his colleagues suppressed the insurgents with unfaltering severity. Whether less drastic, less embittering measures would have been equally effective is no point for a pronouncement from pulpit or fireside. In September 1922 there seemed at least an even chance that "this thing that was trying so hard to be an Irish nation would go down in chaos, anarchy, and futility."[2] A year later it was possible to hold a General Election in reasonable tranquillity. Soon Ireland was taking her place at Geneva as a nation of progressive civilisation, and orderly efficient rule.

Cosgrave stayed in power for ten years of crowded achievement. Of his social and economic policies it is too early to judge. But in

[1] The extracts above are from Alfred Oliphant's obituary of Childers, *Atlantic Monthly*, Vol. IV, Jan.–June 1923, and from Shaw Desmond, *Drama of Sinn Fein*, p. 92. See Desmond Ryan, *Remembering Sion*, for striking portraits of Griffith, Collins and Childers.

[2] Kevin O'Higgins, September 27th 1922.

the constitutional sphere the progress was unqualified and notable. The improvements in Dominion Status effected between the Treaty of 1921 and the Statute of Westminster of 1931 have already occupied many volumes; the part played by the Irish will itself fill more than one. It is true that even after the Statute of Westminster Ireland *qua* party to the Treaty continued to be restricted in one or two special ways,[1] but from the Statute onwards it would be hard to name a single respect in which *qua* Dominion she was prevented from enjoying full practical autonomy.

These things were the work of Cosgrave, O'Higgins, Fitzgerald, McGilligan, and among civil servants, Dermot O'Hegarty. Only in one matter—unhappily of prime importance—did they prove helpless. When the game of the Boundary Commission was played out to its completion the South found themselves with no scrap of all it believed it had been promised. No report of the Commission was ever published, for the Free State Commissioner resigned: an "Agreement" was patched up, and the boundary was left where it was. But Mr Justice Feetham of South Africa, the Chairman appointed by the British Government, published his general conclusions in a long letter to *The Times*, and the people of the South had every opportunity of seeing how for four years their leaders had been misled.

Mr. Feetham made it plain that whatever the statistical facts—and these gave the Commissioners little difficulty—the transfer of substantial areas from Northern to Southern Ireland was in his view ruled out by the wording of the clause. So much for Article 12, the Article which Griffith and Collins understood to be intended to give them "essential unity," the Article without which the Treaty, as an English signatory admitted, "never would have been, never could have been signed."

Soon after the Treaty Collins had suspected that Lloyd George had said different things to himself and Craig, or at the least had allowed him to think one thing and Craig another. "Mr. Collins," it was reported on February 8th 1922, after a meeting between Collins and Craig, "stands on the Boundary Commission, and the Irish Delegation's agreement with Mr. Lloyd George that large territories were involved in the 'Agreement,' and not merely a boundary line as Sir James Craig was given to understand, privately, by several British Ministers." But at the final catastrophe Collins must have turned in his grave. As usual,

[1] See the Defence clauses of the Treaty, and the Article forbidding religious discrimination. The latter, however, restricts Ulster, and in that sense the United Kingdom, equally with the Free State. See also Appendix 7.

individual Englishmen strove desperately against evil arrangements; Baldwin, the Conservative Prime Minister, did all in his power to find satisfactory compensation for the South.[1] Irishmen, however, still laugh sadly or sourly when there is talk to-day of Ireland "breaking the spirit of the Treaty." Are English hands quite clean?

Let us take a more general view of the Cosgrave administration. "Cosgrave," said Mr. Churchill, "to the courage of Collins added the matter-of-fact fidelity of Griffith." Certainly both those qualities were indispensable in whoever was to guide Ireland through these opening years; in the former revolutionaries thrust forward to serve as antidotes to revolution. Cosgrave and his colleagues entered on an inheritance of obligation such as their worst enemy would hardly have prepared for them. The Treaty committed them to the renunciation of old ambitions, the justification of old opponents, the execution of old friends. Among sections of their own countrymen they have raised up against themselves hostilities that while they live may pursue them; it must be their consolation to have made their names respected wherever government is studied. Their cause was linked to a principle of honour, and no one can say that they have not kept the faith.

> "*Yet Freedom! yet thy banner, torn, but flying,*
> *Streams like the thunder-storm against the wind.*"

The aspirations of Ireland were not satisfied by the Treaty. The pro-Treaty Party might argue that they ought to have been satisfied. The fact remains—they were not. Ireland, and this held true after all the progress just described, continued to be denied what a large part of the population persisted in regarding as essential to independence, and what certainly no "independent" nation, England for example, would dream of surrendering except under overwhelming force. She continued to be denied the Republic, and at each election after 1922 the Republican vote increased. Republican extremists embarked on sporadic violence, and provoked repressive legislation. At last, in February 1932, Fianna Fail, the constitutional Opposition, supplanted Cumann na nGaedheal, De Valera took the place of Cosgrave.

[1] The financial clauses of the Treaty were cancelled—probably an advantage to Ireland of some theoretical magnitude though (1) informed Irish opinion is not agreed whether there would have been a balance of net Irish *or net English* liability; (2) it is unlikely that in practice England would have made serious effort to collect a large sum from Ireland.

He was pledged to remove the Oath of Allegiance, whose existence was thought to prevent many Republicans from standing for the Dail. He was also pledged to discontinue payment of some £3,000,000 a year to England of Land Annuities and £2,000,000 a year under other heads—at least until such time as the British Government showed legal cause why Ireland should continue these payments. For his lawyers assured him that in their opinion England had no valid claim. When returned to power De Valera made it plain that he intended to honour to the letter his pledges over the Oath and the Annuities.

We need not go into the niceties of the various efforts at negotiation that followed. It may be that De Valera was a thought peremptory in the first place. But he has been very conciliatory since. Everyone will commiserate with J. H. Thomas, a Labour Minister in a strongly Conservative Government, debarred as no Conservative would have been from taking a generous conciliatory line in keeping with his own Irish record. For our part we cannot forget an afternoon in the Dail in June 1932. De Valera was reading a letter he had written to Thomas in which he suggested arbitration on the Annuities issue, though on the understanding that there would be no restriction on the membership of the Court. As he read, even old Unionists in the gallery applauded. The British might not be able to accept the offer as it stood. At least it was the first olive branch that the Irish Republican movement had held out to England since the Treaty. "I am informed," went on De Valera, "that Mr. Thomas is not going to accept these proposals." There was almost audible disappointment. At that moment Thomas was reading De Valera's letter to the House of Commons and commenting, "this makes things worse than before."

Already when Ireland removed the Oath the British Government had announced a breach of the Treaty and proclaimed their intention of making no agreement at Ottawa with a country so unmindful of its "honourable obligations." Now they clapped a tariff on most Irish exports into England in order to collect thereby the withheld Annuities. They declared themselves ready for arbitration, but every member of the Arbitral Tribunal must be drawn from inside the Empire. They were insistent that arbitration by foreigners in imperial disputes had been ruled out by solemn agreement at the Imperial Conference of 1930. And buoyed up by these affirmations they embarked on the "Economic War" and prepared to fight it out to the end.

There are two immediate points at issue between England and Ireland. Did Ireland break the Treaty when she removed the Oath of Allegiance? Is she under legal obligation to pay the Annuities? There is a corollary debate. Was international as opposed to imperial arbitration ruled out by the report of the Imperial Conference of 1930?

All three controversies are immensely technical. Lawyers advising Cosgrave took sixty-five pages to explain before the 1932 Election why the Annuities were legally due—and that without referring to the "secret" agreement of 1923, on which Thomas appears to hinge his case. For our part, we consider that the Irish Government has, to say the least, made out a good case in all these disputes. Let that pass. But this we do find absurd: that the democracy of one member of the British Commonwealth should through its Government stigmatise the democracy of another as "dishonourable," because the lawyers of the two countries interpret differently some very involved sets of documents, and a general situation *sui generis*.[1]

Few, however, in England or out of it, will judge the present Irish policy unprejudiced by their particular view of the present Irish leader. Everyone by now knows the externals; the long towering frame, the dark unfathomable eyes behind the spectacles, the tense inflexible mouth and chin, the meditative, sorrow-lined face. This, it is just beginning to be known in England, is the hero of Boland's Mill, the last commandant to surrender in Easter Week 1916; the man whom Griffith stood down for, feeling it was the people's wish, whom he and Collins were proud to serve under, whom they strove to the last, even after the Treaty, to preserve as leader for the nation.

This history has centred round negotiations to which he was no party. Yet three pieces of information may be derived from it, three things to cause reflection when some sage leader-writer begins to expound his "hatred of England," his "fanaticism," his "instability and failure to appreciate the meaning of an honourable obligation." At least we have learnt that from the middle of 1921 he laboured unwearingly to find some way of peace with England consistent with Irish independence; that as the negotiations de-

[1] British lawyers of consequence are far from unanimous in taking the British side. Professor Berriedale Keith of Edinburgh University, an unrivalled authority on the constitutional law of the Dominions, was quick to detect British inconsistency in relying on *imperial* conventions in the dispute over the Arbitral Tribunal and on *international* conventions in the dispute proper over the Annuities. In autumn 1933 Ireland removed three relics of British supremacy from her Constitution, including the judicial appeal to the Privy Council. Quasi-automatically the British Government descried breaches of the Treaty. Professor Keith in the *Manchester Guardian* dealt very roughly with their claims.

veloped he let himself be drawn and helped draw others to that extreme point where further concession meant compromise with principle; that he never did so compromise, but that he said from the beginning what he says to-day: That the Treaty robbed Ireland of independence, would be accepted from no feeling of affection or hope of profit but from fear of extermination, and was beyond the power of Ireland, as it would have been beyond the power of any nation of self-respecting manhood, to keep for long.

## CHAPTER II

## THE TREATY TRANSCENDED

> "What we want to do is to stand by the traditions of which we are the heirs in all matters except our relations with Ireland: and to make our relations with Ireland conform to the other traditions of our country."
>
> GLADSTONE.

*The present position—A mockery of statesmanship—The Treaty not a final settlement—The Irish demand—The possibility of satisfying it within the Empire—External Association a compelling alternative—The justice of the Irish case—The difficulty of arguing against it to-day—A great fleeting opportunity—England called on alike by self-interest and by her most characteristic traditions to undo the evil, complete the good of 1921.*

THE present position is pitiful. Both countries are standing up to the "Economic War," both countries have found various compensations. But certain interests in Ireland (those incidentally most friendly to England) are suffering calamitously; the cattle trade so vital to England in wartime is being forced out of existence; while the decline of £14,000,000 a year in English total exports to a country that was previously England's second best market, makes mock of the trade agreements England entered into at Ottawa and elsewhere, and indeed of all serious efforts to expand her export trade.

Nor is the loss only economic, nor the confession only one of ignominy in the merchanting sphere. Acrimony is steadily infecting all mutual kindliness. Future generations will hardly believe their eyes when they read about the origin and continuance of this war;

they will distribute blame between the two countries in the same proportions as they allocate responsibility.

Personal inquiries have satisfied us beyond all shadow of doubt that the present obstacle to settlement is not economic but political. A British Government that pays £3½ million instead of ten times that amount by way of "token" to America would find it hard to be niggardly over the pure finance. It has in fact been quite forthcoming with indications of sympathetic treatment. But to obtain such treatment Ireland must honour "her honourable obligations." "The principle of the thing," says the British Government, "is involved." What they mean is that they can come to no agreement until they know where De Valera and the Republican Party stand on the questions of the Treaty, the Republic, and the future constitutional relationship of Ireland to the British Empire.[1]

If they have any hope that peace with Ireland can be arrived at on the basis of the Treaty as it stands, or rather, on the basis of the Treaty as it is generally interpreted in England, they can put aside those illusions. It is true that there *is* a way of reading the Treaty which would give Ireland everything she wants. In the report of the Imperial Conference of 1926 the Mother Country and Dominions are described as "autonomous communities, freely associated, in no way subordinate to one another"; and Ireland, which under the Treaty is supposed to have the same constitutional status as the other Dominions, and (subject to any express restriction) the same relation to the British Crown and Parliament as Canada, can argue from these and other documents that already she possesses legal, constitutional and moral right to secede from the Empire if she wishes. But the ordinary British view seems to be that under the Treaty Ireland ruled out the right of secession in her own case for all time, or until such time as Great Britain gave permission. Even, therefore, if it were found possible and desirable to preserve formal harmony between a new settlement and that of 1921, it would be necessary for Great Britain to make certain new declarations explaining the ampler sense in which she was now ready to interpret the Treaty.

What does Ireland want? She wants it made plain that historically she is a distinct nation from Britain, not a British off-

[1] The Trade Agreement concluded at the beginning of the year seems to represent some retreat by the British Government from the position described above (which was first assumed at Ottawa in 1932). In itself the Trade Agreement is thoroughly creditable to both Governments concerned, and will, it is to be hoped, prove the first of several of its kind. But, unfortunately, the British attitude to the Annuities dispute seems unchanged, and the determination to collect the Annuities by economic war unshaken.

shoot; that if she continues in any association with Britain it is for the benefit of both countries and not because of any British right whatever over Ireland; that any such association is voluntary and can be terminated with proper notice at the discretion of either country; that under its terms Ireland, co-operating for certain common purposes in the foreign sphere, is left absolutely unrestricted freedom of action in all domestic affairs.

That was the demand with which Ireland came to London in October 1921. It is a demand that goes deeper than the particular symbolism in which it has come to be expressed, or than the particular constitution of the British Empire at any given moment in its unceasing evolution. It is the demand that Irishmen should at last be allowed to count Ireland their own "from the sod to the sky," as Frenchmen count France, Germans count Germany, Englishmen England. It is the demand to be allowed to exorcize the nightmare of the English problem from Irish politics; to be allowed to get on with the work of building up a prosperous Ireland. It is the demand for the undoing of the conquest. It is the demand for national independence.

How far can that demand be satisfied within the Empire? In a physical sense there is no difficulty. For the Dominions already enjoy full internal and external autonomy, the only element of subordination lying in an allegiance to a common British Crown which, however, in all Irish affairs must act on the advice of its Irish Ministers. But, psychologically, we cannot be dogmatic. It may be that if England admitted the justice of the Irish claims just mentioned, and took official steps by new declarations to satisfy Ireland that they were catered for under the present Dominion Status—in particular if England explicitly recognised the right of a Dominion to secede—it may be that if England did these things Ireland would find her aspirations capable of fulfilment within the Empire, or if the word were preferred, the Commonwealth. There is at least one aspiration, reunion with Ulster, which, in the opinion of the official opposition, the United Ireland Party, can be satisfied on a Commonwealth basis and on a Commonwealth basis alone.

But England must face the risk that the words "British Dominion," "British Subject," "British Commonwealth," would, for all the new declarations, still be found impossible headings under which to frame an Irish civilisation. In that event something on the lines of External Association would provide a sensible, a compelling alternative.

What exact scheme would content Ireland is, of course, pure

speculation, but we are hopeful, though we boast no access to the private counsels of the present Irish Government, that we need not go far beyond the various drafts submitted to the British in autumn 1921. Ireland's independence would be recognised, and Saorstat Eireann would be translated by Republic; but Ireland would be associated with the British Commonwealth for purposes of common concern, she would take her place at Imperial Conferences, and Englishmen and Irishmen while not citizens of one anothers' countries would enjoy the same rights as if they were.[1]

The symbolism could satisfy Irish Nationalism and at the same time display Ireland's loyalty to the spirit of the undertaking and the common purposes of the group. It would provide an accurate description of the real relationship, would be inoffensive now, and in time to come perhaps inspiring.

Defence should present no difficulty once the constitutional settlement brought Ireland into voluntary alliance and true friendship with England. At present England enjoys certain naval facilities on the Irish coast and Ireland is allowed no effective Navy. But under the Treaty Ireland has had the right at any time since 1926 to have this last restriction reconsidered "with a view to her undertaking a share in her coastal defence." If the defence of the two islands were once accepted under External Association as a matter of common concern, it should not prove difficult to find a congenial division of labour under which the larger, richer island, the island with the tremendous overseas commitments, bore the major responsibility and expense.

The Ulster problem is harder. De Valera, however, made it plain in 1921 that there could be no question of forcing in the North-East corner against its wishes, and neither he nor Cosgrave has ever wavered since in repudiating coercion. De Valera, it is true, will never concede the theoretical right of Ulster to stay separate from the rest of the Irish nation. But in the kind of agreement we have in mind between the Twenty-Six Counties and Great Britain it should not defy the wit of man to get this point of view put on record without its affecting the immediate practical arrangement.

There is no difficulty then in pointing to a practical solution. What of the justice of the case, and of Ireland's moral right to secede if so she wishes? Thirty years ago Mr. L. S. Amery could

[1] Cf. the Citizenship Bill recently before the Dail. We envisage also preferential trade agreements between Ireland and all members of the British Commonwealth.

write these sentences in an introduction to a *Times* Official History: "Much sympathy has been wasted on small nations 'rightly struggling to be free'; little sympathy is bestowed on the great nations rightly struggling for mastery, for supremacy of higher civilisation and higher political principle." To-day the right of self-determination is a dogma of international morality to which English politicians in public unanimously subscribe.

In private it is fair to say some of them are more apt to be cynical, but surely no one will argue against this modest statement of the claim: "That a nation's desire to be independent establishes a strong initial presumption in favour of its right to independence. That the onus of proof is transferred to those who in any particular case deny the right."

In the case of Ireland is there any argument strong enough to rebut the initial presumption? Twelve years ago in the debates on the Treaty, Sir J. Butcher, now Lord Danesfort, gave as a chief reason for opposing the Treaty the probability that if Ireland became a Dominion she would before long be demanding complete separation from England. And separation, he was able to say looking round without contradiction, would not be tolerated by a single member of the House of Commons. So apparently the arguments against separation were thought overwhelming at that time. Let us pass rapidly in review those that carried weight in the past, not necessarily against separation, but against whatever happened to be the particular extension of Irish liberty proposed.

1. "That Ireland was not a nation and to allow her to break away from the United Kingdom was to break up a living political organism; similar rights might be claimed by Devonshire or Norfolk." Considering the already distant relations between Ireland and England and the degree of separation already arrived at, this "organic" argument, the one brought forward most commonly against Home Rule, has no meaning or reality to-day.[1]

[1] (1) With it disappears an argument which Lord Balfour always stressed: "That Ireland, not a nation now, would become a nation if given the encouragement of Home Rule, and would demand separation." The contention was logical and has proved prescient. But it assumed that separation was an evil; it gives no reasons against it.

(2) A new type of objection is sometimes raised against any "centrifugal tendency" such as that involved in Irish separation, by left-wing thinkers who would normally be strong opponents of Imperialism. They see in such tendencies a movement towards that excessive Nationalism which they think is menacing the world to-day. But they should realise (i) that Ireland is already in practice as separate a political organism from Great Britain as she would be under External Association; (ii) that Ireland has no aggressive aims, and is an enthusiastic believer in the collective system, as expressed in the League of Nations, etc. She has no desire to break away from organised

2. "That Ireland's independence would strike a fatal blow at the defences and therefore at the security of the Empire." There is no reason to fear any such thing. Ireland was ready in 1921 to give effective guarantees that no foreign powers would be allowed to obtain by alliance or otherwise a footing in her country; she was ready to go further and co-operate with the British Empire in matters of common concern. Under the settlements suggested one would expect to see Great Britain retain for a time at least her existing naval facilities, and Ireland join for the first time with national ardour in the defence of the two islands. Under the present Dominion Status there is no compulsion on a Dominion to co-operate with Great Britain even on broad questions of foreign policy. At the lowest estimate Britain would be no worse off under External Association; at the highest, infinitely better off than now.

3. "That Ireland, like India or say, Nigeria, is not fit to govern herself; in particular she cannot be trusted to behave decently to her Protestant minority." No one seriously suggests that Great Britain is responsible for the protection of the Irish Catholics; Ulster is safeguarded by her own constitution; but of the Southern loyalists, who have not received their deserts in these pages, something here must be said.

It would be impertinent for the present writer, a Protestant Irishman living outside Ireland, to congratulate Irish Protestants who reside in their own country on the felicity of their lot. They suffered much during the war against the British, and in their property more still during the Civil War; at the present time, in so far as they belong to the grazier class, the "Economic War," a by-product of Nationalism, as many of them regard it, is costing them dear. Yet their best-known spokesman, Senator Sir John Keane, not long ago bore witness that their life is in many ways happier and safer than in the days of British rule; and if we compare their treatment with that of Catholics in the North (who admittedly constitute a far greater menace to the existing régime), we can conclude that the Irish Free State in its twelve years of life can pride itself on at least one fine achievement—the justice it has provided for minorities.

This justice has not been prompted or enforced by Britain; there is no reason to think that it would be diminished under a Republic; while even under a Republic "reciprocal citizenship" would keep open the ranks of the British services and professions

international society, only to be freed from the suzerainty of a particular Empire, and generally to be put on an equality with other states.

to all Irishmen, including that class which we like to believe has produced as high a level of distinction as any other in the world.

Yet the sentimental ties are strong, and from this standpoint it would be a happy consummation if Gaelic Ireland decided to build a national structure within the framework of the Commonwealth. But in any case the matter has passed out of England's hands. The best service she can render the Irish loyalists is to take steps to end the "Economic War" and to allow their country peace.

4. Finally there are the arguments from prestige. We have often been told in Irish controversies how fatal to British prestige would be a surrender to force (Lord Carson), or alternatively how fatal would be a surrender except to force (Professor Dicey).

The first argument is not here relevant, though it may have been in 1921. We do not believe the second to be true. We ourselves can imagine no finer vindication of the principles of freedom on which the Empire to-day is understood to be founded, than a gesture of renunciation towards Ireland; none more likely to prove fruitful of honour, harmony, and strength.

A year ago last November the Irish Government inquired whether they could take it that England would use no force to stop Irish secession. The British Government gave a non-committal answer. That answer cannot have done any good to British prestige but it may have been felt to save England's face. Britain under the Treaty abandoned responsibility for Ireland, but she did not renounce dominion over her. "It was at the time politically impossible." Pride, in other words, prevented. It would be a gesture worthy of her record in every field but the Irish, and it would cost her nothing, if in this matter of Ireland for once she pocketed her pride.

There then stands Ireland's right of secession. The old contrary arguments are dead, and there are no new ones. The case is unanswerable. And if Ireland were allowed to go under these circumstances, she must be sped with a blessing and not with a lecture or a sneer, without "his Majesty's Ministers in the United Kingdom taking a very grave view . . ."

But a last adversary awaits us. "Yes, yes," he will say, "very interesting, or it would be if I or anyone else were interested in Ireland. Unfortunately Ireland has ceased to count. She doesn't matter any more. Call yourself a Republic if it gives you any pleasure. Secede away if you like, we shan't stop you. But don't expect us to give your children jobs in the British services, or, if they fail in the examinations, British doles. Don't expect us to give your produce preferential Imperial rates. Don't in fact expect to be treated as British citizens if you find what you call our 'symbolism' as repulsive as you say."

There is no answering this reasoning, and if all Englishmen thought likewise there would be nothing but isolation for Ireland with considerable material loss. Some Irishmen would not be sorry, but to us it would be a disaster for both countries if this were the final end. We need not write panegyrics on what Irishmen have done to help build up and defend the British Commonwealth, what Irishmen have contributed to English literature, speech, and thought, how fertile has proved the character and inspiration of the two races when working in close accord. We put only this question: Would any Englishman be proud fifty years hence to acknowledge that he had had the chance of associating Ireland on terms of permanent and close intimacy with England and that he had preferred to see her go her way, embittered, hostile, possibly affiliated elsewhere; and simply because the words in which she wished the relationship described, while providing an accurate description, had an unfamiliar and unattractive ring?

One can write and one can write. Sometimes someone will read. But fixed ideas remain. Strongest of all elements in the attitude that "does not want to have anything more to do with Ireland" is a misunderstanding of the personality of the present Irish President, of his record, and of that of the Republican Party. "Personally," they will say to you, "De Valera may be, we understand he is, courageous, sincere, honourable, devout, disinterested, intelligent, charming. But politically—politically he is a defaulter, and a defaulter obsessed by a fanatical hatred of England. And the same is true of his party. It is impossible to attempt any settlement with a force in politics like that."

This is the honest feeling of many English people who would count as well informed in political affairs. Its existence is due to a profoundly unjust propaganda and a half-unconscious distortion by the Press that goes back to the months following the Treaty, and even to the months of the Truce. When Mr. De Valera's biography and the history of the Republican movement in Ireland are written, a far stronger case will be found presented for him and them than any sketched in these pages. We ourselves have no Irish party allegiance, and we have attempted an objective record. All that we ask is that the reader should turn back and examine whether there is anything in the record of the President or the Republican Party that suggests such fanaticism, such hatred of

England, or such political inconsistency, as to make it hopeless to seek in his company or theirs a final Irish settlement.

The Treaty was a great step forward, but it could never be the final step. Both sides would approach new negotiations in easier circumstances, with fuller consciousness, in a spirit of more chastened though no less fervid patriotism. England would come to them puzzling no longer how to avoid the stigma of surrender to violence, nor how to reconcile radical innovation with her age-long party loyalties, but stripping the issue of all traditional party associations and asking herself a few elementary questions such as these: Is there no such thing as international morality? Is it satisfied by keeping the few conventional precepts of international law? What moral right have we to be in Ireland? What moral right have we to use our superior reserves of violence in limiting Irish independence? If our self-preservation demands some measure of intrusion, what compensation can we find and offer? Does pride still compel us to interfere in any way with cherished Irish symbolism? Must it still create obstacles to the organised expansion of reciprocally advantageous trade?

Ireland would come to settlement resolved to enter into no obligations beyond the power of future Irishmen to keep; yet conscious always of the fact that her land is partitioned, and that until there is peace with England six of her counties will remain cut off. She would come, too, ready like England to lay the first foundations of the new relationship in mutual trading self-interest. Sentiment and affection would not long be delayed.

The Anglo-Irish problem is unlike most others of contemporary politics; it is capable of prompt, obvious solution. For by this time there is no genuine conflict of contending aims or needs. The details of the scheme are not important. The approach is everything. England unharassed by war, fresh from a triumphant restoration of her national credit, must of her own accord turn to Ireland and say to her: We have dismissed our old party prejudices, honest and well-intentioned, but, whether once they were right or whether they were always wrong, now outworn and irrelevant. We question no longer your right to full independence. But we cannot willingly see you become foreigners. We ask you to be something more.

Thus and thus only will she fulfil the dreams so nobly, though up till now so vainly expressed by some of her most valiant Christians, her most majestic law-givers, her favourite sons. Thus and thus only will "Englishmen stand by the tradition of which they are the heirs in all matters except their relations with Ireland"; thus and thus only will they "make their relations with Ireland conform to the other traditions of their country." Thus and thus only will they bring peace so that "island of incomparable beauty, so individual in its genius, so tenacious in love or hate, so captivating in its nobler moods. Thus and thus only shall come lasting reconciliation between the British and Irish peoples; joined, for all their distinguishable race and distinct nationhood, by indissoluble geographical connection, by common trade advantage, ties of marriage, blood, and mingled population, an interwoven heritage of culture, deep natural affinity, common democratic ideals.

But let it not be supposed that time is on the side of peace. A few months more of strife, and an Ireland within the Commonwealth will be impossible; a year or two more, and External Association will seem, looking back, to have been an idle fantastic hope. England has always been too late in Ireland, and once again with every day that passes the Sibylline books are brought nearer to the flames.

One word more. The Irish Nationalist Movement has not, as is sometimes alleged, owed its inspiration to hatred of England; but Irish Nationalists have seldom had much good to say of English "Imperialism," while English sympathisers with the Irish cause have tended to be what used to be called "Little Englanders," and what is now sometimes called "Defeatists." Our angle is different. We see nothing incompatible in being an Irish Nationalist and a believer in the British Commonwealth—so long as the British Commonwealth is founded on these two great principles: the principle of freedom (to secede if need be) for all parts of the Commonwealth that are mature nations; the principle of trusteeship in their own interests for all parts that must as yet be classed as backward communities. In the advance of a real Commonwealth, founded not as hitherto in name only on these two principles, we see the best single hope of order and liberty for the world.

"Nevertheless," it will be persisted, "suppose the cause of all that is highest in modern civilisation, all that is most enlightened in modern progress stands or falls with British stability and vigour. Can such a cause, in these days especially when the international situation is so disquieting, be over-ridden by the interests of a State so small as Ireland?"

That was the old supposed dilemma, but now, as we have tried in necessarily inadequate summary to indicate, that dilemma exists no more. No longer is the question one of Irish freedom versus English security. The only difficulty to-day is one of words and formulas, and with these England, if she be truly great, can afford to be truly generous.

And so, conclusion. Englishmen admit the sorry record of their country in Irish history, but most of them believe that their country acted chivalrously, almost quixotically, in making the Irish Treaty. If we are discussing the action of individual Conservative leaders of England's action compared with her own past in Ireland—yes. But, absolutely, was it so? At the present day it is often said that if Ireland declared a Republic it would matter so little to England that she would use no violence to prevent it. In 1921 it seemed to matter so much to her that she threatened Ireland with immediate war if the Irish Delegates did not within three hours sign the Republic away. England has undone many of the wrongs she has inflicted on Ireland; she has not yet undone the last.

Let us strive for settlement. But meanwhile each country has a task which it can perform without waiting for exact accommodation with the other. Whatever England's policy, it remains for Ireland to do herself justice as a nation. For that she had not yet done. Whatever Ireland's policy, it remains for England to make atonement. For that she has not yet made.

# APPENDIX 1

## ARTICLES OF AGREEMENT FOR A TREATY BETWEEN GREAT BRITAIN AND IRELAND, DECEMBER 6, 1921

1. Ireland shall have the same Constitutional status in the community of Nations known as the British Empire as the Dominion of Canada, the Commonwealth of Australia, the Dominion of New Zealand, and the Union of South Africa, with a Parliament having powers to make laws for the peace, order, and good government of Ireland, and as Executive responsible to that Parliament, and shall be styled and known as the Irish Free State.

2. Subject to the provisions hereinafter set out, the position of the Irish Free State in relation to the Imperial Parliament and Government and otherwise shall be that of the Dominion of Canada, and the law, practice, and Constitutional usage governing the relationship of the Crown or the representative of the Crown and of the Imperial Parliament to the Dominion of Canada shall govern their relationship to the Irish Free State.

3. The representative of the Crown in Ireland shall be appointed in like manner as the Governor-General of Canada, and in accordance with the practice observed in the making of such appointments.

4. The Oath to be taken by members of the Parliament of the Irish Free State shall be in the following form:—

> I . . . do solemnly swear true faith and allegiance to the Constitution of the Irish Free State as by law established, and that I will be faithful to H.M. King George V, his heirs and successors by law, in virtue of the common citizenship of Ireland with Great Britain and her adherence to and membership of the group of nations forming the British Commonwealth of Nations.

5. The Irish Free State shall assume liability for the service of the Public Debt of the United Kingdom as existing at the date hereof and towards the payment of War Pensions as existing at that date in such proportion as may be fair and equitable, having regard to any just claim on the part of Ireland by way of set-off or counter-claim, the amount of such sums being determined in

default of agreement by the arbitration of one or more independent persons being citizens of the British Empire.

6. Until an arrangement has been made between the British and Irish Governments whereby the Irish Free State undertakes her own coastal defence, the defence by sea of Great Britain and Ireland shall be undertaken by His Majesty's Imperial Forces, but this shall not prevent the construction or maintenance by the Government of the Irish Free State of such vessels as are necessary for the protection of the Revenue or the Fisheries. The foregoing provisions of this Article shall be reviewed at a conference of Representatives of the British and Irish Governments, to be held at the expiration of five years from the date hereof with a view to the undertaking by Ireland of a share in her own coastal defence.

7. The Government of the Irish Free State shall afford to His Majesty's Imperial Forces

(*a*) In time of peace such harbour and other facilities as are indicated in the Annex hereto, or such other facilities as may from time to time be agreed between the British Government and the Government of the Irish Free State; and

(*b*) In time of war or of strained relations with a Foreign Power such harbour and other facilities as the British Government may require for the purposes of such defence as aforesaid.

8. With a view to securing the observance of the principle of international limitation of armaments, if the Government of the Irish Free State establishes and maintains a military defence force, the establishments thereof shall not exceed in size such proportion of the military establishments maintained in Great Britain as that which the population of Ireland bears to the population of Great Britain.

9. The ports of Great Britain and the Irish Free State shall be freely open to the ships of the other country on payment of the customary port and other duties.

10. The Government of the Irish Free State agrees to pay fair compensation on terms not less favourable than those accorded by the Act of 1920 to judges, officials, members of Police Forces, and other Public Servants who are discharged by it or who retire in consequence of the change of government effected in pursuance hereof. Provided that this agreement shall not apply to members of the Auxiliary Police Force or to persons recruited in Great Britain for the Royal Irish Constabulary during the two years next preceding the date hereof. The British Government will assume

responsibility for such compensation or pensions as may be payable to any of these excepted persons.

11. Until the expiration of one month from the passing of the Act of Parliament for the ratification of this instrument, the powers of the Parliament and the Government of the Irish Free State shall not be exercisable as respects Northern Ireland, and the provisions of the Government of Ireland Act, 1920, shall, so far as they relate to Northern Ireland, remain in full force and effect, and no election shall be held for the return of members to serve in the Parliament of the Irish Free State for constituencies in Northern Ireland, unless a resolution is passed by both Houses of Parliament of Northern Ireland in favoùr of holding of such elections before the end of the said month.

12. If, before the expiration of the said month, an address is presented to His Majesty by both Houses of Parliament of Northern Ireland to that effect, the powers of the Parliament and the Government of the Irish Free State shall no longer extend to Northern Ireland, and the provisions of the Government of Ireland Act, 1920 (including those relating to the Council of Ireland) shall so far as they relate to Northern Ireland continue to be of full force and effect, and this instrument shall have effect subject to the necessary modifications.

Provided that if such an address is so presented a Commission consisting of three persons, one to be appointed by the Government of the Irish Free State, one to be appointed by the Government of Northern Ireland, and one who shall be Chairman to be appointed by the British Government shall determine in accordance with the wishes of the inhabitants, so far as may be compatible with economic and geographic conditions, the boundaries between Northern Ireland and the rest of Ireland, and for the purposes of the Government of Ireland Act, 1920, and of this instrument, the boundary of Northern Ireland shall be such as may be determined by such Commission.

13. For the purpose of the last foregoing article, the powers of the Parliament of Southern Ireland under the Government of Ireland Act, 1920, to elect members of the Council of Ireland shall after the Parliament of the Irish Free State is constituted be exercised by that Parliament.

14. After the expiration of the said month, if no such address as is mentioned in Article 12 hereof is presented, the Parliament and Government of Northern Ireland shall continue to exercise as respects Northern Ireland the powers conferred on them by the Government of Ireland Act, 1920, but the Parliament and Govern-

ment of the Irish Free State shall in Northern Ireland have in relation to matters in respect of which the Parliament of Northern Ireland has not power to make laws under that Act (including matters which under the said Act are within the jurisdiction of the Council of Ireland) the same powers as in the rest of Ireland, subject to such other provisions as may be agreed in manner hereinafter appearing.

15. At any time after the date hereof the Government of Northern Ireland and the provisional Government of Southern Ireland hereinafter constituted may meet for the purpose of discussing the provisions subject to which the last foregoing article is to operate in the event of no such address as is therein mentioned being presented and those provisions may include:—

(*a*) Safeguards with regard to patronage in Northern Ireland;
(*b*) Safeguards with regard to the collection of revenue in Northern Ireland;
(*c*) Safeguards with regard to import and export duties affecting the trade or industry of Northern Ireland;
(*d*) Safeguards for minorities in Northern Ireland;
(*e*) The settlement of the financial relations between Northern Ireland and the Irish Free State;
(*f*) The establishment and powers of a local militia in Northern Ireland and the relation of the Defence Forces of the Irish Free State and of Northern Ireland respectively,

and if at any such meeting provisions are agreed to, the same shall have effect as if they were included amongst the provisions subject to which the powers of the Parliament and the Government of the Irish Free State are to be exercisable in Northern Ireland under Article 14 hereof.

16. Neither the Parliament of the Irish Free State nor the Parliament of Northern Ireland shall make any law so as either directly or indirectly to endow any religion or prohibit or restrict the free exercise thereof or given any preference or impose any disability on account of the religious belief or religious status or affect prejudicially the right of any child to attend a school receiving public money without attending the religious instruction at the school or make any discrimination as respects State aid between schools under the management of different religious denominations or divert from any religious denomination or any educational institution any of its property except for public utility purposes and on payment of compensation.

17. By way of provisional arrangement for the administration

of Southern Ireland during the interval which must elapse between the date hereof and the constitution of a Parliament and Government of the Irish Free State in accordance therewith, steps shall be taken forthwith for summoning a meeting of members of Parliament elected for constituencies in Southern Ireland since the passing of the Government of Ireland Act, 1920, and for constituting a provisional Government, and the British Government shall take the steps necessary to transfer to such Provisional Government the powers and machinery requisite for the discharge of its duties provided that every member of such provisional Government shall have signified in writing his or her acceptance of this instrument. But this arrangement shall not continue in force beyond the expiration of twelve months from the date hereof.

18. This instrument shall be submitted forthwith by his Majesty's Government for the approval of Parliament and by the Irish signatories to a meeting summoned for the purpose of the members elected to sit in the House of Commons of Southern Ireland and if approved shall be ratified by the necessary legislation.

Signed

On behalf of the Irish Delegation:—
ART. O. GRIOBHTHA.
MICHAEL O. COILEAIN.
RIOBARD BARTUN.
E. S. O. DUGAIN.
SEORSA GABHAIN UI DHUBHTHAIGH.

On behalf of the British Delegation:—
D. LLOYD GEORGE.
AUSTEN CHAMBERLAIN.
BIRKENHEAD.
WINSTON S. CHURSHILL.
L. WORTHINGTON EVANS.
HAMAR GREENWOOD.
GORDON HEWART.

*6th December, 1921.*

## ANNEX

1. The following are the specific facilities required:—

DOCKYARD AT BEREHAVEN.

(*a*) Admiralty property and rights to be retained as at the date hereof. Harbour defences to remain in charge of British care and maintenance parties.

QUEENSTOWN.

(*b*) Harbour defences to remain in charge of British care and maintenance parties. Certain mooring buoys to be retained for use of His Majesty's ships.

BELFAST LOUGH.

(*c*) Harbour defences to remain in charge of British care and maintenance parties.

LOUGH SWILLY.

(*d*) Harbour defences to remain in charge of British care and maintenance parties.

AVIATION.

(*e*) Facilities in the neighbourhood of the above ports for coastal defence by air.

OIL FUEL STORAGE.

(*f*) Haulbowline, Rathmullen—To be offered for sale to Commercial Companies under guarantee that purchasers shall maintain a certain minimum stock for Admiralty purposes.

2. A Convention shall be made between the British Government and the Government of the Irish Free State to give effect to the following conditions:—

(*a*) That submarine cables shall not be landed or wireless stations for communication with places outside Ireland be established except by agreement with the British Government; that the existing cable landing rights and wireless concessions shall not be withdrawn except by agreement with the British Government; and that the British Government shall be entitled to land additional submarine cables or establish additional stations for communication with places outside Ireland.

(*b*) That lighthouses, buoys, beacons, and any navigational marks or navigational aids shall be maintained by the Government of the Irish Free State as at the date hereof and shall not be removed or added to except by agreement with the British Government.

(*c*) That war signal stations shall be closed down and left in charge of care and maintenance parties, the Government of the Irish Free State being offered the option of taking them over and working them for commercial purposes subject to Admiralty inspection and guaranteeing the upkeep of existing telegraphic communications therewith.

3. A Convention shall be made between the same Governments for the regulation of Civil Communication by Air.

# APPENDIX 2

(*Page 38*)

## THE GUERILLA WAR AND BLOODY SUNDAY

We put forward the account in the text of the guerilla war after study of all the sources known to us, in the conviction (1) that it gives a fair picture of the general methods of the two sides; (2) that our version of each particular incident is in accordance with the overwhelming majority of serious evidence. But it is possible that some of those who lived through the horrors of that period, suffering may be, or seeing their friends suffer terribly, will pay little heed to anything new that is written about those years in Ireland, and refuse, if it does not fit in with their ideas, to reckon unprejudiced and judicial. We suggest that they omit the whole of Part II and pass straight on to Part III.

For our part we have frequently had to choose between flatly conflicting narratives (all figures of casualties, etc., are disputed and we have as far as possible eschewed them), but only one day has given serious pause—November 21st 1920, "Bloody Sunday". What exactly were the functions and status of the Englishmen killed that morning? In Ireland it is ordinarily understood that they were in some sense Intelligence Officers or Secret Service men; living in mufti, some, perhaps all of them, under false names; employed in special work in connection with the identification, capture, trial, or execution of prominent Sinn Feiners. Their position is compared to that of British officers acting as spies in Germany during the Great War. The circumstances in which they were killed are admitted to have been revolting, but held to have been dictated by the disparity in strength between the I.R.A. and the British Forces. Beasley, however, an authoritative Irish source for the guerilla period, goes much further than this and associates directly some of those who were killed with the murder of Lord Mayor McCurtain of Cork, and with plans for the secret murder (*i.e.* slaughter in cold blood without trial) of various combatant and non-combatant Sinn Feiners.

On the English side, General Macready writes: "At nine a.m. on Sunday, November 21st, eight houses were simultaneously visited by parties of armed rebels who murdered seven officers, three ex-officers, two R.I.C., and two civilians. . . . This effort . . . was ostensibly a retaliation for the execution of Kevin Barry, the

Sinn Fein leaders being under the impression that those whom they murdered were in some way involved in the man's trial. Of those who were murdered only two were connected with the legal branch of the staff, and they had nothing to do with Barry's case. . . . It was stated that the officers who were murdered were those who ordered reprisals, an assertion as false as that they were concerned in the trial of Kevin Barry." Professor Alison Phillips reprobates the slaughter as strongly as Macready, but tells a slightly different story. "These officers . . . were mainly engaged in court-martial work—and as often as not in the interests of prisoners." He quotes the "Official Report" which stated that "the Sinn Feiners were becoming alarmed at the quantity of information which the authorities were receiving, and desired to destroy the evidence and at the same time terrorise the officers connected with the machinery of justice." Winston Churchill contents himself with observing: "On a November morning fourteen officers, believed by the rebels to be engaged in intelligence work, were shot, unarmed, several in the presence of their wives, in their billets in Dublin."

General Crozier, who arrived on the scene very soon after the officers were killed and personally arrested Tealing, the only Sinn Feiner caught, goes into the matter at some length. (See *Ireland for Ever*, pp. 99–103, 147–9, 218–19.) Substantially he arrives at the same conclusion as Beasley. "Upstairs in one room lay a dead Secret Service man in bed." "Collins," he was told at first in Dublin Castle, "has done in most of the Secret Service people." "Captain A. set up a chain of communications with Captain B. at the War Office, and later arranged the assassination by police of Lord Mayor MacCurtain of Cork and others. . . . Michael Collins established the existence of the germ of a murder gang within the British hierarchy. . . . Collins waited for the plot to widen and unravel, eventually killing many of the 'commissioned assassins,' in November, including Captain A."

It is known, however, that some of the men killed on "Bloody Sunday" were of the highest character. Crozier provides an explanation of any difficulty this may cause by a quotation from Collins: "I found out," he reports Collins as saying to him after the Truce, "that those fellows we put on the spot were going to put a lot of us on the spot, so I got in first. Of course a few of your fellows, whom we didn't want to kill because we had nothing against them, walked on to the spot and had to be done in as they became dangerous evidence."

On a different point it is worth noticing an extract, quoted by

Crozier, from the Report of the American Commission of Enquiry: "We have been impressed by the evidence developed by British Military tribunals in the trial of one Tealing, that one of the British Officers who were killed in Dublin on November 21st 1920, had been living as a civilian in a house in Dublin under the assumed name of MacMahon."

Amid this varied and conflicting information we do not think that a statement of the facts can usefully be taken further than indicated in the text.

## APPENDIX 3

(*Page 195*)

### THE SUB-CONFERENCE, NOVEMBER 24TH

The grave and crucial meeting of November 24th gave rise to some stiff correspondence between Chartres and Tom Jones, of whom Chartres but not Jones had been present at the meeting. "I confirm," wrote Jones on November 25th, "what was stated to you this morning, that we cannot accept this document (Chartres's description of the meeting) as either a complete or accurate account of the conversation which took place. Several instances could be given. For example, it is stated: "Sir Gordon Hewart assured the Irish Delegates that they must not suppose that the British Government was contemplating the alternative of war." What the Attorney-General stated was: 'That the Irish Delegates must not suppose that the British Government was contemplating with equanimity the alternative, which was war.' "

Chartres was not to be suppressed so easily. He flatly denied that his record had been criticised by British Ministers for inaccuracy. On the contrary, said he, "Lord Birkenhead, who read the document carefully and suggested two additions, said that it reflected with 'remarkable fidelity what had passed.' Sir Gordon Hewart, in reply to my enquiry whether there were any errors of statement which should be corrected, replied explicitly that there were none," though in view of inevitable omissions Hewart preferred a short statement of conclusions reached.

Jones next replied that it was impossible for the British to accept as accurate an account that omitted things that had been said and contained things that had not been said—an understandable retort, if one that could be brought against any reconstruction, however accurate in essence, based on longhand notes and memory. Chartres now dropped letter form and lashed out in a memorandum beginning, "If Mr. Thomas Jones persists in misrepresenting a discussion at which he was not present"—finally it was agreed that the Irish Delegates should rely on Chartres's account, the British on an *aide-mémoire* by the Attorney-General confined to a summary of the conclusions reached. On the point of dispute Chartres, one imagines, was technically correct, though it is possible that the Attorney-General at the time conveyed well enough the meaning Jones attributed to him. At any rate, nothing less than an official shorthand report would have been of much use to convict the British, through the mouth of their Attorney-General, of any reluctance to make war in the event of a breakdown.

A glance at Hewart's *aide-mémoire* can conclude the episode. We find him reproducing with sympathetic intelligence the arguments relied on by the Irish. It is when we come to his account of the British reply to them that we begin to rub our eyes. According to Hewart the British three times insisted on allegiance to the Crown, bringing forward no other argument save that allegiance was a test of common citizenship. If this account is correct one is surprised that the Irish did not put up reciprocal citizenship, under which it will be remembered all the material benefits of common citizenship were to be secured to both countries. Leaving this aside we are startled by other discrepancies between Hewart's account and Chartres's. According to Chartres, Birkenhead had adopted a broad politico-sentimental standpoint. "The British people attach the greatest importance to the symbol of the Crown." Hewart drops this tone completely and concentrates on the constitutional difficulties inherent in the Irish proposals. He puts into the mouth of the British Delegates language almost verbally identical with that used in the British memorandum of October 27th. Perhaps, as we saw then, the struggle even so reduces itself to one of symbols, but the language of constitutional impediment has the finer, more technical ring, and Hewart might well think that if an account of the meeting were ever to be published it would add gravity before the world to Britain's case. Of course we accept Hewart's statement that he spoke at the meeting on the lines emphasised in his report. But it is difficult not to think that the main British argument was that attributed by Chartres to Lord Birkenhead: "That the British people attach the greatest importance to the symbol of the Crown."

Unless of course we are to reject Chartres's account as a complete fabrication. But in that case Birkenhead would never have said that it reflected "with remarkable fidelity" what had passed. Or are we to treat this tribute also as a fabrication by Chartres? If so, it was one of singular audacity (seeing that Jones could have referred it at once to Birkenhead), and one in very fair imitation of Birkenhead's manner.

## APPENDIX 4

*Saturday, December 3rd*

(*A*) THE FINAL DRAFT
(*B*) AUTHORITIES FOR OUR ACCOUNT OF THE DISCUSSIONS

### A (*Pages 204 and 206*)

The Final Draft now before the Irish offered them less than the Treaty (as eventually signed and as given in Appendix 1), in the following main respects: (1) Its Oath imposed direct and explicit allegiance to the King, not merely allegiance to the Constitution. (See Clause 4 of the Treaty.) (2) It gave Ireland no immediate rights to possess any armed vessels at all, denied reconsideration of this restriction for ten years, and held out no explicit probability that Ireland's position would be improved at the end of that time. The Treaty allowed her armed vessels for the protection of revenue and fisheries, promised review of this Article in five years instead of ten, and added the encouraging assurance that such review would be entered upon "with a view to the undertaking by Ireland of a share in her own coastal defence." (See Clause 6 of the Treaty.) (3) It gave Ireland only a *local* military defence force. The word "local" is struck out in the Treaty. (See Clause 8 of the Treaty.) (4) It prohibited protective duties between England and Ireland, though this was not to prevent the imposition of duties directed against dumping or other unfair competition. The Treaty gives full fiscal autonomy. (It contains, therefore, no clause to correspond with the restriction in the Final Draft.)

### B (*Page 206*)

We have based our account of this Saturday's discussions (1) on some notes taken at the time by O'Murchadha, acting as secretary to the Cabinet, in the place of O'Hegarty, absent in London. (2) On Stack's Memoirs written rather more than a year later. (3) On various recollections of individuals present, some since made public.

No minutes were kept of Cabinet proceedings, but O'Murchadha, following O'Hegarty's practice, kept his own record of decisions reached, so that he might have something to refer to and so as to be able to tell absent Ministers what had been decided while they were away. The notes were never intended as an official record. On certain vital features of the day's happenings they throw no light, and generally they should not be taken for more than they are—a single man's contemporary but incomplete and not always clear impression of many hours of confusing discussion, terminated by incomplete decisions. Supplementing them however from our other sources we would seem to arrive at an adequate understanding of what took place.

## APPENDIX 5
(*Page 210*)

### WHAT DID GRIFFITH PROMISE?

There is no doubt whatever that at this last Cabinet meeting Arthur Griffith left on the minds of De Valera, Brugha, and others, a firm impression that he had undertaken to sign no document involving Dominion Status without reference back to Dublin. It was only because he understood that a promise of this kind had been given that De Valera abandoned his intention of accompanying the Delegation back to London. Is it, however, certain that Griffith's words could have borne no reasonable interpretation other than that attributed to them by De Valera and Brugha?

To this question, although O'Murchadha says nothing of any pledge given by Griffith, we have reached the conclusion that the answer must be in the affirmative. In the text, therefore, we have represented Griffith (see p. 238) as being tied at the final Conference with the British by two declarations that had by then come to conflict with one another, viz.: (1) The statement that he would not break on the Crown; (2) the promise to sign nothing involving Ireland in Dominion Status[1] without reference back to Dublin.

[1] "Dominion Status", "Allegiance to the Crown", "British subjects", may in the present discussion be regarded as interchangeable expressions.

Griffith, however, is obviously the highest authority on the subject of any pledge he did or did not give, and those who are interested in the question should study the following exchanges which took place in Dail Eireann on January 10th 1922, three days after the Dail had assented to the Treaty. (De Valera had already on January 6th mentioned Griffith's pledge without contradiction, and the matter had apparently been freely discussed in the Private Sessions.)

Mr. ETCHINGHAM: Arthur Griffith cannot deny that he pledged his word to the President of the Republic and the Minister of Defence in the Mansion House, Dublin, on December 3rd, that he would not sign any document until he returned; and he did sign and pledge his word to Lloyd George that none of these documents should be made public. He said he has pledged his word.

Mr. GRIFFITH: That is not so; it is a deliberate misrepresentation—and you know it.

Mr. ETCHINGHAM: I never heard it contradicted before—that the Chairman of the Delegation did not pledge his word in the Mansion House. It is on record.

Mr. CATHAL BRUGHA: Does Mr. Griffith deny that he gave his word to us that he would not sign anything? Does he deny that?

Mr. GRIFFITH: I gave my word that I would not sign that document.

Mr. DE VALERA: We must be clear on this. Nobody here will be able to accuse me of at any time telling any untruth. I say it is a solemn truth that the Chairman of the Delegation, on leaving us at the Cabinet meeting—otherwise things might have been different—gave an undertaking that any document which involved allegiance to the Crown, and involved our being British subjects, would not be signed until it was submitted to Dail Eireann.

Mr. GRIFFITH: I have sat here and I have listened for weeks to misrepresentation. At the Private Session we had all this up, and we are having it at the Public Session now. The first line of attack on us was that we had exceeded our powers. President de Valera admitted that we had not. On that Saturday after I came back I was at the Cabinet meeting, and I told them I would not break on the Crown. I asked President de Valera himself to go to London if he wished. When I was going away the President asked me to try and get the thing back to Dail Eireann. I tried, and I tried all I could, to get the matter kept back for a week. I could not succeed. I was faced with the responsibility of signing or not signing. The responsibility was placed on me and I signed. *I protest against the misrepresentation that I was a man who pledged his word to something*. (Our italics.)

Now can it be said that anywhere here Griffith denies the "solemn truth" averred by De Valera that he promised to sign nothing that "involved allegiance to the Crown and involved [Irishmen] being British subjects" without reference back to the Dail? He is obviously and understandably indignant at any suggestion that he has been in some way dishonourable. But where does he deny the fact alleged by his opponents? The last sentence quoted might at first seem to contain such a denial: "I protest strongly against the misrepresentation that I was a man who pledged his word to something." But it does not seem possible to take this sentence literally, for Griffith has just previously said that he *did* pledge his word to *something*: "I gave my word that I would not sign that document" (*i.e.* the Final Draft in the form it was discussed by the Dublin Cabinet). Can one, therefore, extract more from the sentence in question ("I protest strongly," etc.) than a general expression of resentment at any notion that he had in any way betrayed his trust?

To-day no detached historian would dream of attaching moral blame to Griffith because when faced with unforeseen circumstances in London he made his choice in the way he did. But equally it would be unfair to De Valera, Brugha and others not to emphasise our personal conclusion that Griffith did in fact give the undertaking that they claimed he had given. For if he had not given such an undertaking it would have been from their point of view dereliction of duty and negligence of the interests of the Republic to have allowed him to return to London in charge of the Delegation. If criticism there must be, it should be levelled against (*a*) the general failure in Dublin on Saturday, December 3rd, to lay plans to meet an ultimatum: (*b*) the acceptance of the ultimatum by the Delegates in London as something that left no way of escape.

## APPENDIX 6
(*Page 228*)

### LLOYD GEORGE ON DECEMBER 5TH

Lloyd George was due to see the King at 10 o'clock, but he did not finish with Collins till after 10.10, and then had a few words with C. P. Scott, Editor of the *Manchester Guardian*, so that he can hardly have reached Buckingham Palace before 10.20. At 11.15 he presided over a meeting of the British Delegates, and at 12 over a meeting of the Cabinet. Scott lunched with him afterwards and stayed on talking to Jones "after Lloyd George had gone for a short sleep before the Irishmen came" (see Mr. J. L. Hammond's *Life of C. P. Scott*, p. 284).

## APPENDIX 7
(*Page 273*)

### IRISH CONSTITUTIONAL PROGRESS SINCE 1921

Briefly the position in 1921 was that, as regards internal autonomy, the Dominions enjoyed in all normal times complete practical autonomy, tempered by the knowledge that there were circumstances in which the British Government, or the British Governor-General, might interfere if they or he strongly disapproved of anything that was being done. As regards external autonomy the foreign policy of the Dominions was conducted, as Lloyd George explained to the House of Commons in introducing the Treaty, through "the machinery of the British Foreign Office", and in spite of recent advances was substantially under British control.

To-day since the Statute of Westminster all legal derogations from internal autonomy have vanished, save those such as the Dominions choose voluntarily to retain. A long process of evolution has made Ireland completely independent in foreign affairs; the King's representative in Ireland is an Irish nominee and "Rubber Stamp" with no discretionary power even in theory, and King George V in all Irish affairs acts exclusively on the advice of his Irish Ministers.

Of quasi-restrictions there remain only (1) a common allegiance; (2) possibly a common status as British citizens (though Ireland can define her own citizens and can apparently deprive them if she wishes of British citizenship[1]); and (3) conceivably some sort of unwritten extralegal understanding that the Dominions in major group questions will act in reasonable concert. Further vexed questions are those of (1) neutrality; (2) secession. (1) If England became involved in war there would be no legal or constitutional

[1] Cr. the recent Citizenship Bill.

obligation on the Dominions to lend active assistance. But even to-day they might find that Britain's enemies were able, if they wished, to make out a plausible case at international law for treating all members of the Empire as automatic belligerents.[1] (2) South Africa has claimed since 1926 that a Dominion has a legal right to secede. On this point British constitutional authorities are divided, and British Governments have, up to the present, managed to evade the issue. But whatever may be the rights of the other Dominions, the official British view seems to be that Ireland on signing the Treaty entered into a moral, if not legal, obligation to remain within the Empire until she had Great Britain's permission to secede.

## APPENDIX 8

(*Page 259*)

### THE BOUNDARY CLAUSE (*See Article* 12, *p. 290*)

Mr. Feetham's decision was greeted with understandable cynicism in the South of Ireland, a cynicism still reawakened by any fresh mention of an "Imperial Tribunal". For our part we are prepared to accept the Feetham decision as just as likely as not to be correct; we are prepared to neglect the case that can be made against British Governments from the day that they began to waver before Ulster criticism of this Article in the Treaty debates in 1921 to the day of the Feetham decision four years later. We are content to restrict our indictment to what went before the Treaty. And let us try our hardest to be tolerant and understanding.

In autumn 1921 the British Government was faced with the fact that there were large areas in the North which would prefer to be in the South, and small areas in the South which would prefer to be in the North. They saw no serious difficulty in making minor adjustments, in a rectification of the frontier that would leave neither side much richer or poorer. For this purpose some sort of Boundary Commission was clearly inevitable. But when this had been done the far bigger question would remain whether the large Catholic "surplus" should or should not remain in the North; whether, to put the matter in its popular form, Ulster should keep

[1] Ireland under Clauses 6 and 7 of the Treaty is still subject to certain Defence restrictions in favour of England from which the other Dominions are free. Ireland, therefore, could be treated as an automatic belligerent much more easily than the other Dominions.

Fermanagh and Tyrone. Supposing the facts were as stated (and the Boundary Commission could verify them), the British Government had open to them three courses. (1) They could have decided that the South were entitled to gain the two counties. (2) They could have decided that the North was entitled to keep them. (3) They could have decided that the whole problem, though admittedly of a broad political character, was so wrapped up with hypotheses not yet proven as to be incapable of solution: (*a*) until after the facts had been ascertained, and (*b*) except by the expert body that had itself ascertained them. Of these courses (1) was favourable to the South; (2) to Ulster: under (3) (*a*) and (*b*) each part of Ireland would have taken a sporting chance of the Commission making a political decision in its favour.

Now it is a nice point whether the British did in fact take course (2) or course (3); whether they weighted the Clause in favour of Ulster, in favour of the view that large territories could in no circumstances be transferred (it was thus that Justice Feetham read the Clause), or whether they left it completely open so that Feetham might just as easily have decided the other way. But of one thing there is no doubt. The Sinn Fein leaders unquestionably believed as a result of two months' conversations, as a result above all of Michael Collins's last conversation with Lloyd George, that it was neither of these courses but course (1) that had been adopted; that the Clause was weighted in their favour; that the British Government had taken a definite political decision to give them the two counties[1] and that the Clause was drawn up with that intention.

One point is left. This Clause like the rest of the Treaty was drafted by the British. Did the British Government know what the Sinn Fein Delegates thought was the intention behind it? Chamberlain and Birkenhead did not know. But unless all our documents are fabrications, all our deductions childish, Lloyd George must have known. From two months' conversations with Griffith and Collins he must have known that they would never be prepared to give up the Republic on the mere chance of the Chairman of the Commission proving favourably inclined to them. That if the possibility of a "Feetham decision" was even allowed to cross their minds the Treaty never would be, never could be signed.

"Ah well," a sophisticated critic will tell us, "Griffith and Collins were grown men, chosen to represent their country. They had

[1] Supposing always that there were, as the Sinn Feiners claimed, large areas in the North running down to the frontier whose populations would prefer incorporation in the South.

access to excellent legal advice. Surely they must have been expected to be able to look after themselves?" But even if, which we do not admit, the implied criticism of Griffith and Collins be just, was this the way to welcome Ireland "into the family", or one calculated when the inevitable exposure came along "to end the conflict of centuries".

# CHRONOLOGY

1914 Sept. Home Rule placed on Statute Book, but suspended till end of War. Ulster apparently excluded. No Sinn Fein Members of Parliament at this time.

1916 April. Easter Rising. Republic declared.

1918 Dec. General Election. Sinn Fein wins every seat but one, outside Ulster.

1919 Jan. Republic established.

1919 Jan.–Dec. Development of (*a*) Dail Government.
(*b*) Anglo-Irish War.

1921 June 7. Ulster Government comes into existence under Government of Ireland Act, 1920.

---

1921 June 24. Lloyd George invites De Valera into Conference.

1921 July 11. Truce.

1921 July 14–21. Lloyd George-De Valera conversations in London.

1921 July 20. British present Dominion terms.

1921 Aug. 10. Dail Government refuses Dominion terms.

1921 Aug. 10–Sept. 30. Lloyd-George-De Valera correspondence.

1921 Oct. 11–Dec. 6. Anglo-Irish negotiations in London. Five phases.

(*a*) Tuesday, Oct. 11th–Monday, Oct. 24th.—Seven Plenary Sessions. Inconclusive.

(*b*) Monday, Oct. 24th–Thursday, Nov. 3rd.—Provisional Irish concessions in hopes of British pressure on Craig.

(*c*) Saturday, Nov. 5th–Thursday, Nov. 17th.—British pressure on Craig.

(*d*) Friday, Nov. 18th–Wednesday, Dec. 30th.—British pressure directed against Sinn Fein.

(*e*) Thursday, Dec. 1st–Tuesday, Dec. 6th.—Sinn Fein delegates struggle against, amend, and eventually agree to British Final Draft of Dec. 1st.

1921 Monday, Dec. 5, 7.30 p.m. (approx.). Lloyd George ultimatum: Dominion Status or immediate war.

1921 Tuesday, Dec. 6, 2.20 a.m. Treaty signed.

1921 Thursday, Dec. 8. Dublin Cabinet meeting. De Valera publishes repudiation of Treaty.

1922 Jan. 7. Dail agrees to Treaty, 64 votes to 57.

1922 June 28. Civil War begins in Ireland.

1922 Dec. 6. Irish Free State established.

1922 Dec. 7. Ulster opts out.

1932 Feb. De Valera returned to power at General Election.

1932 July. British levy special duties on Irish produce, in compensation for land annuities withheld on legal grounds. Economic war begins.

# INDEX

[AUTHOR'S NOTE.—*I am much indebted to Mr. Hilary Sumner-Boyd for making this index.*]

## C

H



I



J

N



O



P



R



S

T